FROM LOGOS TO CHRISTOS

Editions SR/Éditions SR

Editions SR/Éditions SR is a general series of books in the study of religion, encompassing the fields of study of the constituent societies of the Canadian Corporation for Studies in Religion/Corporation canadienne des sciences religieuses. These societies are: Canadian Society of Biblical Studies/Société canadienne des études bibliques; Canadian Society of Church Historic Studies/ Association canadienne des études patristiques; Canadian Society for Study of Religion/Société canadienne pour l'étude de la religion.

General Editor
Aaron Hughes

Editions SR
Volume 34

FROM LOGOS TO CHRISTOS

Essays on Christology in Honour of Joanne McWilliam

✠   ✠   ✠

Ellen M. Leonard and Kate Merriman, editors

Wilfrid Laurier University Press

WLU

Wilfrid Laurier University Press acknowledges the financial support of the Government of Canada through the Canada Book Fund for our publishing activities.

Library and Archives Canada Cataloguing in Publication

From Logos to Christos : essays on Christology in honour of Joanne McWilliam / Ellen M. Leonard and Kate Merriman, editors.

(Editions SR series ; vol. 34)
Includes bibliographical references and index.
Issued also in electronic format.
Includes some text in French.
ISBN 978-1-55458-065-1

1. Jesus Christ—Person and offices. 2. Logos (Christian theology). 3. Religion and ethics. I. Leonard, Ellen M., 1933– II. Merriman, Kate, 1948– III. Series: Editions SR ; 34

BT198.F853 2010   232   C2010-901992-X

ISBN 978-1-55458-168-9
Electronic format.

1. Jesus Christ—Person and offices. 2. Logos (Christian theology). 3. Religion and ethics. I. Leonard, Ellen M., [date]– II. Merriman, Kate, 1948– III. Series: Editions SR ; 34

BT198.F853 2010a   232   C2010-901993-8

Cover design by Sandra Friesen. Cover photo of Joanne McWilliam courtesy of her family. Text design by Catharine Bonas-Taylor.

This book is printed on FSC recycled paper and is certified Ecologo. It is made from 100% post-consumer fibre, processed chlorine free, and manufactured using biogas energy.

Printed in Canada

Every reasonable effort has been made to acquire permission for copyright material used in this text, and to acknowledge all such indebtedness accurately. Any errors and omissions called to the publisher's attention will be corrected in future printings.

Recycled
Supporting responsible use
of forest resources
FSC   www.fsc.org Cert no. SGS-COC-003153
© 1996 Forest Stewardship Council

Contents

✛ ✛ ✛

Foreword

✠ ✠ ✠

$\mathbf{M}$Y FIRST RECOLLECTION of Joanne is as an undergraduate taking a summer course taught by her at St. Michael's College in the 1970s. I had heard so much about her, and when I took one of her courses, it was clear that the fame was well deserved. At that time there were very few women teaching in Religious Studies, and we were in awe. Years passed before I would have the chance to get to know her personally, but along the way her reputation grew and grew. The great thing about her lectures was that she never relied on her personality or special effects to catch the classes' interest. It was her dedication as a scholar that caught the attention and won the respect of one and all. Even the most conservative Anglican bishops listened to her, and her address at the General Synod, when the Anglican Church of Canada voted to ordain women to the priesthood, most certainly influenced the vote in favour. Remember that she was speaking as a Roman Catholic laywoman at the time.

Subsequently I remember the buzz of excitement when word spread that Dr. Joanne McWilliam had been received into the Anglican fold and would be teaching at Trinity College, Toronto. There was further excitement when we heard she was applying for holy orders. It fell to a group of Examining Chaplains in Toronto to interview her, and I remember well the slightly nervous question: "Which one of us is going to quiz her on theology?" Needless to say, the theological questions were handled beautifully. No surprise there, but afterwards I remember all commented that prayer was obviously as strong a passion for Joanne as her theology, and wasn't that wonderful beyond words!

Still more time passed, and I came to know Joanne as a colleague at Trinity College. She was now a deacon, and the date for her ordination to the presbyterate had been set. One day, passing in the halls of the Larkin Building, she asked me if I would teach her how to preside at the altar. The earth moved beneath my feet.

With that history, the reader can understand how very pleased we all were when Joanne was appointed to the Primate's Theological Commission of the Anglican Church of Canada. What a sheer delight to hear her and Robert Crouse discuss Patristics. It was refreshing also to hear her engage feminist critique and move elegantly from topic to topic as we developed the three workbooks that the first commission published. The membership of the Theological Commission was very intentionally diverse, yet the respect afforded Joanne was universal. One had only to set foot on the campus of General Seminary in New York to know that she was as highly respected south of the border as in Canada.

With those very personal comments, let me state the obvious: the Church has been blessed beyond words by the life, ministry, and theological contribution of Joanne McWilliam. We have been blessed by her questions: "Can one be a Christian and against the ordination of women?" "Can a person be a Christian and against the blessing of same-sex unions?" The Body of Christ was blessed by her loyalty and her love for her family and friends through the days of controversy and darkness in the academy. And Anglicans and others continue to be blessed by her generosity as a teacher of theology; she continued to teach as a non-stipendiary member of the Divinity faculty right up to her final weeks of life, because she knew that teaching Augustine was imperative to the formation of theological minds. Last but not least, the human family was and is blessed by her deep commitment to justice. It shone forth when she spoke with pride about the lives of her children and grandchildren; it was evident when, just occasionally, you could get her to talk about herself and you discovered that she read widely in the area of social justice and lived her life in accordance with her convictions.

So thank God for the gift of Joanne McWilliam, theologian, priest, wife, mother, grandmother, teacher, mentor, and friend. May the Church honour Joanne's gifts and enormous contribution by being as theologically sound, devout, and faithful as she was.

Bishop Victoria Matthews
Diocese of Christchurch, New Zealand

Contributors

✠ ✠ ✠

Jane Barter Moulaison is Associate Professor of Theology and Church History in the Faculty of Theology, University of Winnipeg, Winnipeg, MB.

Mary Ann Beavis is Professor and Head of the Department of Religion and Culture, St. Thomas More College, University of Saskatchewan, Saskatoon, SK.

J. Kevin Coyle is Professor of Early Church History and Patristics, Faculty of Theology, Saint Paul University, Ottawa, ON.

Cynthia Crysdale is Professor of Theology and Ethics at the School of Theology, University of the South, Sewanee, TN.

Theodore de Bruyn is Associate Professor of Religous Studies, Department of Classics and Religious Studies, University of Ottawa, Ottawa, ON.

Pamela Dickey Young is Professor of Religious Studies, Queen's University, Kingston, ON.

Michael A. Fahey, sj, is Research Professor of Theology, Boston College, Chestnut Hill, MA.

Deirdre Good is Professor of New Testament, General Theological Seminary, New York City, NY.

Roger Haight, sj, is Scholar-in-Residence, Union Theological Seminary, New York City, NY.

Elizabeth A. Johnson, csj, is Distinguished Professor of Theology at Fordham University, New York City, NY.

Ellen M. Leonard, csj, is Professor Emerita of Systematic Theology, Faculty of Theology, University of St. Michael's College, Toronto, ON.

The Right Reverend Victoria Matthews is Bishop of the Diocese of Christ-church in the Anglican Church of Aotearoa, New Zealand, and Polynesia.

Kate Merriman is an Anglican priest at All Saints Church and freelance editor, Toronto ON.

David Neelands is Dean of the Faculty of Divinity of Trinity College and Margaret E. Fleck Chair of Anglican Studies, Toronto, ON.

Paul-Hubert Poirier is Professor of Christian Origins and History of Christianity, Faculté de théologie et de sciences religieuses, Université Laval, Québec, QC.

Peter Slater is Professor Emeritus of Theology, Faculty of Divinity, Trinity College, in the Toronto School of Theology, Toronto, ON. Peter Slater and Joanne McWilliam were married in 1987.

Yves Tissot is Pastor of the Reformed Church of the Canton of Neuchâtel, Switzerland.

J. Robert Wright is St. Mark's Professor of Ecclesiastical History, General Theological Seminary, New York City, NY.

Introduction

✣ ✣ ✣

ELLEN LEONARD, CSJ
KATE MERRIMAN

J OANNE ELIZABETH MCWILLIAM was born in Toronto on 10 December 1928. She died on Canada Day, 1 July 2008. This Festschrift, planned before her death, was a source of happiness for her. She knew that her friends and colleagues would continue their conversations in the areas that were important to her. Christology was one of those areas. Joanne was a teacher, a scholar, a priest, a theologian, a wife, a mother, a grandmother, a mentor, and a friend. She managed to integrate all of these vocations. She was a leader who blazed a trail for other women scholars and priests, serving as a mentor for many of us.

Joanne was an ecumenical Christian. Her mother came from a Presbyterian background; her father was a Roman Catholic from New Brunswick. She was raised and educated as a Roman Catholic. She attended Loretto Abbey for secondary school, and then the University of Toronto, where she received an honours B.A. in Philosophy and History in 1951, earning the Cardinal Mercier Medal in Philosophy. In 1953 she completed an M.A. in Philosophy; in 1966 she received an M.A. in Theology from the University of St. Michael's College; in 1968 she became the first woman to graduate from St. Michael's with a Ph.D. in Theology.

Joanne believed strongly in gender equality. She saw that the official Catholic Church ignored lay experience generally and that it both ignored and rejected women's experience. In her article "The Misuse of Tradition" (1985), she pointed out that "in Western society the only social entity which does not recognize the equal status of women is the Roman Catholic church."[1] In 1975, while still a Roman Catholic theologian, she addressed the General Synod of the Anglican Church of Canada while they were pondering the question of the ordination of women. In 1976 the Anglican Church of Canada ordained its first women priests. In 1985 Joanne joined the Anglican Church of Canada and quietly requested a transfer from St. Michael's College to Trinity College. In one of her last articles, written for the Anglican Church of Canada Task Force on Human Life, she stated: "I use 'church' throughout to refer to the entire Christian community, not only the Anglican Church of Canada."[2] This was always her vision—a wide vision of church rooted in the Scriptures and the Early Church.

In 1987, believing that it was important for women students in Divinity to have a model of an ordained woman faculty member, she offered herself for ordination as a deacon in the Anglican Church. In 1988 she was ordained a priest, becoming the first ordained woman to be tenured on the Faculty of Divinity at Trinity College. In 1987 she married Professor Peter Slater, then Dean of the Faculty of Divinity. In 1998 Joanne and Peter were appointed as Honorary Assistant Priests at Christ Church Deer Park, a position Joanne maintained until her death.

Joanne lectured in philosophy at the University of Detroit from 1954 to 1955, but she spent most of her academic career at the University of Toronto (1969–94), where she carried out many demanding duties as a member of both the Toronto School of Theology and the Graduate Centre for the Study of Religion. She served as Chair of the Department of Religious Studies (1990–92, 1993–94), as Director of Advanced Degree Studies at the Toronto School of Theology (1981–84), and as Associate Director of the Graduate Centre for the Study of Religion (1987–90) and later as Director (1993–94). The Toronto School of Theology and the Centre for the Study of Religion owe Joanne a debt of gratitude. These were formative years for both institutions, as Theology and Religious Studies programs were then being developed. Joanne laid an extraordinary foundation for these programs. She guided their growth with wisdom, foresight, and rigour. Her administrative skills during these years made it possible for hundreds of students to find their way through the various stages of their programs. The careful work she did in guiding the growth of both institutions continues to shape Religious Studies and Theology in Toronto.

When Joanne became an emerita professor, she accepted another challenge: from 1994 to 1999 she was the Mary Crooke Hoffman Professor of Dogmatic Theology at the General Seminary of the Episcopal Church in New York—the first woman to hold this position. She enjoyed those five years in Manhattan.

She and Peter lived in the seminary, praying with the students and faculty, attending lectures and plays, and entertaining family and friends.

In 2003 Joanne received an honorary Doctor of Divinity from Queen's Theological College. She began her address to the graduating class by stating that she was accepting the degree on behalf of the women theologians of her generation. In her address she emphasized that theologians have an obligation to proclaim their faith intelligently and boldly. She described theology as "loving God with one's mind."[3]

Canon Dr. Alyson Barnett-Cowan described Joanne as "that wonderful kind of Christian scholar, one for whom the knowledge of God is the supreme aspiration, one for whom wisdom, not superficial learning, is the goal of education, one for whom passion and compassion are essential marks of the truly learned."[4] Her scholarly work was rooted in the Patristic period, especially Augustine. Many of her publications explore aspects of Augustine's life and thought. An internationally acknowledged expert on the theology of Augustine, she participated in the quadrennial Oxford Patristics Conference and organized a major international conference at Trinity College on the 1,600th anniversary of Augustine's conversion and baptism. Fifteen of the papers from that conference were published in a collection, *Augustine: From Rhetor to Theologian*, edited by Joanne.[5] Included in the collection is her own essay, "The Study of Augustine's Christology in the Twentieth Century."[6]

In 1996 Joanne was appointed by Archbishop Michael Peers to the first Primate's Theological Commission. Joanne served on the commission from 1996 to 2003. The commission produced three workbooks, which Joanne edited.[7] They contain essays and brief articles by the members on critical theological issues. Joanne's own voice can be heard in the exchanges among the members, and her skill as an editor is evident. Each topic included references to a number of theologians. Karl Rahner is cited as "very much a theologian of the church." This also describes Joanne: she was a scholar who placed her theology at the service of the church. Alyson Barnett-Cowan summed up Joanne's unique contribution to the commission: "She understood the deep tradition very thoroughly yet could advance new developments without fear."[8]

Joanne also encouraged others to publish. She served on the Canadian Corporation for the Study of Religion (CCSR) and was the founding co-editor of the *Toronto Journal of Theology* in 1986. She was an active member of the Canadian Theological Society, the Canadian Society for Patristic Studies, and the American Theological Society, serving as president in all of these learned societies.

Joanne served the church and society well. A quote from the Primate's Theological Commission expresses her contribution: "The Christian church, too, has its elite, not set apart by money or class, by hierarchical place or gender, but by a gift that enables them to speak and write of God and the Christian life in a way that speaks to others across time."[9] Joanne had that gift, one that she used with generosity and courage.

It was especially in teaching that her gift manifested itself. Her four children recall her taking advantage of "teachable moments" as they were growing up. Her graduate students recall her high standards and her conscientious attention to detail. Generations of students in both theology and religious studies appreciated her competence and commitment. The papers she gave at TST seminars were lucid and addressed current theological concerns even while working with ancient materials. One graduate student remembered that he experienced and valued "her combination of intelligence, generosity, humour, and tenacity." As a colleague he treasured her "warmth, interest, wit, and shrewd observation." Joanne continued to share her gift as a teacher, offering courses on Augustine to graduate students until the last year of her life.

✠

In light of Joanne's academic work on Augustine and on Christology, and with her input into the planning of this volume in early 2008, the editors have chosen Christology as the theme for this Festschrift in her memory. Joanne's friends and colleagues have honoured her wishes with essays that continue the conversations many had with her during her lifetime and that advance those discussions. The contributions are diverse, reflecting the authors' broad interests and expertise, but they are also unified by the christological focus. The essays in Part I explore the rich and complicated interplay between Christology and tradition. Those in Part II address relationships between ethical concerns and Christology.

In Part I, "Christology and Tradition," the first two writers look for christological understandings in widely disparate elements of popular culture. Theodore de Bruyn examines the evidence for the popular reception of Christology presented in Greek amulets found in Egypt and dating from the fourth to the seventh centuries. Mary Ann Beavis investigates twentieth- and twenty-first-century Canadian culture—the sculpture *Crucified Woman* (1976), the films *Jesus of Montreal* (1989) and *Jesus Christ Vampire Hunter* (2001), and the Canadian hero Terry Fox. What is the Christology that has been received in these cultures? How have they expressed and adapted it?

The next three writers turn to christological developments and debates within the Early Church and assess their doctrinal and credal formulations. Paul-Hubert Poirier and Yves Tissot seek a deeper understanding of the Christology of the third-century Acts of Thomas by comparing Greek and Syriac versions of passages that fall into three categories: Christ in relation to God, or the Father; Christ within the work of salvation; and particular titles applied to Christ. Kevin Coyle traces the development of Augustine's Christology in his anti-Manichaean writings. These studies offer careful analyses of the differences between emerging ecclesial tradition and other—Gnostic and Manichaean—Christologies. Robert Wright adds another dimension to the examination of tradition and how it develops by presenting views on the seventh canon of Ephesus. In this canon, is Ephesus prohibiting any and all textual changes to the creed of Nicaea or only those changes that might imply a different doctrinal stance being demanded especially of converts? Wright looks at this debate in the writings of Adam Zernikaw, a seventeenth-century Lutheran convert to Eastern Orthodoxy; Thomas Richey, a nineteenth-century Episcopalian; and Archbishop Peter L'Huillier, a twentieth-century Orthodox theologian.

The next two writers carry the christological discussion forward into our own time. After critiquing the tradition of Logos Christology, Roger Haight examines alternatives offered by Schleiermacher, Tillich, and Schillebeeckx. Peter Slater compares Augustine and Tillich on the subject of Christ the Transformer of Culture, one of the five models elaborated by H. Richard Niebuhr. Both Slater and Haight note the features of modern and postmodern culture that call for the re-examination of classical Christology.

Finally, David Neelands and Michael Fahey, in the spirit of Joanne herself, bring out ecumenical dimensions in the development of Christology. Neelands shows how Richard Hooker, in his Christology, by drawing on Augustine, the Greek theologians, and Scholasticism, charts a course that comprehends both Reformed and Catholic Christianity. Michael Fahey takes a critical look at the Christology that sees the founding of the Church as the achievement of Jesus during his public life. This understanding neglects both the role of the Holy Spirit in the anointing of believers and conferral of charisms, and the saving will of God the Father. Fahey cites ecumenical consensus statements from a wide range of sources, among them the Faith and Order Commission of the World Council of Churches and Anglican/Orthodox, Reformed/Roman Catholic, and Methodist/Roman Catholic dialogues, all of which reappropriate the Trinity's role in the founding and life of the Church.

The authors in Part II, "Christology and Ethics," take as their starting point current ethical concerns—ecology, heterosexism, violence, hospitality, and political action—and discuss Christology in relation to these. Elizabeth Johnson observes that there has been a dramatic shift of attention "to the heavens and the earth" and that concern for the devastation of the earth at human hands has been most keenly felt in the area of ethics. In her essay she explores lines of thinking and aspects of the tradition that connect Christology with ecological ethics. The ethical issue central to Pamela Dickey Young's paper is heterosexism and the way it privileges men over women and heterosexual marriage over other kinds of committed relationships. She argues that the maleness of Jesus has been used to justify this subordination, and she proposes that male and female be seen as interpretive categories rather than as givens. Cynthia Crysdale develops a way of understanding redemption in Christ that offers the possibility of ending cycles of violence. In distinction from Anselm's atonement theory and its derivatives, she presents an ethic of risk as an alternative to an ethic of control. Deirdre Good unpacks the many dimensions of the seemingly straightforward Christian virtue of hospitality to strangers. Like the two disciples on the road to Emmaus, Jesus' contemporary disciples would do well to journey alongside strangers. It was in the extension of hospitality and the breaking of bread that the disciples were able to experience the risen Lord. In the final essay, Jane Barter Moulaison takes up the inquiry into the nature and limits of political action. She looks at ways in which Augustine's *City of God* has been used as a type of political realism and, instead, presents it as a work of christological realism. Augustine does not develop a theory that relates the earthly city to the distant, heavenly city, but describes their relationship only insofar as Christ is the Lord of both cities.

✠

The editors have many people to thank for their contributions and assistance. Members of Joanne's family—especially her husband, Peter Slater—have been most supportive and co-operative. All the authors responded quickly to the invitation to contribute essays in Joanne's honour, and wrote in ways that are thoughtful and profound and that preserve her rich legacy. We are particularly grateful for the fact that they adhered to the publication schedule—not an easy thing to do for people whose expertise and teaching are so much in demand.

We also wish to thank those who contributed toward the cost of publication: the Canadian Corporation for the Study of Religion; the Centre for the Study of Religion, University of Toronto; Christ Church, Deer Park, Toronto; Sisters of St. Joseph, Toronto; Theodore de Bruyn; University of St. Michael's College, Toronto; and Trinity College, Toronto.

Finally we are grateful to the staff of Wilfrid Laurier University Press—Lisa Quinn, acquisitions editor, Leslie Macredie, website and marketing coordinator, and Rob Kohlmeier, managing editor—for their guidance and expertise, and to Matthew Kudelka, our copy editor.

Notes

1 Joanne McWilliam, "The Misuse of Tradition," in *Women and the Church: A Source Book,* collected and organized by Michael W. Higgins and Douglas R. Letson (Toronto: Griffin House, 1986), 142–50 at 145; reprinted from *Grail: An Ecumenical Journal* 1 (June 1985): 13–23.

2 "The Theological Bases of Community: Creation, the Holy Spirit, the Church," paper presented to the Anglican Church of Canada Task Force on Human Life, March 2008.

3 "Loving God with one's mind" is developed in McWilliam's last published article: "How Theological Is Theological Education?" *Toronto Journal of Theology: The Future of Theological Education in Canada,* Supplement 1 (2009): 131–40.

4 Alyson Barnett-Cowan, homily delivered at Requiem for Joanne McWilliam, Christ Church, Deer Park, 7 July 2008.

5 Joanne McWilliam, ed., *Augustine: From Rhetor to Theologian* (Waterloo: Wilfrid Laurier University Press, 1992).

6 Ibid., "The Study of Augustine's Christology in the Twentieth Century."

7 The title of the series is *Wrestling with God;* Book 1, *Longing for God: Anglicans Talk about Revelation, Nature, Culture, and Authority* (Toronto: Anglican Book Centre, 2001); Book 2, *Turning to God: Anglicans Talk about Sin, Grace, and the Christian Life* (ABC, 2002); Book 3, *Meeting God: Anglicans Talk about Creation, the Trinity, and the Church* (ABC, 2004).

8 Alyson Barnett-Cowan, staff person on committee, e-mail 19 June 2008. For Joanne's understanding of and appreciation for tradition, see "Tradition before the Future," *Toronto Journal of Theology* 9, no. 1 (1993): 51–66.

9 *Longing for God,* 86.

PART ONE

✣ ✣ ✣

Christology and Tradition

1

Ancient Applied Christology
Appeals to Christ in Greek Amulets in Late Antiquity[1]

✠ ✠ ✠

THEODORE DE BRUYN

AN AMULET can be defined as an item that is believed to convey in and of itself, as well as in association with incantation and other actions, supernatural power for protective, beneficial, or antagonistic effect, and that is worn on one's body or fixed, displayed, or deposited at some place.[2] While an amulet can consist simply of organic matter—a figurine, medallion, ring, or other object devoid of text—in Late Antiquity many amulets included a written charm. These texts, for all their diversity, follow a common pattern. They usually invoke the supernatural power or powers by name and then petition or adjure these powers to perform some act of protection, healing, success, revenge, or the like. Sometimes they command lesser powers—mostly demons, occasionally angels—in the name of greater powers.[3] They may also narrate a short account (*historiola*) describing or identifying the power being invoked.[4]

As the influence of the Christian church—its teachings, rituals, clergy, and adherents—grew in the Roman Empire, amulets began to invoke supernatural power in Christian terms. They appealed to the divine in Christian terms, either exclusively or along with traditional Greco-Roman or Jewish deities or powers, and they recounted major events in the "history" of God. Not surprisingly, given the centrality of Jesus Christ to the new faith, christological formulations and narratives made their way into amulets. These formulations and narratives were shaped in significant ways by the credal statements and liturgical expressions of the Church. But they also manifested idiosyncrasies or vagaries that one would expect in the production of remedies by local priests, monks, or other experts more or less familiar with the traditions of the Church.[5] Amulets thus offer us an opportunity to study Christology as it was received and applied in popular practices at the local level.

In this paper I limit my investigation to amulets found in Egypt (a region where, because of its dry climate, many amulets written on papyrus or parchment have been preserved), written in Greek, and dated mostly from the fourth to the seventh centuries.[6] To locate these items, I have relied upon the following *instrumenta studiorum:* the major collections of edited magical papyri,[7] Joseph van Haelst's 1976 catalogue of Jewish and Christian literary papyri,[8] Kurt Treu's and Cornelia Römer's reviews of recently published Christian papyri from 1969 to the present,[9] and William Brashear's 1995 survey of Greek magical papyri.[10] I have also searched papyrological journals and editions of papyri, parchments, *ostraca,* and tablets for amulets and formularies (recipes for amulets) published between 1996 and 2007.

Forms of Address

Since the appeals and adjurations written on amulets are addressed to deities, we would expect that when they invoke the power of Jesus Christ they are echoing forms of invocation found in the prayers of the Church. After all, it was the worship of Jesus by Christians, and the concomitant reflection on this worship, that attributed divinity to him.[11] Thus the names or titles that appear most frequently in amulets are also widely attested in early Christian sources: "Jesus Christ," "Lord Jesus Christ," "Lord Jesus," "Christ," "Lord," "Son," and "Son of God."[12] These may be combined with other common epithets, such as "our Saviour Jesus Christ,"[13] "Saviour Jesus,"[14] or "only-begotten Son."[15] Occasionally amulets use phrases that denote the cosmological position or role attributed to Jesus Christ: "ruler of aeons," "the king of the aeon," "the king Christ, God," "king of heaven," "highest God," and "Emmanuel."[16] Appeals addressed simply to "Jesus" are rare.[17]

Some amulets appeal to God through Jesus Christ or in the name of Jesus Christ,[18] following well-established patterns of Christian prayer.[19] Thus a fragment of the Lord's Prayer that was likely used as an amulet ends with a doxological formula that is also found in the collection of prayers attributed to Serapion: "through your only-begotten Jesus Christ."[20] Other amulets call upon God as "the Father of our Lord (and Saviour) Jesus

Christ,"[21] again echoing an ancient Christian form of address.[22] Many amulets, however, refer directly to Jesus Christ as the one who dispels malignant forces and protects the wearer, consonant with a long-standing Christian practice of casting out demons in the name of Jesus Christ.[23] Amulets invoke the name of Christ to command an evil spirit to flee;[24] they declare that Christ saves the one who wears the amulet;[25] they appeal to him to protect or heal the wearer of the amulet.[26]

In several amulets Jesus Christ's power is invoked by way of acclamation. Thus one amulet, comprising a series of biblical verses and a doxology, opens and closes with the acclamation "Christ!"[27] Another encloses its adjuration and petition with the acclamation "Jesus Christ is victorious!"[28] A third, consisting of a row of three crosses and the letters α and ω alternating in two columns, concludes with the statement "Jesus Christ help" written between crosses.[29] These types of acclamations had become increasingly common in Christian contexts in the fourth century and beyond, and were used in exorcistic and apotropaic as well as doxological and civic modes.[30] They convey an elemental aspect of Christology in amulets: Jesus Christ as a figure who has conquered death and can command demonic agents of sickness and misfortune.[31]

Narratives

An appeal to a deity in an amulet was sometimes cast in the form of, or accompanied by, a narrative (*historiola*) recounting an event in the life of the deity that related to the situation at hand. Such narratives can be regarded as performative utterances that convey power from a mythic past to a human present in order to address the problem or concern. In amulets that invoke Jesus Christ, his power to intervene is established by several types of narratives that operate, in effect if not always in form, as *historiolae*.[32]

Credal Statements

Several amulets open with credal statements describing the career of Christ from his pre-existence to his heavenly reign. One amulet, assigned to the late fifth or early sixth century, opens with a credal declaration: "[Christ was born of the] Virgin Mary, and was crucified by Pontius Pilate, and was buried in a grave, and rose on the third day, and was taken up into the heavens, and ..."[33] Two other amulets, assigned to the fifth and sixth centuries respectively, open with briefer credal acclamations:

Christ was born, amen.	Christ was proclaimed in advance.
Christ was crucified, amen.	Christ appeared.
Christ was buried, amen.	Christ suffered.
Christ arose, amen.	Christ died.
He has woken to judge the living and the dead.[34]	Christ was raised.
	Christ was taken up.
	Christ reigns.[35]

While these two credal statements echo phrases found in the second article of ancient creeds (as well as earlier christological summaries or *regulae fidei*),[36] their wording evidently differs not only from known creeds but also from each other.[37] Their acclamatory or hymnic character suggests that they may have liturgical origins.[38] They may, in fact, have been intended for use in exorcism,[39] since the Crucifixion, burial, Resurrection, and Ascension of Christ were believed to have broken the devil's hold over the human race. By recounting these events, these credal statements render present the power of Christ to save and protect the wearer of the amulet.[40]

An Extended Prayer

Credal statements are necessarily summary in character. We are fortunate, however, to have one amulet that recounts the salvific work of Christ in more detail. It provides an example of a particular christological warrant for calling upon Jesus Christ for exorcistic or apotropaic purposes.

P.Cair.Cat. 10263, a prayer dating from the fourth or fifth century that had apparently been buried with a mummy,[41] preserves a long epiclesis calling upon Christ to protect the wearer from the powers of darkness in their many forms.[42] Christ is invoked as "God of the heavens and God of the earth and God of the saints through [your blood]."[43] He is referred to as "the fullness of the aeon," "the king of the aeon," "the God of the aeon," and "the mercy of the aeon."[44] The epiclesis narrates his coming "through Gabriel in the womb of the virgin Mary,"[45] his birth in Bethlehem and youth in Nazareth, his Crucifixion, his Resurrection and appearances in Galilee, and his ascent to the highest heaven, where he is worshipped by myriads upon myriads of angels echoing the language of the Sanctus. Then follows the invocation, which appeals to Christ as "the blessed lamb through whose blood the souls have been freed as the bronze gates of themselves were opened for him, who has broken the iron bars, who has loosed those bound in the [darkness], who has made Charon impotent, who has bound the hostile rebel that was cast into his own places."[46] Christ's victory in the underworld is the reason that the powers of darkness have no hold over the person named in the prayer.[47] The invocation concludes with a doxology that, like the Sanctus which concludes the epiclesis, accords Christ "power … which prevails forever."[48]

This prayer offers a glimpse of the sorts of narratives that could lie behind the appeal to Christ in amulets. In this instance Christ is presented as God, who, having conquered the Adversary in the Crucifixion, Resurrection, and descent to the underworld, receives all glory upon being received again into heaven (the Sanctus), and exercises all power (the doxology). In fact, several amulets contain doxologies that praise Christ as God in similar terms. One undated amulet opens with a narrative of Jesus saving Peter from the storm. Peter's acclamation "Son of God!" leads directly to the following doxology: "And I say, 'O almighty one, glory to you, God, who creates the angels, ruler of aeons!'"[49] Another amulet of uncertain date juxtaposes two forms of address that likewise reflect the ambivalent status of Christ: it opens with an appeal to God almighty "through our Lord Jesus Christ, the beloved child,"[50] but then concludes with a fulsome (and intriguing) doxology: "O Jesus Christ, you king of all the aeons, almighty, inexpressibly a creator, nurturer, master, almighty, noble child, kindly son, my unutterable and inexpressible name, truly true form, unseen for ever and ever. Amen."[51]

Miracles Performed by Jesus

Besides presenting credal or extended christological narratives that dispel or command evil simply by virtue of the events they recount, amulets preface their petitions or adjurations with accounts of healings and other wonders performed by Jesus on earth.[52] Most of these wonders are drawn from the canonical Gospels; a few are apocryphal.[53]

Some amulets simply recount the wonder as a *historiola* proper before proceeding to a petition or invocation. So, for example, after the credal statement quoted above, P.Turner 49 continues by declaring, "[We believe,] Jesus, that you were healing then every infirmity of the people and every illness. Savior Jesus, we believe that you went then into the house of Peter's mother-in-law, who was feverish, [and you touched her hand and] the fever left her. And now we beseech you, Jesus, also now heal your maidservant, who wears your great name, from every illness and from … fever and from fever with shivering and from headache and from every malignity and from every evil spirit."[54] Likewise, prior to the doxology noted above, P.Berl. inv. 11858 opens with this *historiola*: "[When a strong] wind [came up] and he [i.e., Peter] began to sink, he called out with a loud voice. And he [i.e., Jesus] held out his hand and grabbed him. And when it was calm, he [i.e., Peter] shouted, 'Son of God!'"[55] In a similar fashion, a formulary from the fifth or sixth century incorporates an apocryphal narrative into an adjuration against an ocular discharge: "For our Lord was pursued by the Jews, and he came to the Euphrates river and stuck in his staff, and the water stood still. Also you, discharge, stand still from head to toenails in the name of our Lord, who was crucified ..."[56]

More often, however, amulets appeal to Jesus as the one who has performed such-and-such a healing or wonder; that is, they recount the event in the form of a clausal *historiola*.[57] Thus several amulets appeal to Jesus as the one who, in the words of Matthew's Gospel, healed "every illness and every infirmity" (Matthew 4:23, 9:35, cf. Matthew 10:1).[58] Another asks the one "who has healed again, who has raised Lazarus from the dead even on the fourth day, who has healed Peter's mother-in-law, who has also accomplished many unmentioned healings in addition to those they report in the sacred gospels" to heal the woman wearing "this divine amulet."[59] Similarly, P.Oxy. VIII 1151 alludes to the healing of the paralytic by the pool at the Sheep Gate (John 5:2–9) in calling upon the "God of the sheep-pool" to deliver Joannia from evil.[60] P.Louvre inv. E 7332 *bis* refers to Jesus' power to rebuke the winds and the seas (Matthew 8:26–27) in a petition to relieve a woman of her afflictions.[61] And, finally, P.Ups. 8 and P.Hamb. I 22—a petition by a certain Sabinus and an inscription for his gravestone—both invoke Jesus' healing of the blind in asking God to redress the injuries Sabinus suffered at the hand of his daughter Severine.[62]

These invocations attest to the currency of canonical and apocryphal stories of wonders performed by Jesus while on earth. The stories may have owed their currency in part to the fact that they served as warrants for calling upon Jesus to heal. (It is noteworthy that healings reported in the Gospels are also invoked in prayers for the anointing of the sick in later Coptic rites.)[63] The stories disclose another dimension of Christology, alongside stylized credal acclamations and cosmological narratives of salvation. It is still a Christology of divine power. But the power is manifested in response to evident human need. The value of the stories lies in the conjunction, past and present, of divine healer and human petitioner.

Configurations

The christological aspects of the invocations and narratives in the amulets that we have reviewed are, except for a few instances, unexceptional. The amulets for the most part express common lineaments of Christology—particularly miaphysite Christology—in the period in which they were written. Their contribution to the study of Christology in Late Antiquity does not lie in their sophistication. It lies rather in the evidence they provide of beliefs about Jesus that were popularly held and of the ways in which these beliefs came to be held.

The language used in these amulets to invoke the power of God in Christian terms derives in large part from the liturgy of the Church. This is suggested by many echoes or adumbrations of liturgical usage in amulets, such as the Sanctus,[64] the creed,[65] doxologies,[66] acclamations,[67] litanies,[68] and liturgical archaisms.[69] These liturgical echoes illustrate the effect of ritual acts—especially participatory acclamations—in encapsulating Christian beliefs and expectations in relatively brief formulae.[70] These formulae then lend themselves to applications elsewhere. For example, several amulets appeal to "the blood of Christ" or "the body and blood of Christ" for protection.[71] While the phrase can hark back to the victory of Christ in the Crucifixion,[72] its customary wording is likely owing to the formula of communion in the Eucharist, where the communicant is offered "the body of Christ" and "the blood of Christ" and responds with "Amen."[73] The body and blood of Christ become, in effect, parts for the whole, signifying the past victory and present power of Christ. They are invoked as such to protect one's person and one's home.[74] (The crosses, staurograms, and Christograms that precede, conclude, and otherwise accompany Christian texts in amulets function as even simpler signifiers of the victory and power of Christ.)[75]

The brief, stylized form of these types of signifiers, along with the power attributed to them or their referents, made them particularly handy for use in amulets. It also allowed them to be configured in irregular ways. For example, an amulet for the protection of a home and its occupants begins by invoking a string of Egyptian and Jewish powers—"Hor, Hor, Phor, Phor, Iao Sabaoth Adonai, Eloe, Salaman, Tarch[ei]"[76]—and concludes with the injunction "Be on guard, Lord, son of David according to the flesh, the one born of the holy virgin Mary, holy highest God, of the Holy Spirit. Glory to you, heavenly king. Amen."[77] The formulation of the human and divine origins of Christ recalls the language of the Nicene Constantinopolitan creed.[78] The inversion of the credal phrasing, as well as the allusion to Romans 1:3, suggests that the invocation was mediated through some other liturgical form (perhaps a hymn) or appropriated with some freedom.

Some of these idiosyncracies in christological expression in amulets may be the result of a scribe following a recipe or using a formula without being aware of its origins. Indeed, this is the case with a separated leaf of a papyrus codex in the Berlin collection that preserves six recipes for spells.[79] The first recipe appears to be derived from a Christian liturgical exorcism.

It consists of lines that invoke Jesus directly (in the manner of an exorcism) and lines that recount the incarnation of the Son and the wonders performed by him (recalling the narratives discussed above). But at some point prior to the transcription of the recipe the credal verses and the responsory lines fell out of sequence, and as a result the recipe presents a garbled version of the original litany.[80]

Recipes like this one constituted a diverse fund of incantations to be employed in amulets. The results are often "syncretistic" in the sense that Christian elements are juxtaposed with Egyptian and Jewish elements—sometimes dramatically so, as in the case of an amulet that appeals equally to Jesus Christ and the white wolf.[81] Occasionally, as in the case of Dioscorus of Aphrodite's copy of an amuletic text,[82] we catch glimpses of an individual using and modifying a recipe in accordance with his or her religious beliefs. More often this process is hidden from us. We are left only with aspects of Christology appropriated from the liturgy of the Church and refracted through the living memory of a scribe, the reified wording of a formulary, and the ad hoc production of incantations. Nevertheless, the resulting artifacts present Christologies that in their succinct formulation and mundane application may bring us closer to the "take away message" of the liturgy of the Church for many Christians.

Postscript

When I began my doctoral studies under the supervision of Joanne McWilliam, I had intentions of writing a dissertation on Augustine's sermons. Though I eventually settled on another project, I read widely in the sermons and, on occasion, wrote about Augustine's homiletic discourse. My present interest in the Christianization of amulets may seem far removed from that early work on Augustine and from Joanne's own expertise in his Christology. But it was Augustine who first sparked that interest through his portrayal of Christians who used—or resisted the temptation to use—amulets. I like to think that Joanne would have enjoyed the irony of this unintended influence of the bishop of Hippo, and that it would have drawn from her the sort of wry comment that one so often experienced in her company and that I recall with much affection.

Notes

1 Research for this paper was supported by a grant from the Social Sciences and Humanities Research Council of Canada and by release from teaching from the Faculty of Arts of the University of Ottawa. I gratefully acknowledge this assistance.

2 For definitions of the term "amulet" and descriptions of what the term comprises, see, among others, R. Wünsch, "Amuletum," *Glotta* 2 (1910): 219–30; Ernst von Dobschütz, "Charms and Amulets (Christian)," in *Encyclopedia of Religion and Ethics*, ed. James Hastings (New York: Charles Scribner's Sons, 1908–27), III:413–30; F. Eckstein and J.H. Waszink, "Amulett," in *Reallexicon für Antike und Christentum* (Stuttgart: Hiersemann, 1950), I:397–411; Campbell Bonner, *Studies in Magical Amulets, Chiefly Graeco-Egyptian* (Ann Arbor: University of Michigan Press, 1950), 2; and Roy Kotansky, "Incantations and Prayers for Salvation on Written Greek Amulets," in *Magika Hiera: Ancient Greek Magic and Religion*, ed. Christopher A. Faraone and Dirk Obbink (New York: Oxford University Press, 1991), 107–37 at 107–8. My specification of "protective, beneficial, or antagonistic effect" is similar to the analysis of types of amulets in Von Dobschütz, "Charms and Amulets," 416–21.

3 See David Jordan, "A Prayer Copied by Dioskoros of Kômê Aphroditês (*PGM* II 13a)," *Tyche* 16 (2001): 82–90 at 90–91.

4 See David Frankfurter, "Narrating Power: The Theory and Practice of the Magical *historiola* in Ritual Spells," in *Ancient Magic and Ritual Power*, ed. Marvin Meyer and Paul Mirecki (Leiden: Brill, 1995), 457–75.

5 On the role of Christian experts in the production of amulets, see David Frankfurter, "Ritual Expertise in Roman Egypt and the Problem of the Category 'Magician,'" in *Envisioning Magic: A Princeton Seminar and Symposium*, ed. Peter Schäfer and Hans G. Kippenberg (Leiden: Brill, 1997), 115–35 at 125–30.

6 In what follows, references to papyrological editions, corpora, and series are abbreviated according to John F. Oates et al., eds., *Checklist of Greek, Latin, Demotic and Coptic Papyri, Ostraca and Tablets*, 5th ed. (American Society of Papyrologists, 2001), updated on the World Wide Web at John F. Oates et al., *Checklist of Greek, Latin, Demotic and Coptic Papyri, Ostraca and Tablets*, http://scriptorium.lib.duke.edu/papyrus/texts/clist.html, September 2008. Items published in editions, corpora, and series are referred to by volume number in roman numerals and item number in arabic numerals, followed, where relevant, by line numbers in Arabic numerals. In the event of possible confusion I indicate "p." for pages. For items not published in or not superseded by editions, corpora, and series, I provide bibliographical details at the first reference. When an item is republished in a corpus or series, I also identify it by the principal edition (e.g., P.Amst. I 26 = *Suppl. Mag.* I 22) or by the collection and inventory number (e.g., P.Heid. inv. G 1386 = *Suppl. Mag.* I 28) to aid recognition.

7 Karl Preisendanz and Albert Henrichs, eds., *Papyri Graecae Magicae: Die griechischen Zauberpapyri*, 2nd ed., 2 vols. (Stuttgart: Teubner, 1974), hereafter *PGM;* and Robert W. Daniel and Franco Maltomini, eds., *Supplementum Magicum*, 2 vols. (Opladen: Westdeutscher, 1991–92), hereafter *Suppl. Mag.* Because my investigation focuses on Egypt, I do not include items with Christological references published in Roy Kotansky, ed., *Greek Magical Amulets: The Written Gold, Silver, Copper, and Bronze Lamellae. Part I: Published Texts of Known Provenance* (Opladen: Westdeutscher, 1994); see nos. 35, 52, 53, and 68, all of which were found outside of Egypt and

several of which manifest Jewish or Jewish-Christian traits. Many of the texts republished and translated (in German) in *PGM* were previously republished and translated (in French) by Charles Wessely, ed., *Les plus anciens monuments du christianisme écrits sur papyrus, II*, Patrologia orientalis 18.3 (Paris: Firmin-Didot, 1924), 341–509. English translations of many of the texts discussed in this paper can be found in Marvin Meyer and Richard Smith, eds., *Ancient Christian Magic: Coptic Texts of Ritual Power* (San Francisco: Harper San Francisco, 1994), hereafter *ACM*.

8   Joseph van Haelst, *Catalogue des papyrus littéraires juifs et chrétiens* (Paris: Publications de la Sorbonne, 1976).

9   Kurt Treu, "Christliche Papyri," *Archiv für Papyrusforschung* 19 (1969): 169–206; 20 (1970): 145–52; 21 (1971): 207–14; 22 (1973): 367–95; 24/25 (1976): 253–61; 26 (1978): 149–59; 27 (1980): 251–58; 28 (1982): 91–98; 29 (1983): 107–10; 30 (1984): 121–28; 31 (1985): 59–71; 32 (1986): 87–95; 34 (1988): 69–78; 35 (1989): 107–16; 36 (1990): 95–98; 37 (1991): 93–98; Cornelia E. Römer, "Christliche Texte," *Archiv für Papyrusforschung* 43 (1997): 107–45; 44 (1998): 129–39; 45 (1999): 138–48; 47 (2001): 368–76; 48 (2002): 349–50; 50 (2004): 275–83; 51 (2005): 334–40; 53 (2007): 250–55.

10   William M. Brashear, "The Greek Magical Papyri: An Introduction and Survey; Annotated Bibliography (1928–1994)," in *Aufstieg und Niedergang der römischen Welt*, Part 2, *Principat*, vol. 18.5, ed. Wolfgang Haase and Hildegard Temporini (Berlin: Walter de Gruyter, 1995), 3380–684 at 3480–82 and 3492–93.

11   For a convenient introduction to the origins of Christian devotion to Jesus, see Larry W. Hurtado, *At the Origins of Christian Worship* (Grand Rapids: Eerdmans, 1999), 63–97, and the literature cited there.

12   "Jesus Christ": P.Amst. I 26 = *Suppl. Mag.* I 22, 1; P.Coll.Youtie II 91 = *Suppl. Mag.* I 30, 4; P.Heid. inv. G 1386 = *Suppl. Mag.* I 28, 2; P.IFAO s.n. = *Suppl. Mag.* II 61, 4; P.Köln inv. 521a, 9 (Dierk Wortmann, "Neue Magische Texte," *Bonner Jahrbücher* 168 [1968]: 56–111 at 106); P.Köln inv. 851 = *Suppl. Mag.* I 34, 1; P.Köln inv. 2861 = *Suppl. Mag.* I 20, 5–6; P.Köln IV 171, 7; P.Oxy. VI 924 = *PGM* II 5a, 15; P.Oxy. VIII 1152 = *PGM* II 6a, 3–4; P.Prag. I 6 = *Suppl. Mag.* I 25, 9–10; P.Vindob. inv. G 329 = *PGM* II 12, 7, 14, with F. Maltomini, "Un 'utero errante' di troppo? *PGM* II 12 riconsiderato," *Zeitschrift für Papyrologie und Epigraphik* 160 (2007): 167–74, and Cornelia Eva Römer, "Gebet und Bannzauber des Severus von Antiochia gegen den Biss giftiger Tiere, oder: Maltomini hatte recht," *Zeitschrift für Papyrologie und Epigraphik* 168 (2009): 209–12; P.Vindob. inv. G 338 = *PGM* II 11, 1; P.Wessely Prag. Graec. 1 = *PGM* II 21, 26–27, 41.

"Lord Jesus Christ": P.Berl. inv. 17202, 7 (William M. Brashear and Roy Kotansky, "A New Magical Formulary," in *Magic and Ritual in the Ancient World*, ed. Paul Mirecki and Marvin Meyer [Leiden: Brill, 2002], 3–24); P.Louvre E 7332 *bis*, 1 (William M. Brashear, with Adam Bülow–Jacobsen, *Magica Varia* [Brussels: Fondation Égyptologique Reine Élisabeth, 1991], 63–70); P.Vindob. inv. G 29831 = *MPER* N.S. XVII 10, 5; P.Wessely Prag. Graec. 1 = *PGM* II 21, 7–8.

"Lord Jesus": P.Vindob. inv. G 337 = *PGM* II 10, 47.

"Christ": P.Batav. 10 = *Suppl. Mag.* I 35, 1–8; P.Oxy. VIII 1151 = *PGM* II 5b, 3, 23, with Dieter Hagedorn, "Bemerkungen zu Urkunden," *Zeitschrift für Papyrologie und Epigraphik* 145 (2003): 224–27 at 226; PSI VI 719 = *PGM* II P19, 1, 6. Cf. also n71 below for amulets that appeal to the body and blood of Christ.

"Lord": P.Berl. inv. 17202, 1a, 11; P.Heid. inv. G 1101 = *SB* XVI 12719 = *Suppl. Mag.* I 32, 8; P.IFAO s.n. = *Suppl. Mag.* II 61, 4; P.Louvre E 7332 *bis*, 4; P.Osl. I 5 = *PGM* II 3, 8, with Marcus N. Tod, "The Scorpion in Graeco-Roman Egypt," *Journal of Egyptian Archaeology* 25 (1939) 55–61 at 58–60, and Robert W. Daniel, "Some ΦΥΛΑΚΤΗΡΙΑ," *Zeitschrift für Papyrologie und Epigraphik* 25 (1977): 144–54 at 150–53; P.Oxy. VIII 1151 = *PGM* II 5b, 23; P.Vindob. inv. G 337 = *PGM* II 10, 21, 34–35.

"Son" (in the context of a trinitarian formula): P.Lond.Lit. 231 = *PGM* II 5d, 1; P.Oxy. VI 924 = *PGM* II 5a, 15; P.Ross.Georg. I 24 = *PGM* II 15a, 18–22; P.Turner 49 = *Suppl. Mag.* I 31, 4; P.Vindob. inv. G 337 = *PGM* II 10, 42. "Son" (in other contexts): P.Vindob. inv. G 337 = *PGM* II 10, 2; P.Vindob. inv. G 26034 + 30453, 9 (H. Hunger, "Ergänzungen zu zwei neutestamentlichen Papyrusfragmenten der Österreichischen Nationalbibliothek," *Biblos* 19 [1970] 71–75 at 72–75, reuniting the two fragments P.Vindob. inv. G 26034 + 30453 under the name P.Vindob. inv. G 30453).

"Son of God" and variants: P.Berl. inv. 11858 = *PGM* II 23, 10; P.Oxy. VIII 1151 = *PGM* II 5b, 5, 23–25: the latter, "Son and Word of the living God"; P.Prag. I 6 = *Suppl. Mag.* I 25, 3–4; P.Ups. 8 = *Suppl. Mag.* II 59, 13 and P.Hamb. I 22 = *Suppl. Mag.* II 60, 3: "Son of the great God whom man never beheld."

13 P.Vindob. inv. G 329 = *PGM* II 12, 7–8.

14 P.Turner 49 = *Suppl. Mag.* I 31, 2; P.Vindob. inv. G 338 = *PGM* II 11, 1.

15 P.Berl. inv. 21911 = *SB* XIV 11494 = *Suppl. Mag.* I 26, 1–2 = BKT IX 206; P.Duke inv. 778, 21–22 (Csaba A. La'da and Amphilochios Papathomas, "A Greek Papyrus Amulet from the Duke Collection with Biblical Excerpts," *Bulletin of the American Society of Papyrologists* 41 [2004]: 93–113); P.Köln IV 171, 6–7; P.Lond.Lit. 231 = *PGM* II 5d, 3–4.

16 In addition to the epithets at P.Cair.Cat. 10263 = *PGM* II 13, 1, 7, 8, 18, P.Berl. inv. 11858 = *PGM* II 23, 11–14, and P.Wessely Prag. Graec. 1 = *PGM* II 21, 41–49, discussed below, see also P.Berl. inv. 11858 = *PGM* II 23, 25: "the king Christ, God"; P.Louvre E 7332 *bis*, 7: "Lord my God"; P.Osl. I 5 = *PGM* II 3, 10–11: "highest God," "king of heaven"; P.Ups. 8 = *Suppl. Mag.* II 59 and P.Hamb. I 22 = *Suppl. Mag.* II 60; "Emmanuel": P.Ups. 8 = *Suppl. Mag.* II 59v: "Emmanuel."

17 Jesus alone is invoked in a second-century *lamella* in a private collection in London (Roy Kotansky, "An Early Christian Gold *lamella* for Headache," in Mirecki and Meyer, *Magic and Ritual in the Ancient World*, 37–46 at 39, line 2. Cf. also P.Turner 49 = *Suppl. Mag.* I 31, 2, 3, where, however, other christological and trinitarian forms of address are also found.

18 P.Cair.Cat. 10696 = *PGM* II 5c, 4–5; P. Köln inv. G 2861 = *Suppl. Mag.* I 20, 5–6, where one reads simply ὀνόματι Ἰη(σο)ῦ Χρ(ιστο)ῦ in place of the usual ἐν ὀνόματι; P.Wessely Prag. Graec. 1 = *PGM* II 21, 7–8.

19 See Joseph A. Jungmann, *The Place of Christ in Liturgical Prayer*, 2nd ed., trans. A. Peeler (Staten Island: Alba House, 1965), 144–71.

20 P.Köln IV 171, 6–7, with comm; cf. Maxwell E. Johnson, *The Prayers of Sarapion of Thmuis: A Literary, Liturgical, and Theological Analysis* (Rome: Pontificio Istituto Orientale, 1995), 46–80.

21 BGU III 954 = *PGM* II 9, 2–3; P.Köln VIII 340, 35–37; P.Vindob. inv. G 29831 = *MPER* N.S. XVII 10, 3–5.

22 The formula "our Lord and Saviour Jesus Christ" appears in early witnesses of the
    liturgy of St. Mark: P.Stras. inv. gr. 254r, 9; P.Lond.Lit. 232r, 8–9 (as reconstructed);
    P.Vindob. inv. G 26134 = *MPER* N.S. XVII 50r, 5–6. See Geoffrey Cuming, *The Liturgy
    of St Mark* (Rome: Pontificium Institutum Studiorum Orientalium, 1990), xxiii–xxix,
    61–63, and Jürgen Hammerstaedt, *Griechische Anaphorenfragmente aus Ägypten und
    Nubien* (Opladen: Westdeutscher, 1999), 24, 45, 97. Cuming, 69–74, assigns the
    version of the liturgy incorporating "our Lord and Saviour Jesus Christ" to the
    mid–fourth century, and the version incorporating "our Lord and God and Sav-
    iour Jesus Christ" to the mid–fifth century. The later formula would appear to lie
    behind the phraseology of P.Vindob. inv. G 329 = *PGM* II 12, 6–7.

23 See, e.g., Acts 16:18, 19:13; Justin, *Second Apology* 6.6, 8.4, *Dialogue with Trypho* 30.3;
    Origen, *Against Celsus* 1.6, 1.25, 1.67; Athanasius, *Life of Antony*, 63; cf. Wilhelm
    Heitmüller, *"Im Namen Jesu": Eine sprach–u. religionsgeschichtliche Untersuchung zum
    Neuen Testament, speziell zur altchristlichen Taufe* (Göttingen: Vandenhoeck & Ruprecht,
    1903), 222–65; K. Thraede, *"Exorzismus," in Reallexicon für Antike und Christentum*
    (Stuttgart: Hiersemann, 1950–), VII:44–117 at 63–66, 102–5; Bernd Kollmann,
    *Jesus und die Christen als Wundertäter: Studien zu Magie, Medizin und Schamanismus in
    Antike und Christentum* (Göttingen: Vandenhoeck & Ruprecht, 1996), 351–53. It is
    noteworthy that the only prayer addressed to Christ in the *Apostolic Constitutions*
    is a prayer of exorcism; see *Apostolic Constitutions* 8.7.8 and cf. Marcel Metzger, ed.,
    Les constitutions apostoliques, vol. 2, Sources Chrétiennes 329 (Paris: Les Éditions
    du Cerf, 1986), 30. Cf. the exorcistic litanies at n68 below.

24 P.Oxy. VIII 1151= *PGM* II 5b, 1–3; cf. P.Prag. I 6 = *Suppl. Mag.* I 25, 3–5.

25 P.Batav. 20 = *Suppl. Mag.* I 35, 8.

26 P.Coll.Youtie II 91 = *Suppl. Mag.* I 30, 4; P.Köln inv. 851 = *Suppl. Mag.* I 34, 1–11;
    P.Oxy. VIII 1151= *PGM* II 5b, 23–38; PSI inv. 365 = *PGM* II 18, 12–15, with Franco
    Maltomini, "Osservazioni al testo di alcuni papiri magici greci. (III.)," *Studi clas-
    sici e orientali* 32 (1982): 235–41 at 239; P.Vindob. inv. G 26034 + 30453, 9–10.

27 PSI VI 719 = *PGM* II 19, 1, 6.

28 P.Prag. I 6 = *Suppl. Mag.* I 25, 1, 9–10.

29 P.Köln inv. 521a, 9–10.

30 For an overview see Th. Klauser, "Akklamation," in *Reallexicon für Antike und Chris-
    tentum* (Stuttgart: Hiersemann, 1950), I:215–33 at 225–31. On the use of the νικᾳ-
    acclamation in religious and secular contexts, see O. Weinreich, "Neue Urkunden
    zur Sarapis–Religion," in *Ausgewählte Schriften I: 1907–1921* (Amsterdam: B.R. Grüner,
    1969), 410–42 at 427–28 and 440–42; Erik Peterson, ΕΙΣ ΘΕΟΣ: *Epigraphische,
    formgeschichtliche und religionsgeschichtliche Untersuchungen* (Göttingen: Vanden-
    hoeck & Ruprecht, 1926), 152–58; Bonner, *Studies in Magical Amulets*, 176. On
    βοήθει–declarations, see Bonner, *Studies in Magical Amulets*, 180.

31 In accordance with this recognition of Jesus Christ's power over demonic forces,
    some amulets appeal simply to "the power of Jesus Christ." See P.Amst. I 26 =
    Suppl. Mag. I 22, 1 and P.Oxy. VI 924 = *PGM* II 5a, 14–15; cf. Arthur D. Nock, "Stud-
    ies in the Graeco-Roman Beliefs of the Empire," *Journal of Hellenic Studies* 45 (1925):
    84–101 at 85–95, and Peterson, ΕΙΣ ΘΕΟΣ, 198.

32 See David Frankfurter, "Narrating Power," 464–65.

33 P.Turner 49 = *Suppl. Mag.* I 31, 1: [Χ(ριστὸ)ς ἐγεννήθη ἐκ τῆς παρθ]ένου Μαρία
    κ(αὶ) ἐστ(αυ)ρ(ώ)θη ὑπὸ Ποντίου Πιλάτου κ(αὶ) ἐτάφη εἰς μνημῖον κ(αὶ) ἀνέστη
    εν τῇ τρίτῃ ἡμέρα κ(αὶ) ἀνελήμφθη ἐπὶ τοὺς οὐρανοὺς κ(αὶ) ε....

34 P.Haun. III 51 = *Suppl. Mag.* I 23, 1–6: Χριστὸς ἐγεννήθη, ἀμήν. Χριστὸς ἐσταυρόθη, ἀμήν. Χριστὸς ἐτάφη, ἀμήν. Χριστὸς ἀνέστη, ἀμή<ν>. γεγέρθη κρῖνε ζῶντας καὶ νεκρούς.

35 P.Batav. 20 = *Suppl.Mag.* I 35, 1–7: Χ(ριστὸ)ς προεκ[ηρύχθη], Χ(ριστὸ)ς ἐφάνη, Χ(ριστὸ)ς ἔπαθεν, Χ(ριστὸ)ς ἀπέθανεν, Χ(ριστὸ)ς ἀνηγέρθη, Χ(ριστὸ)ς ἀνελήμφθη, Χ(ριστὸ)ς βασιλεύει. Each phrase is preceded by a staurogram (⳨).

36 On early Christological summaries, see Richard N. Longenecker, *New Wine into Fresh Wineskins: Contextualizing the Early Christian Confessions* (Peabody: Hendrickson, 1999), 13–20, and John N.D. Kelly, *Early Christian Creeds*, 3rd ed. (London: Longman, 1972), 62–99. On the distinction between these summaries and later creeds, see now Liuwe W. Westra, *The Apostles' Creed: Origin, History, and Some Early Commentaries* (Turnhout: Brepols, 2002), 37–39 with 40–41nn77–78. The varying formulations of the second article of ancient creeds are conveniently summarized in Hans Lietzmann, "Symbolstudien III," in *Kleine Schriften III: Studien zur Liturgie- und Symbolgeschichte zur Wissenschaftsgeschichte*, Texte und Untersuchungen zur Geschichte der altchristlichen Literatur, vol. 74 (Berlin: Akademie, 1962), 194–211. For complete texts of ancient *regulae fidei* and creeds, see August Hahn and G. Ludwig Hahn, eds., *Bibliothek der Symbole und Glaubensregeln der alten Kirche*, 3rd ed. (1897; reprint, Hildesheim: Georg Olms, 1962).

37 A comparison of the phraseology used in P.Turner 49 with known creeds reveals small anomalies: the epithet παρθένου precedes rather than follows Μαρία; the pronoun ὑπό is used in place of the more common ἐπί; the explanation εἰς μνημῖον is added to ἐτάφη; and ἀνελήμφθη ἐπὶ τοὺς οὐρανούς is used where other creeds have ἀνελθόντα εἰς τοὺς οὐρανούς. P.Haun. III 51 employs many of the same verbal forms as P.Turner 49: ἐγεννήθη, ἐσταυρώθη, ἐτάφη, ἀνέστη. P.Batav. 20, on the other hand, has fewer parallels with either these two or known creeds (cf. P.Batav., pp. 98–99.)

38 The acclamatory character of P.Haun. III 51 and P.Batav. 20 may be inferred from the repetition Χριστός and, in the case of P.Haun. III 51, the response of ἀμήν (cf. P.Haun. III 51, 1 comm.). The credal opening of P.Turner 49, where each verb is accompanied by a single prepositional phrase, has a hymnic cadence. On the combination of fixity and freedom that characterized the development of liturgical forms and credal formulae, see Kelly, *Early Christian Creeds*, 98–99, 167–68, 193–94.

39 The use of summaries of the career of Christ, together with the name of Jesus, in exorcism is attested already by Justin, *Dialogue with Trypho*, 85.2, and Origen, *Against Celsus*, 1.6. Acclamatory creeds similar to those just discussed are also found in Greek prayers and amulets preserved in medieval and modern manuscripts; cf. A. Vassiliev, ed., *Anecdota Graeco-Byzantina: Pars Prior* (Moscow: Universitatis Caesareae, 1893), 339; Armand Delatte, *Anecdota Atheniensia*, vol. 1: *Textes grecs inédits relatifs à l'histoire des religions* (Liège: Vaillant-Carmanne; Paris: Édouard Champion, 1927), 146, 616; Fritz Pradel, *Griechische und süditalienische Gebete, Beschwörungen und Rezepte des Mittelalters* (Giessen: Alfred Töpelmann, 1907), 13.23–14.6 with 48–49.

40 I thus differ from G.H.R. Horsley, *New Documents Illustrating Early Christianity. A Review of the Greek Inscriptions and Papyri Published in 1978* (Sydney: Ancient History Documentary Research Centre, Macquarie University, 1983), 114–19 at 116, who holds that the credal statements serve to establish the *bona fides* of the wearer as Christ's follower.

41 P.Cair.Cat., p. 34.

42 P.Cair.Cat. 10263 = *PGM* II 13, 1–8.

43 Cf. Adolf Jacoby, *Ein neues Evangelienfragment* (Strassburg: Karl J. Trübner, 1900), 32n1, and 36. Jacoby sees a modalistic theology in this identification of Christ with the creator. But the attribution to Christ of all God's creative and salvific works is not out of keeping with Eastern soteriology. See Albert Gerhards, "Prière adressée à Dieu ou au Christ? Relecture d'une thèse importante de J.A. Jungmann à la lumière de la recherche actuelle," in *Liturgie, spiritualité, cultures: Conférences Saint–Serge, XXIXe semaine d'études liturgiques, Paris, 29 Juin – 2 Juillet 1982*, ed. A.M. Triacca and A. Pistoia (Rome: Edizioni Liturgiche, 1983), 101–14 at 107–09. The Alexandrian anaphora of Gregory of Nazianzus, to which Gerhard refers, is conveniently reprinted in Anton Hänggi and Irmgard Pahl, eds., *Prex eucharistica: textus e variis liturgiis antiquioribus selecti*, 2nd ed. (Fribourg: Éditions universitaires Fribourg Suisse, 1968), 358–73 at 358–62.

44 P.Cair.Cat. 10263 = *PGM* II 13, 1, 7, 8, 18.

45 P.Cair.Cat. 10263 = *PGM* II 13, 2-3; cf. Joseph Barbel, *Christos Angelos: Die Anschauung von Christus als Bote und Engel in der gelehrten und volkstümlichen Literatur des christlichen Altertums. Zugleich ein Beitrag zur Geschichte des Ursprungs und der Fortdauer des Arianismus* (Bonn: Peter Hanstein, 1941), 253.

46 P.Cair.Cat. 10263 = *PGM* II 13, 8–12; English translation in *ACM*, p. 36, slightly modified; cf. *PGM* II 13, 9 with J. Kroll, *Gott und Hölle: Der Mythos vom Descensuskampfe* (Leipzig; Berlin: B.G. Teubner, 1932), 109–11, who reads δι' ὅ in place of διό (p. 109, n7).

47 On the diverse early Christian accounts of Christ's descent to the underworld, see, in addition to Kroll, *Gott und Hölle*, Carl Schmidt, *Gespräche Jesu mit seinen Jüngern nach der Auferstehung*, Texte und Untersuchungen zur Geschichte der altchristlichen Literatur 43 (Leipzig: J.C. Hinrichs, 1919), 453–576; John Arnott MacCulloch, *The Harrowing of Hell: A Comparative Study of an Early Christian Doctrine* (Edinburgh: T & T Clark, 1930); Rémi Gounelle, *La descente du Christ aux enfers: Institutionnalisation d'une croyance* (Paris: Institut d'Études Augustiniennes, 2000).

48 P.Cair.Cat. 10263 = *PGM* II 13, 18.

49 P.Berl. inv. 11858 = *PGM* II 23, 10–14.

50 P.Wessely Prag. Graec. 1 = *PGM* II 21, 7–8: διὰ τοῦ κυρίω (l. κυρίου) ἡμῶν Ἰη(σο)ῦ Χρ[η](στο)ῦ (l. Χρ[ι](στο)ῦ) ἀγαπημένου (l. ἠγαπημένου) παιτός (l. παιδός). Adolf von Harnack, "Die Bezeichnung Jesu als 'Knecht Gottes' und ihre Geschichte in der Alten Kirche," in *Kleine Schriften zur alten Kirche: Berliner Akademieschriften 1908–1930* (Leipzig: Zentralantiquariat der Deutschen Demokratischen Republik, 1980), 2:730–56, originally published in *Sitzungsberichte der Preussischen Akademie der Wissenschaften zu Berlin 28* (1926): 212–38, assembles the earliest witnesses referring to Jesus as παῖς θεοῦ and analyzes the change in meaning from the "servant of God" to "child of God," the latter being associated with the "only-begotten Son of God." Later overtaken by Nicene Trinitarian and Christological terminology, the phrase ἠγαπημένου παιδός is preserved in prayers in the earliest church orders: *Apostolic Tradition* 4.4, *Didascalia* 42, and *Apostolic Constitutions* 8.39.4 and 8.41.8 (among many instances); cf. Metzger, *Les constitutions apostoliques*, SC 329:32–33.

51 P.Wessely Prag. Graec. 1 = *PGM* II 21, 41–49: Ἰη(σοῦ)ς Χρη(στό)ς, <σ>ὺ βασιλεὺς τῶν διώνων (l. αἰώνων) πάντ[ων], παντοκράτωρ, ἀμυθήτοις

(l. ἀμυθήτως) κτίσ[τα], τροφεῦ, δέσποτα, παν[τ]οκράτωρ, εὔπαις, υἱὸς εὐνοῶν, ἀστένακτόν μοι (l. μου) κ(αὶ) ἀμμύθητον (l. ἀμύθητον) ὄνομα, ἀλληθὸς (l. ἀληθὲς) ἀλληθῶς (l. ἀληθῶς) εἶτος (l. εἶδος) ἀ[όρ]ατο[ν εἰ]ς αἰώνας ἐώνων (l. αἰώνων), ἀμήν.

52 Frankfurter, "Narrating Power," 469, distinguishes between "those *historiolae* that function by virtue of their narrative—what I would call *historiolae* proper—and those that function as a subsidiary invocation to a directive utterance, a command or prayer—what we might call 'clausal *historiolae*.'"

53 See further Theodore de Bruyn, "Apocryphal and Canonical Christian Narratives in Greek Papyrus Amulets in Late Antiquity," in *Christian Apocryphal Texts for the New Millennium: Achievements, Prospects, and Challenges*, ed. Pierluigi Piovanelli (Leiden and Boston: Brill, forthcoming).

54 P.Turner 49 = *Suppl. Mag.* I 31, 2–4, English translation, pp. 87–88.

55 P.Berl. inv. 11858 = *PGM* II 23, 1–11; English translation in *AMC*, p. 34.

56 P.Heid. inv. G 1101 = *Suppl. Mag.* I 32, 8–11, English translation, p. 92.

57 Cf. n52 above.

58 P.Coll.Youtie II 91 = *Suppl. Mag.* I 30, 2-3; P.Oxy. VIII 1151 = *PGM* II 5b, 25–27; P.Turner 49 = *Suppl. Mag.* I 31, 2. Matthew 4:23 is also quoted in the manner of a self-standing *historiola* in P.Oxy. VIII 1077 = *PGM* II 4 and in BKT VI 7.1, 17–20. See further Theodore de Bruyn, "Appeals to Jesus as the One 'Who Heals Every Illness and Every Infirmity' (Matt 4:23, 9:35) in Amulets in Late Antiquity," in *The Reception and Interpretation of the Bible in Late Antiquity*, ed. Lorenzo DiTommaso and Lucian Turcescu (Leiden: Brill, 2008), 65–81.

59 PSI inv. 365 = *PGM* II 18, 5–12; English translation at *ACM*, p. 38.

60 P.Oxy. VIII 1151 = *PGM* II 5b, 7–14.

61 P.Louvre E 7332 *bis*, 1–2.

62 P.Ups. 8 = *Suppl. Mag.* II 59, 13–14, and P.Hamb. I 22 = *Suppl. Mag.* II 60, 3–4.

63 Henricus Denzinger, ed., *Ritus orientalium Coptorum Syrorum et Armenorum in administrandis sacramentis*, 2 vols. (1863–64; reprint, Graz: Akademische Druck– u. Verlagsanstalt, 1961), 2:489–90, 492–93, and 497; cf. *Coptic Offices*, trans. Reginald Maxwell Woolley (London: Society for Promoting Christian Knowledge, 1930), 95–96, 99–100, and 106.

64 On the Sanctus in early Egyptian anaphoras, including the liturgy of St. Mark, and its incorporation into amulets, see Theodore de Bruyn, "The Use of the Sanctus in Christian Greek Papyrus Amulets," in *Papers Presented at the Fourteenth International Conference on Patristic Studies Held in Oxford 2003: Liturgia et Cultus, Theologica et Philosophica, Critica et Philologica, Nachleben, First Two Centuries*, ed. Frances M. Young, Mark J. Edwards, and Paul M. Parvis, Studia Patristica 40 (Leuven: Peeters, 2006), 15–20.

65 As discussed above; cf. also BGU III 954 = *PGM* II 9, 28–29.

66 E.g., P.Bad. IV 60, 9–12; P.Duke inv. 778, 22–25; P.Lond.Lit. 231 = *PGM* II 5d, 1–2; P.Ross.Georg. I 23 = *PGM* II 16, 19–24; PSI VI 719 = *PGM* II 19, 5–6.

67 E.g., in addition to the Christological acclamations discussed above, the acclamations "Amen" (many instances), "Alleluia" (BKT VI 7.1, 23; P.Köln inv. 851 = *Suppl. Mag.* I 34, 12–15; P.Vindob. inv. G 337 = *PGM* II 10, 33), "One holy Father, one holy Son, one holy Spirit" (P.Bon. I 9, 5–7 and P. Köln VI 257 = *Suppl. Mag.* I 21, 1–2; cf. Cuming, *Liturgy of St Mark*, 55 with 141–42), and "Father, Son, Mother"

(P.Oxy. VI 924 = *PGM* II 5a, 15; cf. John D. Turner, *Sethian Gnosticism and the Platonic Tradition* [Leuven: Peeters, 2002], 63–64).

68 See Brashear and Kotansky, "New Magical Formulary," 10–13, on P.Berl. inv. 17202 (discussed further below), P. Louvre E 7332 *bis*, and P.Vindob. inv. G 19909 = *PGM* II 6d = Brashear, *Magica Varia*, 66.

69 Cf. n50 above.

70 See Roy A. Rappaport, *Ritual and Religion in the Making of Humanity* (Cambridge: Cambridge University Press, 1995), 107–38 and 277–312.

71 BKT VI 7.1, 21–22; P.Lond.Lit. 231 = *PGM* II 5d, 5; P.Ross.Georg. I 24 = *PGM* II 15a, 21–23; P.Vindob. inv. G 19889 = *PGM* II 2a, 8; cf. also Kotansky, *Greek Magical Amulets*, I 35, 8–10, found in Yalvaç, Turkey (ancient Pisidian Antioch), and J. Cozza Luzi, "Ein altchristliche Phylacterium aus Blei," *Römische Quartelschrift* 1 (1887): 197–208, found in Reggio, Calabria. Cf. Franz J. Dölger, "Ein Türsegen mit der 'Blut Christi'-Formel unde eine 'Blut Jesu Christi'-Litanei," and "Beschwörungen bei 'Leib und Blut Christi' auf einem Bleitäfelchen und einem Papyrus–Amulett," in *Antike und Christentum: Kultur- und religionsgeschichtliche Studien*, 2nd ed., 6 vols. (Münster: Aschendorff, 1974–75), 5:246–54 and 255–61.

72 P.Ross.Georg. I 24 = *PGM* II 15a, 21–27.

73 The phraseology of the amulets resembles the formula of communion attested at *Apostolic Constitutions* 8.13.15 and indirectly suggested by Cyril of Jerusalem, *Mystagogical Catecheses* 5.20–22.

74 Cf. Dölger, "Beschwörungen," 256–58.

75 The later practice in the liturgy of St. John Chrysostom of elevating the portion of the eucharistic bread stamped with the acclamation "Jesus Christ is victorious!" written in the four quadrants of a cross concentrates in one action the many signifiers discussed here. On this practice see F.E. Brightman, *Liturgies Eastern and Western*, 2 vols. (Oxford: Clarendon Press, 1896) 1:393; Franz J. Dölger, "Heidnische und christliche Brotstempel mit religiösen Zeichen," in *Antike und Christentum*, 1:1–46 at 21–38; G. Galavaris, *Bread and the Liturgy: The Symbolism of Early Christian and Byzantine Bread Stamps* (Madison: University of Wisconsin Press, 1970), 62–76.

76 P.Osl. I 5 = *PGM* II 3, 2; cf. P.Oxy. VII 1060 = *PGM* II 2, 2 and P.Oxy. VIII 1152 = *PGM* II 6a, 1–3, also amulets to protect a home and its occupants, for a similar opening.

77 P.Osl. I 5 = *PGM* II 3, 9–11: φύλαξον, κύριε, υἱὲ τοῦ Δαυὶδ κατὰ σάρκα, ὁ τεχθεὶς ἐκ τῆς ἁγίας παρθένου Μαρίας, ἅγιε, ὕψιστε Θεέ, ἐξ ἁγίου πνεύματος. δόξα σοι, οὐράνιε βασιλεῦ. ἀμήν.

78 Giuseppe L. Dossetti, *Il simbolo di Nicea e di Costantinopoli: Edizione critica* (Rome: Herder, 1967), 246: σαρκωθέντα ἐκ πνεύματος ἁγίου καὶ Μαρίας τῆς παρθένου.

79 P.Berl. inv. 17202.

80 Brashear and Kotansky, "New Magical Formulary," 10–13.

81 P. Köln inv. 851 = *Suppl. Mag.* I 34.

82 P.Cair.Masp. II 67188v = *PGM* II 13a, with Leslie S.B. MacCoull, "P. Cair. Masp. II 67188 Verso 1–5. The *Gnostica* of Dioscorus of Aphrodito," *Tyche* 2 (1987): 95–97, and Jordan, "A Prayer."

2

Jesus of Canada?
Four Canadian Constructions of the Christ Figure[1]

✠ ✠ ✠

MARY ANN BEAVIS

Have you ever been here on a Sunday when it's packed? Have you seen the Haitian charladies, the Guatemalan refugees, the elderly and forsaken? It's a gathering of universal misery. They don't care about the latest archaeological findings in the Middle East. They want to hear that Jesus loves them and awaits them—Does that justify selling plastic statues of Jesus and bottles of St. Joseph's oil for $15?—That Jesus is less than a rock poster. And is holy oil less effective than cocaine at $125 a gram? Not everyone can afford psychoanalysis. So they come here to be told "Go in peace, your sins are forgiven." It comforts them, a bit. That's something. This is where we hit the depths ... loneliness, illness, madness. (Fr. Leclerc, *Jesus of Montreal*)

RECENT SCHOLARSHIP on American popular culture has analyzed the role of popular representations of Jesus in relation to national identity. In *American Jesus: How the Son of God Became a National Icon*, Stephen Prothero argues that since the eighteenth century, Jesus has become a "national icon" whose shifting resurrections and reincarnations have included the enlightened sage, the sweet saviour, the manly redeemer, the superstar, the Mormon elder brother, the black Moses, the rabbi, and the Oriental Christ.[2] Stephenson Humphries-Brooks has examined the development of "cinematic saviours" in American Jesus movies (e.g., *King of Kings*, *The Greatest Story Ever Told*, *Jesus Christ Superstar*, *Jesus of Nazareth*, *The*

Last Temptation of Christ) and Christ-figure films (e.g., *Ben-Hur*, *Spartacus*, *Shane*, *High Plains Drifter*, *Pale Rider*, *The Matrix*, *Braveheart*) as exemplars of a developing "American christology," culminating in Mel Gibson's *The Passion of the Christ* (2004).[3] The contemporary American Christ figure, Humphries-Brooks argues, is a "Jesus with a gun," an action-figure hero who fits post-9/11 America, a Christ-like protagonist who skirts sacrilege by not being directly identified with Jesus of Nazareth:

> The fundamental structure of the Christ myth is broken apart and reassembled, but never directly attributed to the Jesus character. Hollywood has been happy to give us Jesus as the Christ who descends from the heavens, gathers disciples, teaches, works miracles, is betrayed, suffers unjustly at the hands of religious and political authorities, is crucified, dies, and is buried and resurrected to ascend to the heavens. It has not given us Jesus as the Warrior Lamb of God who returns to gather his elect and vanquish the evil forces that oppose him. The satisfaction of the final judgment instead has been provided by iconic heroes, never named Jesus, who are therefore free to explore at various points in their career the close connection assumed by America between justice and vengeance.[4]

The Passion, in contrast, fully conflates Jesus with the action hero, an idealized personification of America, bruised and beaten but ultimately triumphant over the enemy: "the adoption of the action movie genre to the Jesus story necessitates a thorough structuring of the film world into for or against, good versus evil. Jesus becomes the American action hero carrying with him the expectation of such heroes who always suffer silently and triumph in the end."[5] Prothero and Humphries-Brooks would agree that the American Jesus has become a product for consumption, in traditional Christian worship but even more as an iconic expression of American identity.[6]

Prothero asserts that while interest in Jesus is not limited to the United States, America has taken the cultural "immanentization" of Jesus to unprecedented heights, to the point that "Christians do not have a monopoly, even on the central figure of their tradition."[7] Over the past two hundred years, the American Jesus has been both a legitimator of mainstream American values and an iconoclast who challenges and subverts them, a figure belonging not to just one religious tradition but to many.[8] As the Jewish New Testament scholar Samuel Sandmel observed, the "Jesus of Western culture" belongs to secular culture as a whole, irrespective of the religious commitments of its members; as a Jew, Sandmel had no religious relationship to Jesus, yet he acknowledged the impossibility of avoiding the cultural Jesus.[9]

To date, no comparable studies of the role of Jesus as a *Canadian* cultural icon have appeared. The only example I have been able to locate is a brief 1970 article by Dick Harrison, "The American Adam and the Canadian Christ," which contrasts the American novelistic archetype of the "authentic American as a figure of heroic innocence and vast potentiality, poised at the start of a new history"[10] with the tendency of Canadian authors to build their novels around a "central redemptive figure" who stands not at the beginning of a new epoch "but in the midst, carrying the weight of an imperfectly understood past history and uncomfortably aware of his own implication in its sins. Frequently he is sacrificed in an attempt to bring forth a new order, and not infrequently he is given explicit overtones of Christ, the new Adam."[11] Harrison sees such figures in, for example, these disparate novels: Hugh MacLennan's *The Watch That Ends the Night* (1959), Morley Callaghan's *Such Is My Beloved* (1934), Malcolm Lowry's *Under the Volcano* (1947), Leonard Cohen's *Beautiful Losers* (1966), and Sheila Watson's *The Double Hook* (1959). The consistent characteristics of the "Canadian Christ" that Harrison finds throughout these works are "his uncomfortable sense of the need of human redemption, his despair at setting the universe in order even for himself, his frequent ambiguity and failure, and final passivity."[12] This particular construction of the Christ figure may, as Harrison speculates, be attributable to the pessimism and irony of twentieth-century fiction in general,[13] but it is in striking contrast to the consistently more positive, heroic cast of the American counterpart. He also notes that the redeemer figure is portrayed in a "romantic cast" characteristic of Canadian fiction.[14]

Canada, like the United States, is a predominantly "Christian country," albeit more secular and liberal in its national values.[15] Portrayals of Jesus regularly feature on the cover of Canada's national newsmagazine, *Maclean's*, along with sensational subtitles: "Jesus Has an Identity Crisis" (31 March 2008); "Did He Really Die on the Cross?" (3 April 2006); "Jesus: What Do We Know About Him?" (8 March 2004); "Jesus at 2000" (20 November 1999); "Who Was Jesus?" (21 December 1992). The accompanying articles are controversial and attract the expected mix of outraged (from conservative Christians) and supportive (from liberal Christians and non-Christians) letters to the editor.[16] The Provincial Museum of Alberta's millennial exhibition *Anno Domini: Jesus Through the Centuries* attracted national attention.[17] Books like Tom Harpur's *The Pagan Christ* ("our blind faith in literalism is killing Christianity"), Gretta Vosper's *With or Without God* ("God does not answer our prayers. Jesus is not the saviour who saved the world by dying for our sins"), and Barrie Wilson's *How Jesus Became Christian:*

St. Paul, the Early Church, and the Jesus Cover-up ("move over Dan Brown, there's another Jesus conspiracy theorist in town") are published by Canadian publishers and grace the bookshelves of Canadian bookstores.[18] Nino Ricci's demythologizing Jesus novel *Testament* received the expected reactions of praise from the secular press[19] and disdain from conservative Christians.[20] In the Canadian print media, then, Jesus functions as a public icon whose sacred status is continually both exploited and challenged.

The question whether some dominant construal of the Christ figure as described by Humphries-Brooks operates in Canadian culture in the first decade of the twenty-first century is an intriguing one. Does the failed redeemer identified by Harrison in 1970 still characterize secular Canadian Christology, or have new archetypes emerged? It is obviously beyond the scope of this essay to undertake a comprehensive survey of Canadian cultural expressions of the Christ figure. As opposed to a more or less realistically portrayed "Jesus of history," a Christ figure is defined here as a figure significantly manifesting elements from the biblical Jesus tradition and the history of Christology; as defined by Ronald Holloway, "the Christ figure … follows the main thread of the Christ story, while disguising it through a surface narrative and relying on the viewer to provide the necessary continuity. The figure is strong enough to exist by itself, but points to a meaning far beyond this existence for ultimate truth."[21] Here, I will offer four examples of Canadian cultural Christ figures that have received both national and international recognition and that are secular as opposed to religious: Almuth Lutkenhaus-Lackey's *Crucified Woman* (1976); the character Daniel in Denys Arcand's *Jesus of Montreal* (1989); the cult film *Jesus Christ Vampire Hunter* (dir. Lee Lemarbre, 2001); and the Canadian hero Terry Fox, particularly as constructed by the 2005 made-for-TV movie *Terry* (dir. Don McBrearty).

Crucified Woman

According to the artist, this sculpture, completed in 1976, was intended not as religious art, but rather to portray suffering ("I am a woman," the artist observed).[22] It gained some notoriety in 1979 when it was displayed in the chancel of Toronto's Bloor Street United Church.[23] Doris Jean Dyke, who was chair of that church's arts committee when the sculpture was displayed, describes its appearance:

> The sculpture is a bronzed, elongated female figure in cruciform, naked with outstretched arms. The seven-foot figure is placed securely on a four-foot concrete base. There is no cross. The feet point downward, the breasts

are taut, and the head drops to one side. There is beauty in the naked female body of the sculpture; there is pain and suffering in the face. The position of the hands, the nakedness, the absence of the cross, the absence of nail marks, the female, rather than the male, body are departures from traditional norms of representation of the crucifixion.[24]

It was subsequently donated to Emmanuel College, Toronto, in 1986, where it stands in the garden and has served as a site of the yearly December vigils commemorating the "Montreal Massacre" of fourteen women that took place at the École Polytechnique on 6 December 1989. In 1995 the sculpture was featured on the cover of *Maclean's* to illustrate the cover story "Is God a Woman?"[25]

Though evocative of traditional Crucifixion scenes, *Crucified Woman* is not simply a "female Jesus" but a Christ figure. As such, she has attracted both rapturous praise and righteous indignation. The novelist Margaret Laurence famously expressed her appreciation of the piece: "'Crucified Woman' is almost dancing, on the earth, the life dance of pain and love … To me, she represents the anguish of the ages, the repression, the injustice, the pain that has been inflicted on women, both physically and emotionally. 'Crucified Woman' also speaks to me of the comfort and help I have known from my mothers and the unconditional love I feel for my own children."[26] One less appreciative churchgoer commented: "A crucified woman is mocking the very basis of the Christian religion, the fact that Jesus Christ died on the cross and rose again. To take the ultimate sacrifice that Jesus made for the people of this world and make it into a sculpture calculated to create controversy and get publicity is to me— blasphemous."[27] After the sculpture was installed in the Emmanuel College garden, several male professors expressed discomfort with it: "One of the professors at Victoria said he would not be able to walk by it. Another wanted it placed where he could not see it from his window. Many did not care one way or another but opined that those that did not like it did not have to look at it. One professor said he was sexually aroused—it was too erotic."[28]

Though the sculpture was experienced as novel and shocking by viewers in the 1970s and 1980s, and is no doubt still considered sacrilegious by conservative Christians, the motif of the crucified woman is far from unique. Rachel Anderson points out that during the "era of the High Medieval and Renaissance period of 1100–ca. 1630 CE, a time of inflamed and eroticised devotional piety that absolutely adored the tortured and bloody body of Christ on the cross, when almost all art was religious art … the pictorial tradition of the Christian crucified woman appears to have arisen and to have established its own set of meanings."[29] Two other periods, 1800 to 1930 and 1960 to the present, have also seen efflorescences of the motif.[30] The second wave of feminism in the 1970s inspired a spate of explicitly feminist artworks depicting a female Crucifixion, such as Edwina Sandys's *Christa* (1974), *Crucifixion, Shoalhaven* (Arthur Boyd, 1979–80), *Christine on the Cross* (James M. Murphy, 1984), and Margaret Argyle's *Bosnian Christa* (1993).[31]

The wide range of public responses to the image is explained by Anderson: "Images of crucified women are necessarily potent; they combine two of the most intensely evocative motifs of Western culture, the image of the Crucified Christ and the image of the alluring Female Body. The result of their combination yields an extraordinarily freighted image."[32] One element in this volatile mix is the erotic load attached to the combination of sex and violence; crucified women are a popular motif in pornography, as attested by the porn site http://www.crucified-women.com (billing itself as "The Largest Collection on the Net").[33] Another relevant factor is the explicitly feminist orientation of works like *Crucified Woman* and *Christa*, which, as Julie Clague argues, expose "the reality of the cross as a site of patriarchal violence" through graphic images of female suffering.[34] The juxtaposition of the "sacred" image of the Crucifixion with "obscene" and "feminist" images of the tortured female body evokes the latent anti-feminism and misogyny inherent in "Christian" culture. Why else is the image of a woman suffering on a cross so much more distressing than the sacred icon of the crucifix?

Jesus of Montreal

Jesus of Montreal (1989) is one of the best-known Canadian films, having been nominated for the Oscar for Best Foreign Language Film (1990), and having won seventeen other awards, including three from Cannes and twelve Genies (including Best Picture).[35] This film is assigned a chapter in almost all scholarly books on Jesus movies[36] and is regularly studied in university Bible and film courses.[37] It has been called a "film of transition" in that it is both a Jesus movie and a Christ-figure film.[38] The plot revolves around a contemporary re-enactment of the life of Jesus, ostensibly based on the Gospels and "recently discovered historical evidence." In terms of genre, the "life of Jesus" part of the film is an avant-garde revival of the medieval Passion Play, a series of *tableaux vivantes* from the Gospels, traditionally put on during Holy Week and culminating in the Crucifixion and Resurrection.

The hero of the film is a young man, Daniel Coulombe ("Daniel Dove"), who has been hired by the priest of a large Montreal parish to revivify a stale Lenten devotion illustrating the Stations of the Cross. Daniel quickly gathers together a small troupe of four other actors, two women and two men, and creates an ingeniously staged outdoor spectacle, starring Daniel as Jesus, that immediately becomes the hit of the season. Despite rave reviews from the media, the priest, Fr. LeClerc, is incensed at the unorthodox retelling of the sacred story and decides, backed by the official Church, to close it down. Daniel and his friends defy the authorities and put on one final show. Tragically, Daniel is mortally injured by an overenthusiastic fan, who accidentally knocks down the cross where Daniel/Jesus is hanging as police officers arrive to arrest the cast for trespassing on church property.

The Jesus figure of the movie is obviously the hero of the Passion Play and is portrayed in terms that would be radical even for the Jesus Seminar. Jesus, the script claims, was the illegitimate son of a Roman soldier and Mary of Nazareth, a powerful magician and philosopher whose story is more authentically conveyed in the Apocryphal Gospels than in the Bible. The play, based on "recent new discoveries" and "computer assisted analysis," maintains that the canonical Gospels were written a hundred years after the Crucifixion and that the disciples' post-Resurrection visions of Jesus did not begin until ten years later—claims that any competent biblical scholar would refute.

The Christ figure is Daniel, whose life outside the play begins to parallel that of the traditional Jesus of Scripture and tradition. Daniel, a mystery man with an obscure past, is heralded by an actor friend, who pronounces him the "really good actor." After receiving his commission from Fr. Leclerc, Daniel gathers disciples (four, like the four Gospels), who become increasingly devoted to him and to their artistic mission. As in traditional paintings of Jesus, Daniel always wears white. The female actors, single mother Constance (Lazure, who always wears blue) and glamorous Mireille (Fontaine, who is first seen walking through a fountain), are Mother Mary and Mary Magdalene figures. Daniel is arrested for opposing the sexual exploitation of female actors at an audition in a scene redolent of the cleansing of the temple (especially John 2:13–17). His fatal injury is inflicted while he is tied to the cross; the two women stay with him to the end. After his death, Daniel's eyes and heart are transplanted and give vision and new life to the recipients. The actors regroup to found a theatre in the name of their beloved friend.

Stern, Jefford, and Debona (1999) offer a persuasive interpretation of the film as a biting critique of Montreal society in the late twentieth century:

One technique or stylistic element the viewer might notice is the frequent use of panoramic views of Montreal, including those from the hill of the shrine and from the office building where various characters meet with the lawyer/agent, but especially during the crucifixion scenes in the Passion Play ... After all, the movie is entitled *Jesus of Montreal*, not *Jesus of Contemporary Western Urban North American Culture*. One of our students watched this movie with great interest. He had lived and worked in Montreal for twenty years. He noted that at one time Montreal was the most Catholic of Canadian cities but had now become the most secular. A traditional Catholic spirituality had been replaced by a relentless joie de vivre, a constant quest for enjoyment or pleasure. The city had lost its soul, he concluded.[39]

While the Jesus figure of the Passion Play is foreign and edgy, the Christ figure, Daniel, embodies the traditional spiritual values that the city needs in order to restore itself to holiness: salvation must be found within the human spirit; don't give up hope in the meaningfulness of existence; walk in solidarity with others; forget yourself and help one another; live the simple life; love one another. Daniel's harrowing apocalyptic ramblings in the subway foretell the inevitable downfall of the shallow, trivial, exploitative American empire and its Quebec outpost, Montreal:

All these buildings, these great structures, not a stone will be left some day ... When you see the abomination of desolation if you're on the plain, flee to the mountains. If you're on the balcony, don't go inside for your things. If you're on the road, don't return home. Woe to those who are with child! Pray that your flight be not in winter. If anyone says to you, "Christ is here" or "There ..." believe it not. Believe it not. False Christs ... false prophets ... The powers of the heavens shall be shaken. Not the day, nor the hour ... You know not when the Judgment ...Watch!

In the meantime, *Jesus of Montreal* offers hope for individual salvation—in the form of authentic human existence based on values of caring, trust, and hope. In fact, the Christ figure Daniel comes close to offering the kinds of spiritual consolation described by Fr. LeClerc in the speech quoted at the beginning of this chapter: the latest scholarship on the historical Jesus, as represented in the Passion Play, is not what people want; rather, they crave the love and compassion of the Christ of faith, to be told "Go in peace, your sins are forgiven."

Jesus Christ Vampire Hunter

A very different Canadian Jesus movie is *Jesus Christ Vampire Hunter* (2001), a send-up of traditional Jesus movies. The title conflates the famous *Jesus Christ Superstar* (1973) and the hit TV series *Buffy the Vampire Slayer* (1997-2003). Like *Superstar*, *Vampire Hunter* is a musical; like Buffy, this Jesus kicks demonic butt.

Despite its low budget and poor production values, *Vampire Hunter* has won film festival awards: the Fargo Film Festival award for Best Cult Film (2002), and from the Santa Cruz Film Festival (2002), Best Science Fiction / Fantasy / Horror Film.[40] It has been widely reviewed online,[41] including by Canuxploitation: Your Complete Guide to Canadian B-Films (http://www.canuxploitation.com/review/jesus.html, accessed 8 August 2008). It was screened at the 2002 meeting of the Society of Biblical Literature in Toronto.

The premise of the film is suitably outrageous: the lesbians of Ottawa are being attacked by vampires, and punk-coiffed Father Alban and his colleague Father Eustace are concerned. They know that only Jesus Christ himself has the power to stop the carnage, and they know where to find him: on a local beach, doing baptisms. Their stilted dialogue with the Saviour is not that far from many traditional Jesus movies ("I'm here to build a kingdom, Alban, my father's kingdom—I cannot see to the battlements before the foundation is laid, or else the foundation will inevitably collapse"). Like Buffy, this Jesus fights evil with martial arts, especially kick-boxing; there are several extended (and rather tedious) scenes of the Lord battling gangs of vampires, and one where he beats up a band of atheists ("Real enough for you?" he gloats). His disciples include a gun-toting Mary Magnum ("I'm on your side, rabbi—see, no fangs!"), who belongs to a branch of Christianity that knows "women in the church haven't always been so horizontal"; El Santo, a professional wrestler ("be sure you get my good side, or you'll be on my bad side"); and the jazz singer Blind Jimmy Leper. His archenemies include the vampire Johnny Golgotha and the mad surgeon Dr. Praetorius, who grafts human skin onto vampires so that they can tolerate sunlight ("new wine in new wineskins"). Occasionally, Jesus and company burst into song, recalling the 1970s musicals *Godspell* and *Superstar*:

> It's all good / It's all right / Everybody get laid tonight / He came from heaven, / two stakes in his hand / To smite the vampires / and free that land. / Come now and join him, all ye strong and bold / We'll fight together, / like the days of old. / Behold his Glory, / come praise the light /

That has delivered us, / from the endless night. / Come sound the trumpet, / prepare the feast / And make the joyful shout, / to he who slayed the beast.[42]

Both Jesus' parents make an appearance: mother Mary checks up on him through a talking, glow-in-the-dark statuette; "Dad" communicates through the medium of a bowl of cherries (God: "Jesus ..." Jesus: "Is that you, bowl of cherries?" God: "Do bowls of cherries talk, Jesus?").

Not surprisingly, critics regularly deplore the film's cheesy quality, amateurish acting, and relentless shallowness. Yet the film abounds in quips ("If I'm not back in five minutes, call the Pope!"), and shows considerable biblical knowledge, sometimes resulting in some memorable exegesis: at one point, Jesus eats garlicky schawarma so that he can slay the vamps "with the breath of his mouth" like the apocalyptic Lord of 2 Thessalonians 2:8 ("And then the lawless one will be revealed, whom the Lord Jesus will destroy with the breath of his mouth, annihilating him by the manifestation of his coming").[43] In a novel retake of the Good Samaritan, a wounded Jesus is ignored by an off-duty cop but rescued by a blonde transvestite ("Jesus, honey, you're a mess!").

An anonymous reviewer for Canuxploitation.com commented that he (or she) took the movie more seriously than expected:

> What makes *JCVH* such an effective movie is that it makes itself almost believable. I noticed myself taking this picture much more seriously than other Canadian B-movie parodies like *Big Meat Eater* and *Revenge of the Radioactive Reporter*. Because *JCVH* is filmed to resemble an older drive-in movie, I associated it with the slightly more serious cult films from the 60s and 70s that we all laugh at, not with. Sometimes it doesn't seem like it's supposed to be funny at all, just an oddly scripted gem that hasn't aged well.[44]

Though Jesus has accomplished considerable slayage by the end of the movie, he forgives at least some of his enemies (to the evil Dr. Praetorius: "Not even this separates you from my love"). The parish priests worry that their lesbian parishioners are vulnerable because the Church doesn't want to investigate the deaths of these "ladies of Sappho"; the church should learn to leave judgment to God, Jesus opines.[45] To a vampire-priest who explains that his gang targets lesbians because they are deviants, Jesus replies, "there's nothing deviant about love." He resurrects ex-vampire Maxine Schreck so that she and Mary Magnum can pursue a romantic relationship. Jesus' final sermon to a crowd of onlookers and media would be at home in many liberal churches:

Back when I was hanging out with the apostles, I used to say, if you can, bear the whole yoke of the Lord, but if you can't, do what you can. And if you choose Christianity, don't follow me, follow my teachings. Think about it, make up your own mind, it's the message that's important, not the messenger. I don't need to give you new laws, I'm just telling you what you already know ... It's the part of you that feels bad when you don't give that homeless guy that spare change. Trust yourself, learn to love, learn to forgive. And remember—five keeps the neighbourhood alive!

Despite its horror-movie premise and comic tone, the film is irreverent, not blasphemous, and its message, such as it is, is surpisingly close to Daniel's in *Jesus of Montreal*.

In representing Jesus as the consummate superhero, *Vampire Hunter* lampoons not just traditional Jesus movies, but the kind of macho American Christ figure critiqued by Humphries-Brooks: "The absorption of the Jesus movie into the action hero genre means that the film naturally and necessarily divides the world into a conflict between good and evil. The hero triumphs, and is supposed by the viewer to continue his triumph off screen, or ... to ride off to resurrection and revenge another day."[46] Since many pop-culture superheroes (including Buffy the Vampire Slayer) have characteristics of the Christ figure,[47] a superhero Jesus is not much of a stretch. Indeed, the film is as much a spoof of the superhero-as-Christ-figure as it is of Jesus movies. Stanley Donner, director of two *Superman* movies, admitted: "It's a motif I had done at the beginning when Brando sent Chris [Reeve] to earth and said 'I send them my only son.' It was God sending Christ to earth."[48] Jesus not only saves; Jesus sells.

Terry Fox

Of the four "Canadian Christ figures" discussed here, Terry Fox is the only one who is not an artistic creation, but an iconic culture hero, named one of the top ten "greatest Canadians" by CBC Television.[49] In 1980, Fox, a twenty-one-year-old cancer survivor and amputee, set out from the Newfoundland coast on a cross-country run to raise a dollar per Canadian for cancer research, with minimal publicity and little financial support. Initially accompanied by a single friend in a donated van, he met with both discouragement and accolades on his way from the Maritimes through Quebec, but was greeted enthusiastically in Ontario, where the Canadian Cancer Society had mounted a major publicity campaign. After rapturous welcomes in Ottawa and Toronto, Fox proceeded west. By the time he reached the halfway mark in Sudbury, his health had deteriorated, and the run came to an end at Thunder Bay, where he was diagnosed with lung cancer. Terry died less than a year later, on 28 June 1981.

As a bona fide Canadian hero, Fox is amenable to interpretation in mythic terms. His story resonates with the legendary Gilgamesh, who sets out to overcome death but who must ultimately bend to its inevitability. However, in a culture whose predominant hero figure, both secular and religious, is Jesus Christ, it is to be expected that Terry would be interpreted in Christ-like terms, since in Western culture "Jesus of Nazareth is the universal Homo, the essential Vir, the Son of human nature ... Blending in himself all races, ages, sexes capacities, temperaments, Jesus is the archetypal man, the ideal hero, the consummate incarnation, the symbol of perfected humanity,... history's true Avatar."[50] The contours of Fox's life are amenable to such a construal: a young man from a working-class family in a small town (Port Coquitlam, British Columbia) sets out on a cross-country mission to vanquish a deadly disease. Fox wrote in a letter to a potential sponsor: "I'm not saying that this will initiate any kind of definitive answer or cure to cancer, but I believe in miracles. I have to."[51] Initially accompanied by a single companion (his best friend, Doug Alward), he attracts other supporters and meets with both opposition and acclaim "on the way." After "triumphal entries" into the capital cities of Canada and Ontario, his quest ends in death and apparent failure. But after the run ends, Fox's fundraising goal is exceeded; after his death, a foundation is established in his name, and his message spreads throughout the world: "Terry Fox runs are held yearly in 60 countries now and more than 360 million have been raised for cancer research. His legacy lives on."[52] Statues of the one-legged runner dot the nation, including one on Parliament Hill.

There is no evidence that Fox himself had any messianic leanings or that he was particularly religious; nor is he generally regarded by the Canadian public as a Christ figure. Nonetheless, the 2005 biopic *Terry*, made to commemorate the twenty-fifth anniversary of Fox's historic run, is tinged with christic undertones. Note that the screenplay was carefully reconstructed from primary sources: diary entries, personal letters, eyewitness accounts, and news and documentary footage.[53] It is highly doubtful that the filmmakers intended to portray him as a Christ figure. Nonetheless, in the film, the obvious christic resonances in Fox's story are subtly struck.

The movie begins with Terry initiating his mission at the water's edge, when he dips ("baptizes") his prosthetic leg in the Atlantic, at St. John's, Newfoundland. (Later, when Terry's friend Doug says he has called Saint John [New Brunswick], "just to check," Fox quips, "Did I hear that right?")[54] It is clear that Terry's mission is on behalf of cancer victims who are outcasts owing to public fear of the disease.[55] His special concern for children is highlighted, and he gives priority to meetings with children's groups (one child comments, "My mom called me the miracle baby, but you're the miracle man"; in Wawa, Ontario, Terry is greeted by children singing "He's got the whole world in his hands").[56] With its setting primarily on the Trans-Canada Highway, there are many scenes of cross-shaped electrical poles stretching into the distance; one such scene is strikingly set up after Fox is run off the road by a semi in eastern Quebec. In between the hosannas he receives in Ottawa and Toronto,[57] Terry enjoys a "last supper" with his parents and friends,[58] where his mother admits that she doesn't know what to think about her extraordinary son.[59] Fox's several inspiring speeches are accompanied by hymn-like music. Terry's private meeting with his Canadian idol, hockey demigod Bobby Orr, is a sort of transfiguration scene where Fox asks for advice from the older hero on when to quit.[60] Near the end of his run, Terry sees a wolf at the side of the road, a portent of his death. A police officer warns Terry about the steepness of Montreal River Hill;[61] as he runs up the 3 kilometre incline in pain from tendonitis, Fox's condition worsens. In Thunder Bay, when Terry admits that he needs to see a doctor, he is shown leaning across the open door at the back of the van, arms spread out in cruciform. At several points in the film, Fox's physical and mental suffering are highlighted, as is his humanity—he has a keen sense of humour, he loses his temper,[62] he likes to be admired by girls.[63] The faithful Doug accompanies his friend throughout the run, a sort of beloved disciple ("St. John") to the end.[64] Terry Fox, reads the tagline on the DVD cover, "raised the spirit of a nation."[65] A *TV Times* article proclaims Fox "Canada's son."[66]

Leaving aside whether *Terry* deliberately, coincidentally, or unconsciously (most likely, a combination of the latter two) portrays its hero in Christ-like terms, the christological motif the film most poignantly evokes is that of the Suffering Servant.[67] The director, Don McBrearty, remarks that "he and his crew quickly learned Fox's odyssey was often a nightmare: freezing cold, then blistering heat; lonely and treacherous—but in the end, it was also intensely gratifying because it proved a single person can do so much, one small step at a time."[68] According to McBrearty, the film was emotionally the toughest project he had ever worked on. The dangers and difficulties of the run are emphasized throughout the film—for example, as a *National Post* article observes:

> The screenplay does not spare Quebec ... depicting how Fox and his small entourage were not only ignored by the media across the province, but harassed by police, even threatened with arrest if he did not abandon the

main highways for side roads. At one point he is nearly run over by an indifferent transport truck, all the while suffering dizzy spells, a racking cough (portent of things to come) and a bleeding leg. One newspaper even accused him of surreptitiously skipping two thirds of the Quebec run, a slam that was later retracted.[69]

Both the filmic Terry and the real-life man can rightly be described as sacrificing safety and comfort for a salvific goal. It is impossible to contemplate Fox's achievement without respect and admiration, tinged with regret for his premature death.[70]

Conclusions

The four Canadian Christ figures discussed above are portrayed in very different forms: a feminist sculpture, a québécois art film, a low-budget cult film, and a real-life Canadian hero. Ostensibly, the messages conveyed by these cultural Christs are diverse. *Crucified Woman*, though not created as a religious work, was eventually adopted by religious institutions (Bloor Street United Church and Emmanuel College) and has recently been claimed as emblematic of a Canadian contextual feminist theology: "The sculpture raises theological questions about suffering, embodiment, the place of art in worship and the meaning of incarnation."[71] *Jesus of Montreal* parallels a radical revisioning of the historical Jesus with the more traditionally Christ-like figure of Daniel, who is emblematic of a return to authentic human values. *Jesus Christ Vampire Hunter* is a comic tribute to B-movies that uses the trope of the superhero to send up conventional cinematic Christs and superheroic Christ figures. Terry Fox, a recognized "great Canadian," has been mythologized into a Christ figure, reflecting his heroic status in recent history.

If Harrison's 1970 article on the Canadian Christ figure in literature is a valid reflection of Canadian secular Christology at that time, then the examples discussed here indicate development in directions beyond the failed redeemer figure who haunts the pages of mid-twentieth-century novels. However, like the works discussed by Harrison, the three artistic productions discussed in this chapter—the sculpture and the two films— exist in tension with their secular American counterparts. *Crucified Woman* has encountered considerably more appreciation and acceptance than Edwina Sandys's *Christa*, which, Prothero observes, "lives on (barely) in obscurity, tucked away in the undercroft of Christ Church in New Haven, Connecticut."[72] *Jesus of Montreal* is a sort of sequel to Arcand's *The Decline of the American Empire* (1986); among other things, it critiques the spiritual hollowness of a city dominated by an imperial culture. *Vampire Hunter*, almost prophetically, pokes fun at the kind of American superhero Jesus epit-omized in Gibson's *The Passion of the Christ* (2004).

While most of the secular Canadian Christ figures considered above are iconoclastic, including Harpur's *Pagan Christ* and the "all-human" figure of Nino Ricci's *Testament*, there is a lingering respect for the values associ-ated with Jesus of Nazareth, if not for traditional christological doctrines. Even the most outrageous and intentionally tacky example, *Jesus Christ Vampire Hunter*, ends on a surprisingly inspirational note. As Ricci observes of unorthodox treatments of Jesus from Renan to Andrew Lloyd Webber, "few of these … for all the radicalness they may have had in their own time, were quite able to shed the mantle of divinity that cloaked the tradi-tional Jesus."[73]

Interestingly, the iconoclasm is reserved for the Christ figures that are clearly artistic creations. The Gospel preached by the "real" human char-acter, Daniel, in *Jesus of Montreal* is existential but recognizably Christian. And the real-life human being, Terry Fox, subtly cast in christic terms since his death in 1981, has achieved a post-mortem sanctity denied most more explicit "Canadian Christs." As a speech recorded in *Hansard* observes, there was "a spiritual thing" about Terry Fox, "who is inspired by forces that we should come to understand much better than we do."[74]

Notes

1   I partnered with Joanne McWilliam for several years as Publications Officer for the Canadian Corporation for the Study of Religion (CCSR) and as co-editor of Edi-tions SR. Joanne was always a congenial and hard-working colleague, and part-nering with her in service to the Canadian academic community was a pleasure and a privilege. One of my last tasks as CCSR Publications Officer was to request funding for this Festschrift in the series that Joanne and I co-edited. I am grate-ful that Joanne knew about and approved of the project, and I thank Ellen Leonard and Kate Merriman for their many hours of work in bringing it to fruition.

2   Stephen Prothero, *American Jesus: How the Son of God Became a National Icon* (New York: Farrar, Straus, Giroux, 2003).

3   Stephenson Humphries–Brooks, *Cinematic Savior: Hollywood's Making of the Ameri-can Christ* (Westport: Praeger, 2006).

4   Ibid., 115.

5   Ibid., 132.

6   See Humphries–Brooks, *Cinematic Savior*, 133–38; Prothero, *American Jesus*, 291–303.

7   Prothero, *American Jesus*, 302.

8   Ibid., 300–2.

9   Prothero, *American Jesus*, 266, citing Samuel Sandmel, *We Jews and Jesus: Exploring Theological Differences for Mutual Understanding* (New York: Oxford University Press, 1965), 111.

10 Dick Harrison, "The American Adam and the Canadian Christ," *Twentieth Century Literature* 16, no. 3 (1970): 161–67 at 161; here, Harrison is citing R.W.B. Lewis's description of the "American Adam" archetype.

11 Harrison, "Canadian Christ," 161–62.

12 Ibid., 167.

13 Ibid.

14 Ibid.

15 See Michael Adams, *Fire and Ice: The United States, Canada, and the Myth of Converging Values* (Toronto: Penguin Canada, 2004).

16 The terms "conservative" and "liberal" here are used as blanket terms to denote evangelical Protestants and traditionalist Catholics, on the one hand, and "mainline" Protestants and progressive Catholics on the other, with the former favouring a higher Christology than the latter.

17 See the exhibit's catalogue, David Goa, Linda Distad, and Matthew Wangler, *Anno Domini: Jesus Through the Centuries—Exploring the Heart of Two Millennia* (Edmonton: Alberta Community Development, 2000).

18 Tom Harpur, *The Pagan Christ: Recovering the Lost Light* (Toronto: Thomas Allen, 2004); Gretta Vosper, *With or Without God* (Toronto: HarperCollins, 2008); Barrie Wilson, *How Jesus Became Christian: St. Paul, the Early Church, and the Jesus Cover-Up* (Toronto: Random House Canada, 2008). The parenthetical quotations are from the cover liner of Harpur's book, the Amazon.ca product description of Vosper's (http://www.amazon.ca/Without-God-Gretta-Vosper/dp/1554682282/ref=pd_bbs_1?ie=UTF8&s=books&qid=1215794742&sr=8-1), and *Kirkus Reviews* (on Wilson), quoted on Amazon.ca (http://www.amazon.ca/How-Jesus-Became-Christian-Cover-up/dp/0679314938/ref=pd_bxgy_b_text_b?ie=UTF8&qid=1215794742&sr=8-1). Websites accessed 8 August 2008. The books by Harpur and Wilson are both amenable to critique on historical-critical grounds; they have also provoked the kinds of predictable religious reactions defined in n16 above.

19 Nino Ricci, *Testament* (Toronto: Random House Canada, 2002).

20 For excerpts of reviews from Canadian newspapers, see http://www.amazon.com/gp/product/product-description/0385658540/ref=dp_proddesc_0?ie=UTF8&n=283155&s=books, accessed 8 August 2008. Ron Charles of the *Christian Science Monitor* remarked that Ricci was lucky that Christian authorities don't issue fatwas (30 June 2003); http://www.powells.com/review/2003_06_30.html, accessed 8 August 2008.

21 Ronald Holloway, *Beyond the Image: Approaches to the Religious Dimension in the Cinema* (Geneva: Oikoumene, 1977), 187; for discussions of the Christ figure in film, see Lloyd Baugh, *Imaging the Divine: Jesus and Christ-Figures in Film* (Franklin: Sheed & Ward, 2000), 109–12; see also Anton Karl Koslovic, "The Structural Characteristics of the Cinematic Christ Figure," *Journal of Religion and Popular Culture* 8 (Fall 2004), http://www.usask.ca/relst/jrpc/art8-cinematicchrist.html, accessed 8 August 2008.

22 Marci McDonald and Sandra Farran, "Is God a Woman?" *Maclean's* 109, no. 15 (1995): 46–51 at 51.

23 See Doris Jean Dyke, *Crucified Woman* (Toronto: United Church Publishing House, 1991).

24 Ibid., 25.

25 McDonald and Farran, "Is God a Woman?" 46–51.

26 Margaret Laurence, *Dance on the Earth: A Memoir* (Toronto: McClelland and Stewart, 1989), 115–17.

27 Quoted in Dyke, *Crucified Woman*, 8.

28 Dyke, *Crucified Woman*, 23. For a broader selection of comments, see idem, 1–24.

29 Rachel Anderson, "The Crucified Woman: A Paradox of Prurience and Piety," research paper, 21 May 2007, 6. http://hdl.handle.net/1773/3101, accessed 8 August 2008.

30 Anderson, "Crucified Woman," 6.

31 See Julie Clague, "The Christa: Symbolizing My Humanity and My Pain," *Feminist Theology* 14, no. 1 (2005): 83–108.

32 Anderson, "Crucified Woman," 3.

33 As observed by Anderson, "Crucified Woman," 5, accessed 8 August 2008.

34 Clague, "The Christa," 83.

35 See http://www.imdb.com/title/tt0097635/awards, accessed 8 August 2008; it was nominated for seven other awards.

36 E.g., W. Barnes Tatum, *Jesus at the Movies: A Guide to the First Hundred Years* (Santa Rosa: Polebridge, 1997), 177–90; Richard C. Stern, Clayton N. Jefford, and Guerric Debona, *Savior on the Silver Screen* (New York: Paulist Press, 1999), 299–336; Baugh, *Imaging the Divine*, 113–29; Adele Reinhartz, *Jesus of Hollywood* (Oxford: Oxford University Press, 2007), 31–39.

37 For sample syllabi, see RS2YY3E, McMaster University (http://www.socsci.mcmaster.ca/relstud/emplibrary/RS%202YY3E%20Final%20Winter%202008.pdf); RE 397, Colby College (http://www.colby.edu/rel/syllabif05/re397f05.html); English 354, California Polytechnic State University (http://cla.calpoly.edu/~smarx/courses/354/index.html); "Jesus: Real to Reel," Institute of Pastoral Studies, Loyola University (http://post.queensu.ca/~rsa/REELSYLL.HTM). Websites accessed 8 August 2008.

38 Baugh, *Imaging the Divine*, 113–29.

39 Stern et al., *Savior*, 318.

40 http://www.imdb.com/title/tt0311361/awards, accessed 8 August 2008. According to the DVD cover, it has also won awards from the Slamdance Film Festival and Zombiedance.

41 See http://www.imdb.com/title/tt0311361/externalreviews, accessed 8 August 2008.

42 Lyrics from http://www.leoslyrics.com/listlyrics.php?hid=78MyTcx4rOc%3D, accessed 8 August 2008.

43 NRSV.

44 http://www.canuxploitation.com/review/jesus.html, accessed 8 August 2008.

45 The description of the Catholic Church's attitude toward lesbians calls to mind the notorious incident in 2003, when Cardinal Aloysius Ambrozic of Toronto refused to hand Sr. Christina Cathro her doctoral diploma from St. Michael's College because the title of her dissertation, listed in the program, was "Contributions of Lesbians' Journeys to Spiritual Direction and Theological Reflection." The Chancellor of the University of Toronto did the honours.

46 Humphries-Brooks, *Cinematic Savior*, 130.

47 See Bruce David Forbes, "Batman Crucified: Religion and Modern Superhero Comic Books," online essay (http://www.wacc.org.uk/wacc/content/pdf/1329);

Anton Karl Koslovic, "Superman as Christ Figure: The American Pop Culture Messiah," *Journal of Religion and Film* 6, no. 1 (2002), http://www.unomaha.edu/jrf/superman.htm; Wendy Love Anderson, "What Would Buffy Do?" *Christian Century* (17 May 2003), http://findarticles.com/p/articles/mi_m1058/is_10_120/ai_102140735. Websites accessed 8 August 2008.

48 Quoted by Koslovic, "Superman."

49 See http://www.cbc.ca/greatest/top_ten, accessed 8 August 2008.

50 George Dana Boardman, quoted in Prothero, *American Jesus*, 300.

51 Quoted on CBC, The Greatest Canadian website: http://www.cbc.ca/greatest/top_ten/nominee/fox-terry.html, accessed 8 August 2008.

52 http://www.cbc.ca/greatest/top_ten/nominee/fox-terry.html, accessed 8 August 2008.

53 According to the DVD insert.

54 Cf. Mark 1:9–11; Luke 3:21–22; John 1:29–34.

55 E.g., Luke 19:10; Matthew 11:28; Mark 1:32; Matthew 5:2–11; Luke 6:20–26.

56 Mark 10:13–16; Matthew 19:13–15; Luke 18:15–17.

57 Mark 11:1–10; Matthew 21:1–11; Luke 19:8–14; John 12:12–19.

58 Mark 14:22–25; Luke 22:14–23; 1 Corinthians 11:23–26.

59 Luke 2:51b.

60 Mark 9:2–8; Matthew 17:1–8; Luke 9:28–36; 2 Peter 1:16–18.

61 Cf. Matthew 27:33; Mark 15:22; Luke 23:33; John 19:17. The Terry Fox Foundation's account of Terry's journey describes the uphill run this way: "The Montreal River Hill, just south of Wawa, is three km long. Those who knew it were making the analogy of the hill being Goliath and Terry being David." http://www.terryfoxrun.org/english/marathon/timeline/default.asp?s=1, accessed 8 August 2008.

62 According to a nationalpost.com article, the Fox family was offended by an earlier (1983) HBO Terry Fox movie because it portrayed him as too ill tempered (http://www.shawn-ashmore.com/print/nationalpost03.html, accessed 8 August 2008); the 2005 film "portrays Terry in a more heroic light."

63 Though Fox kept up a regular correspondence with his girlfriend, Rika, throughout the run (according to the DVD insert), this relationship is downplayed in the film; as Koslovic notes, asexuality is a feature of cinematic Christ figures: "After all, the biblical Jesus had no wife or girlfriend or engaged in sexual practices that are recorded in the Bible, except the common assumption of his celibacy" ("Cinematic Christ Figures," 36). While Terry clearly likes girls and they seek him out, the movie downplays the romantic and sexual side of his life.

64 John 19:26.

65 Acts 2:1–4.

66 Alison Cunningham, "Canada's Son," *TV Times* (9–15 September 2005), 5.

67 Cf. Mark 10:45; Matthew 20:28.

68 http://www.shawn-ashmore.com/print/globemail03.html, accessed 8 August 2008.

69 http://www.shawn-ashmore.com/print/nationalpost03.html, accessed 8 August 2008.

70 Fox's implicit Christ-figure status is illustrated by a student's comment when I suggested in a Religion and Popular Culture class that Terry might have been alive today if it hadn't been for the run's physical toll on his body. The student, who was initially quite resistant to the notion that Fox was a kind of Christ figure, blurted

out: "But he *had* to die!" In another class (Bible and Film, 2008), the students uttered an "Ah!" of recognition when I showed a slide of a Terry Fox sculpture after asking them what a Canadian Christ figure would be like.

71 Ellen Leonard, "The Emergence of Canadian Contextual Feminist Theologies," in *Feminist Theology with a Canadian Accent: Canadian Contextual Feminist Theology*, ed. Mary Ann Beavis with Elaine Guillemin and Barbara Pell (Ottawa: Novalis, 2008), 23–38 at 35.

72 Prothero, *American Jesus*, 85.

73 Nino Ricci, "On Writing *Testament*," online essay; http://www.ninoricci.com/On Writing Testament.htm, accessed 8 August 2008.

74 20 March 1987, Morning Sitting. http://www.leg.bc.ca/hansard/34th1st/34p_01s _870320a.htm, accessed 8 August 2008.

3
La christologie d'un apocryphe: une christologie apocryphe?
Le cas des *Actes de Thomas*

✠ ✠ ✠

PAUL-HUBERT POIRIER
YVES TISSOT

DANS L'INTRODUCTION à sa traduction des *Actes de Thomas* parue dans la nouvelle édition des *Neutestamentliche Apokryphen* de W. Schnee-melcher, Han J. W. Drijvers estime que ces *Actes* ne connaissent à proprement parler aucune sotériologie entendue au sens d'une doctrine d'un sauveur[1]. Des concepts comme ceux de péché ou de grâce ne s'y rencontreraient pas, pas plus que n'y seraient mentionnées l'incarnation, la crucifixion, la résur-rection ou l'ascension du Christ. Cependant, dans une précédente étude consacrée aux formes primitives de la christologie antiochienne[2], le même auteur voyait dans les *Odes de Salomon* et les *Actes de Thomas* deux témoins privilégiés dont l'apport permettrait de combler le «vide historique» existant entre les conceptions du second siècle relatives à la personne et à l'œuvre du Christ, et la christologie antiochienne classique telle qu'elle s'est déve-loppée à la fin du IVᵉ siècle dans l'école d'Antioche. D'autre part, en 1952, C. L. Sturhahn[3] a consacré une thèse à la christologie des Actes apocry-phes, dont un des chapitres traite de la christologie des *Actes de Thomas*. Sturhahn s'est intéressé avant tout à ce qu'il appelle les énoncés kérygma-tiques («Kerygmata») des *Actes de Thomas*, au double point de vue de la christologie et de la conception des sacrements. Il distingue deux types de «Kerygmata», les uns relevant du christianisme commun («allgemeinchrist-lich»), les autres, gnosticisants. En ce qui concerne la christologie, il range parmi les premiers tous les passages à résonance néotestamentaire, ou qui se réfèrent aux récits synoptiques de la passion. À la seconde catégorie, il attribue des passages comme ceux du chap. 45,3, où le sauveur vainc les démons en les trompant par un déguisement charnel, du chap. 72,1, qui, dans le texte grec, affirme que le sauveur est «devenu comme (ὡς) un homme», ou du chap. 153,1, qui qualifie Jésus de «polymorphe». Pour Sturhahn, même si les *Actes* reprennent des éléments christologiques traditionnels, ils les relativisent pour les mettre au service d'une christologie gnostique au centre de laquelle domine la figure d'un *salvator salvandus* qui, en dépit de son abaissement, appartient néanmoins au monde supérieur. Nous verrons plus loin ce qu'il faut penser de ces appréciations. Pour le moment, tournons-nous vers les *Actes de Thomas*[4].

Leur lecture, même rapide, montre qu'ils offrent, surtout dans les nombreuses hymnes et prières qu'ils renferment, un très riche matériau christologique, dans lequel les titres du Christ occupent certes une grande place, mais dont les développements plus ou moins longs sur l'œuvre du Christ ou sur sa relation au Dieu-Père ne sont pas absents. L'étude de ce matériau est cependant rendue difficile par la situation textuelle des *Actes de Thomas*. Ceux-ci sont en effet attestés par deux versions dont aucune, dans l'état actuel des choses, ne peut être considérée comme originale par rapport à l'autre, et le fait est que ces versions sont le point d'aboutissement d'une histoire rédactionnelle particulièrement complexe[5]. Par ailleurs, le genre littéraire des *Actes de Thomas* — un long récit romanesque dans lequel ont été insérés des discours, des hymnes et des prières — ne facilite guère l'étude pour elle-même d'une question théologique ou dogmatique comme celle de la christologie. Il est en effet difficile de délimiter et d'extraire de leur contexte narratif des développements dont l'examen ferait apparaître *la* christologie des *Actes*. Mais on ne peut non plus, au risque d'aboutir à une énumération répétitive de thèmes et de titres, se contenter de suivre le fil du récit et de relever, au fur et à mesure de leur apparition, les éléments de christologie que recèleraient les *Actes de Thomas*.

Pour notre part, nous avons retenu un certain nombre de passages des *Actes de Thomas*, qui nous ont paru avoir un contenu ou une incidence christologique particulièrement forte. Ces passages ont été, aux fins de la présente analyse, regroupés sous trois chefs, selon qu'ils parlent (1) du Christ dans sa relation à Dieu ou au Père, ou (2) du Christ dans l'«économie» de l'incarnation ou l'œuvre du salut, ou encore (3) qu'ils appliquent au Christ des titres particuliers. Chacun des passages présentés ou discutés sera donné en synopse de manière à faire apparaître les particularités des versions syriaque et grecque, sans que nous ayons cherché à reconstituer, par-delà ces versions, ce qu'auraient pu être les *Actes* primitifs. Notre étude, qui portera par conséquent sur les *Actes de Thomas* tels qu'ils nous sont parvenus, soit en grec soit en syriaque, ne saurait fournir qu'une vision partielle de leur christologie, dans la mesure où celle-ci est indissociable de la trame narrative des *Actes* et inextricablement liée aux autres aspects doctrinaux qu'ils présentent. Nous espérons néanmoins qu'elle contribuera modestement à l'examen approfondi de la christologie des *Actes de Thomas* que souhaitait H. J. W. Drijvers[6].

Le Christ dans sa relation à Dieu ou au Père

Nous considérerons tout d'abord un ensemble de textes qui décrivent la situation du Christ par rapport au Père, ou encore, son statut avant son envoi auprès de l'humanité. Le premier de ces textes est une prière de l'apôtre Thomas en faveur d'un jeune couple qu'il vient de convertir à l'encratisme. Attestée, avec des variantes, en syriaque et en grec, cette prière énonce plusieurs des thèmes christologiques propres aux *Actes de Thomas*, dont nous ne retiendrons que ceux qui concernent son existence en Dieu ou auprès du Père:

Syriaque	Grec
10 [1]Seigneur,	**10** [1]Mon Seigneur et mon Dieu[7],
compagnon de tes serviteurs,	toi le compagnon de route de tes serviteurs,
guide et conducteur	toi qui guides et diriges
de ceux qui croient en toi,	ceux qui croient en toi,
refuge et repos des opprimés,	toi le refuge et le repos des affligés,
espoir des pauvres	toi l'espoir des pauvres
et sauveur des faibles,	et le rédempteur des prisonniers,
guérisseur des âmes	toi le médecin des âmes
malades,	gisant dans la maladie
	et le sauveur de toute la création,
vivificateur des mondes	toi qui vivifies le monde
et sauveur des créatures!	et qui donnes force aux âmes,
C'est toi qui connais ce qui doit arriver	tu connais les événements à venir,
et tu l'accomplis en nous!	toi qui par nous réalises ces événements
C'est toi qui manifestes	toi, Seigneur, qui dévoiles
les mystères cachés	les mystères cachés
et qui révèles les paroles secrètes!	et qui révèles les paroles qui sont secrètes.
C'est toi le planteur du bon arbre	tu es, Seigneur, le planteur du bon arbre
et par tes mains sont	et par tes mains sont engendrées
toutes les œuvres.	toutes les bonnes actions.
C'est toi	Tu es, Seigneur,
qui es caché	
dans toutes tes œuvres!	celui qui est en toutes choses,
	et qui passe par toutes choses,
	et qui est inhérent à toutes ses œuvres
et tu es connu par	et qui est révélé
leurs actions!	par l'activité de toutes choses.
[2]Jésus, Fils parfait de l'amour parfait,	[2]Jésus Christ, toi le Fils de la miséricorde et le Sauveur parfait,

tu devins Christ

et tu as revêtu le premier homme.
Tu es la puissance,
la sagesse, l'intelligence, la volonté et
le repos de ton Père, en la gloire de
qui tu es caché et par qui tu es révélé
dans ton agir. Vous êtes un sous deux
noms.

Christ
Fils du Dieu vivant,

toi la force sans crainte (…)

Après l'énoncé d'un certain nombre de titres christologiques sous une forme litanique, cette prière évoque l'envoi, la descente et la remontée de Jésus, «fils parfait de l'amour parfait» (syriaque), «fils de la miséricorde» (grec). Alors que le grec s'en tient à un schéma relativement simple, qui fait de Jésus «l'ambassadeur envoyé depuis les hauteurs et descendu jusqu'à l'Hadès» (10,3-4) pour en faire remonter ceux qui y avaient été enfermés (passage sur lequel nous reviendrons ci-dessous), le syriaque amplifie à partir de l'opposition du caché et du manifesté pour décrire la situation de Jésus auprès du Père: «Tu es la puissance, la sagesse, l'intelligence, la volonté et le repos de ton Père, en la gloire de qui tu es caché et par qui tu es révélé dans ton agir. Vous êtes un sous deux noms!» (10,2). On a ici l'affirmation d'une unité du Père et du Fils qui confine, par-delà la différence des noms, à une identité au sein de laquelle le Fils n'est plus désigné que par une pentade d'attributs paternels.

Cette dialectique de l'unité, ou de l'identité, des personnes malgré la diversité des noms revient ailleurs dans les *Actes*, par exemple, au début d'une longue invocation de Thomas à Jésus:

Syriaque
48 [1]Jésus, voix sublime,
qui t'es levé depuis l'amour parfait
sauveur du tout,
libérateur et bienfaiteur de monde,
fortificateur des morts!
Jésus, droite du Père
qui renversas le mauvais
et le repoussas jusqu'à la limite
inférieure
et réunis ses biens
dans un lieu de rassemblement béni!
Jésus, roi qui règnes sur tout
et qui soumets tout,
Jésus, qui es dans le Père
et le Père en toi,
et vous êtes un
en puissance et en volonté,
en gloire et en essence ;

Grec
48 [1]Jésus très-haut, voix
qui s'élève de la miséricorde parfaite,
Sauveur de tous,

droite de la lumière,
qui renverse le Mauvais
dans sa nature,

et rassembles toute sa nature
en un seul lieu,

à cause de nous tu fus appelé par des noms divers,	toi le polymorphe,
tu es Fils	toi le Monogène,
et tu as revêtu un corps,	toi le premier-né d'une multitude de frères,
²Jésus, qui fus un abstinent	²
et dont la grâce pourvoit à tout	
comme un Dieu, Fils du Dieu très-haut,	Dieu issu du Dieu très-haut,
qui fus un homme méprisé et humble.	toi, l'homme méprisé jusqu'à ce jour.

Dans ce chap. 48, comme au chap. 10, le grec présente une rédaction beaucoup moins développée que le syriaque. Dans le grec comme dans le syriaque, Jésus est qualifié de «voix» (φωνή), celle qui s'est levée à partir de «la miséricorde parfaite» (grec) ou de «l'amour parfait» (syriaque); il est «le Monogène» (grec), le Dieu issu «du Dieu très-haut». Mais alors que le grec se contente de qualifier Jésus de polymorphe, le syriaque, prenant appui sur Jean 10,30, affirme l'unité de Jésus et du Père. Par ailleurs, il n'y est pas question de polymorphie, mais de polyonymie au regard de l'économie accomplie par Jésus: «*à cause de nous* tu fus appelé par des noms divers».

Un peu plus loin, à la fin d'une épiclèse adressée à l'Esprit, celui-ci[8] est appelé, mais dans la seule version syriaque, «puissance du Père et sagesse du Fils, car vous êtes un en tout» (50,2). Ici encore, la diversité des noms et des attributs s'efface devant l'unité du Père, du Fils et de l'Esprit. Nous citerons encore un passage, propre au syriaque, où le même thème est développé d'une manière particulièrement remarquable:

> **70** ²«Glorifié sois-tu, Dieu de vérité et Seigneur de toutes les natures que, dans ta volonté, tu as désirées!
>
> Tu as fait toutes tes œuvres, tu as achevé toutes tes créatures et tu les as produites selon l'ordre de leur nature, et tu as établi ta crainte sur toutes afin qu'elles soient soumises à ton commandement.
>
> Ta volonté a frayé un chemin depuis ton mystère jusqu'à la manifestation et elle s'est occupée de toute âme que tu as faite.
>
> Elle fut dite par la bouche de tous les prophètes, par toutes sortes de visions, de voix et de sons, et Israël n'a pas obéi à cause de son inclination mauvaise.
>
> ³Et toi, parce que tu es le Seigneur de tout, tu prends soin des créatures pour étendre sur nous ta miséricorde en celui qui est venu par ta volonté et a revêtu le corps, ta créature, corps que tu as voulu et formé selon ta sagesse glorieuse ; lui que tu as disposé dans ton mystère et que tu as fait surgir dans ta manifestation.
>
> Tu lui as donné le nom de Fils, lui qui est ta volonté, puissance de ta pensée, car vous êtes sous des noms distincts, Père, Fils, et Esprit, à cause de l'administration de tes créatures, en vue de la croissance de toutes les natures.

> Vous êtes un en gloire, en puissance et en volonté, et vous êtes séparés sans
> être divisés, et un, tout en étant distincts.
> Tout subsiste en toi et t'est soumis, parce que tout t'appartient.

D'après cette hymne de louange mise dans la bouche de Thomas, le «Dieu de vérité et Seigneur de toutes les natures» a voulu se manifester, et cette volonté, entité quasi personnifiée, s'est frayé un chemin depuis le mystère divin jusqu'à sa manifestation, fut proclamée par les prophètes et a été la cause de la venue de celui qui «a revêtu le corps»; qui résidait dans le secret et que Dieu a «fait surgir dans sa manifestation». Ici, on a nettement l'impression que la désignation et l'individuation de l'envoyé comme entité distincte, à savoir comme Fils, et l'imposition conséquente d'un nom, ne se sont produites qu'en vue de l'économie, «à cause de l'administration des créatures». Ce caractère secondaire des dénominations ne concerne d'ailleurs pas que le Fils, elle vaut pour les trois personnes de la Trinité. Mais, de manière plutôt inattendue, le texte pare à l'accusation de sabellianisme auquel les formulations que nous venons d'évoquer pourraient prêter le flanc en recourant à un énoncé surprenant d'équilibre: «Vous êtes un en gloire, en puissance et en volonté, et vous êtes séparés sans être divisés, et un, tout en étant distincts», qui n'est pas sans rappeler une phrase du chap. 48,1 cité ci-dessus: «vous (c.-à-d. le Père et le Fils) êtes un en puissance et en volonté, en gloire et en essence».

Il y a d'ailleurs plusieurs passages des *Actes*, outre ceux que nous avons produits, dans lesquels le Fils est associé au Père et à l'Esprit dans un modèle «trinitaire» ou triadique, selon que l'on considère le syriaque ou le grec. Ainsi, au chap. 39, Thomas termine une prière litanique adressée à Jésus par la doxologie suivante:

Syriaque	Grec
39 [3]Nous te glorifions!	**39** [3]Nous te glorifions
Et, par toi, nous exaltons	et nous te chantons, toi
ton sublime Père, lui qui est invisible,	et ton Père invisible
et l'Esprit saint qui couvre	et ton saint Esprit et la mère de
toutes les créatures.	toutes créatures.

Dans cette doxologie, le grec a sûrement préservé une formulation plus primitive que le syriaque, qui a de toute évidence subi une révision orthodoxe. Il est d'ailleurs possible que le grec ait également fait l'objet d'une révision partielle qui aurait abouti, en voulant expliciter «mère» par «Esprit», à la juxtaposition de l'Esprit à la mère. C'est ce que donne à penser la comparaison avec une autre épiclèse, prononcée sur le pain par l'apôtre Thomas, à la fin de laquelle n'est mentionné que le seul nom de la mère, suivi de celui de Jésus. Là aussi, le syriaque a été lourdement révisé, comme le montre la synopse des deux versions:

Syriaque	Grec
133 «[1]Nous faisons mémoire sur toi du nom du Père, nous faisons mémoire sur toi du nom du Fils, nous faisons mémoire sur toi du nom de l'Esprit, nom sublime	**133** «[1]Nous nommons sur toi
	le nom de la Mère, du mystère ineffable des Puissances et des Autorités
qui est caché à tous!»	cachées. Nous nommons sur toi le nom de Jésus.»
[2]Et il dit: «Par ton nom Jésus, que vienne la puissance de bénédiction et de louange et qu'elle habite sur ce pain.»	[2]Et il dit: «Que descende la puissance de bénédiction et qu'elle soit établie dans le pain.»

Il ressort clairement des textes qui ont été allégués jusqu'à présent que, si l'inscription du Fils dans la Trinité classique paraît bien être secondaire dans les *Actes de Thomas*[9], ceux-ci affirment néanmoins clairement la préexistence du Fils auprès du Père. Cette préexistence est d'ailleurs la condition obligée de l'envoi du Fils d'auprès du Père, un thème que les *Actes* se plaisent à développer. Cet envoi est d'abord la «procession» du Fils unique à partir du Père, qui se traduit aussitôt, pour ne pas dire simultanément, par son envoi salvifique auprès de l'humanité, expression de la «philanthropie»[10] divine, comme on le voit en finale de cette invocation que Thomas adresse à Jésus:

Syriaque	Grec
122 [1]Qui est comme toi, Dieu, toi dont l'amour et la tendresse ne se refusent à personne? Qui te ressemble par la tendresse et la pitié, sinon ton Père qui a délivré ses mondes de la nécessité et de l'erreur, amour qui a vaincu le désir, vérité qui a anéanti le mensonge, toi le beau en qui n'apparaît rien de haïssable, toi l'humble qui a renversé l'orgueil, toi le vivant qui a anéanti la mort, et repos qui a supprimé le labeur? Gloire à l'Unique qui provient du Père! Gloire à la tendresse	**122** [1]Qui est comme toi, Dieu, toi qui ne refuses ta tendresse et ta sollicitude à personne? Qui est semblable à toi, pareillement miséricordieux? Toi qui as délivré tes brebis[11] des maux, toi la vie qui a maîtrisé la mort, toi le délassement qui a mis fin à la fatigue. Gloire au Monogène issu du Père. Gloire au miséricordieux

qui fut envoyée par la tendresse!	qui a été envoyé du cœur de Dieu.
Gloire à ta tendresse qui fut sur nous!	

Dans un passage d'interprétation difficile et propre au syriaque — il s'agit de la confession d'un jeune homme ressuscité — l'envoi du Fils est situé dans une vaste fresque qui évoque la création, la chute et le salut:

> **34** [1b]À toi la gloire, Dieu miséricordieux, grand et glorieux, auteur et fondateur de toutes les créatures! Tu as fixé limite et mesure à toutes tes créatures, et tu as fixé pour elles les variations qui sont utiles à leurs natures. Ainsi que l'a voulu ta divinité, c'est toi qui as fait l'homme par l'ouvrage de tes mains, pour qu'il domine; [1c]tu as créé pour lui une autre créature pour qu'il combatte avec elle dans la liberté que tu lui as donnée, et l'homme oublia sa nature d'être libre et il se soumit à son semblable. Celui-ci devint pour l'homme un ennemi parce qu'il découvrit que l'homme avait oublié sa nature. L'ennemi se réjouit parce qu'il trouva un accès contre son semblable et il pensa qu'il deviendrait maître sur tous les esclaves. [1d]Et toi, le miséricordieux, dans ton grand amour tu as répandu sur nous ta grâce et tu as envoyé vers la race de notre humanité ta parole, ordonnatrice de toutes les créatures, par l'intermédiaire de ton Fils glorieux; et lui, par la liberté que tu lui as donnée, ta grâce l'aidant, vint et nous trouva dans ces œuvres que notre humanité avait faites depuis le premier jour. [1e]Tu ne nous a pas imputé nos fautes mais tu nous a fait vivre par ta grâce.

D'après ce texte, c'est la «parole, ordonnatrice de toutes les créatures» qui est «envoyée» à l'humanité «par l'intermédiaire du Fils». Une telle distinction entre la parole (identique au Verbe préexistant?) et le Fils est toutefois absente de la grande hymne de louange qui suit l'Hymne de la Perle dans le manuscrit syriaque de Londres:

> **113B** [1]« Glorifié sois-tu, Père, Seigneur du tout, essence ineffable,
> qui es caché à tous les mondes dans la clarté de ta gloire !
> Loué sois-tu, Fils, premier-né de la vie,
> qui procèdes du Père sublime et es parole de vie!

Le même texte affirme d'ailleurs la préexistence du Fils auprès du Père «avant les mondes»:

> [7]Glorifié sois-tu, Père tout-puissant,
> qui habites dans la splendide lumière, qui es caché dans ta gloire et
> qui es révélé à tous par ta grâce!
> Loué sois-tu, Fils parfait,
> qui es semé sur la terre vivante et qui, dès avant les mondes, es dans
> ton Père saint!

L'engendrement du Fils, accompli «dans le silence et la paix de la réflexion» (113B,4) est cependant toujours lié, de près ou de loin, à la révélation que le Père fait de lui-même, d'abord par les prophètes (113B,3) puis, en plénitude, par le Fils (113B,5).

Jusqu'ici, la plupart des textes allégués étaient propres au syriaque; aussi citerons-nous pour conclure une profession de foi christologique commune au grec et au syriaque, dans laquelle l'affirmation monothéiste du Deutéro-Isaïe (45,5.21) est appliquée non plus au Père mais au Fils:

Syriaque	*Grec*
25 ¹Je te confesse,	**25** ¹Je te rends grâces,
Seigneur Jésus le Christ:	Seigneur Jésus,
	de ce que tu as révélé ta vérité
	à ces hommes.
toi seul es Dieu de vérité,	Car tu es le seul Dieu de la vérité,
et il n'y en a pas d'autre ;	et il n'y en a pas d'autre.
toi, tu connais	Et tu es celui qui connais
ce que l'homme ne connais pas.	toutes les choses inconnues de la plupart.

Pareille transposition revient au chap. 33,1, mais dans un passage attesté en syriaque seulement.

Le Christ dans l'«économie» du salut

L'œuvre réalisée par le Christ dans son incarnation, depuis sa naissance jusqu'à son ascension, fait l'objet de plusieurs mentions plus ou moins développées dans les *Actes de Thomas*. Prédite par la loi et les prophètes, elle figure au centre de la prédication de Thomas telle que la rapporte un passage résumant son activité évangélisatrice dans un style qui rappelle celui des synoptiques:

Syriaque	*Grec*
59 ²(L'apôtre) ne cessait jamais de prêcher,	**59** ²(L'apôtre) ne cessait de prêcher,
de leur dire et de leur montrer	de dire aux fidèles et de leur montrer
que Jésus est le Christ	que c'était ce Jésus Christ
dont les Écritures ont parlé:	que les Écritures avaient proclamé,
la loi et les prophètes en ont montré les figures¹², les mystères et les images;	
qu'il a été donné comme alliance pour le peuple afin que ce dernier soit, grâce à lui, gardés du culte des idoles, et comme lumière pour les peuples, afin que, par lui, se lève sur eux la grâce de Dieu; et tous ceux qui garderont ses commandements trouveront le repos dans son royaume et seront comblés de gloire;	

il est venu, il a été crucifié
et il est ressuscité le troisième jour.
Il leur racontait
et leur expliquait cela
depuis Moïse jusqu'au dernier des prophètes,
parce que tous ont prêché sur Jésus,
et Jésus vint
et accomplit en œuvre
ce qu'ils avaient prêché.

qui est venu, a été crucifié
et après trois jours est ressuscité des morts.

Il leur éclairait ensuite,
commençant par les prophètes,

les choses qui concernent le Christ,
qu'il fallait qu'il vînt
et qu'à son sujet fussent accomplies
les prophéties qui le concernaient.

D'après la confession du jeune marié converti à l'encratisme, dans l'acte premier, le salut apporté par le Christ consiste à éveiller à la connaissance de soi et à permettre le retour à un état premier:

Syriaque
15 [1]Je te confesse, Dieu nouveau,
qui es venu ici
par l'intermédiaire d'un pérégrin.

Je te glorifie, Dieu qui as été proclamé
par l'intermédiaire d'un homme hébreu,
toi qui m'as éloigné de la corruption
et qui as semé en moi la vie,
toi qui m'as sauvé de la maladie

qui durait en moi depuis toujours,

toi qui t'es montré à nous
et j'ai perçu
ce que je suis,
toi qui m'as délivré de la chute
et m'as fait avancer vers la perfection,
toi qui m'as sauvé
de ces choses qui passent
et qui m'as rendu digne
de celles qui ne passent pas,
toi qui t'es avancé jusqu'à
ma petitesse
pour que nous parvenions à ta grandeur,

[2]toi qui ne m'as pas fermé tes entrailles
quand j'étais perdu,
mais qui m'as montré
à me chercher moi-même
et à éloigner de moi
ce qui n'était pas de moi,

Grec
15 [1]Je te rends grâces, Seigneur,
toi qui as été prêché
par l'étranger
et qui as été trouvé chez nous,

toi qui m'as éloigné de la corruption
et qui as semé en moi la vie,
toi qui m'a débarrassé de cette maladie
difficile à traiter et à guérir
et attachée à moi pour l'éternité,
et qui as inséré en moi
la santé de la tempérance,
toi qui t'es montré à moi
et qui m'as révélé tout l'état
dans lequel je suis,
toi qui m'as racheté de la chute
et m'as fait passer vers le meilleur,
qui m'as débarrassé
des choses temporelles
et m'as jugé digne
des choses immortelles et éternelles,
toi qui t'es abaissé jusqu'à moi
et à ma petitesse
pour m'établir près de ta grandeur
et t'unir à moi

[2]toi qui n'as pas retenu ta miséricorde
loin de moi, l'homme perdu,
mais qui m'as montré
comment me chercher moi-même

et savoir ce que j'étais
et ce que je suis maintenant
et comment je suis,
pour que je devienne de nouveau
ce que j'étais,

toi qui, alors que je ne te connaissais pas,
m'as cherché,
toi qui,
alors que je n'avais pas conscience de toi,
t'es avancé jusqu'à moi,
toi que je perçois
maintenant,

toi que je ne connaissais pas
et qui m'as cherché toi-même,
toi
de qui je n'avais pas conscience
et qui m'as pris toi-même près de toi
toi que j'ai perçu
et maintenant
je ne puis pas ne pas penser à toi, toi dont
l'amour bouillonne en moi et je ne puis le
dire comme il faut, ce que je puis dire est
court et tout à fait peu de chose et n'est pas
proportionné à sa gloire.
Pourtant il ne me blâme pas

et je ne peux dire
ce que je ne connais pas,
toi au sujet de qui,
si je parle avec audace,
je ne pourrai en finir,
car c'est à cause de ton amour
que je suis audacieux.

d'avoir l'audace de lui dire
même les choses que je ne connais pas.
Car c'est par mon amour pour lui
que je dis aussi ces choses.

Cet accent mis sur la connaissance de soi évoque bien sûr la gnose, mais il est avant tout caractéristique de l'esprit philosophique et religieux des premiers siècles de notre ère, tel qu'il s'exprime, entre autres mais non exclusivement, dans le *Corpus hermeticum*[13] et dans les *Sentences de Sextus*[14].

Les étapes de la manifestation du Christ ici-bas sont évoquées de façon précise par les *Actes*, qui reprennent les traditions canoniques mais également des données connues par les apocryphes. Un premier passage présente les événements de l'enfance et de l'adolescence de Jésus :

Syriaque
79 [1]Croyez en l'apôtre du Fils élu,
Jésus le Christ,
lui qui est né
afin que ceux qui sont nés
vivent par sa naissance,

qui a grandi
afin que la croissance parfaite
soit visible en lui,
qui est entré à l'école
afin que par lui la sagesse parfaite
soit connue[15],
qui a instruit son professeur[16],
– parce qu'il était le maître de vérité
et le chef des sages –,
qui est allé dans le Temple
et qui a présenté une offrande,
pour que l'on voie que
c'est en lui que
toutes les offrandes sont sanctifiées.

Grec
79 [1]Croyez
en Jésus. Croyez dans le Christ
qui a été engendré,
pour que ceux qui ont été engendrés
vivent par sa vie,
lui qui est devenu un petit enfant
et a été élevé
afin que la perfection de l'âge viril
soit manifestée par lui.

Il a enseigné ses propres disciples,
car il est le maître de la vérité
qui instruit les sages,
lui qui a apporté son don
au Temple
pour montrer que

toute offrande est sanctifiée.

Le passage suivant, qui apparaît juste avant la grande prière de Thomas précédant son martyre, met en lumière, pour citer le syriaque, la double condition du «médecin de toutes les douleurs cachées et manifestes, et [du] vivificateur des âmes qui lui demandent de l'aide»:

Syriaque	Grec
143 [1]Croyez au médecin	**143** [1]Croyez au médecin
de toutes les douleurs	de toutes les maladies
cachées et manifestes,	visibles et invisibles
et au vivificateur	et au sauveur
des âmes qui lui demandent de l'aide:	des âmes qui invoquent son secours.
[2]lui, le noble et le fils de roi,	[2]Il est le (fils) libre des rois.
qui devint esclave et pauvre;	Il est le médecin de ses brebis.
lui, le médecin de sa créature,	
malade du fait de ses serviteurs;	
lui, le purificateur	
de ceux qui croient en lui,	
méprisé et raillé	
par ceux qui ne l'ont pas écouté;	
lui, qui libère ses possessions	
de l'esclavage, de la corruption,	
de l'asservissement et de la perte,	Il est celui qui est outragé
asservi et raillé	par ses propres esclaves.
par ses serviteurs;	
[3]lui, le père de la grandeur,	[3]Il est le père de la grandeur
le Seigneur des créatures	et le seigneur de la nature
et le juge du monde,	et le juge.
< ... >[17];	
lui qui vint de la hauteur,	Il est né le très haut issu du Très Grand,
	Fils monogène de la Profondeur,
qui est apparu par Marie la vierge	il a été appelé fils de la Vierge Marie
et est appelé fils	et il a été désigné comme le fils
de Joseph, le charpentier;	de Joseph le charpentier.
lui dont nous avons vu	Il est celui dont nous voyons
de nos yeux la petitesse du corps,	la petitesse par les yeux du corps,
de qui nous avons reçu	mais dont nous avons perçu
la grandeur dans la foi;	la grandeur par la foi,
	et nous l'avons vue dans ses actes.
lui dont nous avons touché	Il est celui dont nous avons palpé
de nos mains le corps saint	le corps humain même de nos mains,
et dont nous avons vu	mais dont nous avons vu
de nos yeux l'aspect défiguré;	l'aspect changer de nos propres yeux,
[4]lui de qui nous ne pûmes, par nous seuls,	[4]bien que nous n'ayons pu
voir sa forme divine sur la montagne;	voir sur la montagne sa figure céleste.
lui qui fut appelé séducteur,	
	Il est celui qui a fait trébucher
	les archontes
	et qui a fait violence à la mort.
lui le véridique qui ne ment pas	Il est la vérité qui ne ment pas
et qui donne l'impôt et la capitation	et qui a au terme payé le tribut

pour nous et pour lui;
lui que l'ennemi craignit lorsqu'il le vit:

il fut effrayé
et il lui demanda
qui il était et ce qu'on disait de lui,
et il ne l'établit pas sur la vérité
parce que la vérité n'était pas en lui;
lui qui, étant le Seigneur du monde,
a éloigné de lui-même
les convoitises du monde, ses possessions
et tous ses plaisirs,

et a averti
ceux qui l'écoutent et croient en lui
de ne pas en user.

pour lui et ses disciples,
à la vue duquel l'archonte a eu peur
et les puissances qui sont avec lui
ont été troublées,
et l'archonte a témoigné à son sujet
qui il est et d'où,
mais il n'a pas su le vrai,
car il est étranger à la vérité.
Il est celui qui, ayant autorité sur le monde

et sur les plaisirs du monde
et ses richesses et le délassement,
<a rejeté>[18] tout cela
et exhorte
ses sujets
à ne pas en user.

Notons que, dans ce texte, le syriaque, en disant de Jésus qu'il «est apparu par Marie la vierge et est appelé fils de Joseph le charpentier»[19], semble plus orthodoxe que le grec, qui affirme qu'«il a été appelé fils de la Vierge Marie et [...] désigné comme le fils de Joseph, le charpentier». Déjà, au chap. 32,3, où le syriaque avait «fils de Marie», le grec portait «fils de Dieu». Là comme ici, on a l'impression que le grec se fait plus discret sur la naissance terrestre de Jésus.

La passion et la mort de Jésus retiennent également l'attention des *Actes de Thomas*, qui les mentionnent à plusieurs reprises, mais de manière plus explicite dans les deux passages suivants tirés d'une même invocation de Thomas à Jésus:

Syriaque
47 ²Jésus, mystère caché
qui me fut révélé,
c'est toi qui m'as révélé
tes mystères

plus qu'à tous mes compagnons
et tu m'as dit ces <trois>[20] paroles
elles par lesquelles me voici brûlant,
et je ne peux les dire.
Jésus, homme
né,
tué,
mort!
Jésus, Dieu, fils de Dieu,
vivificateur, faisant revivre les morts!

(...)
48 ²(Jésus), Fils du Dieu très-haut,

Grec
47 ²Jésus, mystère caché
qui nous a été révélé,
tu es celui qui nous a révélé
une infinité de mystères,
celui qui m'a mis à part
de tous mes compagnons
et qui m'a dit trois paroles
par lesquelles je suis embrasé,
et je ne puis les dire à d'autres,
Jésus, homme

assassiné,
cadavre enseveli,
Jésus, Dieu de Dieu,
Sauveur qui ressuscite les morts
et guérit les malades.

(...)
48 ²Dieu issu du Dieu très-haut,

qui fus un homme méprisé et humble!
Jésus, qui ne te détournes pas de nous
quand nous te prions,
qui fus cause de vie
pour toute l'humanité!

toi l'homme méprisé jusqu'à ce jour,
Jésus Christ qui ne nous méprises pas
quand nous t'invoquons,
toi qui es devenu la cause de toute vie
pour le genre humain,
toi qui as été jugé et gardé en prison
à cause de nous
et qui délivres tous ceux qui sont dans les
chaînes,

Jésus qui fus appelé séducteur
à cause de nous,
tu es celui qui as arraché à séduction
les hommes qui étaient tiens!

toi qui as été appelé imposteur

et qui délivres les tiens
de l'erreur.

Tout comme le syriaque qualifie Jésus de «vivificateur», la grande louange du chap. 113B, propre à cette seule version, fait allusion au sang «vivant» et «victorieux» du Fils (v. 6, 13, 14, 17), répandu pour les pécheurs (v. 17), de même qu'au «signe de ses blessures» et à «l'aspersion de son sang sur nous» par lesquels il efface les péchés (v. 12). La croix, «étendard» du Christ et «croix de lumière» (v. 16) est elle aussi qualifiée de «vivante et vivifiante» (v. 21).

Dans la perspective des *Actes*, comme d'ailleurs de toute la littérature chrétienne ancienne, la rédemption ou le rachat (cf. chap. 72,2) se fait aux dépens du démon qui, par la faute de l'homme, s'était acquis sur lui comme un droit de propriété. En «devenant Christ et en revêtant le premier homme» (chap. 10,2, propre au syriaque), le Fils de Dieu s'était en quelque sorte soumis au démon mais en apparence seulement, car sa divinité, cachée sous le voile de l'humanité, devait se révéler poison mortel pour l'ennemi. Ce thème du trompeur trompé est particulièrement développé par les *Actes* dans une plainte du démon vaincu par l'apôtre du Christ:

Syriaque
45 [1]Que nous veux-tu,
apôtre du Très-Haut?
Que nous veux-tu,
serviteur de Jésus le Christ?
Que nous veux-tu,
participant des saints mystères de Dieu?
Pourquoi veux-tu notre destruction,
alors que notre temps n'est pas arrivé?
Pourquoi cherches-tu
à prendre le pouvoir
qui nous a été donné,
alors que jusqu'à maintenant,
notre confiance repose sur lui?

Que nous veux-tu,
(toi) qui es venu pour nous expulser?

Grec
45 [1]Qu'as-tu à faire avec nous,
apôtre du Très-Haut?
Qu'as-tu à faire avec nous,
conseiller du saint Fils de Dieu?
Qu'as-tu à faire avec nous,
conseiller du saint Fils de Dieu?
Pourquoi veux-tu nous perdre,
notre temps n'étant pas encore arrivé?
Pourquoi veux-tu
nous enlever notre autorité?

Car jusqu'à cette heure
nous avions de l'espoir
et du temps de reste.
Qu'as-tu à faire avec nous?

Toi, tu as pouvoir	Tu as pouvoir, toi,
sur ceux qui t'obéissent,	sur les tiens,
et nous, nous avons pouvoir	et nous,
sur ceux qui se soumettent à nous.	sur les nôtres.
²Pourquoi veux-tu agir	²Pourquoi veux-tu user
envers nous avec violence,	de tyrannie contre nous,
avant notre temps,	
alors que toi, tu ordonnes aux autres	toi surtout qui enseignes aux autres
de n'agir envers personne avec violence?	de ne pas user de tyrannie?
Pourquoi convoites-tu	Pourquoi demandes-tu
ce qui ne t'appartient pas?	des biens étrangers,
Car ce qui t'appartient ne te suffit pas.	n'étant pas satisfait des tiens?
Pourquoi imites-tu ton Seigneur	Pourquoi es-tu semblable au Fils de Dieu
Dieu, qui a caché sa grandeur et	
s'est rendu visible dans un corps?	
Nous avons pensé à son sujet	
qu'il était mortel	
et il s'est transformé	
et a agi envers nous avec violence.	qui nous a fait du tort?
	Tu lui ressembles en effet tout à fait
Car tu es né de lui, n'est-ce pas?	comme si tu étais né de lui.
Lorsqu'en effet nous avons pensé	Nous avons pensé
que nous le jetterions sous notre	le mettre lui aussi sous le joug comme les
pouvoir,	autres;
il s'est transformé	mais il s'est retourné
(et) nous a renversés dans la	et nous a assujettis.
profondeur.	
³En effet, nous ne le connaissions pas,	³Car nous ne le connaissons pas.
car il nous avait abusés	Il nous a trompés
par son aspect humble,	par sa forme très hideuse,
par son indigence et sa pauvreté,	sa pauvreté et son indigence.
et nous avons pensé,	Le voyant tel,
lorsque nous le vîmes,	nous avons pensé
qu'il était un homme parmi les autres.	qu'il était un homme avec un corps de chair,
Nous n'avons pas reconnu	ne sachant pas
qu'il était le vivificateur de toute	qu'il est celui qui vivifie les hommes.
l'humanité.	

On aurait tort de croire qu'une expression aussi imagée de la geste rédemptrice du Christ soit réservée aux apocryphes. On la trouve en effet reprise par un des plus grands théologiens grecs du IVᵉ siècle, Grégoire de Nysse, dans son *Discours catéchétique* (chap. 21-26)[21]. Cette thématique est d'ailleurs proche de celle du *descensus ad inferos*, elle aussi présente dans nos *Actes*, où elle est décrite d'une façon tout à fait classique, par exemple, dans une prière d'initiation prononcée par Thomas:

Syriaque	*Grec*
156 ²C'est toi qui descendis au Shéol	**156** ²(…) toi qui es descendu dans l'Hadès
avec forte puissance	avec une grande puissance,
et les morts te virent	
et revinrent à la vie.	

Le seigneur de la mort n'a pu résister. Tu es monté dans une grande gloire, et tu as fait monter avec toi tous ceux qui avaient pris refuge en toi. Tu leur as ouvert une route vers la hauteur et tous ceux qui ont été sauvés par toi ont marché sur tes pas; tu les as introduits dans ton bercail et tu les as mêlés à tes brebis.	de qui les archontes de la mort n'ont pu supporter la vue, et qui es remonté en grande gloire, toi qui, ayant rassemblé tous ceux qui ont fui vers toi, leur as préparé la route, et tous ceux que tu as rachetés ont marché sur tes traces, toi qui, les ayant introduits dans ton troupeau, les as mêlés à tes brebis.

L'occurrence, dans la version grecque de ce chapitre, de l'expression «les archontes de la mort – οἱ τοῦ θανάτου ἄρχοντες» pourrait – bien être le vestige d'une représentation du *descensus* plus primitive que celle de la version syriaque, représentation selon laquelle le Sauveur, en remontant, triompherait des archontes présidant aux sphères célestes. On rejoindrait alors la perspective du chap. 10, dont la version grecque, nettement moins développée que le syriaque, évoque une (première) descente du sauveur auprès des «archontes», suivie d'une autre dans l'Hadès:

Syriaque	*Grec*
10 ³Tu es apparu comme faible et ceux qui t'ont vu ont pensé à ton sujet que tu étais un homme qui avait besoin de secours. Tu as montré la gloire de ta divinité par ta patience envers notre humanité,	**10** ³
lorsque tu as renversé le Mauvais de sa violence. Par ta voix,	(toi la force sans crainte) qui a renversé l'Ennemi, toi la voix qui est entendue des archontes, qui a ébranlé toutes leurs puissances,
tu as appelé les morts et ils ont repris vie. À ceux qui vivent et croient en toi, tu a promis un héritage dans ton royaume. C'est toi qui fus ambassadeur et qui fus envoyé des hauteurs célestes, parce que tu peux faire la volonté vivante et parfaite de celui qui t'envoie! Tu es glorieux, mon Seigneur, dans ta puissance! Ta dispensation fait du nouveau dans toutes tes créatures et dans toutes les œuvres que ta divinité a établies! ⁴Nul autre ne peut accomplir la volonté de ta grandeur ni se dresser contre ta personne. Comment es-tu?	toi l'ambassadeur envoyé depuis les hauteurs

Tu es descendu au Schéol,	et descendu jusqu'à l'Hadès,
tu as touché ses confins,	
et tu as ouvert ses portes;	toi qui, ayant ouvert les portes,
tu as fait monter	as ramené de là-bas
ses captifs	ceux qui avaient été enfermés
	de longs temps
	dans la chambre secrète des ténèbres
et tu leur as frayé	et leur as montré
une route vers la hauteur	la remontée qui mène vers le haut (…).
en la personne de la divinité.	

Les deux versions de ce passage, considérées séparément, sont aussi cohérentes l'une que l'autre, mais, dès qu'on les compare l'une à l'autre, le syriaque paraît surchargé de développements qui brisent le mouvement du texte. À l'inverse, il lui manque la mention des archontes et de leurs puissances, comme s'il avait subi sur ce point une révision orthodoxe. C'est une vision tout aussi orthodoxe du *descensus* que l'on rencontre dans un autre passage, que le syriaque est seul à donner: «Toutes bouches et toutes langues, les mondes et les créatures cachés et révélés glorifient le Père, adorent le Fils et louent ton Esprit Saint. Tes anges te glorifient dans la hauteur, par l'intermédiaire de ton Christ, qui devint dans le Schéol paix et espérance pour les morts, qui vécurent et furent ramenés à la vie» (113B,22).

Toute l'économie salvifique accomplie par le Christ telle que se la représentent les *Actes de Thomas*, est en quelque sorte récapitulée dans une hymne de louange à Jésus, mise dans la bouche de Thomas et qui ramasse la plupart des éléments que les textes précédemment cités ont permis de dégager:

Syriaque	*Grec*
80 [1]Jésus, que penser	**80** [1]Quelles choses j'aurai dans l'esprit
au sujet de ton œuvre,	au sujet de ta beauté, Jésus,
et comment t'annoncer,	et quelles choses aussi je dirai de toi,
Je ne le sais!	je ne le sais.
	Ou plutôt je ne le peux.
	Car je ne puis les dire, ô Christ,
Ô toi, aimable,	toi qui es
silencieux, calme	en repos,
et parlant,	
	et seul sage,
voyant ce qui est dans le cœur	toi qui seul connais le dedans des cœurs
et sondant ce qui est dans la pensée!	et qui seul connais les pensées.
Gloire à toi, miséricorde!	A toi la gloire, miséricordieux et doux!
Gloire à toi, Verbe vivant!	À toi la gloire, sage Logos!
Gloire à toi, caché	
qui as multiplié les ressemblances[22]!	
Gloire à ton amour,	Gloire à ta compassion
qui s'est répandu sur nous!	qui est née parmi nous!
Gloire à ta miséricorde	Gloire à ta pitié
qui fut sur nous!	étendue sur nous!

[2]Gloire à ta grandeur,
qui, à cause de nous, devint petite!
Gloire à ton élévation,
qui, à cause de nous, s'est abaissée!
Gloire à ta force,
qui, à cause de nous, s'est affaiblie!
Gloire à ta divinité,
qui, à cause de nous, a revêtu
notre humanité!
Gloire à ton humanité,
qui, à cause de nous, s'est renouvelée
et qui mourut
afin de nous faire vivre!
Gloire à ta résurrection
du séjour des morts,
qui fut pour nous
relèvement et retour à la vie!
Gloire à ta montée au ciel
par laquelle tu nous as frayé un chemin
vers la hauteur;
et tu nous as promis et juré
que nous siégerions à ta droite
et à ta gauche
et qu'avec toi nous serions juges!

Toi, Verbe céleste,
tu es lumière cachée de la pensée
et l'ascèse
de la voie de vérité,
toi qui chasses les ténèbres
et détruis l'erreur.

[2]Gloire à ta grandeur
qui s'est fait petite pour nous!
Gloire à ton très haut règne
qui s'est fait humble pour nous!
Gloire à ta force
qui s'est faite faible pour nous!
Gloire à ta déité
qui pour nous a été vue
dans la ressemblance des hommes!
Gloire à ton humanité

qui est morte pour nous
afin de nous donner la vie!
Gloire à ta résurrection
des morts:
grâce à elle il y a pour nos âmes
résurrection et repos!
Gloire et louange à ta remontée au ciel:
grâce à elle tu nous as montré la montée
vers le haut,
nous promettant
d'être assis à ta droite

et de juger
les douze tribus d'Israël!
Tu es le Verbe céleste du Père,
tu es la lumière cachée de la compréhension,
toi qui montres
le chemin de la vérité,
toi qui poursuis les ténèbres
et qui effaces l'erreur.

Il n'y a qu'un moment de l'œuvre de salut à ne pas apparaître dans ce texte, il s'agit de la parousie finale du Christ et du jugement qu'il réalisera alors sur l'humanité tout entière. Cet épisode n'est cependant pas ignoré par les *Actes*, puisqu'il figure en conclusion d'une exhortation de Thomas, à la fin du deuxième acte:

Syriaque
28 [3]Attendez la venue de Jésus,
espérez en lui
et croyez en son nom
parce que c'est lui le juge
des morts et des vivants,
et c'est lui qui rendra
à chacun selon ses œuvres,
lors de sa seconde venue.

Grec
28 [3]Attendez la venue du Seigneur
et mettez vos espérances en lui
et croyez à son nom.
Car il est le juge
des vivants et des morts,
et il rétribue
chacun selon ses œuvres,
et, dans sa venue
et son épiphanie dernière,
nul homme n'aura d'excuse
sur le point d'être jugé par lui,
comme s'il n'avait pas entendu.

Très exploité par les *Actes de Jean*, où il fait l'objet d'un long discours (chap. 87-93.103-105)[23], le thème de la polymorphie du sauveur n'est pas absent des *Actes de Thomas*. Il y est cependant beaucoup moins développé, et lorsqu'il l'est, c'est en fonction d'un autre thème qui, lui, est bien caractéristiques de nos *Actes*, celui de la gémellité de Thomas et de Jésus. Explicitement appliquée à Jésus une seule fois[24], au chap. 153,1, l'épithète de polymorphe souligne le fait que Jésus se rend présent à l'humanité dans toute sa pauvreté et sa petitesse: «Gloire à toi, Jésus polymorphe! Gloire à toi, qui apparais comme notre pauvre humanité! Gloire à toi, qui nous fortifies, nous encourages, nous corriges et nous réjouis, qui te tiens auprès de nous en toutes nos afflictions, nous fortifies dans la faiblesse et nous encourages dans l'épouvante!» (d'après le syriaque, le grec étant identique).

Les titres du Christ dans les Actes de Thomas

Dans son étude consacrée à la tradition syriaque ancienne[25], Robert Murray a répertorié dans les *Actes de Thomas* près de cent quarante titres du Christ[26], qu'il a classés sous les rubriques suivantes[27]: titres le présentant (1) comme être divin, (2) comme incarné, (3) comme révélateur, (4) en tant qu'il justifie et sanctifie, titres le mettant en relation (5) avec les chrétiens pris individuellement ou (6) avec l'Église vue comme un tout, et enfin, (7) titres eschatologiques. L'importance des titres christologiques des *Actes de Thomas* lui est apparue telle qu'il les a pris comme point de référence pour la constitution du tableau dans lequel il a mis en parallèle, à côté des titres attestés par les *Actes*, ceux qui apparaissent dans les *Odes de Salomon*, chez Aphraate et Éphrem, ainsi que dans les *Psaumes* manichéens et les *Homélies* pseudo-macariennes. D'après Murray, l'essentiel du contenu doctrinal des *Actes de Thomas* peut être ramené aux listes de titres qu'ils appliquent à Jésus et par lesquels ils décrivent son œuvre de «vivificateur». Il a d'autre part souligné la parenté qui lie les *Actes*, dans leur recours à des litanies de titres et d'épithètes, à la littérature sumérienne ancienne et aux *Psaumes* manichéens. Le jugement porté par Murray sur l'importance des titres christologiques dans les *Actes de Thomas* nous apparaît tout à fait fondé, et l'inventaire qu'il en a dressé peut être considéré comme exhaustif. Il resterait bien sûr à en faire une étude d'ensemble[28], mais le classement qu'a opéré Murray et dont nous avons reproduit ci-dessus les rubriques révèle déjà dans les *Actes* une doctrine christologique relativement équilibrée, que l'on peut comparer, par exemple, à celle d'Éphrem le Syrien.

L'enquête de R. Murray nous dispensant de procéder à un relevé des titres christologiques des *Actes de Thomas*, nous nous contenterons d'attirer l'attention sur quelques-uns d'entre eux, et tout d'abord sur la question de la possibilité même de nommer Jésus. On chercherait en vain dans nos *Actes* une théorie des noms — ou du Nom — divins ou christologiques. On y trouve néanmoins formulé un problème auquel la théologie chrétienne ancienne, orthodoxe ou non, s'est intéressé, à savoir celui de l'adéquation à leur objet des noms utilisés pour désigner Dieu ou le Christ. Les *Actes* y font une allusion précise dans le dialogue de Thomas, dit aussi Judas, avec le roi Mazdaï juste avant le martyre de l'apôtre:

Syriaque	*Grec*
163 ²Mazdaï lui dit: «Qui est ton maître, quel est son nom et de quel pays es-tu?» Judas lui dit: «Mon maître, c'est ton maître et celui du monde entier, le maître du ciel et de la terre.» Mazdaï lui dit: «Comment est son nom?» Judas lui dit: «Tu ne peux entendre son nom véritable en ce temps-ci, mais le nom qui lui fut donné est Jésus le Christ.»	**163** ²Misdaios lui dit: «Quel est ton maître? Quel est son nom? Et de quel pays?» «Mon Seigneur», dit Thomas, «mon maître est le tien aussi, il est le Seigneur du ciel et de la terre». Et Misdaios dit «Comment l'appelle-t-on?» Et Judas: «Tu ne peux entendre son vrai nom dans ce temps-ci. Je vais te dire le nom que pour un temps on lui a appliqué, c'est Jésus le Christ.»

La distinction opérée par Thomas entre le ἀληθινὸν ὄνομα et le πρὸς καιρὸν ὄνομα du Christ, c'est-à-dire le nom qui lui fut *donné* ou *appliqué* et non celui qu'il *possède*, rejoint celle qu'établit l'*Évangile selon Philippe* entre «nom caché» et «nom manifesté»[29]. Cela dit, les *Actes de Thomas* ne se privent pas de «nommer» Jésus, ils le font même d'abondance. Mais, lorsque Thomas parle de «ces eaux sur lesquelles j'ai proclamé ton nom, Jésus, notre vivificateur» (chap. 52,2, syriaque seulement), il se peut fort bien que le nom qui a été «proclamé» soit autre que celui par lequel l'apôtre s'adresse à Jésus, et qui demeure imprononçable.

Parmi les nombreux noms et titres donnés au Christ par les *Actes de Thomas*, il en est un qui peut surprendre, celui de «Père». Il revient à quatre reprises dans le grec (chap. 26,2; 30,2; 97; 143,1) et deux fois dans le syriaque (chap. 30,2 et 143,1)[30]. La seconde attestation propre au grec (prière de Magdonia) applique le titre de Père au Christ d'une telle manière qu'elle justifierait le syriaque d'avoir corrigé le texte:

Syriaque	*Grec*
97 Mon Seigneur, mon Dieu et mon vivificateur, Christ, toi, accorde-moi la force de vaincre	**97** Seigneur, Dieu Maître, Père miséricordieux, Christ Sauveur, donne-moi la force de vaincre

l'audace de Karish;	le désir honteux de Charisios
toi, donne-moi de garder la sainteté,	et donne-moi de garder la pureté
celle dans laquelle, toi, tu t'es plu	dont tu te réjouis,
et par laquelle, moi,	afin que moi aussi, par elle,
je trouverai la vie éternelle.	j'obtienne la vie éternelle.

La quatrième occurrence est à vrai dire moins choquante dans la mesure où l'appellation de Père intervient dans une énumération et non au début d'une prière, et dans la mesure aussi où le terme «Père» n'a d'autre fonction que de mettre en valeur la domination universelle du Christ sur la création:

Syriaque	Grec
143 [1]Croyez au médecin	**143** [1]Croyez au médecin
de toutes les douleurs	de toutes les maladies
cachées et manifestes,	visibles et invisibles
et au vivificateur	et au sauveur
des âmes qui lui demandent de l'aide:	des âmes qui invoquent son secours.
(…)	(…)
[3]lui, le père de la grandeur,	[3]Il est le père de la grandeur
le seigneur des créatures	et le seigneur de la nature
et le juge du monde.	et le juge.

L'expression «père de la grandeur» n'est pas propre aux *Actes de Thomas*. Elle est en effet bien attestée dans le manichéisme[31], où elle revient dans les sources grecques[32], coptes (*Psautier, Kephalaia, Homélies*)[33], syriaques[34] ou iraniennes[35]. Son apparition dans les *Actes* est-elle pour autant attribuable à l'intervention d'un lecteur ou d'un réviseur manichéen[36]? C'est loin d'être sûr, car, d'une part, l'expression se retrouve dans les *Homélies* du Pseudo-Macaire[37] et, d'autre part, l'application au Christ du titre de Père est bien attestée dans la littérature chrétienne des deux premiers siècles[38]; on la retrouve notamment dans les *Actes de Jean*[39] et dans l'homélie *Sur la Pâque* de Méliton de Sardes[40].

Les épiclèses ou prières sur l'huile d'onction que contiennent les *Actes de Thomas* font connaître un autre titre christologique, que R. Murray n'a pas intégré à son inventaire. Il s'agit de l'utilisation du terme «huile» en référence au Christ. L'identification de l'huile et du nom du Christ est suggérée dans un passage commun aux deux versions des *Actes*, dans lequel Thomas fait la louange de l'huile baptismale:

Syriaque	Grec
132 [2]Gloire à toi, fruit bien-aimé!	**132** [2]Gloire à toi, amour de miséricorde!
Gloire à toi, nom du Christ!	Gloire à toi, nom du Christ!
Gloire à toi, puissance cachée	Gloire à toi, puissance
qui demeure dans le Christ!	établie dans le Christ!

Elle est aussi sous-jacente à un autre passage, propre au syriaque, qui identifie l'huile non plus à son nom, mais à Jésus lui-même:

Syriaque	Grec
121 ¹Huile sainte qui nous a été donnée pour l'onction, et mystère caché de la croix qui est apparu en elle! C'est toi le redresseur des membres courbés, c'est toi, notre Seigneur Jésus,	**121** ¹Huile sainte qui nous a été donnée pour notre sanctification, mystère caché dans lequel la croix nous a été montrée, tu es le redresseur des membres incurvés, tu es celui qui rabaisse les exploits orgueilleux, tu es celui qui montre les trésors cachés, tu es le rejeton de la gentillesse (…).
qui es la vie, la santé et la rémission des péchés.	

Ailleurs, l'épiclèse accompagnant l'onction n'est plus adressée à l'huile, mais directement au nom du Christ:

Syriaque	Grec
27 ²Viens, saint nom du Christ!	**27** ²Viens, saint nom du Christ qui es au-dessus de tout nom!
Viens, puissance de la miséricorde d'en haut! Viens, amour parfait!	Viens, puissance du Très-Haut et miséricorde parfaite!

Au chap. 157, en revanche, si la louange sur l'huile commence par l'invocation du «fruit» de l'olivier, elle se poursuit par une demande faite à Jésus de venir résider sur l'huile, «sur laquelle nous faisons mémoire de ton nom» (157,2).

L'identification de l'huile au nom du Christ, ou l'allusion à celui-ci dans les prières sur l'huile, repose évidemment sur le rapprochement, sous leur forme syriaque, du nom de l'huile, *mešḥā*, et de celui du Christ, *mšiḥā*. Le fait qu'un pareil rapprochement soit également attesté dans la version grecque, où un tel jeu étymologique n'est pas possible, semble plaider en faveur d'une dépendance de celle-ci par rapport à la version syriaque.

Le dernier titre christologique que nous évoquerons illustre bien les difficultés que soulève la comparaison des versions syriaque et grecque des *Actes de Thomas*. Il s'agit des titres de «Seigneur», «père», «maître» ou «juge», auxquels sont ajoutés parfois «des âmes» ou «de toutes les âmes». Il apparaît dans la formule d'introduction d'une prière de Thomas au début de l'acte III:

Syriaque	Grec
30 ²Notre Seigneur, Seigneur des morts et des vivants, des vivants qui se tiennent debout, des morts qui reposent.	**30** ²Seigneur, juge des vivants et des morts, des vivants qui sont ici présents et des morts qui ici gisent,

Seigneur,	maître et père de toutes choses,
Seigneur des âmes,	père
de celles qui se trouvent dans les corps,	non des âmes qui sont dans des corps,
et père de toutes les âmes,	
de celles qui sont sorties du corps,	mais de celles qui sont sorties du corps,
	tu es en effet le maître et le juge des âmes
	qui sont dans les souillures,
viens, mon Seigneur, en cette heure,	viens à cette heure
à cause de la poussière	
que tes mains saintes ont formée.	
	où je t'invoque et montre ta gloire
	eu égard à celui qui est ici gisant

Le contraste entre les deux versions ne pourrait être plus marqué dans leur manière d'affirmer, d'un côté, que le Christ est le Seigneur de toutes les âmes, qu'elles soient dans le corps ou hors du corps, et, de l'autre côté, qu'il n'exerce sa seigneurie que sur celles qui sont sorties du corps[41]. Tout indique que le syriaque a subi une révision orthodoxe à l'effet d'étendre la domination du Christ à l'ensemble des âmes. Ce qui ne signifie pas pour autant que le grec n'ait pas été retouché: en effet, l'incise «tu es en effet le maître *et* le juge des âmes qui sont dans les souillures» semble préciser l'affirmation qui précède dans le texte en ajoutant que Jésus ne saurait être le père des âmes qui sont dans le corps parce qu'il est leur maître et juge. La situation se complique cependant si l'on considère qu'au chap. 67, le grec s'écarte de ce qu'on lit au chap. 30,2:

Syriaque	*Grec*
67 Seigneur de tous les mondes	**67** Seigneur, maître de toute âme
	qui est dans un corps,
qui t'attendent	
et Dieu de toutes les âmes	Seigneur, père des âmes
qui espèrent en toi (…)	qui mettent leurs espoirs en toi
	et qui attendent ta miséricorde (…)

Dans l'apparat critique de son édition, Maximilien Bonnet[42] se demande si la phrase ὁ δεσπόζων πάσης ψυχῆς τῆς ἐν σώματι οὔσης ne devrait pas être corrigée à la lumière du chap. 30 (p. 147, 9-10 de son édition). Mais avant de procéder à une telle correction, il faudrait être sûr que le texte des *Actes de Thomas* n'a pas fait l'objet, de-ci de-là, de retouches indépendantes et contradictoires, de sorte que, dans le cas présent, il serait difficile de décider lequel des deux chapitres, 30 ou 67, a conservé le texte «original». Quoi qu'il en soit, si on la compare au syriaque, la rédaction grecque du chap. 67 semble particulièrement surchargée et pourrait avoir effectivement subi des retouches rédactionnelles.

La comparaison des versions syriaque et grecque des *Actes de Thomas* montre, au moins pour les quelques extraits que nous avons cités, que ces deux versions non seulement présentent des différences notables l'une par rapport à l'autre, mais aussi qu'elles ont subi des retouches de divers ordres qui ont eu pour effet d'atténuer certaines conceptions ou expressions à propos desquelles on pouvait trouver à redire. La plus évidente de ces retouches a conduit à l'introduction de formules clairement trinitaires dans le syriaque (voir chap. 39,2 et 133,1), à des endroits où le grec atteste une triade formée par le Père, le Fils et la Mère, analogue à celle que connaît le gnosticisme séthien[43]. Mais on peut aussi mentionner l'effacement par le syriaque de la mention des «archontes» qui reviennent à plusieurs reprises dans le grec (aux chap. 10,3; 143,4; 156,2).

D'autre part, le syriaque manifeste une nette tendance à l'explicitation théologique que l'on ne remarque pas dans le grec. Cela est particulièrement clair dans la manière de souligner l'unité et la distinction du Père et du Fils (et éventuellement de l'Esprit), comme le passage suivant: «Tu (*sc.* le Dieu Père) lui as donné le nom de Fils, lui qui est ta volonté, puissance de ta pensée, car vous êtes sous des noms distincts, Père, Fils, et Esprit, à cause de l'administration de tes créatures, en vue de la croissance de toutes les natures. Vous êtes un en gloire, en puissance et en volonté, et vous êtes séparés sans être divisés, et un, tout en étant distincts» (chap. 70,3; dans le même sens, voir chap. 10,2 et 48,1, citant Jn 10,30).

Mais, nonobstant les retouches dont ils ont manifestement fait l'objet, les *Actes de Thomas* témoignent d'une doctrine christologique relativement homogène et équilibrée, affirmant, par-delà les écarts des deux versions, la préexistence du Christ auprès du Père, la réalité de son incarnation, ainsi que la nécessité et l'efficacité de son œuvre salvifique. Il s'agit cependant d'une christologie qui s'exprime dans un langage non technique, volontiers poétique et symbolique, qui se plaît à multiplier les titres et les épithètes. Lorsque cette christologie recourt à la juxtaposition de termes opposés, ce n'est pas tant pour professer un dualisme de l'humain et du divin que pour exprimer le double aspect, ou la double nature, du Christ incarné, comme, par exemple au chap. 47,3, qui loue Jésus, «homme assassiné, cadavre enseveli, Jésus, Dieu de Dieu, Sauveur qui ressuscite les morts et guérit les malades, Jésus, toi qui a été en besoin comme un pauvre et qui sauves comme n'ayant besoin de rien, Jésus, qui prends les poissons pour le déjeuner et pour le dîner, et rends tous satisfaits avec un peu de pain, Jésus qui, comme un homme, t'es reposé des fatigues de la route et, comme un dieu, as marché sur les flots»(d'après le grec). Sturhahn[44] a mis ce passage en parallèle avec quelques lignes de la quatrième catéchèse *ad illuminandos* de Cyrille de Jérusalem, dans laquelle l'évêque montre, avec les mêmes images, que «le Christ était double»[45]. Ce rapprochement est tout à fait approprié non seulement du fait de la similitude des formules, mais aussi parce que les *Actes de Thomas* appartiennent à une littérature de propagande et d'édification toujours très proche de la catéchèse et de la prédication. En revanche, la plupart des traits que Sturhahn attribue à la gnose apparaissent relever davantage de représentations imagées, archaïques, voire mythologisantes, dont les *Actes* sont loin d'avoir le monopole, comme nous l'avons montré à propos du thème de la tromperie du démon.

Cela dit, est-il possible de situer dans le temps la christologie des *Actes de Thomas*? Une réponse définitive à cette question supposerait résolus plusieurs problèmes relatifs à la composition des *Actes*, ce qui est loin d'être le cas. On peut néanmoins avancer, sur la base des deux versions que nous possédons, que les énoncés christologiques des *Actes*, aussi bien par leur style, notamment leur recours à des énumérations litaniques, que par leur contenu, ne peuvent guère être postérieurs au troisième siècle, et même à la première moitié de ce siècle. En effet, tant sur le plan de la forme que des idées exprimées, ces énoncés s'inscrivent bien entre le *Peri Pascha* de Méliton de Sardes et les *Odes de Salomon*, d'une part, et les *Psaumes* manichéens, d'autre part. Seule une étude d'ensemble et une édition renouvelée des *Actes de Thomas*[46] permettront d'être plus précis, sur ce point comme sur bien d'autres. Mais on peut d'ores et déjà affirmer que, si la christologie des *Actes de Thomas* est bien celle d'un apocryphe, elle n'est pas pour autant plus singulière que celles des textes qui leur sont contemporains. Elle l'est en tout cas moins que la christologie des Actes apocryphes antérieurs, comme les *Actes de Jean* et ceux d'*André*[47].

Notes

1 «Thomasakten», dans W. Schneemelcher, éd., *Neutestamentliche Apokryphen in deutscher Übersetzung*, II. Band, Tübingen, J. C. B. Mohr, 1989, p. 295; trad. angl., «The Acts of Thomas», dans W. Schneemelcher, éd., *New Testament Apocrypha*. Revised Edition, English Translation edited by R. McL. Wilson, II, Cambridge/Louisville, James Clarke/Westminster-John Knox, 1992, p. 329.

2 «Early Forms of Antiochene Christology», dans C. Laga, J. A. Munitiz, L. Van Rompay, éd., *After Chalcedon* (Orientalia Lovaniensia Analecta, 18), Leuven, Departement Oriëntalistiek/Uitgeverij Peeters, 1985, p. 108.

3 *Die Christologie der ältesten apokryphen Apostelakten. Ein Beitrag zur Frühgeschichte des altkirchlichen Dogmas*, Göttingen, Vandenhoeck & Ruprecht, 1952, p. 51-89.

4 Édition de la version syriaque par W. Wright, *Apocryphal Acts of the Apostles*, Londres, Williams and Norgate, 1871, vol. 1, p. 172-333; édition de la version grecque par M. Bonnet, *Acta Apostolorum Apocrypha*, II, 2, Leipzig, Hermann Mendelssohn, 1903, p. 99-288; traduction française du syriaque par P.-H. Poirier et Y. Tissot, «Actes de Thomas», dans F. Bovon, P. Geoltrain, dir., *Écrits apocryphes chrétiens* I (*Bibliothèque de la Pléiade*, 442), Paris, Éditions Gallimard, 1997, p. 1321-1470;

traduction française (parfois modifiée) du grec par A. J. Festugière, *Les Actes apocryphes de Jean et de Thomas* (*Cahiers d'Orientalisme*, 6), Genève, Patrick Cramer, 1983, p. 41-117. La synopse des versions syriaque et grecque des *Actes* a été établie par Y. Tissot. La numérotation des chapitres est celle de Bonnet, mais la numérotation des paragraphes est propre à la traduction française parue dans la *Bibliothèque de la Pléiade*. Sur la situation des *Actes de Thomas* dans la littérature apocryphe relative à cet apôtre, voir P.-H. Poirier, «The Writings Ascribed to Thomas and the Thomas Tradition», dans J. D. Turner, A. McGuire, éd., *The Nag Hammadi Library After Fifty Years* (*Nag Hammadi and Manichaean Studies*, 44), Leiden, E. J. Brill, 1997, p. 295-307.

5   Voir Y. Tissot, «Les Actes apocryphes de Thomas: exemple de recueil composite», dans F. Bovon, M. Van Esbroeck, *et al.*, *Les actes apocryphes des apôtres. Christianisme et monde païen* (*Publications de la Faculté de théologie de l'Université de Genève*, Genève, Labor et Fides, 1981, p. 223-232.

6   «Early Forms of Antiochene Christology», p. 108, n. 21.

7   Le grec affirme clairement la divinité du Christ en reprenant la formule de Jn 20,28; celle-ci revient en 81,1 (grec), 97 (syriaque, le grec diffère légèrement), 167,2 (grec et syriaque).

8   Ou plutôt celle-ci, car, pour le syriaque, l'Esprit est une entité féminine.

9   Un autre indice du caractère secondaire des mentions de la Trinité est fourni par le chap. 132,1, où le syriaque porte: «(le baptême) qui affermit l'homme nouveau dans la Trinité», alors que le grec a simplement: «(le baptême fait) se dresser sous une triple forme (τρισσῶς) l'homme nouveau».

10 Ce terme apparaît dans la version grecque, en 123,2 et 156,3.

11 Nous comprenons ainsi le grec κτήματα (éd. M. Bonnet, *Acta Apostolorum Apocrypha*, p. 232,2, qui propose, en apparat, de corriger en κτίσματα).

12 Cf. chap. 49,2 (syriaque seulement): «Nous invoquons ton saint nom, qui fut prêché par les prophètes comme l'a voulu ta divinité. Tu es annoncé dans le monde entier par tes apôtres, selon ta grâce, et tu t'es révélé aux justes par ton amour.»

13 Cf. J.-P. Mahé, «Introduction VI. L'hermétisme», dans J.-P. Mahé, P.-H. Poirier, dir., *Écrits gnostiques. La bibliothèque de Nag Hammadi* (*Bibliothèque de la Pléiade*, 538), Paris, Éditions Gallimard, 2007, p. lvii-lxii..

14 Cf. P.-H. Poirier «Les Sentences de Sextus (NH XII, 1)», dans J.-P. Mahé, P.-H. Poirier, dir., *Écrits gnostiques*, p. 1590.

15 Cf. Lc 2,46; 1 Co 2,6; *Évangile de la vérité* (NH I,3), 19,18, trad. A. Pasquier, E. Thomassen, «Évangile de la vérité (NH I, 3; XII, 2)», dans J.-P. Mahé, P.-H. Poirier, dir., *Écrits gnostiques*, p. 59.

16 Cf. *Histoire de l'enfance de Jésus* (Τὰ παιδικὰ τοῦ Κυρίου) ou *Évangile de l'enfance selon Thomas* 6, trad. S. Voicu «Histoire de l'enfance de Jésus», dans F. Bovon, P. Geoltrain, dir., *Écrits apocryphes chrétiens* I (*Bibliothèque de la Pléiade*, 442), Paris, Éditions Gallimard, 1997, p. 198-200.

17 Un second membre de phrase est requis pour assurer le parallélisme de la phrase, mais il manque aussi en grec.

18 Il n'y a pas de verbe en grec; Festugière traduit la conjecture de M. Bonnet (*Acta Apostolorum Apocrypha*, p. 250): ἀπέθετο.

19 Voir également le début des *Actes de Thomas* (chap. 2,2), où Jésus est également désigné comme «fils de Joseph le charpentier, de la ville de Bethléem en Judée».

20 La mention des «trois» paroles, absente du manuscrit syriaque de Londres, apparaît dans ceux de Berlin et de Cambridge; voir la note *ad loc.* dans P.-H. Poirier, Y. Tissot, «Actes de Thomas», p. 1372.

21 Trad. R. Winling, *Grégoire de Nysse. Discours catéchétique* (*Sources chrétiennes*, 453), Paris, Les Éditions du Cerf, 2000, p. 240-265.

22 On notera ici l'apparition du thème de la polymorphie; cf., à ce sujet, H.-J. Klauck, «Christus in vielen Gestalten: Die Polymorphie des Erlösers in apokryphen Texten», dans Id., *Die apokryphe Bibel. Ein anderer Zugang zum frühen Christentum* (*Tria Corda, Jenaer Vorlesungen zu Judentum, Antike und Christentum*, 4), Tübingen, Mohr Siebeck, 2008, p. 302-374, spécialement p. 333-339.

23 Cf. É. Junod, J.-D. Kaestli *Acta Iohannis*, II. *Textus alii, commentarius, indices* (*Corpus christianorum, Series apocryphorum*, 2), Turnhout, Brepols, 1983, p. 466-493 et 698-700.

24 Si l'on excepte les chap. 80,1 et 48,1; dans ce dernier cas, le qualificatif de polymorphe n'apparaît qu'en grec, alors que le syriaque fait référence à la multiplicité des noms pris par Jésus à cause de nous. Appliqué à Jésus, le terme πολύμορφος se trouve aussi en 153,1.

25 *Symbols of Church and Kingdom. A Study in Early Syriac Tradition*, Cambridge, Cambridge University Press, 1975.

26 *Ibid.*, p. 161 («over 130»).

27 Dans la «Table III. *Titles of Christ*», *ibid.*, p. 354-363.

28 Comme le note Murray, «this subject could easily fill a whole book» (*ibid.*, p. 162).

29 NH II, 56,3-4, trad. L. Painchaud, «Évangile selon Philippe (NH II, 3)», dans J.-P. Mahé, P.-H. Poirier, dir., *Écrits gnostiques*, p. 348.

30 Murray (*Symbols of Church and Kingdom*, p. 355), qui ne considère que les *Actes* syriaques, ne note que l'occurrence du 143,1.

31 Voir, à ce propos M. Tardieu, *Le manichéisme* (*Que sais-je?*, 1940), Paris, Presses universitaires de France, 1997, p. 94-95 et 102.

32 Voir Clackson, S., Hunter, E., Lieu, S. N. C., Vermes, M., *Dictionary of Manichaean Texts*, I (*Corpus Fontium Manichaeorum*, Subsidia, 2), Turnhout, Brepols, 1998, p. 43a.

33 Voir P. Van Lindt, *The Names of Manichaean Mythological Figures* (*Studies in Oriental Religions*, 26), Wiesbaden, Otto Harrassowitz, 1992, p. 3-7; cf. R. Murray, *Symbols of Church and Kingdom*, p. 355, pour le *Psautier*.

34 L'expression figure à plusieurs reprises dans le compte rendu de la cosmologie manichéenne fourni par Théodore bar Koni, au livre XI de son *Liber scholiorum*; voir F. De Blois, E. C. D. Hunter, D. Taillieu, *Dictionary of Manichaean Text*, II (*Corpus Fontium Manichaeorum*, Subsidia), Turnhout, Brepols, 2006, p. 1a, pour les références.

35 Voir W. Sundermann, «Namen von Göttern, Dämonen und Menschen in iranischen Versionen des manichäischen Mythos», *Altorientalische Forschungen* 6 (1979) 99 (= Id., *Manichaica Iranica. Augewählte Schriften*, Band 1 [*Serie Orientale Roma*, 89, 1], Rome, Istituto Italiano per l'Africa e l'Oriente, 2001, p. 125).

36 Sur la relation entre les *Actes de Thomas* et le manichéisme, cf. P.-H. Poirier, «Les Actes de Thomas et le manichéisme», *Apocrypha* 9 (1998) 263-290.

37 Comme le note R. Murray, *Symbols of Church and Kingdom*, 1975, p. 355.

38 Voir à ce propos R. Cantalamessa, «Il Cristo "Padre" negli scritti del II-III sec.», *Rivista di Storia e Letteratura Religiosa* 3 (1967) 1-27, et V. Grossi «Il titolo cristologico "Padre" nell'antichità cristiana», *Augustinianum* 16 (1976) 237-269.

39   Chap. 98, éd. et trad. É. Junod, J.-D. Kaestli, *Acta Iohannis*, I. *Praefatio, Textus* (*Corpus christianorum, Series apocryphorum*, 1), Turnhout, Brepols, 1983, p. 208-209.

40   9,63, éd. et trad. O. Perler, *Méliton de Sardes. Sur la Pâque et fragments* (*Sources chrétiennes*, 123), Paris, Les Éditions du Cerf, 1966, p. 64-65.

41   Cependant, la contradiction entre le syriaque et le grec disparaît si l'on suit, pour celui-ci, le texte du manuscrit D : πατὴρ δὲ οὐ τῶν ἐν σώμασι οὐσῶν ψυχῶν μόνον, ἀλλὰ καὶ τῶν ἐξελθουσῶν.

42   *Acta Apostolorum Apocrypha*, p. 184.

43   Cf. là-dessus J. D. Turner, *Sethian Gnosticism and the Platonic Tradition* (*Bibliothèque copte de Nag Hammadi*, section «Études», 6), Québec/Louvain-Paris, Les Presses de l'Université Laval/Éditions Peeters, 2001, p. 171-172, 210-214, 313-314.

44   C. L. Sturhahn, *Die Christologie der ältesten apokryphen Apostelakten*, p. 65.

45   4,9, PG 33,468 A: διπλοῦς ἦν ὁ Χριστός.

46   Que nous préparons pour la *Series Apocryphorum* du *Corpus Christianorum* (Turnhout, Brepols).

47   Sur ces derniers, voir J.-M. Prieur, *Acta Andreae*. Praefatio – Commentarius (*Corpus christianorum, Series apocryphorum*, 5), Turnhout, Brepols, 1989, p. 394.

4

Jesus in Augustine's Anti-Manichaean Writings

✛ ✛ ✛

J. KEVIN COYLE

T HERE ARE more studies on Augustine of Hippo and his thought than anyone could easily count; yet the examiners of his Christology, whose number happily includes Joanne McWilliam,[1] have been relatively few.[2] This deficit may be due to Augustine's having left us no treatise on Christology per se[3]—not an exceptional omission in the Latin world at his time: before him, only Tertullian had come near to producing a christological treatise, and that in the very precise context of anti-Gnostic (docetic) polemic.[4]

There have also been more or less recent studies on *Manichaean* Christology,[5] including some that bring Augustine and that Christology together. Even without a specific treatise, Augustine does have a lot to say about Jesus Christ, and we may suppose that firm convictions about him lie behind Augustine's remarks on what is wrong with Manichaean Christology. In terms of Manichaean studies, Augustine has always been considered of major significance, for two reasons: before his conversion to Catholicism, he spent nearly a decade as a follower of Manichaeism; and he supplies more information about it—including citations from Manichaean sources—than anyone else in Latin literature. It is doubtful, in fact, that Manichaeism would hold quite the same fascination for Western scholars had Augustine not once been one of its subscribers.[6]

Here, in a way similar to what I did in the case of the God-language of his anti-Manichaean polemic,[7] I wish to examine the way Augustine speaks of Christ in the same polemical context. This could be of some help in further determining not only Augustine's own appropriation of the topic, but also how Manichaeism itself approached Jesus. Though some work has been done on this point, very little of it has pertained to the Western Roman Empire. We do find, though, liberally spread across the past seventy years, some rather forceful expressions of confidence in the Augustinian authority when Manichaeism is the point of reference. For instance, in 1938 Francis Crawford Burkitt said that "the main result of the wonderful finds at Turfan and elsewhere has been to confirm the presentation of Augustine, and to exhibit the religion of Mani as something heretical indeed, judged by catholic standards, but nevertheless a form of Christianity. Central to it is the worship of 'Jesus.' Without Jesus, no Manichaean religion."[8] Gilles Quispel was only slightly less expansive when in 1972 he declared, with reference to the attribution to Mani of the title "Apostle of Jesus Christ," that "the Western Manichaeism he [Augustine] was familiar with had better preserved the original doctrine of its founder than the Eastern documents found at Turfan."[9]

Augustine's Perspective

Now, if one difficulty with theories of Manichaean christocentricity lies in the reliability of sources (and, of course, their interpretation), another emanates from the way in which Augustine is called on to support such theories. This became clear to me from something Julien Ries wrote in 1964:

> Augustine, a former disciple of Mani, knew the central place of Jesus in the doctrine he was contesting. When we read his treatises, however, we sometimes have the impression that his polemic aims more at refuting the two principles, exegesis which would destroy the Scriptures, false conceptions of the soul, sin, and God's immutability. An able debater, deeply informed on Manichaean doctrine, did he not lead his adversaries to positions more vulnerable than those of christology? This problem deserves research.[10]

Hermeneutical doors begin to unlock with that last sentence, but perhaps not in ways Ries intended. There *is* a christological question that merits research; but the inquiry deserves to be extended to some of the premises whereon Ries's own statement rests: How much doctrine had Augustine himself learned as a Hearer, and therefore how much did he know when he disputed with his former religion?[11] Did he in fact recognize "the central place of Jesus" in Manichaean doctrine? And did he deem that place to be so unassailable that he avoided targeting it in his anti-Manichaean

polemic? What I present here claims to be no more than a simple prolegomenon to broaching those questions. The focus will be on Augustine's
debates with Fortunatus, Felix, and Faustus, with some reference to other
Augustinian works that engage Manichaeism and that afford some data on
the matter.

It is clear, first of all, that Augustine does not avoid the issue of
Manichaean Christology for very long. As Alberto Viciano has noted, there
is a christological side to Augustine's anti-Manichaean polemic, though I
am more reserved about his view that "the anti-Manichaean christological debate has the Lord's humanity for its main focal point."[12] But it is also
true that the ground his opponents have staked out largely determines any
direct references Augustine makes to the place of Jesus in Manichaeism.
Thus, with the exception of a few passing references in earlier writings,[13]
his attention to the Manichaean Jesus really commences with the public
debate held with the Manichaean presbyter Fortunatus in 392.[14] In the
first debate, Christology is not really the issue: the main focus is on the
origin of evil. Yet from the outset Fortunatus refers to "Christ," usually in
terms of a saviour or liberator.[15] If he is dangling a bait here, it is one to
which Augustine fails to rise. François Decret takes Augustine's lack of
response to mean that he finds nothing wrong with Fortunatus' presentation, deeming it instead "parfaitement orthodoxe."[16] But Augustine's silence
could also be taken to mean that it only seemed orthodox at the time, that
Augustine's own Christology had not developed sufficiently by then for
him to detect flaws in Fortunatus' presentation of the *uerbum natum a con-
stitutione mundi*,[17] even when Fortunatus provided an evasive explanation
of what he meant by the Word being "born."[18] Yet already here, in 392,
Augustine has the salvific role of Christ in mind: through him God has forgiven sin.[19]

In 396 Augustine took on Mani's *Foundation Letter*.[20] The brief treatment of Christ here is triggered by Mani's use of the title "Apostle of Jesus
Christ." Augustine's response refers to Jesus here and there before allud-
ing more directly to Manichaean notions, coupled with Catholicism's
response: "The man Jesus Christ was not sent by the Son of God, that is,
by the power and wisdom of God, but was, according to the Catholic faith,
assumed in such a way that the wisdom of God appeared in that very man
in order to heal sinners."[21] Here Augustine invokes 1 Corinthians 1:24,
because it is a favourite Pauline text among Manichaeans;[22] but he also
refers to it in order to insist on the identity of the human Jesus with the
divine Son of God. Despite the identity, "human" here really means human,
though born of a virgin. Thus the ironic comparison with Mani and his

claim to be both "Apostle of Jesus Christ" and the one in whom the Paraclete resided: "[Y]ou do not think it shameful to preach that Mani, a man
assumed by the Holy Spirit, was born from the union of the two sexes, yet
you are afraid to believe that the man assumed by the only-begotten wisdom of God was born of a virgin? If human flesh, if intercourse with a
man, and if the womb of a woman could not defile the Holy Spirit, how
could the womb of a virgin defile the wisdom of God?"[23] Then comes that
famous passage where Augustine accuses Manichaeans of setting more
store on their feast of the Bema than on that of Easter.[24] No true Christians they, whatever their claims, because their worship does not focus on
the incarnate, risen Christ.

In his debate with the Manichaean *doctor* Felix, held perhaps at the
end of 404 (though an earlier date is possible),[25] Augustine does not so
much address docetic aspects of Manichaean Christology[26] as Mani's claim
to be the "apostle of Jesus Christ" and the attribution to him of "Paraclete," aspects that do not directly engage the question addressed here.
Felix makes several references to Christ as liberator, and Augustine picks
up on them.[27] He is beginning to perceive the possibilities in the connection between the Incarnation (or, better, Resurrection) and its salvific
effects.[28] Yet only just: given the chance to go further with the theme, he
prefers to remain on the topic already under discussion—without, however, excluding the soteriological:

> Felix said: "From what has Christ purified us? From what has he set
> us free?"
> Augustine said: "Christ did not set free a part of God, the nature of
> God, but set free by his mercy a creature that he made and that fell into
> sin by free choice. He purified a being that had been able to be polluted;
> he set free a being that had been able to be taken captive; he healed a being
> that had been able to become ill. But now we are speaking about God …"[29]

In lines well known from his long reply to the Manichaean bishop Faustus of Milevis, composed sometime between 397 and 400,[30] Augustine
quotes his opponent as saying, "It does not follow that if I accept the gospel,
I therefore accept that Christ was born. The reason is that the gospel came
into being by Christ's preaching, and in it he never says he was born of
human beings."[31] Augustine's reply is very much about Christology, beginning with the issue of Incarnation and Faustus' argument that the Incarnation is not affirmed in any part of the "gospel" he recognizes.[32] It is the
latter point—what "gospel" is—that Augustine first scores in his reply,
before attacking the notion of the "Primal Man," whose son Manichaeans

believe Jesus to be. Finally, he affirms the Catholic belief in the Incarnation.[33] So three elements are at issue here: the integrity of the scriptural canon, the Manichaean cosmogonical myth, and the reality of Christ's humanity. The latter point is extended into the next book, where Faustus again denies it on the grounds of discrepancy between the Matthean and Lukan infancy narratives. In reply Augustine repeats his faith in the Incarnation, then reconciles the genealogies in Matthew and Luke before debating the wider issue of whether the New Testament can be reconciled with the Old. (There are also sidebars on such topics as ecclesiology; but the subtext is always Christ.) Then in the twentieth chapter we find Faustus' famous profession of faith, including his belief in the "twinned" Son who, according to Paul, is the power and the wisdom of God, with his power resident in the sun and his wisdom in the moon.[34] It is in this guise that he worships Christ, says Faustus.[35] But then, asks Augustine, how many "Christs" do Manichaeans really believe in?[36] In fact, he can name three: One is "the suffering Jesus who hangs from every tree," that is, the Light that must suffer while imprisoned in matter, crucified on the "Cross of Light,"[37] the being Faustus calls the *patibilis Iesus qui est uita ac salus hominum, omni suspensus ex ligno,*[38] and who is also known as the Living Soul, a son of the Primal Man.[39] The second is the Jesus who is presented in the Gospels as crucified under Pontius Pilate, but who, because he had only the appearance of humanity, did not suffer, undergoing instead a *mystica passio,* as Faustus puts it:[40] this is the "Christ of Light" (*Christus lumen*).[41] And the third Christ is the (freed) light residing in the moon and sun ("Jesus the Splendour").[42]

Augustine addresses all of these, especially the first. *Iesus patibilis*—a term he lifts from Faustus and that only the two of them employ[43]—essentially means the entrapped divine light that is therefore "crucified" on the cross of the entire material world, as Augustine clarifies in a homily delivered in 414 or 415.[44] By then, his soteriological focus has emerged clearly. Likely earlier, when Augustine responds (suggested dates range from 398 to 406) to a letter received from the Manichaean Hearer Secundinus, in which Secundinus defends his religion's docetic doctrine[45] with the declaration that "if the Lord had had flesh, all our hope in him would have been cut away,"[46] rather than limit himself to the Incarnation, Augustine chooses to reply in a soteriological vein: in that case, he says, there is no consoler (Paraclete!) or saviour but Mani.[47]

Before going further, we should recall the irony that Faustus accuses persons of Augustine's religious persuasion of being "half-Christian" (or "half-Jew") for accepting the teachings of the wrong Jesus.[48] In this view, the Jesus of Catholic Christianity was satanic, the "enemy," who deliberately engineered his own Crucifixion.[49] This is supported by three Manichaean sources—all of them Western, if not exclusively African: the letter of Secundinus to Augustine;[50] a citation from the *Foundation Letter*;[51] and a Coptic Jesus–psalm.[52]

A closer look at his response to Secundinus shows that Augustine seeks to make Christology a focal point even when Manichaeans do not. Secundinus wrote to his erstwhile fellow-believer in 404, and Augustine's reply must have come soon after.[53] Secundinus opens his letter by expressing his gratitude "to the ineffable and most sacred Majesty and to his first-born, Jesus Christ, the king of all lights."[54] This is a most Manichaean way of expressing the divine Father–Son relationship—one that avoids any hint of Incarnation and that dwells on the Light-kingdom of Manichaean cos-mogony.[55] About one-third of the way through his letter, Secundinus exhorts Augustine not to be "the lance of error by which the side of the savior is pierced [see John 19:34]. For you see that he is crucified in the whole world and in every soul."[56] This, under the guise of the Johannine account of the Crucifixion, is the *Iesus patibilis* that we saw earlier with Faustus. Manichaeans, Secundinus adds, "have, therefore, escaped by following the spiritual savior. For the audacity of the devil burst forth to such a degree that, if our Lord had flesh, all our hope would have been cut away."[57] Secundinus expresses no more than these two christological points, but both boil down to the Incarnation as part of the saving act—enough to bring Augustine's reaction. Christ, he says, is not only "king of lights" (whatever Secundinus means by that) but rather (quoting 1 Timothy 1:17) king of the ages, whom Augustine perceives as without a superior or cre-ated equal (3). As to being firstborn, this does not simply mean that he is "first in chronological order," but that "he is consubstantial with the Father and exists before every creature" with "no brothers from the same sub-stance … He is the only begotten and the firstborn—only begotten, because he has no brothers, but firstborn because he has brothers,"[58] those with whom he shares human nature. Augustine continues to develop this dual theme of our adoption by grace and Christ's immutability and eternity with the Father: God with God, through whom all that is has been created (6–7). Yet he is born of a virgin, united with flesh (9), which Augustine mentions several other times (22–23, 25). As to the *Iesus patibilis*, Augustine does not address it, perhaps because, as he says, he has dealt with many of Secund-inus' points elsewhere (12). That is why there is no really soteriological aspect to his reply, either.

Conclusion

What was it about Manichaean Christology that most concerned Augustine? Without doubt, he targeted and repudiated the docetism he perceived there. He could hardly have done otherwise, if he were to take seriously the lynch-pin of his Catholicism—Jesus' Incarnation, death, and Resurrection. Yet strictly speaking, docetism applies to only one of the Manichaean "Christs" that Augustine finds in Faustus. If it had been the single christological issue raised in the debate with Fortunatus in 392, by the time of *Contra Faustum*, in the closing years of the fourth century, it had been incorporated into a wider agenda. There is a consistency in the way that the Manichaeism known to Augustine makes the reality of Christ's flesh a key polemical point in debates with Christians.[59] Once Augustine becomes aware of its implications, he begins to engage that point on similar grounds, but then starts to shift the focus to the *consequences* that render a docetic Christology unacceptable.[60] When can we locate the shift to the more soteriological? Possibly in *De agone christiano*, written in 396 or 397, where he made the point that there can be no real redemption by Christ if Christ's flesh was not real.[61]

To judge from the reply to Faustus, then, the chief problem Augustine was coming to identify in Manichaean Christology was, not the docetic Jesus, but *Iesus patibilis*, who literally contains the seeds of salvation without actually effecting it.[62] That being so, Augustine asks, could a Manichaean Jesus truly be a saviour? "Not a saviour of you, but needing salvation by you," he says to Faustus.[63] By then, not the presence of Christ in Manichaean teaching, but the role that teaching allots to Christ is what really matters; for in that teaching Jesus exercises no truly salutary role.[64] The Manichaean Christ (by whatever definition) could not, in Augustine's view—and despite references such as that by Faustus to *Iesus uita ac salus hominum*,[65] and to *liberator noster Iesus*,[66] by Secundinus to a *spiritalis saluator*,[67] or by Felix to "Christ who came to save the soul from sin"[68]—be construed as in any sense a real saviour. He requires salvation himself, this *confixus et conligatus et concretus Christus*, as Augustine labels him.[69] The *true* saviours are the Manichaean Elect, through whose digestive tracts entrapped divine Light is freed from matter[70] and Christ himself is thereby saved.[71]

"Everything in Manichaeism is about salvation," Henri-Charles Puech has observed.[72] But who effects it? In the end that seems to be the crux of the matter for Augustine. Is Christ, then, a saviour in Manichaeism? The answer must depend on what is meant by the term. It is a question François Decret is compelled to ask of Faustus: "le terme de *saluator* appliqué ici au

Christ, quelle réalité couvre-t-il?" Decret answers that the role to which the "spiritual Jesus" is confined is that of messenger.[73] For Fortunatus, at least, the concept has much to do with Gnostic views of a messenger who *brings* saving *gnosis*;[74] but the salvific role goes to *Iesus patibilis*—precisely the one that Augustine labels *saluator saluandus*.

If Jesus as saviour is not central to Manichaeism, it remains to ask what Augustine's position implies. Were Manichaeans Christian for him, or not? His answer was that—even if never far from their mouths[75]—the appearance of Jesus' name among them could not suffice to make Manichaeans Christians, according to any criterion he could accept. *Blasphematores Christi*, he calls them,[76] adding for good measure: "and therefore not to be saved by Christ"; and—turning Faustus' taunt against him—he calls Manichaeans "pseudo-Christians."[77] How could Jesus be a greater saviour than Mani, when it was Mani who had come, if not to displace, then at least to complete the revelation of Jesus?[78] Augustine might have initially fumbled over the precise identity of the Manichaean Christ(s)—an understandable error, since, as Nils Pedersen says in a masterpiece of understatement, "Mani's Jesus is not an unambiguous figure";[79] but his error appears to have eventually been corrected: a Manichaean Jesus might be the bearer of a saving *gnosis*,[80] which is to say, of information on how salvation is to be achieved;[81] but Manichaeans have no truly *saving* Christ, and in the end that is sufficient in Augustine's view to render ineffective whatever Christ they may espouse.

Postscript

I had just received my doctorate and begun teaching when I met Joanne for the first time in 1975. The occasion was doubly auspicious—it was in Oxford, where the International Patristic Conference was taking place and where the Canadian participants decided to found a society of their own: the Canadian Society of Patristic Studies / Association canadienne des études patristiques. Joanne was thus a founding member and became a tremendous asset to it, always supportive, serving in a number of capacities (including as its president from 1987 to 1991), particularly encouraging younger members, and attending the society's annual gathering so long as her health allowed. In addition, of course, she was a renowned patristic scholar in her own right. I am proud that she was a colleague as well as a friend.

Notes

1 For these, consult the bibliography of her works in this volume.

2 Foremost among these is that of T. van Bavel, *Recherches sur la christologie de saint Augustin: L'humain et le divin dans le Christ d'après saint Augustin,* Paradosis 10 (Fribourg: Éditions universitaires, 1954). See also O. Scheel, *Die Anschauung Augustins über Christi Person und Werk* (Tübingen: J.C.B. Mohr, 1901); E. Franz, *Totus Christus: Studien über Christus und die Kirche bei Augustinus* (Bonn: Rheinischen Friedrich-Wilhelms-Universität, 1956); and A. Grillmeier, *Christ in Christian Tradition* 1 (London: Mowbray's, 1975), 405–13.

3 The closest he gets to dealing with the topic at any length is in his *Epistula 137 ad Volusianum*, on which see Grillmeier, *Christ in Christian Tradition* 1: 410–11.

4 Tertullian, *De carne Christi.*

5 M. Franzmann lists these in *Jesus in the Manichaean Writings* (London: T. & T. Clark, 2003), 2–3. To her list can be added W. Sundermann, "Christ in Manicheism," in *Encyclopædia Iranica* 5, ed. E. Yarshater (Costa Mesa: Mazda, 1992), 535–39; and J. BeDuhn, "The Manichaean Jesus," forthcoming in *Alternative Christs,* ed. O. Hammer (Cambridge and New York: Cambridge University Press, 2009), 51–70, which I was unable to consult.

6 For a brief overview of Manichaeism and its relation to Augustine, see "Mani, Manicheism," in *Augustine Through the Ages: An Encyclopedia,* ed. A.D. Fitzgerald (Grand Rapids: Eerdmans, 1999), 520–25.

7 J.K. Coyle, "God's Place in Augustine's Anti-Manichaean Polemic," *Augustinian Studies* 38 (2007): 87–102.

8 F.C. Burkitt, "Manichaica," *Journal of Theological Studies* 35 (1934): 182–86 at 184. See also P. de Menasce, "Augustin manichéen," in *Freudesgabe für Ernst Robert Curtius zum 14. April 1956* (Bern: Francke, 1956), 79–93 at 87: "Sa sympathie, sa compassion iront plutôt à ceux de ses amis qu'il avait entraînés avec lui dans l'erreur, mais plus jamais il ne concédera au manichéisme d'être autre chose qu'un christianisme aberrant. Christianisme cependant: avec, au centre du système sotériologique, la personne, la mission du Sauveur Jésus."

9 G. Quispel, "Mani, the Apostle of Jesus Christ," in *Epektasis: Mélanges patristiques offerts au Cardinal Jean Daniélou* (Paris: Beauchesne, 1972), 667–72 at 671; repr. in idem, *Gnostic Studies* 2, Uitgaven van het Nederlands historisch-archaeologisch Instituut te Istanbul 34, no. 2 (Istanbul: Nederlands historisch-archaeologisch Instituut, 1975), 230–37 at 236.

10 J. Ries, "Jésus-Christ dans la religion de Mani: Quelques éléments d'une confrontation de saint Augustin avec un hymnaire christologique copte," *Augustiniana* 14 (1964): 437–54 at 454: "Augustin, un ancien disciple de Mani, connaissait la place centrale de Jésus dans la doctrine qu'il combattait. En lisant ses traités on a cependant l'impression que sa polémique vise davantage la réfutation des deux principes, de l'exégèse destructrice des Saintes Écritures, des fausses conceptions de l'âme, du péché, de l'immutabilité de Dieu. Controversiste habile et très au fait de la doctrine manichéenne, n'amenait-il pas ses adversaires sur des positions plus vulnérables que celles de la christologie? Ce problème mériterait une recherche."

11 See J.K. Coyle, "What Did Augustine Know About Manichaeism When He Wrote His Two Treatises *De moribus*?" in *Augustine and Manichaeism in the Latin West:*

Proceedings of the Fribourg-Utrecht International Symposium of the International Association of Manichaean Studies, ed. J. van Oort, O. Wermelinger, and G. Wurst, *Nag Hammadi and Manichaean Studies* 49 (Leiden: Brill, 2001), 43–56.

12   A. Viciano, "Aspects christologiques du 'Corpus Paulinum' dans la controverse antimanichéenne de saint Augustin," in *Manichaica Selecta: Studies Presented to Julien Ries on the Occasion of His Seventieth Birthday,* ed. A. van Tongerloo and S. Giversen, *Manichaean Studies* 1 (Leuven: 1991), 379–89 at 383: "le débat christologique antimanichéen axe principalement sur l'humanité du Seigneur."

13   E.g., *De moribus ecclesiae catholicae* 7, no. 12 (Corpus scriptorum ecclesiasticorum latinorum 90, 14.24–25), completed in 388 or 389. Hereafter CSEL.

14   The date appears firm. See "Fortunatum Manicheum, Acta contra," in Fitzgerald, *Augustine Through the Ages,* 371–72 at 371.

15   Aug., *C. Fort.* 3 (CSEL 25/1, 85.21), 7 (88.9), 11 (90.2), 17 (95.21), 18 (96.6), 20 (100.2), 21 (102.26 and 103.7), and 22 (106.25). F. Decret, "La doctrine centrale du *spiritalis salvator* dans les sources manichéennes africaines," in *Studia manichaica: IV. Internationaler Kongreß zum manichäismus, Berlin, 14.–18. Juli 1997,* ed. R.E. Emmerick, W. Sundermann, and P. Zieme, Berlin-Brandenburgische Akademie der Wissenschaften, Berichte, und Abhandlungen, Sonderband 4 (Berlin: Akademie Verlag, 2000), 138–53 at 141, notes that "le prêtre manichéen, qui pas une seule fois ne cite le nom de Mani, recourt constamment au Christ." On Fortunatus' Christology, see 146–47; and idem, *Aspects du manichéisme dans l'Afrique romaine: Les controverses de Fortunatus, Faustus et Felix avec saint Augustin* (Paris: Études Augustiniennes, 1970), 274-78.

16   F. Decret, "La christologie manichéenne dans la controverse avec Fortunatus," in *Studi sul cristianesimo antico e moderno in onore di Maria Grazia Mara* 2, ed. M. Simonetti and P. Siniscalco (Rome: Collegium Internationale Augustinianum, 1995 = *Augustinianum* 35), 443–55; repr. in idem, *Essais sur l'Église manichéenne en Afrique du Nord et à Rome au temps de saint Augustin: Recueil d'études,* Studia Ephemeridis Augustinianum 47 (Rome: Institutum Patristicum Augustinianum, 1995), 269–80. This represents a change from 1970, when it was Fortunatus' *scriptural* argument that Decret found perfectly orthodox; see his *Aspects,* 233.

17   Fortunatus in Augustine, *C. Fort.* 3 (85.21–22). On Augustine's early Christology, see W. Geerlings, "Der manichäische 'Jesus patibilis' in der Theologie Augustins," *Tübinger Theologische Quartalschrift* 152 (1972): 124–31; O. du Roy, *L'intelligence de la foi en la Trinité selon saint Augustin: Genèse de sa théologie trinitaire jusqu'en 391* (Paris: Études Augustiniennes, 1966), esp. 200–69; van Bavel, *Recherches,* 13–16.

18   See Aug., *C. Fort.* 8 (88.13–16): "FORT. dixit: Ita apostolus dixit, quomodo sentire debeamus de nostris animis, quod Christus nobis ostendit, si fuit Christus in passione et morte, et nos; si uoluntate patris descendit in passionem et mortem, et nos."

19   Aug., *C. Fort.* 20 (98.8–10): "ipsa indulgentia peccatorum, quam nobis deus per dominum nostrum Iesum Christum donauit."

20   On the date of Augustine's reply, see "Epistulam Manichaei quam vocant fundamenti, Contra," in Fitzgerald, *Augustine Through the Ages,* 311–12 at 311. On this Manichaean writing, see also E. Feldmann, *Die "Epistula Fundamenti" der nordafrikanischer Manichäer: Versuch einer Rekonstruktion* (Altenberge-Soest: Akademische Bibliothek, 1987).

21 Aug., *Contra epistulam manichaei quam uocant Fundamenti* 6 (CSEL 25/1, 200.5–9): "Iesus Christus homo non a filio dei, id est uirtute et sapientia dei, per quam facta sunt omnia, missus est, sed ita susceptus secundum catholicam fidem, ut ipse esset dei filius, id est in illo ipso dei sapientia sanandis peccatoribus adpareret." Translation by R. Teske, *The Manichean Debate*, The Works of Saint Augustine: A Translation for the 21st Century, I/19 (Hyde Park: New City, 2006), 238.

22 See J.K. Coyle, *Augustine's "De moribus ecclesiae catholicae": A Study of the Work, Its Composition, and Its Sources*, Paradosis 25 (Fribourg: University, 1978), 242–43.

23 Aug., *C. epist. fund.* 7 (200.16–22): "cur hominem susceptum ab spiritu sancto Manichaeum non putatis turpe natum ex utroque sexu praedicare, hominem autem susceptum ab unigenita sapientia de natum de uirgine credere formidatis? Si caro humana, si concubitus uiri, si uterus mulieris non potuit inquinare spiritum sanctum, quomodo potuit uirginis uterus inquinare dei sapientiam?" Trans. Teske, *The Manichean Debate*, 238. On the docetic aspect of Manichaean Christology, see Coyle, *Augustine's "De moribus,"* 46–7.

24 *C. epist. Fund.* 8 (203.1-4).

25 Most commentators opt for this date, but others place it in 398: see S. Zarb, *Chronologia operum s. Augustini secundum ordinem retractationum digesta* (Rome: 1934), 16–17; P. Jolivet and M. Jourgeon, *Six traités anti-manichéens*, Bibliothèque Augustinienne 17 (Paris: Desclée de Brouwer, 1961), 787–88 (= note complémentaire 59); and Decret's discussion in *Aspects*, 78n2.

26 But see *Contra Felicem* 2.9 (CSEL 25/2, 838.1–18). On Felix's Christology see Decret, *Aspects*, 291–93.

27 *C. Felicem* 2.11 (830.22 – 831.7): "Quos Christus redemit a diabolo … inueniens peccatores sub peccato, redemit confitentes a superbiente."

28 *C. Felicem* 2.11 (841.1–2): "ille autem ostendit eam [uitam laboriosam] in carne sua, non merito iniquitatis suae, sed officio misericordiae suae."

29 *C. Felicem* 2.16 (845.21–28): "FEL. dixit: Christus unde nos mundauit? unde nos liberauit? AUG. dixit: Christus non partem dei, non naturam dei liberauit, sed facturam, quam fecit, in peccatum cadentem per liberum arbitrium sua misericordia liberauit. Eam rem mundauit, quae pollui poterat, eam rem liberauit, quae captiuari poterat, eam rem sanauit, quae infirmari poterat. Modo autem de deo, de natura dei, de substantia dei, de eo quod deus est, loquimur." Trans. Teske, *The Manichean Debate*, 310.

30 Zarb, *Chronologia operum*, 45, sets the time of composition in 397 to 398; O. Perler, *Les voyages de saint Augustin* (Paris: Études Augustiniennes, 1969), 443, between 397 and 399; and Decret, *Aspects*, 61–63, between 398 and 400. On the Christological aspects of this work, see Decret, "La doctrine centrale," 143–45.

31 In Augustine, *Contra Faustum* II,1 (CSEL 25/1, 253.19–21): "neque enim sequitur, ut, si euangelium accipio, idcirco et natum accipiam Christum. Cur? Quia euangelium quidem a praedicatione Christi et esse coepit et nominari, in quo tamen ipse nusquam se natum ex hominibus dicit." Translations from this work are my own.

32 On the Manichaeans' New Testament, see Coyle, *Augustine's "De moribus,"* 147–49.

33 Aug., *C. Faust.* II,2–4.

34 Aug., *C. Faust.* XX,2 (536.14–17): "qui quoniam sit et ipse geminus, ut eum apostolus nouit Christum dicens esse dei uirtutem et dei sapientiam, uirtutem quidem eius in sole habitare credimus, sapientiam uero in luna."

35   Aug., *C. Faust*. XX,4 (537.29–538.2): "sed nec uestrum quidem schisma si me dixeris, uerum est, quamuis Christum uenerer et colam, qui alio eum ritu colo et alia fide quam uos."

36   Aug., *C. Faust*. XX,11 (550.14–19): "Postremo dicite nobis, quot christos esse dicatis. Aliusne est, quem de spiritu sancto concipiens terra patibilem gignit, omni non solum suspensus ex ligno, sed etiam iacens in herba, et alius ille, quem Iudaei crucifixerunt sub Pontio Pilato, et tertius ille per solem lunamque distentus?"

37   See Aug., *C. Faust*. XIV,3 (405–06). On the background of this notion, see A. Böhlig, "Zur Vorstellung vom Lichtkreuz in Gnostizismus und Manichäismus," in *Gnosis: Festschrift für Hans Jonas*, ed. B. Aland (Göttingen: Vandenhoek & Ruprecht, 1978), 473–91; repr. in idem, *Gnosis und Synkretismus: Gesammelte Aufsätze zur spätantiken Religionsgeschichte* 1, Wissenschaftliche Untersuchungen zum Neuen Testament 47 (Tübingen: Mohr, 1989), 135–63. See also I. Gardner, *The Docetic Jesus*, Coptic Theological Papyri 2: Edition, Commentary, Translation [Textband] (Vienna: Hollinek, 1988), esp. 78–85.

38   Aug., *C. Faust*. XX,2, (536.20). See also a Coptic Manichaean psalm to Jesus in C.R.C. Allberry, *A Manichaean Psalm-Book, Part II*, Manichaean Manuscripts in the Chester Beatty Collection 2 (Stuttgart: Kohlhammer, 1938), 121.32–33: "The trees and the fruits—in them is thy holy body. My Lord Jesus." Also, a Psalm "of the Wanderers" (ibid., 155.24): "Jesus that hangs to the tree." Gardner, *The Docetic Jesus*, 74–76 (see also 81–85), notes Coptic Manichaean passages where Jesus seems to undergo real suffering on a cross: but I think that they refer to Jesus on the Cross of Light.

39   See E. Rose, *Die manichäische Christologie*, Studies in Oriental Religions 5 (Wiesbaden: O. Harrassowitz, 1979), 93–103; J. Ries, "Les titres néotestamentaires du Christ dans la liturgie gnostique de Médinet-Mâdi," in *Studia Biblica III: Sixth International Congress on Biblical Studies, Oxford, 3–7 April 1978*, ed. E.A. Livingstone, Journal for the Study of the New Testament, Supplement Series 3 (Sheffield: JSOT, 1980, 321–36 at 322–23 and 326–27; N.A. Pedersen, "Early Manichaean Christology, Primarily in Western Sources," in *Manichaean Studies: Proceedings of the First International Conference on Manichaeism, August 5–9, 1987, Department of History of Religions, Lund University, Sweden*, ed. P. Bryder (Lund: Plus Ultra, 1988), 157–90 at 174–77; and I. Gardner, "The Manichaean Account of Jesus and the Passion of the Living Soul," in van Tongerloo and Giversen, *Manichaica Selecta*, 71–86 at 80–2. Of the Living Soul, Secundinus says in his letter to Augustine (CSEL 25/2, 895.25–26): "Uides enim illum et in omni mundo et in omnia anima esse crucifixum." On the Living Soul as a son of the Primal Man in Coptic sources, see P. van Lindt, *The Names of Manichaean Mythological Figures: A Comparative Study on Terminology in the Coptic Sources*, Studies in Oriental Religions 26 (Wiesbaden: O. Harrassowitz, 1992), 66–67.

40   Aug., *C. Faustum* XXXIII,1 (784.27). See also XXXII,7 (766.20–21): "crucis eius mysticam fixionem"; and *Contra epist. Fund*. 8 (CSEL 25/1, 202.16–18).

41   See Rose, *Die manichäische Christologie*, 74–79 and 117–31; Decret, "La christologie manichéenne," 451–52; Ries, "Les titres," 323; and Pedersen, "Early Manichaean Christology," 170–71.

42   On the latter Christ, see Pedersen, "Early Manichaean Christology," 162–66 and 172–74; Rose, *Die manichäische Christologie*, 154–76; Ries, "Les titres," 322 and

325–26; and van Lindt, *The Names*, 133–48. Pedersen, 163, sees Jesus the Splendour portrayed in the Coptic Kephalaia as "an emanation from the second Father, the Third Messenger." In Africa this manifestation/aspect of Christ seems to be identified with the Third Envoy: see Rose, 17–18: "Bei ihnen besteht außerdem noch die fast unüberwindliche Schwierigkeit, daß nicht immer feststellen läßt, auf welche bestimmte Gottheit sie in dem oder anderen Fall gehen. Das Namen- und Vorstellungsmaterial ist für viele Götter bis zu einem solchen Grade gleichartig, daß es unmöglich ist, aus solchen Quellen eine individuelle Vorstellung eines einzelnen Gottwesens zu erlangen, wie es Waldschmidt-Lentz für Jesus versucht haben." Note that the three "Christs" or "aspects of Jesus" reported by Augustine are never found all together in Manichaean writings. They are, of course, found separately: see the references in Coyle, *Augustine's "De moribus,"* 44–45. On Augustine's characterization of the Manichaean "Christs" see also Decret, *Aspects*, 297–99.

43 Rose, *Die manichäische Christologie*, 89. This does not necessarily mean that the doctrine behind the term is exclusive to North African Manichaeism: see Decret, *Aspects*, 11–13; idem, "La doctrine," 248–49; E. Smagina, "Das manichäische Kreuz des Lichts und der *Jesus patibilis*," in van Oort et al., *Augustine and Manichaeism*, 243–49.

44 Aug., *Enarratio in ps. 140* 12 (CCL 40, 2035.25): "Et ipse est Christus, dicunt, crucifixus in toto mundo." The date is determined by S. Zarb, "Chronologia Enarrationum s. Augustini in Psalmos," *Angelicum* 24 (1947): 265–84 at 275–84. On *Iesus patibilis*, see Geerlings, "Der manichäische 'Jesus patibilis,'" 125–26; Gardner, *The Docetic Jesus*, 78–80; F. Decret, *L'Afrique manichéenne (IVe–Ve siècles)*, t. 2 (Paris: Études Augustiniennes, 1978), 216–18 (= n83); idem, "La doctrine centrale," 150–53; idem, *Aspects*, 284–86.

45 See Decret, "La doctrine centrale," 148–50; Viciano, "Aspects christologiques," 384–86.

46 *Epistula Secundini* 4 (CSEL 25/2, 897.19–20): « Si dominus noster carnalis foret, omnis nostra fuisset spes amputata. »

47 Aug., *Contra Secundinum* 25 (CSEL 25/2, 943.16–17): "Consolatorem igitur et saluatorem Manichaeo excepto nullum esse posse dixisti." See also *In Iohannis euangelium tract. 8.5–7* (CCL 36, 84.10–86.25); *Serm. 362* 13.13 (PL 39, c. 1619); and the references collected by Decret, *Aspects*, 297, nn3–4.

48 Aug., *C. Faust.* I,2 (251.23); XXIII,3 (788.19). See also XV,1 (417): by accepting the Old as well as the New Testament, Catholics have made Christianity a "centaur."

49 Aug., *De haeresibus* 46.15 (CCL 46, 317.151): "Christum autem fuisse affirmant, quem dicit nostra scriptura serpentem." See also *C. Faustum* XV,9 (436.15–17).

50 Secundinus, *Epist. ad Augustinum* (CSEL 25/2, 897.8–17): "Ipse enim non ignoras, quam pessimus sit quamque malignus quique etiam tanta calidiate aduersus fideles et summos uiros militat … Et ut ad ultimum crucis subplicium ueniretur, in perniciem ipsius scribas pharisaeosque accenderit, ut Barnabam [sic] dimitti clamarent et Iesum crucifigi."

51 Quoted by Evodius, *De fide* 28 (CSEL 25/2, 964.7–9): "Inimicus quippe, qui eundem saluatorem iustorum patrem crucifixisse se sperauit, ipse est crucifixus."

52 In Allberry, *A Manichaean Psalm-Book*, 123.5: "thy cross, the enemy being nailed to it."

53 On the date, see "Secundinum Manicheum, Contra," in Fitzgerald, *Augustine Through the Ages*, 759–60 at 759.

54 Secundinus, *Epistula ad Augustinum* (CSEL 25/2, 893.6–7): "Habeo et ago gratias ineffabili ac sacratissimae maiestati eiusque primogenito omnium luminum regi Iesu Christo." Trans. Teske, *The Manichean Debate*, 357.

55 On Jesus as "light" in Manichaeism, see Ries, "Jésus-Christ dans la religion de Mani," 449–52.

56 Secundinus (895.24–26): "noli esse erroris lancea, qua latus percutitur saluatoris. Uides enim illum et in omni mundo et in omni anima esse crucifixum." Trans. Teske, *The Manichean Debate*, 358–59.

57 Secundinus (897.18–20): "euasimus igitur, quia spiritalem secuti sumus saluatorem. Nam illius tantum erupit audacia, ut si noster dominus carnalis foret, omnis nostra fuisset spes amputata." Trans. Teske, *The Manichean Debate*, 360.

58 Augustine, *Contra Secundinum* 5 (CSEL 25/2, 911.20–24): "consubstantialis est patri et est ante omnem creaturam, ex eadem substantia fratres haberet. itaque eum et unigenitum et primogenitum eum diuina testentur eloquia—unigenitum, quia sine fratribus, primogenitum, quia cum fratribus." Trans. Teske, *The Manichean Debate*, 367.

59 See the references in Coyle, *Augustine's "De moribus,"* 46–47; also, the comments of Decret, "La christologie manichéenne," 445–49; Gardner, *The Docetic Jesus*, 64–65 and 74–78; and Pedersen, "Early Manichaean Christology," 169–70.

60 A puzzle here is the limited use he makes of the pericope 1 Corinthians 15:3–22 in the entire discussion on docetism. It appears mainly at the beginning and the end of the *docetic* portion, in *C. Fort.* 22 (CSEL 25/1, 105.21–106.1, verses 19 and 21), and *C. Faustum* II,2 (255.9, verse 11) and XI,3 (317.4–11, verses 9–12). The key verse (14: "If Christ has not been raised, our preaching is useless, and so is your believing") never appears in this context.

61 See Aug., *De ag. chr.* 18.20 (CSEL 41, 120.16–121.10): "Nec eos audiamus, qui non uerum hominem suscepisse dicunt filium dei neque natum esse de femina, sed falsam carnem et imaginem simulatam corporis humani ostendisse uidentibus. Nesciunt enim, quomodo substantia dei administrans uniuersam creaturam inquinari omnino non possit, et tamen praedicant istum uisibilem solem radios suos per omnes feces et sordes corporum spargere et eos mundos et sinceros ubique seruare. Si ergo uisibilia munda uisibilibus inmundis contingi possunt et non inquinari, quanto magis inuisibilis et incommutabilis ueritas per spiritum animam et per animam corpus suscipiens toto homine adsumpto ab omnibus eum infirmitatibus nulla sua contaminatione liberauit!... Isti totum corpus eius falsam carnem fuisse contendunt, ut non sibi uideantur imitari Christum, si non suis auditoribus mentiantur."

62 So H.-C. Puech, "La conception manichéenne du salut," in idem, *Sur le manichéisme et autres essais* (Paris: Flammarion, 1979), 5–101 at 90–91: "De surcroît, la Passion du Christ n'est qu'une illustration du crucifiement cosmique subi, d'après le mythe, par le *Jesus Patibilis*: elle est un acte historique qui exprime, sous forme saisissante, la doctrine du « Sauveur–Sauvé ». Comme l'écrit Alexandre de Lycopolis, « à la fin, le *Noûs* (qui est Jésus) par sa crucifixion a donné à connaître (*anastaurôthénta paraskhesthai gnôsin*) que c'est d'une manière semblable (*toïôdé tropôi*) qu'aussi la puissance divine est fixée (*énêrmosthai*), crucifiée (*énestaurôsthai*) à la Matière »."

Ce n'est donc pas, comme pour le chrétien, dans une participation à Jésus incarné et crucifié que le manichéen retrouvera son salut, mais grâce à l'enseignement et à l'exemple d'un Jésus qui n'a revêtu une apparence physique que pour se manifester au monde dans le temps et dont la mission a été, avant tout, d'éveiller et d'éclairer les âmes." This article revises Puech's "Der Begriff der Erlösung im Manichäismus," *Eranos-Jahrbuch* 4 (1936): 183–285, which was reprinted in G. Widengren, ed., *Der Manichäismus*, Wege der Forschung 168 (Darmstadt: Wissenschaftliche Buchgesellschaft, 1977), 145–213, and appeared in English as "The Concept of Redemption in Manichaeism," in J. Campbell, ed., *The Mystic Vision*, Papers from the Eranos Yearbooks 6 (Princeton: Princeton University Press, 1968), 247–314.

63 Aug., *C. Faustum* II,5 (CSEL 25/1, 258.14–15): "Non iam saluatorem uestrum sed a uobis saluandum."

64 See Aug., *Enarr. in ps. 140* 12 (CCL 40, 2035.24–28): "Tales sunt electi, ut non sint saluandi a deo, sed saluatores dei. Et ipse est Christus, dicunt, crucifixus in toto mundo. Ego in euangelio saluatorem acceperam Christum; uos autem estis in libris uestris saluatores Christi. Estis plane blasphematores Christi, et ideo a Christo non saluandi."

65 See above, p. 71.

66 Aug., *C. Faustum* XIII,1 (CSEL 25/1, 378.1).

67 Secundinus, *Ep. ad Augustinum* (CSEL 25/2, 897.18), employing an expression that strongly suggests a determination to rule out any aspect of corporality, whether in the Saviour or in the saved. See also the texts referred to in the following note. As a Hearer, Secundinus might have simply been professing what he truly believed, or at least as much of Manichaean doctrine as he had thus far received. For it is interesting that the truly sacred books of the Manichaeans seem to have been available only to the Elect. Paul and the Gospels were the references of choice when dealing with the uninitiated. In fact, Manichaeism may be the venue where Augustine had his first serious encounter with Scripture. Is it not, then, possible that in Christian regions Manichaean missionaries chose to expose both potential converts and new Hearers to concepts they would be familiar with from Scripture—albeit tailored to Manichaean specifications—and that only the insider group of Elect would know the "true," complete Scriptures, that is, the canon born of Manichaeism itself, containing the pristine doctrines? This is what F. Decret suggests in "La doctrine du « Iesus patibilis » dans la polémique antijudaïque des manichéens d'Afrique," in idem, *Essais*, 241–67 at 244: "L'« apôtre » de Mani [Adimantus] ne fait jamais recours aux *auctores* de la secte, qui eussent été mal reçus par des auditeurs de formation chrétienne, mais, dans la tradition des Antithèses de Marcion, il s'emploie, avec habilité et en faisant preuve d'une remarquable connaissance des Écritures juives et chrétiennes." See also 246. This would explain that references to Jesus in Eastern Manichaean texts, while not necessarily less abundant, are frequently less clear than in Manichaean documents circulating in the Roman Empire. As one moves westward, in fact, there is more abundant evidence of adaptation. Thus Julien Ries, while making much of "le recueil christologique de Médînet Mâdi," whose texts present a liturgy that « s'attache tout particulièrement à l'action cosmique de Jésus, » adds that they portray as well a "théologie solaire manichéenne" that "nous semble tributaire notamment de certaines doctrines égyptiennes ainsi que du culte de Mithra" ("Les titres," 325–26).

68   Aug., *C. Felicem* 2.21 (CSEL 25/2, 851.16–17): "et polluta est anima et uenit Christus liberare eam et eam liberauit a peccato." See also 10 (838.31–32 and 839.3–4), 16 (845.21), 18 (847.9–10), and 20 (849.31–32 and 850.24–27).

69   Aug., *C. Faust.* 2.5 (CSEL 25/1, 258.13–14).

70   Aug., *C. Faust.* 2.5 (CSEL 25/1, 258.15–259.10). See J.D. BeDuhn, "A Regimen for Salvation: Medical Models in Manichaean Asceticism," *Semeia* 58 (1992): 113–14 and 119–27; idem, *The Manichaean Body in Discipline and Ritual* (Baltimore: Johns Hopkins University Press, 2000), esp. 145–48 and 169–79.

71   See Aug., *Enarr. in ps. 140* 12, cited above (n64).

72   Puech, "La conception," 6: "Tout dans le manichéisme est salut." On the Manichaean notion of salvation, see his entire article.

73   Decret, *Aspects*, 283–85.

74   So Decret, *Aspects*, 277. See especially Fortunatus, in Aug., *C. Fort.* 20 (CSEL 25/1, 100.2–3): "auctore deo saluatore nostro, qui nos docet et bona exercere et mala fugere"; 21 (103.7): "post aduentum saluatoris et post hanc scientiam rerum"; and Faustus, in *C. Faustum* II,1 (254.14–15): "scias me ... accipere euangelium, id est praedicationem Christi."

75   Aug., *Confessiones* 3.6.10 (CCL 27, 31.4–5). See the Coptic psalm in Allberry, *A Manichaean Psalm-Book*, 170.18: "It is Jesus that we seek, on whom we have modelled ourselves."

76   Aug., *Enarr. in ps. 140* 12 (above, n64). But this label is not reserved for Manichaeans: see *Enarr. in ps. 90* 10; *Contra mendacium* 5.8.

77   Faustus refers to Catholic Christians as "semi-christiani" (Aug., *C. Faust.* I.2, CSEL 25/1, 251.23). Augustine's riposte follows (I,3, 253.6–8). See also Felix's declaration, "quando uoluero, ero christianus" (Aug., *C. Felicem* 2.12 (CSEL 25/2, 841.27), and Augustine's retort (842.3): "quando uolueris, esto." Decret's affirmation therefore needs to be qualified: "pas une seule fois l'auteur ne considère la secte comme un courant extérieur au christianisme ... Il reste que le polémiste regarde le manichéisme comme un courant chrétien, même s'il le considère désormais comme un christianisme dévoyé." F. Decret, "Saint Augustin témoin du manichéisme dans l'Afrique romaine," in *Internationales Symposium über den Stand der Augustinus-Forschung vom 12. bis 16. April 1987 im Schloß Rauischholzhausen der Justus-Liebig-Universität Gießen*, Cassiciacum 39/1, ed. C. Mayer and K.H. Chelius (Würzburg: Augustinus-Verlag, 1989), 88–89; repr. in idem, *Essais*, 16–17.

78   See Coyle, *Augustine's De moribus*," 23–26; and Puech, "La conception," 6–9, 50–52, and 82–93.

79   Pedersen, "Early Manichaean Christology," 157. E. Rose, "Die manichäische Christologie," *Zeitschrift für Religions- und Geistesgeschichte* 32 (1980): 219–31 at 223–28, categorizes Augustine's three "Christs" into five manifestations, while Pedersen counts "six different Jesus-hypostases, all of them connected with the main aspects of the way to salvation for the soul" (see also 162).

80   See Puech, "La conception," 8–10.

81   See Coptic Psalm 248 (Allberry, *A Manichaean Psalm-Book*, 56.15–57.33).

5

The Seventh Canon of Ephesus

✠ ✠ ✠

J. ROBERT WRIGHT

J OANNE MCWILLIAM was one of that rare breed of academics who are as conversant in modern theology as they are in early Church history. She always sought the facts to back up her theological rationalizations. As a result, the impact of her teaching and writing was strengthened and more greatly appreciated—even if at times it may have appeared at first impression to consist of seemingly dry detail or of apparently idle speculation—because with her one always knew that a solid foundation was bound to undergird whatever she chose to write or speak about. And it was this feature that gave students and scholars alike a confidence as they approached her lectures or her literary output. She had something to say, and she said it well.

I began to reflect upon this characteristic of her work when I first read the essay titled "Augustine at Ephesus?" that she generously contributed in an undeserved tribute to me that was published back in 2006.[1] Beginning that essay with the observation that St. Augustine was already dead by the time of the third ecumenical council at Ephesus in 431, and concluding it with the comment that, because of the issues involved there, "Augustine was fortunate to miss Ephesus," she had important things to say about his understanding of how Jesus Christ could be both God and man. As evidence she illustrated his thought on the distinction between, but also coexistence of, divinity and humanity in Christ that the council affirmed in its use of the term *theotokos;* she did so by citing two of Augustine's profound observations one after another: "Christ was born of a woman not as he is, the blessed God over all, but in that feeble [nature] which he took from us" [and] "As man, born of Mary, God was his god. As God the Word, eternally born, [his] relationship was to a Father."[2] Professor McWilliam then moved to her contention that "if Augustine had been there [at Ephesus] he would have found it difficult, if not impossible, to join either side wholeheartedly."[3]

Her point, I think, is well taken, and the purpose of the present chapter is to offer still another dimension to her careful sifting of the theological and historical issues involved. Was Augustine really "fortunate to miss Ephesus," or were there other developments generated by the Ephesine council that might have actually pleased Augustine and that may also interest successors and admirers of Professor McWilliam as they ponder what Augustine might have thought of the totality of that council's work? Granted that dead persons tell no tales, and that no one can really be sure what Augustine would have said about ecclesial debates and decisions at Ephesus subsequent to his death, is there yet more evidence to be taken into account as later scholars weigh its actions? Does its commonly assumed theological decision about Nestorius and *theotokos* exhaust all of its contribution to Christology, or is there some further historical—or even canonical—evidence that may have a bearing on our evaluation of that council and possibly affect our estimate of what Augustine might have thought of it had he lived to see it?

Around the same time that I first read Professor McWilliam's essay "Augustine at Ephesus?" I was invited by the Slavic and Baltic Division of the New York Public Library to contribute to an analysis of a recently accessioned and quite unique manuscript from the seventeenth century of some 2,049 pages penned in Latin. Written as a treatise against what its author regards as the papal addition of the *filioque* clause into the Nicene Creed, it was composed by a rather angular Lutheran convert to Eastern Orthodoxy named Adam Zernikaw (1652–93/4). This polemic and extremely one-sided work, composed at Baturyn (Ukraine) about the year 1682 with the precision of a Western legal mind by an author who was then only about thirty years of age, is titled *De Processione Spiritus Sancti a Solo Patre*. Its author tends to attribute most of the evils of the Church of his time to the Roman papacy, though his scholarly apparatus is quite impressive. The unique and hitherto unrecorded copy of the manuscript now in possession of the New York Public Library contains hundreds of named references and citations of councils and early church writers such as Justin Martyr, Clement of Alexandria, Origen, Gregory Thaumaturgus, Cyril of Alexandria, Athanasius,

Dionysius the Areopagite, Abbot Alcuin, John of Damascus, Gregory of Tours, Photius, Bellarmine, Bessarion, Baronius, "the Jesuits," and (frequently in the margins) Tyconius.

Zernikaw's *De Processione* has recently been reintroduced to the scholarly world elsewhere—an event in which I played one small part.[4] It is not the intention of the present chapter to contribute still another excursus about the merits and fortunes of the *filioque*. Our attention now needs to focus upon the seventh of the nineteen tractates into which Zernikaw divides his voluminous work, for here he asserts it to be "shown, by that decree of ecumenical synods (his reference is Ephesus and Chalcedon) lest any other definition of the faith be introduced in the churches besides that of Nicaea, that not only is it commanded not to introduce anything contrary, but also it is prohibited to insert anything within the Holy Symbol itself (Nicene Creed); and therefore even if it were true that the Holy Spirit proceeds from the Son, by no means would it be possible to introduce that into the Holy Symbol." Zernikaw's Latin is a bit archaic and contorted and difficult to translate (my own version here is quite literal), but his meaning is clear, for his reference is to the seventh canon of the council of Ephesus, which was subsequently endorsed at Chalcedon. So this now brings us to the question of what Ephesus said in this canon and whether Augustine would have considered himself totally fortunate to be already dead before it was convoked. Granted Professor McWilliam's point about Augustine's likely distaste for the theological debates at Ephesus, what would he have thought about this seventh canon? Surely, all the historical or canonical evidence must be considered—and not merely his known theological positions on the major controversies—if one is to give a total surmise of what Augustine might have thought at that juncture near the end of his life on this earth, had he lived on into the Council of Ephesus.

The first six canons of Ephesus clearly involve the discussions about Nestorius, and Professor McWilliam is no doubt correct about the ambivalence if not distaste that Augustine might have felt if he had become submerged in those murky waters. For the sake of argument we may also assume that Augustine had no intense theological interest in the eighth and final canon, on the jurisdictional rights of Cyprus. But the seventh Ephesine canon is not really a canon at all but a *horos* or "determination" of a different sort; and it has certainly had a unique life of its own, as can be seen merely from the prominence given to it by Zernikaw in his treatise from the seventeenth century. The seventh canon of Ephesus reads as follows: "It is not permitted to produce or write or compose any other creed except the one which was defined by the holy fathers who were gathered together in the Holy Spirit at Nicaea. Any who dare to compose or bring forth or produce another creed for the benefit of those who wish to turn from Hellenism or Judaism or some other heresy to the knowledge of the truth, if they are bishops or clerics they should be deprived of their respective charges and if they are laymen they are to be anathematized."[5] Here, it would seem, is a determination over which Augustine would not have had the reservations that Professor McWilliam confidently attributed to him *post mortem* as regards the christological debates at Ephesus itself, though of course one can never take for granted the assumptions of great theological minds on any given point, especially if they are allowed to wander apart from the moorings of history and the canonical traditions.

The seventh canon of Ephesus has had a history of its own, quite interesting in its own right, and not so closely connected to the christological concerns that Professor McWilliam correctly suggests would have weighed heavily on Augustine's mind had he lived on into the summer and early fall of 431. Zernikaw quotes the text of the seventh Ephesine canon on folio 482 recto of the New York Public Library's copy of his treatise, and it is possible that Zernikaw learned of it from the writing of his friend Thomas Smith, Anglican priest and former chaplain to the English ambassador in Constantinople, whose *Account of the Greek Church*[6] begins its discussion of the *filioque* with an account of the same canon of Ephesus. In a general way, it can be said that over the course of history debate has focused on the question of whether Ephesus in this canon was prohibiting (as the Greek writers tend to claim) any textual changes at all from the "original" creed of Nicaea—which would have ruled out much of the creed's third paragraph as subsequently expanded, as well as certain other points—or whether the canon was only ruling out (as the Latins claimed) any change in textual wording that might imply some different doctrinal stance now being demanded especially of converts other than the stance that had already been taken against Arianism.[7] This is not the place to develop the history of that debate, but the point needs to be stressed that this canon is also part of the legacy of the Ephesine council: it involves the subtle interplay of history and theology in a way in which (for our own time) Professor McWilliam showed considerable aptitude; and even apart from the question of *filioque*, it concerns a subject that might well have attracted Augustine—a debate from which he would not have wanted to be excluded.

An especially noteworthy example of the importance ascribed to the seventh canon of Ephesus in subsequent Anglican history—which has very little to do with the focus of theological debate at Ephesus but very much indeed to do with the text of this canon from the same council—is the discussion given to its *horos* in the work of Thomas Richey, my own distant predecessor as Professor of Ecclesiastical History in the General Theological Seminary from 1879 to 1902.[8] Writing in the best Anglican liberal-catholic tradition, in which Professor McWilliam also found herself much at home, Professor Richey divided his book into considerations of "historical" and "doctrinal" questions. His overall concern was to support the insertion of the *filioque* into the creed; at the same time, he did not wish to contradict the seventh canon of Ephesus, and he developed this position by asserting that the creeds were living and growing realities of the Church's experience rather than absolute and fixed definitions. He further asserted that the Church never expected complete uniformity to any single formula of belief, that even the creeds coming out of Nicaea and Constantinople were themselves the products of historical evolution, and that just as subsequent ages have seen some historical development of wording, there has nonetheless been an underlying consistency of doctrinal affirmation. Commenting on the differences of approach in East and West, he observed that historical developments within the churches of the East were usually met by decrees that did not necessitate changes in credal wording, whereas such developments in the West in some cases called for alterations in the credal text.

Thus far Richey stands in contrast to Zernikaw, the seventeenth-century convert to Orthodoxy, who in his seventh tractate held—as we have remarked—that the papacy and by implication the entire Church of the West was in violation of the conciliar faith of Ephesus and its seventh canon, having unilaterally added a single word to the Nicene text. We may also note in passing that already in the fifteenth century, the Orthodox (Greek) side had said something very similar at the council of Ferrara in 1438, where the seventh canon of Ephesus was invoked to demonstrate the non-canonical nature of the addition of the *filioque*.

Still more recently, a much more scholarly and much less fundamentalistic and polemical interpretation of the seventh canon than that of Zernikaw has been developed from an Orthodox point of view. This occurs in the comments on the seventh Ephesine canon published in 1996 by the late Archbishop Peter L'Huillier in his extensive and masterful commentary on ecclesiology in the canons of the early ecumenical councils. About one hundred years after Richey, after many years of study of the original historical and canonical documents, he reached conclusions very similar to those of Richey himself—namely, that the fathers of Ephesus did not want to forbid completely the composition of other dogmatic formulations where they might seem necessary. He summarized: "Nothing allows us to think that they [the fathers of Ephesus] wanted to prohibit competent organs of the Church from publishing, if it was felt necessary, new symbols and dogmatic decrees; this is effectively what happened in later history."[9]

Adam Zernikaw in the seventeenth century, notwithstanding whatever he knew of the circumstances surrounding the unilateral Western insertion of the *filioque* at the third council of Toledo in 589 and its later entry into the Nicene Creed at Rome with papal approval, raised acutely the question of what Ephesus might have meant by its seventh canon and also, by implication, the broader question of what authority should be attributed to conciliar canons, especially when there are differences of interpretation. It is still a question that all the churches face today. For myself, I do not think that Augustine, had he still been alive in 431, would have withdrawn from the opportunity to discuss all this in the context of the seventh Ephesine canon. I believe that historians will be able to discern a consistency of interest regarding it that can include not only Thomas Richey and Peter L'Huillier but also Aurelius Augustinus and Joanne McWilliam.

Notes

1 Joanne McWilliam, "Augustine at Ephesus?" in *One Lord, One Faith, One Baptism: Studies in Christian Ecclesiality and Ecumenism in Honor of J. Robert Wright*, ed. Marsha L. Dutton and Patrick Terrell Gray (Grand Rapids: Eerdmans, 2006), 56–67.

2 Augustine, *Contra Faustum* 3.6; idem, *Enarratio in ps.* 21.10–11, both cited in McWilliam, "Augustine at Ephesus?" 65.

3 Ibid., 56.

4 Edward Kasinec and J. Robert Wright, "A Manuscript Copy of Adam Zernikaw's 'De Processione' (Baturyn, 1682) at the New York Public Library," in *Confraternitas: Festschrift in Honor of Iaroslav Isaievych*, ed. Mykola Krykun and Ostap Sereda (Lviv [Ukraine]: Ivan Krypiakevych Institute of Ukrainian Studies of the National Academy of Sciences of Ukraine, 2006–7), 353–62.

5 Norman P. Tanner, ed., *Decrees of the Ecumenical Councils*, (London: Sheed and Ward; Washington: Georgetown University Press, 1990), 1:65, which gives the original Greek and Latin texts on the same page. Alternative English translation in J. Stevenson, ed., *Creeds, Councils, and Controversies: Documents Illustrative of the History of the Church AD 337–461* (London: SPCK, 1966), 296. Original Greek and Latin texts also published in J. Alberigo et al., eds., *Conciliorum Oecumenicorum Decreta* (Bologna: Istituto per le Scienze Religiose, 1973), 65. Note that the word occurring twice in this canon and translated here as "creed"—namely, the Greek word *pistis*, which in the Latin version comes out as *fides*—appears in some English translations as "faith," which allows it to have a broader meaning that is also more vague than its narrower translation by the word "creed."

6 Thomas Smith, *Account of the Greek Church* (London: 1680), 197. Zernikaw is known to have been studying patristic sources at the Bodleian Library in September 1676 (Kasinec and Wright, "A Manuscript Copy," n4).

7 Still another line of interpretation, advanced by a former Anglican Bishop of London, J.W.C. Wand, that the council in this statement intended to prohibit the requirement of some other creed than Nicaea for the reception of converts rather than the composition of any new creed at all, seems less likely. Wand, *Doctors and Councils* (London: The Faith Press, 1962), 190.

8 Thomas Richey, *The Nicene Creed and the Filioque* (New York: E. & J.B. Young, 1884). The substance of this work is divided in two parts: first "the historical argument," and then "the doctrinal issue."

9 Archbishop Peter L'Huillier, *The Church of the Ancient Councils: The Disciplinary Work of the First Four Ecumenical Councils* (Crestwood: St. Vladimir's Seminary Press, 1996), 163.

6
Logos Christology Today
✟ ✟ ✟

ROGER HAIGHT, SJ

J OANNE MCWILLIAM spent a good deal of her academic career studying various aspects of Patristic Logos Christology and trinitarian theology. Few conceptual symbols in Christian theology rival the importance of Logos in Christian theology. Like all classical symbols, Logos, or more familiarly "the Word of God," continues to be reinterpreted in new cultures and thus retain its significance. I offer this essay as one to which she would have responded with spontaneity and not without criticism.

Because Logos is a classical symbol with ancient Hebrew and Greek resonances, it has had to defend its relevance within a growing sense of historicity. An appreciation of historical change in modernity led to formulae for understanding the development of doctrine beyond Nicaea and Chalcedon, and the more radical sensibilities for difference and particularity that mark postmodernity have often challenged the relevance of the universal, comprehensive character of Logos. The purpose of this chapter is to demonstrate by example that Logos is under considerable pressure in systematic theology today and to suggest ways in which its meaning may yet again be modified and reappropriated in new theological frameworks of interpretation.

The argument unfolds in three logical phases across five parts. In the first, I list several problems that surround uses of Logos language today. The second phase contains three parts. It turns to three systematic theologians—Friedrich Schleiermacher, Paul Tillich, and Edward Schillebeeckx—who engage Logos language and reinterpret the classical usage in significantly different ways. In the third and concluding phase, I offer some constructive reflections in the light of the contributions of these theologians that are meant to contribute to the ongoing discussion of Logos.

Problems Entailed in Logos Christology

There have always been problems connected with Logos Christology; indeed, this theological construct was *conceived* in controversy. Even though it remains a norm against which all Christologies should be compared, it will never be free from debate, even among those who defend some version of it. In this part I briefly lay out some of these problems as they are felt today. This does not mean they are new. And those who accept a Logos Christology as their own usually profess it in a way they believe absorbs or responds to these problems. But an increasing number of others believe these problems require a different language when it comes to expressing their belief in the divinity of Jesus Christ and the nature of God.

Mythological Construals of Logos Christology

The most obvious problem with Logos Christology lies in the tendency to read it in the literal terms of a myth. The point of this observation is not to make "myth" a negative category but to note the tendency for the idea of God as Logos becoming a human being to become a kind of "comic book" narrative. This entails thinking of the three persons of the trinity as individuals, constituting a numerical three, one of whom became incarnate in Jesus.[1] The objectification of language and the role of the imagination in all knowing spontaneously lend support to this misunderstanding. When preachers refer to the doctrine of the trinity and the doctrine of Incarnation entailed in the constitution of the person of Jesus Christ as mysteries, the referent often appears in mathematical terms: How can one be three, or the one person, Jesus, really be both a human being and God? On the one hand, preachers frequently blame these mysteries on theologians; on the other, theologians do not usually attend to such elementary and obvious mistakes. But this does not mean that they go away. What exactly does "Logos" refer to?

Logos Christology Is Abstract

This complaint about Logos Christology is perhaps the oldest, and its most common neuralgic point. It can be brought to bear from two points of view. The first refers to the abstract and metaphysical language of the doctrine and the consequent level of discussion it involves. Jesus of Nazareth is pre-supposed in this discussion, but in order to express Jesus' relation to God and ultimately his divinity, it is said that the Word of God is incarnate within him. John's Gospel contains the clearest affirmation that "the Word was with God" and that "the Word became flesh" in this world in Jesus. Once this datum is in place, the conversation shifts to an abstract and deeper metaphysical level of the identity of "the Word" and the conditions of the possibility of God as Word being the driving force of Jesus' life in history. Granting certain premises, this conversation is meaningful, but it is not kerygmatically forceful or edifying; it is precisely metaphysical.

The abstract metaphysical character of the Christological problem reveals the second aspect of the problem: it is abstract in the sense of what it leaves behind and what is missing. The metaphysical conversation does not deal with the historical Jesus, his ministry, his teachings in parable and apho-rism, his exorcisms and general "going around doing good." This is not a problem in principle, but it represents a real diversion of attention. The pre-existent Logos of God, its character, how it becomes present and oper-ative within Jesus, make up the issues that in fact take over the conversa-tion so that Jesus of Nazareth recedes to the background. But it is to Jesus that Christians relate. They do not relate to a divine nature; rather, a divine nature or dimension of God is meant to "explain" why Christians relate to Jesus as the mediator of God's salvation.

The Hypostatization of a Metaphor

The logic of the development of the doctrine that Jesus is the Incarnation of the pre-existent Word of God can be explained by two tendencies. The first is the inclination to read written speech objectively. Religious beliefs always lead back to someone's religious perception and speech. When this is considered valuable enough to be remembered or committed to writing, the community that is later socialized into these religious expressions tends to take them as representing objective knowledge. The second tendency is for metaphor generally and personification in particular to pass from fig-urative iconic language to objective factual knowledge. A good example of this is the personification of God's wisdom as a person. The personification is all the more dramatic by being a woman, Sophia, who is depicted as a real figure. Analogously, is the idea that Jesus is God's word a personifica-tion of God's effective and wise power of speech? Or does it refer to the individuated form of divine being designated "Logos" inhabiting Jesus? What makes all this difficult is the structure of metaphor itself, whose form and power of communication is gained precisely by seemingly literal affirmation: "That kid *is* a tiger!" Somewhere along the way, Jesus as the personification of God's revealing power or Word was hypostatized. It is not clear whether this had already taken place before or even in the writing of John's prologue or afterwards. It is clear, however, that Justin Martyr is dealing with an individual Logos. One also has to decide whether this development was itself a revelation, or an inevitable cultural mistake, or simply an example of symbolic speech about transcendent reality. In any case, it left emergent Christology with the problem of the "second God" whose ready answer was subordinationism.[2]

Is Logos Redundant?

Frequently, when the Fathers write about Jesus in history, the referent of the language is the Logos or divine Son. This occasionally becomes obvious when divine powers are spontaneously predicated of the Jesus of history. But as I indicated in the last paragraph, that was less of a problem before Nicaea, because Logos was not strictly a second God; the divinity incarnate in Jesus was less than that of Yahweh or the Father. This general sentiment became especially clear in the strong reaction against Sabellius for suggesting that the Father could have been incarnate in Jesus in such a way that God suffered. The Sabellian construction clearly preserved the divinity of Jesus Christ more decisively than did subordinationism; but the passibility of God was the greater anomaly. When Nicaea declared the Son to be of the same nature as the Father, that should have meant that Incarnation of the Word would be as unthinkable as that of the Father: so the Arians thought. Or should we rather think that Sabellius was not so wrong after all—that the radical incarnation of God, Father or Son, should not be compared to the mutual inherence of two finite beings? The Incarnation of God is more like that which occurs in creation out of nothing. The radical being present of God to finite creatures entails no competition at all because it is of a completely different order of causality, one that sustains creaturely existence itself. If the Logos is of the same nature as the Father, the concept seems to be redundant, or the distinction of the Logos from the Father unnecessary.

Multiple Incarnations of Logos

The technological and cultural shrinking of our world has made the theology of religions a central theme for Christian theologians, and it comes into focus in Christology. The problem is most intense for those who wish to find a formula that preserves the classical tradition of affirming Jesus' divinity even while preserving the uniqueness and autonomous validity of other religions. Among several theological theories that have this as their goal, one finds the view that God as Logos has become incarnate in more than the one instance of Jesus of Nazareth.[3] This position reasserts the traditional Christian understanding of Incarnation but extends its application in a non-competitive way to other media or figures bearing God's salvation. This view is attractive because it so neatly achieves its purpose; but it has residual side effects. On the one hand, it clearly "explains" why other religions may be considered by Christians as autonomous and analogous to Christianity. On the other, the idea of multiple Incarnations of Logos alters the character of the symbol. Logos appears to point to a more common and readily encountered presence of God, one that scarcely differs in that respect from God as Spirit.

Is "Person" Language Applied to God Dysfunctional?

The language of "person" applied to God and the very idea that God is a "person" are coming under new pressure. Christian theology and ordinary speech have traditionally called Father, Son, and Spirit "persons." And God is generally depicted as a person. Of course theology is quick to add that the term "person" when applied to the persons of the trinity has a meaning quite different from ordinary speech and specifically from psychological understandings of an individual person. But that does not prevent the use of gendered pronouns for God, thus drawing God back into the sphere of men and women. In a past, smaller world and universe—one construed by what today appears as unsophisticated science—it may have been natural to think of God as the all-powerful person who created the world. But does not application of the category of "being a person" to God appear archaic and incongruous today? The problem does not lie in characteristics of personality such as intelligence and freedom being applied to God: it is hard to imagine the creative power behind the emergence of personal existence as being in itself less than its created effects. But the idea that God is a person, with the limits that are built into that concept, seems too confining for the creator of the universe as it is known today. This problem, which applies to all affirmations about God, appears particularly acute in this designation of God's being. It raises the question of how and what a language, whose technical meaning is different from the commonsense usage, actually communicates to ordinary people, Christians included. By "dysfunctional" I mean a language that in reality systemically distorts that which it intends to communicate. One way of addressing this issue is simply to allow the name, God, to remain gender free—that is, to transcend gender and being a person altogether—while at the same time implicitly including within "God" all that personality entails. In short, one way or another we have to get beyond Logos or the divine Son being a person within the Godhead and, more generally, thinking of God as a person.

These six issues do not exhaust the difficulties surrounding the concept of Logos. But they raise some serious questions to which use of Logos as a constructive symbol must attend. The discussion now shifts to three modern theologians who have engaged the logic of Logos at a profound level.

Schleiermacher's Alternative Trinitarian Theology

Friedrich Schleiermacher is probably better known for his lack of a theology of the trinity than for constructive interpretation, but he wrote about the trinity and made a significant contribution to trinitarian thinking. Though his theology is undeveloped, it is not so in principle and could have been drawn out. My goal here is to outline Schleiermacher's alternative to traditional trinitarian theology, which still strongly affirms the divinity of Jesus Christ and avoids some of the problems listed at the head of this chapter. I will do this by giving an overview of how Schleiermacher handles the doctrine of trinity and then showing how he preserves the realism of Incarnation without hypostatization of the Logos, and how his "system"—as distinct from his own convictions—can be used to appreciate religious pluralism.[4]

According to Schleiermacher, the doctrine of the trinity is derivative. By that I mean that the doctrine developed so that it depends, in the order of knowing, on the doctrines of the divinity and redeeming work of Jesus Christ and the Spirit. The history of doctrine and the debate at Nicaea contradict the idea that the doctrine of trinity is prior to the doctrines of Jesus Christ and salvation. Citing Schleiermacher, it is simply not true "that acceptance of the doctrine of the Trinity is the necessary precondition of faith in redemption and in the founding of the kingdom of God by means of the divine in Christ and in the Holy Spirit" (CF 72, 749).

For Schleiermacher, the content of the doctrine of the trinity lies in the doctrines of the divinity of Jesus Christ and the Holy Spirit. These two doctrines, after the doctrine of creation, define the essence or substance of Christian faith. Schleiermacher deeply and exhaustively developed his explanation of the Incarnation. The union of true God with humanity in the person of Christ and in the Church "are the essential elements in the doctrine of the trinity," and "the whole view of Christianity set forth in [his] church teaching stands or falls" with these two essential doctrines (CF 170, 738).[5] In other words, the doctrine of the trinity does not add anything essential beyond what is already contained in the doctrines of creation, Jesus Christ, and the Spirit in the Church.

Schleiermacher insists on the defensive and protective function of the doctrine of the trinity. Both historically and in its logic it is decisively anti-Arian: it was formulated to protect the essential and radical divinity of Jesus Christ against any subordination. This is also the logic of its formulation—that is, as a negation of the Arian understanding. Both the aim of the doctrine and its origin go precisely to the content of the true divinity of Jesus Christ and the Spirit in the Church (CF 170, 739). The doctrine as Schleiermacher construes it also protects monotheism against any implication of tritheism in Christian language. For example, he generally steers away from arguing the doctrine of Christ's divinity on the basis of John's prologue.

Finally, the doctrine of the trinity plays an integrating role in the Christian imagination. The doctrine of the trinity is the keystone of Christian doctrine. It consists in equating the union of God with human nature in Christ and the union of God as Spirit in the Church with the divine essence in itself. This represents what is essential in the doctrine of the trinity (CF 170, 739).

How does Schleiermacher conceive the Incarnation if such an Incarnation is not that of the hypostatized Logos? The Christian doctrine of Jesus Christ, Son of God, says that God not only is present in and to all creation as creator, but also is present to the world in a special way by Incarnation. The doctrine of creation out of nothing entails God's being present equally in all creation; there is nothing between the creature and the creator. No presence can be deeper or closer than the power of being itself. Thus Schleiermacher goes to some length in trying to explain how a more intense, personal, and revealing or self-manifesting presence of God in Jesus might be understood.[6] He explains this special presence on the basis of the being and level of activity of the receiver of God's being. In other words, the three "persons" of the trinity are not present within the Godhead but are determined by that in which God is active and which responds to God. These are the whole of creation, Jesus, and the Church as community.

On the assumption that Schleiermacher is sympathetic to Sabellius, so that his interpretation of Sabellius represents in some measure his own appropriation of trinitarian language, one can read his position in several texts. Sabellius could use trinitarian language, Schleiermacher notes: he "could admit three *prosopa*, but not three *hypostatic* ones" (SA XIX, 69). The "persons" thus referred to the union of the one God with various things outside God. Sabellius could refer to a trinity or use trinitarian language, but the system of predication did not consist in referring to three distinct hypostases or "persons" but to the distinct unions of the one God with creatures.

Developing this further, Schleiermacher writes: "In governing the world in all its various operations on finite things, the Godhead is *Father*. As redeeming, by special operations in the person of Christ and through him, it is *Son*. As sanctifying, and in all its operations on the community of believers, and as a Unity in the same, the Godhead is *Spirit*" (SA XIX, 70). "With [Sabellius] it was a peculiar union of the Godhead with something else; easily and simply to be distinguished, which defined the province of each member of the Trinity. In accordance with this, the Unity might be glorified as Father, Son, and Spirit; and in this glorification the whole of Christian piety might be concentrated, as believed both in the *monarchia* and the *oikonomia*" (SA XIX, 72). In this system of understanding, the unity of God is favoured. But the particular distinct presences of God outside of God's self, distinct from one another by virtue of the subject receiving God's presence, allow one to differentiate trinity. "The Son was not, in his view, the same as the Father, because he was united with something different from that with which the Father was united, and acted in a different sphere ... But the real *Godhead* in the Father and in the Son was, in his view, one and the same" (SA XIX, 67).

Schleiermacher himself thought that Christianity was the highest form of religious consciousness. Nevertheless, his reflection on the Incarnation that bypasses three "persons" within the Godhead can be viewed as relevant to a pluralistic theology of religions. Regarding the premise that the revelation of God in Jesus Christ is a revelation of the nature and character of God, of the way God really is, one can say that Jesus Christ reveals the way God acts generally. It is according to God's nature to self-manifest to and enter into dialogue with human beings. And if God is to be known with any specificity, and not merely as the object of a vague impulse or desire on our part, God must be revealed in particular contexts, symbols, places, events, and persons. At the very least, the Incarnation of God in Jesus Christ means that God is such that God can be and is revealed within the finite symbols of this world. This reading of trinitarian doctrine leads one to appreciate God being active in other religions' traditions as God was active in Judaism in the law and the prophets and analogously as God was revealed in Jesus. This is the way God relates to human existence. Therefore other persons, other books, and other histories provide vehicles for God "appearing to" and thus defining a people religiously. Other religions do not have the story of Incarnation in Jesus, but they have stories and figures analogous to it.

Tillich's Spirit Christology

In some respects Paul Tillich's Spirit Christology seems to be an alternative to the Logos Christology that took form under the tutelage of John's prologue and that has dominated the tradition. At the same time, Tillich retains a trinitarian theology of God and a role for Logos language in speaking of Jesus as the Christ. But like all Spirit Christologies, Tillich's transcends a typical three-stage or descending and ascending movement associated with incarnational Logos Christology. His existential interpretation of Christian doctrines and his symbolic realism combat all mythological thinking in a naive negative sense. I will briefly represent Tillich's Spirit Christology in three stages that deal with his blunt statement of his Spirit Christology, the trinitarian background in which it functions, and how Spirit Christology relates to Logos language about the Christ. I am not breaking new ground here but simply reporting Tillich's theology, virtually in his own words.

Spirit Christology

The best way to introduce Tillich's Spirit Christology is to quote his own terse introductory statement: "The divine Spirit was present in Jesus as the Christ without distortion. In him the New Being appeared as the criterion of all Spiritual experiences in past and future. Though subject to individual and social conditions his human spirit was entirely grasped by the Spiritual Presence; his spirit was 'possessed' by the divine Spirit or, to use another figure, 'God was in him.' This makes him the Christ, the decisive embodiment of the New Being for historical mankind."[7]

Tillich makes the case for the appropriateness of his Spirit Christology by a turn to the synoptic gospels, which portray the Spirit as operating in all aspects of Jesus' ministry: the Spirit is the constant source of Jesus' power. The infancy narratives depict even Jesus' procreation by the divine Spirit (III, 144–45). More deeply, the two signs or manifestations of the effects of Spirit within Jesus are his complete "self-sacrificial love," or the principle of *agape* or self-transcending love, and his perfect faith. "The faith of the Christ is the state of being grasped unambiguously by the Spiritual Presence" (III, 146).[8]

Tillich draws out some of the theological implications of his Spirit Christology. The first is that it is the power of God that makes Jesus the Christ: "[I]t is not the spirit of the man Jesus of Nazareth that makes him the Christ, but ... the Spiritual Presence, God in him, that possesses and drives his individual spirit. This insight stands guard against a Jesus-theology that makes the man Jesus the object of Christian faith ... [I]t is Jesus *as* the Christ in whom the new Being has appeared" (III, 146).

A second reflection on this Christology states that Jesus "is not an isolated event—something which, so to speak, fell from heaven ... Spirit-Christology acknowledges that the divine Spirit which made Jesus into the Christ is creatively present in the whole history of revelation and salvation before and after his appearance." In other words, "the Spiritual Presence in history is essentially the same as the Spiritual Presence in Jesus as the Christ. God in his self-manifestation, wherever this occurs, is the same God who is decisively and ultimately manifest in the Christ" (III, 147).[9] Thus Tillich postulates a continuity between the operation of the Spirit in Jesus and in the rest of humankind.

But third, the presence of the Spirit in Jesus is unique and the decisive climax of God's revelatory power in history. Jesus is the norm of all the self-disclosures of God in history. "Therefore, his manifestation anywhere before or after Christ must be consonant with the encounter with the center of history" (III, 147). "Every new manifestation of the Spiritual Presence stands under the criterion of his manifestation in Jesus as the Christ" (III, 148).

Tillich is therefore a modern; Christ is the centre of a unified history; Tillich's framework is a total metahistorical conception. Tillich maintains the "unique" in the sense of "only once" character of the Spirit's presence in Jesus. No revelation of or in the Spirit can transcend Jesus. "Obviously, such an expectation's realization would destroy the Christ-character of Jesus. More than one manifestation of the Spiritual Presence claiming ultimacy would deny the very concept of ultimacy" (III, 148).

Trinitarian God

For Tillich, the symbol of God as Spirit does not render the category Logos redundant. The symbols of God as creative power, as saving love, and as ecstatic transformation are "reflections of something real in the nature of the divine for religious experience and for the theological tradition. They are not merely different subjective ways of looking at the same thing. They have a *fundamentum in re*, a foundation in reality, however much the subjective side of man's experience may contribute" (III, 283). He does not rule out the possibility that the divinity of Jesus Christ can be expressed without recourse to Logos, but the main reason for affirming trinity correlates with the idea of a "living God": "it is impossible to develop a doctrine of the living God and of the creation without distinguishing the 'ground' and the 'form' in God, the principle of abyss and the principle of the self-manifestation in God" (III, 288). "Life" entails movement, dynamic self-positing and self-reflection, so that the dimensions of trinity, without any concern for the number three, correlate with the living God.[10]

The Relation of Spirit and Logos in Christ

This leaves us with the questions of the meaning of "Logos" for Tillich and how Logos stands in relation to God as Spirit or Spiritual Presence and to Jesus. The answer to the first question is carefully crafted by Tillich. He defines the term Logos by referring to "the self-manifestation of God"[11] and by distinguishing six analogous uses or meanings, including its application to God creating through Logos, to being revealed in the course of history, and to Scripture and preaching. But the two foundational meanings for trinity and Christology, Tillich's first and fourth senses, are sharply drawn, and I cite them in full.

> The "Word" is first of all the principle of the divine self-manifestation in the ground of being itself. The ground is not only an abyss in which every form disappears; it also is the source from which every form emerges. The ground of being has the character of self-manifestation; it has *logos* character. This is not something added to the divine life; it is the divine life itself. In spite of its abysmal character the ground of being is "logical"; it includes its own *logos*. (I, 157–58)

> Fourth, the Word is the manifestation of the divine life in the final revelation. The Word is a name for Jesus as the Christ. The Logos, the principle of all divine manifestation, becomes a being in history under the conditions of existence, revealing in this form the basic and determinative relation of the ground of being to us, symbolically speaking, the "heart of the divine life." The Word is not the sum of the words spoken by Jesus. It is the being of the Christ of which his words and his deeds are an expression. (I, 158)

Turning now to the relation of Logos to Jesus, difficulties arise precisely around the concept of Incarnation. What does it mean for Logos, the second *hypostasis* of the trinity, to take flesh? The key to a response to this question lies in the symbolic character of all predications of God—a character that forbids projecting onto Logos a finite individuality, which the imagination spontaneously tends to do. Logos as a dimension of divine life infinitely transcends the individual person, Jesus. "[O]ne cannot attribute to the eternal Logos in himself the face of Jesus of Nazareth or the face of 'historical man' or of any particular manifestation of the creative ground of being. But certainly, the face of God manifest *for* historical man is the face of Jesus as the Christ. The trinitarian manifestation of the divine ground is christocentric for man, but it is not Jesu-centric in itself. The God who is seen and adored in trinitarian symbolism has not lost his freedom to manifest himself for other worlds in other ways" (III, 289–90).

Finally, the relation between Logos and Spirit in Tillich's Christology shows that his Spirit Christology is not simple but dialectical. While the Logos is the self-manifestation of God within the person of Jesus, it is God as Spirit or the Spiritual Presence that effects that self-manifestation within the person of Jesus. Spirit precisely symbolizes the dynamic power of God. The Spirit symbolizes divine power within Jesus that effects his being the Logos or self-manifestation of God.

Schillebeeckx's Creation Faith and Christology

Edward Schillebeeckx began his career as a neo-Thomist in the 1940s, but after Vatican II he radically altered his theological method by turning to the secular world and history and integrating this encounter into his interpretation of Christian symbols. His new theological method gave a large place to the doctrines of creation and eschatology in his representation of a Christology from below. In the following I will show how his creation faith exerted a decisive influence on his understanding of Christology. I will first lay out his theology of creation and then show how he used creation faith as a way ultimately to bypass Logos and its hypostatization to express the divinity of Jesus Christ in a way that is open to the autonomous validity of other religions.[12]

Creation Faith

"Belief in God the creator is never an explanation, nor is it meant to be."[13] The symbol of creation represents faith in the nature and character of God and is the result of a revelation of God that takes place within religious experience. This experience is mediated through a recognition of the radical contingency of oneself and the larger existence in which we participate. "Nature and history are the authorities in which and through which God discloses himself as creator, in and through our fundamental experiences of finitude" (GAU, 91). Schillebeeckx shows that the experience of contingency can be interpreted in faith as an opening up to a transcendent ground of being and meaning.

More precisely, the possibility of speaking of a creator God is founded in a "basic trust" that is displayed by the human project itself. Basic trust in existence, life, and history operates within collective human achievement as the basis and condition of its possibility. This fundamental trust operates against all difficulties and frustrations; it asserts that the future of human existence is meaningful. The Christian interpretation of this secular trust names it a hope for salvation. This is no proof of anything. "The so-called proof of the existence of God which is based on the experience of contingency is therefore only the reflective justification, made afterwards, of the conviction that this unconditional trust in the gift of a meaningful human future is not an illusion, not a projection of frustrated wishful thinking."[14] But once internalized this conviction wields critical power. Creation is not God; nothing created can be related to as though it were divine. Creation faith, recognizing the finitude and contingency of created reality, realizes that nothing created can be absolutized.

Creation faith means that God is immediately present to all reality. "From a Christian perspective, the world and human existence are totally other than God, but within the presence of the creator God" (GAU, 93). As transcendent creator and absolute being, God is not distant and absent from God's creation. Creation out of nothing means that there is no medium between God and creation. God is directly present to God's creation as its cause and ground. "The boundary between God and us is our boundary, not God's" (GAU, 94). God creates out of love, and God is immanent and present to God's creation. All things exist within God's creative power so that God in turn is the within of all creation.

Human beings participate in God's creating. Creation is not an event of the past but an always actual, ongoing process. The significance of creation not being an explanation is that one cannot say that the creator established a preordained, unchanging order of things. Rather, creation includes a constant process of change through contingent events and chance. Human existence emerged in this creative process so that human freedom and intelligence now participate in the process itself. "God creates man as the principle of his own human action, who thus himself has to develop the world and its future and bring them into being within contingent situations" (GUA, 95). In this way, creation has become a task for human freedom; it is something that human freedom is intended to take up. "This does not do away with the saving presence of God, God's immanence in creation. But this creative power of God never breaks in from outside. God's power is inwardly present."[15] For Schillebeeckx, creation in human beings has become history. It is open to the future and is changing. God and creation, therefore, cannot be used to canonize past events and arrangements as static norms for the future. Life is a narrative; it moves out of the past and into the future; to live is to look ahead and continually draw the past forward to illumine the future. In sum, creation faith translates through freedom into commitment to this world and history (GFM, 76).

Freedom in modernity and postmodernity is understood as creativity; it is more than the power to choose; it transcends existentialist commitment; it is the power to create new reality. As creator, God created this human power. Therefore God desires that it be used. And God has confidence in it. God has entrusted creation to human beings not merely as caretakers of a past condition but as cocreators with God of the future. "Human existence itself is responsible for what happens on earth and is to make order and *shalom* out of chaos ... Within the limits of creaturely existence, human beings are entrusted with the world and history, and in that context Yahweh bestows on humans God's complete confidence."[16]

Jesus Christ as Concentrated Creation

Schillebeeckx's formal Christology contains his appropriation of the councils of Nicaea and Chalcedon. The teaching of those councils states that Jesus as a single person is both truly human and truly divine. This doctrine symbolizes for Christian tradition the essential character of Christian faith. Where does Schillebeeckx's Christology stand in this tradition? Schillebeeckx shifted his language about this central doctrine, and a brief outline of the first two stages in his development will help shed light on his third and final position.

Before Vatican II, in his *Christ the Sacrament of the Encounter with God,* Schillebeeckx used traditional objective trinitarian terminology of a divine Word or Son descending and becoming incarnate in this world by assuming a human nature or humanity that constituted Jesus of Nazareth. Jesus was God acting in history in an overt but empirically unrecognizable way.[17]

Schillebeeckx's book *Jesus* contains a second stage. After his extensive reflection on the historical ministry of Jesus, Schillebeeckx added a reflection on the classical doctrinal language, as an afterthought, mainly because he thought people would expect it. He did not want to leave his discussion of Jesus without saying something about his divinity and the traditional language about it.[18] In this reflection he proposes that traditional theology adopt the conception of a mutual and simultaneous "enhypostatic union" between the Logos and the human person Jesus. While his conceptual analysis clashes sharply with the historical method of the book, Schillebeeckx explains the relationship between the two kinds of reflection in terms of primary and secondary religious language. Primary religious language is the more or less proximate expression of primal Christian experience. Such experience usually relates to the person of Jesus, either the memory of him as a concrete person or an image of him. Secondary reflection—what Schillebeeckx calls reflection to the power of two—consists in critical appropriation of primary expression and, as such, is tied to the primary language that relates back to Jesus. Primary language is normative for secondary; and Jesus is normative for primary christological language. The purpose of second-order reflection is to explain and protect these first-order assertions. The relation between these two languages is a way of situating the meaning of "enhypostatic union," about which I will say something further on.

In 1974 Schillebeeckx published the short essay "The 'God of Jesus' and the 'Jesus of God,'" in which he characterized the primary experience that Christians had of Jesus.[19] This experience is simultaneously an experience of God mediated through Jesus and an interpretive experience of Jesus. Jesus is encountered as one who reveals God as saviour, a God who as creator is intrinsically and by nature saviour. At the same time, especially in the experience of Jesus risen, Jesus is experienced and interpreted as of God, as sent by God, as a medium of God and God's salvation. This short essay gets at the heart of the experience of Jesus as mediator of salvation from God as the basis of all Christology.

Moving to secondary language, Schillebeeckx says that Jesus is both "parable of God and paradigm of humanity" (*Jesus*, 626). God was acting in Jesus in such a way that Jesus is the focus and medium for this twofold revelation. Jesus reveals God; faith can read the character of God as authentically represented in Jesus' preaching and his acts of love. And one can experience in his ministry as well the model of what human existence should be. If a theoretical or second-order Christology explains and protects such an experience of and relation to Jesus, it is orthodox. In other words, this basic religious proposition is the norm and criterion for second-order theology and doctrines. This makes the idea that Jesus is the parable of God and the paradigm of human existence a contemporary translation of the Chalcedonian formula of truly divine and truly human.[20] Schillebeeckx's proposal of a mutual or simultaneous enhypostatic union means a co-inhabitation of the individual Jesus in God and of God as Word in the individual Jesus. Schillebeeckx says that this is possible because it does not generate two individuals, as it would in two finite subjects being united. In the case of creator and creature there is no parity; the creature is already in the creator, and the creator is immanent in the creature, sustaining it. Thus on the level of Jesus' freedom and autonomy as a creature there is no competition but a mutual indwelling. This formulation is a theoretical construal that allows Jesus his individual personhood and thus protects his status as a human creature and at the same time his real mediation of true God.

The third stage in Schillebeeckx's development is stated at the end of the *Interim Report,* where he poses the question, Is Jesus God? (IR, 140–43). He does not answer this question straightforwardly, the way a neoscholastic theologian might. A direct yes to such a misguided question would compromise the tension of the Chalcedonian formula: Jesus is both human and divine. Rather, his answer is twofold and consistent with his whole interpretation of Jesus. On the one hand, the significance of Jesus is that he really reveals God; he points away from himself so that one encounters God and God's salvation in and through him. Salvation from God is revealed in Jesus. But the medium or person Jesus in whom this saving God is revealed cannot be separated from the revelation. "We cannot separate God's nature and God's revelation. Therefore in the definition of what God is, the man Jesus is indeed connected with the nature of God" (IR, 142).

Schillebeeckx's formula for this final position is that "'Christology' is *concentrated* creation: belief in creation as God wills it to be" (IR, 128). I take this to mean that God's creative and saving presence is so active in Jesus that Jesus mediates that power and presence; it empowers him and he mediates it to others in a conscious and efficacious way. Jesus is not the Christ because he strives harder and thus becomes the sacrament of God. It is God at work within him that makes him Christ and saviour.

What does this Christology say about religious pluralism? Schillebeeckx has gone beyond the now standard "inclusivist" anonymous Christianity of the churches and toward a pluralist theology of religions. In his Christology the positive revelations and truths found in the religions help us look at Jesus with new eyes, and a re-examination of Jesus and the God of Jesus enables us to see these religions with new eyes. The pluralism that Schillebeeckx embraces is not sheer plurality or relativism, but the one salvation from the God of creation experienced in the many religions.

Concluding Constructive Reflections

I began this discussion with some of the problems that afflict the language of Logos in the ordinary speech and theology of Christians. The three theologians surveyed bear witness to various aspects of the strain placed on the term Logos. They differ significantly among themselves and cannot be synthesized without remainder. But they all contribute valuable perspectives to the issue. In this conclusion I return to the problems announced at the outset of this chapter and offer comment on the neuralgic points. I do this by turning ideas from these theologians into some concluding constructive observations.

It seems plain enough that Christian theology has consciously to transcend a mythological understanding of the term "Logos." All three theologians considered here have left naive appropriation of the symbol far behind. This entails explicit disavowal of any numerical understanding of the doctrine of trinity. The mathematics of "one in three" simply misses the point of trinitarian language; more seriously, it positively distorts the doctrine and forms a blockage to finding a path within it. We need a consistent, conscious recognition of the transcendent character of God, with the attendant appreciation that all language about God is symbolic and does not represent God the way literal or univocal speech communicates ideas about finite this-worldly reality. Under these conditions, the language of "person" about the dimensions of the Godhead corresponding to trinity has become inappropriate and dysfunctional, for person currently refers to individuals and thus numerical plurality in the Godhead. Transcending mythological language also means that hypostatization of the symbols "Word of God," "Wisdom of God," and "Spirit of God" is deeply misguided. Treating this symbolic language as referring to discrete entities beyond the figurative speech of metaphor and personification leads directly to imagining God as a plurality.

These reflections do not necessarily entail the need to leave the language of Word and Spirit behind. The theologies of both Schleiermacher and Tillich provide a basis for trinitarian language. For Schleiermacher, God is really present and is really revealed in Jesus and in the community, and this provides the way for the Church to tell the Christian story in terms of the encounter with God in creation, the saving activity of God in Jesus, and the sanctifying presence of the Spirit in the community. In Tillich's view, creating, self-manifesting, and dynamic spiritual presence point to real dimensions of the divine life of God. Logos, as God's self-manifestation, refers to a real and distinguishable aspect of God. This is a coherent use of language, though not everyone will follow Tillich in this last step.

Another observation runs along the same lines as the first. Historical consciousness has urged that Christology begin its critical constructive work with a consideration of Jesus of Nazareth. The human being Jesus stands at the head of the development of Christology, and it is he who is the historical referent of this discipline. Practically speaking, every objection to this strategy of Christology from below builds upon the fear that such a point of departure will turn reductionist and be unable to come to an interpretation of Jesus as the Christ, an object of faith. But that is certainly not the case necessarily, because in fact the first Christologies followed this path exactly. In many cases, the objection itself may be embedded implicitly in a misapprehension that the divine element in Jesus is available in some source other than precisely within the human person, the humanity itself, of Jesus. Divinity or God's presence in Jesus is the within of Jesus and not an overt quality "added on" to his historical reality. The Spirit causing Jesus to be God's self-manifestation or Logos occurred within history, not "above" it or "outside" it. Schillebeeckx's reflection on the non-competitive union between divine and human hypostases sheds a great deal of light on this problem; so too does his creation Christology: there is no gap or competition between God's presence and the fully human Jesus.

This brings us to issues connected with the theology of religions. At this point I fix attention on those Christian theologies of religion that are bent on understanding Jesus Christ in a way that does not negate but supports the autonomous validity of other religions. Some of these theologies turn to a theology of the Spirit operative in the world "from the beginning" before the appearance of Jesus. Others speak of multiple incarnations of the Logos in a manner analogous to the universal operation of the Spirit. In both cases, the distinctive functions of Word and Spirit are becoming confused. Is it the case that either one will do because both are pointing to the experience of God's efficacious presence in the world?

Insights gained from Schillebeeckx's creation theology and Tillich's symbolic realism can be combined to address this issue. For Schillebeeckx's panentheism, all things exist within the embrace of God's creating power, so that God is the within of all created reality. From this point of view, the presence of the reality of God, the whole of God, sustains from within the whole of reality and each individuated particle within it. And from Tillich's perspective, the whole of God is marked by the character of the fullness of unlimited being (the pure act of being itself, the Abyss)—that is, intrinsically ordered or reflective and manifest to itself, while at the same time being dynamic activity. These dimensions of the transcendent, infinite, and living God do not correspond without remainder to the distinctions that the human mind has devised to designate experience of God as creator, Word, and Spirit. Only when these dimensions of God are hypostatized and made to be distinct in God according to human distinctions do they become problematic. This leads to the following constructive conclusion.

Christian theology and catechetics need terms that preserve the doctrine of the trinity in a non-mythological way. This would be a language that returns the focus of the imagination to one God and that does not isolate the so-called persons prior to their reference to dimensions of the one living God. This would be a language that distinguishes traditional dimensions in God and that at the same time can be used to tell the Christian story without suggesting tritheism. One way of at least addressing this issue and mitigating its problematic aspects would be to place God at the centre of one's speech about God: "God as creator" is the God who creates; "God as Word" or "God as revealing Word" is the same God who appears in various guises or media in history and who for Christians is decisively revealed in Jesus; "God as Spirit" or "God as dynamic Spirit" is the same God stirring human beings from within to self-transcending response.

This language deliberately begs the question of the real distinction between these dimensions within the Godhead. The symbolic character of God language means that all such distinctions as they are conceived in our finite language must be denied.[21] How exactly their constellation within the real life of God corresponds to their reaffirmation is hidden within the mystery of God and unknown.

Notes

1 The word "trinity" in the essay is not capitalized because I take it as the name of a doctrine and not of God.

2 See Roger Haight, *Jesus Symbol of God* (New York: Orbis, 1999), 245–49, 473–76.

3 Raimundo Panikkar, *The Unknown Christ of Hinduism* (Maryknoll: Orbis, 1981), 31–61; Michael Amaladoss, "The Pluralism of Religions and the Significance of Christ," in *Asian Faces of Jesus*, ed. R.S. Sugirtharajah (Maryknoll: Orbis, 1993), 85–103; idem, "The Mystery of Christ and Other Religions: An Indian Perspective," *Vidyajyoti: Journal of Theological Reflection* 63 (1999): 327–38.

4 I draw this representation of Schleiermacher's theology of the trinity from the following sources: Friedrich Schleiermacher, *The Christian Faith* (New York: Harper Torchbooks, 1963), cited in the text as CF by paragraph and page; idem, "On the Discrepancy Between the Sabellian and Athanasian Method of Representing the Doctrine of the Trinity," *Biblical Repository and Quarterly Observer* 18 (April 1835): 265–353; 19 (July 1835): 1–116 (orig. *Theologische Zeitschrift*, 1822), trans. and commentary by M. Stuart, cited in the text as SA by volume and page. This material is drawn from my essay "Trinity and Religious Pluralism," *Journal of Ecumenical Studies* 44 (2009): 525–40.

5 The content of the doctrine of the trinity that is drawn from Schleiermacher's portrayal of the Christian economy of salvation reinforces its derivative character. Schleiermacher states the derivative character of the doctrine this way: "Hence it is important to make the point that the main pivots of the ecclesiastical doctrine— the being of God in Christ and in the Christian church—are independent of the doctrine of the trinity" (CF #170, 741). "Independent" here entails being prior to and subsumed into the synthesizing doctrine of trinity so that they are the essential ingredients of it. I have represented Schleiermacher's Christology in *Jesus Symbol of God*, 303–9, and his ecclesiology in *Christian Community in History, II, Comparative Ecclesiology* (New York: Continuum, 2005), 316–36.

6 Schleiermacher writes that theology needs a distinction between "how we are to conceive of the divine Being, as existing in union with a particular Being [Jesus], and as universally present and existing everywhere" (SA 18, 349). One has to determine "how the existence of God in Christ stands related to that indwelling of his in all human beings, which is essentially connected with his omnipresence and universal agency" (SA 19, 23).

7 Paul Tillich, *Systematic Theology I–III* (Chicago: University of Chicago Press, 1967), III:144; cited hereafter in the text by volume and page. Jesus, Tillich continues, was "the bearer of the Spirit without limit" (III:145). The Spirit "created the Christ within Jesus" (III:147).

8 It is more difficult to think of Jesus having faith in a Logos Christology. But a conception of Jesus without faith tends toward docetism. A Spirit Christology is able to preserve Jesus' human faith (III:146).

9 "The assertion that Jesus is the Christ implies that the Spirit, which made him the Christ and which became his Spirit (with a capital 'S'), was and is working in all those who have been grasped by the Spiritual Presence before he could be encountered as a historical event" (III:147).

10 The important thing in the doctrine of trinity is not the number three, but "the unity in a manifoldness of divine self-manifestations. If we ask why … the number 'three' has prevailed, it seems most probable that the three corresponds to the intrinsic dialectics of experienced life and is, therefore, most adequate to symbolize the Divine Life. Life has been described as the process of going out from itself and returning to itself. The number 'three' is implicit in this description, as the dialectical philosophers knew" (III:293).

11 The key phrase for understanding Logos is "God manifest," in God's self, in the Bible, in Jesus, in the history of revelation. "'God manifest'—the mystery of the divine abyss expressing itself through the divine Logos—this is the meaning of the symbol, the 'Word of God'" (I:159).

12 This material is drawn from my earlier unpublished essay on the Christology of Edward Schillebeeckx titled "Christology in the Face of Postmodernity."

13 Edward Schillebeeckx, *God Among Us: The Gospel Proclaimed* (New York: Crossroad, 1983), 91; cited in the text as GAU.

14 Edward Schillebeeckx, *God the Future of Man* (New York: Sheed and Ward, 1968), 74–75 at 75; cited in the text as GFM.

15 Edward Schillebeeckx, *For the Sake of the Gospel* (New York: Crossroad, 1990), 93.

16 Edward Schillebeeckx, *Interim Report on the Books* Jesus *and* Christ (New York: Crossroad, 1981), 109; cited in the text as IR.

17 Edward Schillebeeckx, *Christ the Sacrament of the Encounter with God* (New York: Sheed & Ward, 1963), displays this understanding well at 13–39.

18 See Edward Schillebeeckx, *Jesus: An Experiment in Christology* (New York: Seabury, 1979), 636–74; cited in the text as *Jesus*.

19 Edward Schillebeeckx, *The Language of Faith: Essays on Jesus, Theology, and the Church* (Maryknoll: Orbis, 1995), 95–108.

20 Dorothy Jacko, "Salvation in the Context of Contemporary Secularized Historical Consciousness: The Later Theology of Edward Schillebeeckx," PhD diss., University of St. Michael's College, Toronto School of Theology, 1987, 189. See Robert Schreiter, "Jezus als parabel van God en paradigma van menselijkheid,"

in *Meedenken met Edward Schillebeeckx,* ed. H. Haring, T. Schoof, and A. Willems (Baarn: H. Nelissen, 1983), 158–70.

21 I have in mind the prescription of Thomas Aquinas, which he draws from Dennis the Areopagite: "Such names as these, as Dionysius shows, are denied of God for the reason that what the name signifies does not belong to Him in the ordinary sense of its signification, but in a more eminent way. Hence Dionysius says also that God is above all substance and all life." Thomas Aquinas, *Summa Theologiae,* I, q.13, a.3, ad 2 in Anton C. Pegis, *Basic Writings of Saint Thomas Aquinas* (New York: Random House, 1945), 117.

7

Christ the Transformer of Culture
Augustine and Tillich

✟ ✟ ✟

PETER SLATER

IN AN ESSAY on "Augustine's *City of God* XIX and Western Political Thought," Oliver O'Donovan remarks that Augustine "lacks a theory of progress" in human history, adding that "sadly" he viewed with "complacency ... the institution of slavery."[1] According to O'Donovan, this conclusion clashes with an earlier view of Augustine promoted by H. Richard Niebuhr that Augustine should be counted among proponents of "Christ the Transformer of Culture." In Niebuhr's *Christ and Culture*, "transformation" constitutes the fifth (and best?) Christian stance toward "culture" or "civilization,"[2] the type exemplified in modern times by F.D. Maurice. The other types, according to Niebuhr's chapter headings, are "Christ against Culture," "The Christ of Culture," "Christ above Culture," and "Christ and Culture in Paradox." Niebuhr admitted that Augustine defied neat pigeon-holing, exhibiting aspects of all five types or "motifs" in his polemical and apologetic texts.[3]

The identity of "the Christ" is more assumed than argued for by Niebuhr. According to him, "concepts and propositions" cannot adequately portray "a principle which presents itself in the form of a person" (*C&C*, 14). How we name contrasts changes over time. Some juxtapose reason and revelation where others concentrate on Gospel and Law. All contrasting pairs of terms draw attention to differing interpretations given through the ages to descriptions of what makes faith in divine grace more than a work of human religiosity. How grace works is not finally explicable, but there are clues in nature and above all in the Bible. Biblical insights concerning Christ and culture include elements of information, reformation, conformation, *and* transformation.

In this paper, I revisit Augustine's position and review Tillich, as a modern Augustinian; I then consider recent issues raised concerning their presuppositions. Augustine and Tillich represent respectively a classical and a modern mindset concerning the weight given to form and dynamics in a tradition that draws on Neoplatonic philosophy, adapted to explicate the Bible as our primary entrée into divine wisdom and salvation history.

Augustine

My generation owes its estimate of Augustine's legacy to C.N. Cochrane's *Christianity and Classical Culture: A Study of Thought and Action from Augustus to Augustine*. Cochrane presented Augustine as the culmination of revolutionary Christian thinking prompted by Arianism, the polemics of Athanasius, and the apologetics of the Cappadocians. Their Trinitarian theologies addressed classical conundrums concerning reason and experience, subjectivity and objectivity, life attuned to the senses and to contemplation.[4] The critical move, according to Cochrane, was their Trinitarian formula for making divine being incommensurate with any kind of finite being within the universe. However spiritual its substance, however intimately this permeates all existence, divine being must not be thought of in pantheistic terms as simply the sum of all energy in the universe or the underlying mainstay of all its parts and aspects. The Godhead of Father, Son, and Holy Spirit defies rational apprehension yet is savingly known to faith seeking understanding, most definitively through the Incarnation of the Son.

Countering the classical conception of emanation, the doctrine of creation *de nihilo* broke a stalemate in Hellenistic thinking, which was acculturated to cyclical polytheistic conceptions of the natural world.[5] The accent on faith as precondition of understanding, so emphasized by Augustine, invited participation from all segments of society while acknowledging the cognitive concerns of educated converts. As Arthur Darby Nock pointed out, conversion in the world of early Christianity often meant conversion to a moral philosophy of life, not to "religion" in the sense of rites associated with family and civic shrines.[6]

Looking beyond appearances for substantive springs of thought and action, most "pagan" intellectuals already repudiated polytheism. The contrast between popular and critical conceptions then was similar to that still found in much of India.[7] At the cultic level, the many find expression at myriad local temples and household altars. To the philosophical, the One, or the source beyond the one and the many, is the actual reality of all. The biblical doctrine of creation cuts against cultic and philosophical polytheistic assumptions, both by its monotheistic injunction against idolatry and by its ontological insistence on the gulf between creator and creation.[8] For Augustine, the doctrine of creation was a major step in his conversion from Manichaeism to Catholicism. Using the image of the Prodigal Son, he construed conversion in terms of the turning of the will directed by its loves. (His idea of actual evil is as perversion, not privation: the latter term only explains the *possibility* of evil in a good creation.)[9] Conversion means striving for eternal harmony, which is only possible through grace.

Niebuhr's characterization of Augustine is an avowed unpacking of Cochrane's. Under the "transformer" chapter heading, primary emphasis is on the "conversion" of culture. As opposed to unqualified dualist or accommodationist positions, *a "conversionist" stance is marked by its doctrines of creation, corruption, and salvation.* These assume "a view of history that holds that to God all things are possible in a history that is fundamentally not a course of merely human events but always a dramatic interaction between God and human agents" (*C&C*, 194). To what extent Augustine belongs in the fifth category turns on the much discussed issue of his conversion (or conversions), on developments in his Christology, and on his mature conception of sacred and secular history, articulated in the *City of God*.

Regarding conversion, the challenges are to characterize fairly conversion from what and to what, and to examine how thoroughgoing a particular conversion was. To what extent did apologetic intentions hide a convert's actual position, and to what extent did parts of his or (rarely, among early authors) her preceding culture remain "unbaptized"? In Augustine's case, his relation to pagan Platonism remains much debated.[10] Any historical answer is complicated by the fact that we depend on his own retrospective account of his conversion in the *Confessions*. Against hagiography, modern critics adopt a hermeneutics of suspicion. We must not read Augustine's text as objective history. Also, we must query any self-serving thrust of his versions of events, which nevertheless remain our primary source.[11] We must also be suspicious of overly anti-hagiographic accounts and our accounts of these! Here one sympathizes with Niebuhr's avoidance of endlessly regressing histories. Despite such caveats, there seems no reason to doubt that Augustine's conversion was from a Manichaean to a Catholic version of Christianity, with Neoplatonists acting as midwives.

Regarding christological developments in Augustine's thought—which was the subject of Joanne McWilliam's unfinished *magnum opus*—a primarily theological focus tends to gloss over historical nuances. Niebuhr, for instance, aligns Augustine with the Johannine strand of biblical theology, commenting that "his Christology remains weak and undeveloped when compared with Paul's or Luther's. He often tends to substitute the Christian religion—a cultural achievement—for Christ; and frequently deals with the Lord more as the founder of an authoritative cultural institution, the church, than as savior of the world through direct exercise of his kingship." Here Niebuhr is looking ahead to what he valued in F.D. Maurice. The passage continues: "also faith in Augustine tends to be reduced to obedient assent to the church's teachings, which is doubtless very important in Christian culture but nevertheless no substitute for confidence in God" (C&C, 217). In fact, as his unpopular doctrine of predestination reminds us, Augustine's Manichaean tutelage meant that he was initially much more immersed in Pauline than in Johannine theology.[12]

In his essay on "The Christological Substructure of Augustine's Figurative Exegesis," Michael Cameron notes development in the course of Augustine's anti-Manichaean writings from a "spiritual" to an "incarnational" paradigm, which, as the name implies, was generated by an advance in his Christology.[13] Cameron remarks that his "thesis goes against standard scholarly opinion of Augustine's christology," represented by Joanne McWilliam's statement that "Christology did not lead the way but changed in response to other changes in his thinking."[14] She observed that in any given context, Augustine's pastoral and/or polemical concerns were the mainsprings of his public restatements of doctrines. Had he lived to attend the Council of Ephesus, for instance, he may well have agreed with Nestorius' insistence on Jesus' full humanity, as against Alexandrian high christologies. But his obsession with Pelagianism, and the alleged association of Nestorius with a Pelagian position, may have moved Augustine to underplay the more Antiochene thrust of his mature Christology in that context.[15] Her conclusion, after a lifetime of research, was that "Augustine never insisted on one description of the incarnation as the only correct one." Theologically, his conversion included ever deepening appreciation of what it means to insist on the full humanity of God the Word incarnate.

Augustine's soteriology added to early emphasis on the Incarnate Word as teacher the salvific import of the Lord's humility in opposition to the devil's pride. The realization that evil originated in spiritual deficiency, not a material cause, was an important part of his conversion from Manichaeism. The Pauline texts so often cited were accepted by both Manichaean and Catholic Christians. Augustine reconstrued the formers' reading of the spirit–flesh contrast and experience of conflicting wills. He appealed to Platonism as the most acclaimed philosophical tradition of his day. It gave him a notion of spiritual substance that broke the hold on his imagination of Manichaean ontology. Following earlier Church Fathers, Augustine reworked Platonism to support a conception of the creation of time and space by the eternally "simple" triune substance of God (*City* XI, xix, 354). Theologically, he applied the notion of time as the moving image of eternity to the two "natures" of the Christ. The supralapsarian antidote to prodigally diverted wills was an infusion of eternal blessedness at the right time. The root Platonic metaphor of light, not sound, invoked the image of the sun/the Good forever emitting its influence without losing its power.

Contemporary Augustinian scholars attend to the pastoral content and intent of most of the Augustine corpus in a way that most earlier scholars did not.[16] Over his long life, Augustine never gave as much priority to logical consistency as some would have him do. His *City of God*, in particular, is an encyclopedia of religion, sprinkled with pastoral assurances for victims of rape, entertaining fables of faith healing, and apologetic conclusions concerning sin, evil, the glory of Rome, and the life of the world to come. Charlemagne had it read to him during supper for entertainment as well as for thoughts on how to be a Christian emperor.[17]

According to Niebuhr, "Christ is the transformer of culture for Augustine in the sense that he redirects, reinvigorates, and regenerates that life of man, expressed in all human works, which in present actuality is the perverted and corrupted exercise of a fundamentally good nature; which, moreover, in its depravity lies under the curse of transiency and death … because it is intrinsically self-contradictory" (*C&C*, 209). Existentially, the focus is on individual selfhood and ultimate destiny, not social structures. In the *City of God*, Augustine treats communities as collections of individuals, united by a common love.[18] Culturally, the account of conversion draws on Platonic notions of eternity and time in such a way that value is primarily located in ideal forms and hierarchical ordering, not historical progress. The Christly model in that culture privileged monastic over married life and made material differences of no account in the end-time. In Book XIX he characterized the divinely ordained end for God's elect, which alone—according to him—satisfies the natural human drive or urge for lasting happiness, as "eternal life" or "eternal peace."[19]

What is clear is that, like Irenaeus, Augustine took an allegorical reading of "spoil the Egyptians" (Exodus 3:22 and 11:2) as warrant for "the right to select truth from pagan texts without accepting polytheism." That "Exodus passage," Henry Chadwick notes, "was ridiculed by the Manichees."[20] Through baptized ex-Manichaean, philosophically Neoplatonic eyes,

Augustine reads as key the Pauline text, "As in Adam all die, so in Christ shall all be made alive again" (I Corinthians 15:22). Since Adam and Eve were expelled from Eden before they had offspring, Augustine concluded that we are condemned to share their destiny—missing the fruit of immortality and suffering the life of transient pilgrims—unless we are chosen to become reborn members of the Body of Christ. Even then, in this world, we pay the price of pride or self-love, only anticipating the rewards of humble obedience hereafter. By right, all of us "in Adam" are condemned to eternal death. By sheer grace, some are redeemed "in Christ," since God's will in creation cannot ultimately be thwarted (e.g., *City* XIV, xi–xv, 457–64).

Since Origen and others took literally that all will be made alive again, modern liberals, like Niebuhr following Maurice, hold against Augustine his hard line on predestined damnation of the majority. Was it culture, not faith, that drove him to conclude that the "all" who are saved in the Christ means "whoever is saved," not "everybody"? If so, that culture was Christian, not pagan. But it was sectarian Christian. In Roman times Christians were a minority, affirming their biblical identity with the chosen few of Israel's righteous remnant, to whom alone God's promise of salvation was made. In this world we are called to be suffering servants, looking to share the Risen Lord's universal triumph overtly only in the future. As a Manichaean, Augustine grew up with a sectarian mentality and was unchanged in this respect by conversion to a Catholic allegiance. Like many converts, he was more aggressively Catholic than many of his contemporaries.

O'Donovan and Niebuhr hone in on justice issues, with regard to slaves in this world or the non-elect. In Augustine, *justice and goodness* are indivisibly grounded *in the being of God*. The conception of eternally simple—not composite—and therefore incorruptible divine being is the hallmark of the Neoplatonic strand in his philosophical theology. Whatever God wills for us now or hereafter is just, even if we fail to understand how. Knowing from Jesus that God is just and good, we can take on faith that God is eternally so, since God is immutable. The only ultimately satisfying good for us is God's eternal goodness.

All theologians reflect their era. In Augustine's case, the times were chaotic. It is not surprising that his ontology privileged order. His classical conception of eternal being and his experience of politics militated against looking for lasting social transformations in history. His theology muted the momentous shift due to biblically inspired faith in the Early Church from ontological to eschatological dualism. Succeeding generations, owing much to Augustine, have reoriented their readings of biblical texts. For instance, we read Paul's epistles through quite different frames than those he assumed when writing them.[21]

A traditional view used to be that everything theologically significant on doctrinal subjects was said before AD 451 by the Church Fathers in council. After that came schisms. That view enshrines presuppositions about timeless truth, such as we find in Augustine.[22] It has roots in a Hellenistic strand of the biblical record, especially concerning translation of the Septuagint.[23] It is not the only biblical doctrine of revelation. As Tillich points out, every appeal to scriptural authority, classical, modern, or "postmodern," has to be reargued by each new generation.[24] In classical tradition, people searched the Scriptures for timeless truth, bent on eternal life.

Strong proof of eternity for Augustine is the timelessness of mathematical truth. His constant criteria of goodness were measure (including numbers), form, and order. No being lacks some degree of measure, form, and order. Therefore, all must be somewhat good and cannot be wholly bad. That the number of the elect is eternally fixed, replacing the number of fallen angels, was for him implied in the conceptions of divine goodness and justice. In this world, justice entails penal conditions for saints as well as sinners, partly to keep saints on their toes and partly as the historical consequence of Adam's primal sin in this life. Augustine's was a strong doctrine of divine punishment based on his reading of the "Old" Testament as standing orders for this world. He regarded slavery as part of our transient penal condition, not part of the natural order of creation. In the hierarchy of created being, all humanity is on an ontological par, but that applies to our citizenship in the City of God, not the *civitas terrena* (*City*, XIX, xv, 693). In this again, Augustine followed Paul.

In Augustine's inherited culture, fate was a conception tied in with astrology, trading on fascination with numbers. He had no problem affirming both free will and predestination.[25] For him, after his conversion, there was a clear line drawn between mechanical material causes and spiritual causes, in a way that ruled out astral control over human actions.[26] The origin of evil must be due to spiritual initiatives, however flawed, not physical embodiment. Only recently have Augustine's theological heirs broken on biblical grounds with his conception of predestination by eternal decree, replacing the classical conception of eternity with a contrast between God's time and fallen time.[27]

Whatever was made of Augustine's two-cities typology by subsequent theologians, what his classic text sets forth is a biblically based account of *salvation history* turning on the providentially directed individual decisions of the godly and the ungodly in this life. In early Hebrew culture, tribal identity tied individual destiny to that of one's prince or patriarch. We are "in" Adam, Israel is "in" Abraham, Isaac, and Jacob (whereas the reprobate are "in Esau"), and so on.[28] That the Christ is not just a son of David but the second or last Adam is what marks us as new creatures and subjects of God's eternal kingdom. Contrary to such foundational accounts, however, later prophets assured children that their fate was not wholly determined by their fathers' decisions (Ezekiel 18). As with all exegetes, Augustine's reading of key texts was selective.

Regarding history, Augustine's separation of the history of the earthly city from sacred history was groundbreaking. His was not a modern conception of secular history, but he advanced the process of disenchanting the fields and forests, thereby clearing cultural space for the development of modern science—including, eventually, economics, sociology, and history as social sciences.[29] His conception of miracles and the fulfillment of prophecy, which he took to be biblical, still led him to allow for a hidden heavenly hand behind the forces of nature, as in the rising of a sudden wind favourable to Theodosius (*City* V, xxvi, 179–80). But he argued convincingly that earthly cities were no longer to be considered sacred and that earthly rulers were no longer to be worshipped as lesser gods. As the backdrop for his accounts of conversion, his conception of the heavenly city put a premium on individual personal morality, not corporate ethics. In this, he discerned the hand of God in history differently from Hegel and the post-Kantians, whose philosophies set the stage for Barth and Tillich.

Tillich

Tillich counted himself an Augustinian, not a Thomist, in that he looked inwardly for God in our sense of self, rather than outwardly to the cosmos.[30] His generation had to reckon with Kant and Hegel. Hegel saw himself as a pioneer in placing the Book of History alongside Scripture and the Book of Nature, as revelatory records of the Word of God. Most European theologians in the twentieth century rejected Hegelianism but could not ignore Hegel's challenge as it related to the historicity of ideas. Most started from some version of dialectical idealism, but in contrast to classical idealists, the existentialists especially gave ontological priority to temporal events, not eternal structures.[31]

As with Augustine, a traditional biblical metanarrative informed Tillich's faith. However, totalitarianism in his time led him and his contemporaries to privilege freedom rather than order. Against Marxist and neo-Hegelian dialectics, he rejected belief in inexorable social progress. He rued the fact that his fellow Germans, proud of their "Christian civilization," were so complicit in occasioning two world wars. He insisted with Barth and Bonhoeffer that the true Führer was Jesus, not Adolf Hitler.[32]

Among Christian apologists on the Protestant side, Tillich was pre-eminent. The ontology that he converted for theological purposes was that of Schelling, rather than Hegel, modified in a realist direction by the challenge of Marxism. He said yes to the prophetic protests of Marxists against Hegelian God-talk. (Compare Gandhi's contemporary response to Tagore that, to a starving man, God must come as food and wages.)[33] What Tillich rejected in Marxist and Freudian materialism was the mechanistic imaging of substructures and superstructures. Also important to him were depth psychology and existentialist emphasis on authentic decision making as definitive of personal destiny. Augustine's anti-Manichaean insistence on spiritual substance reappears in Tillich's regular reminder that God is personal or "transpersonal," not a thing, not one finite being among others. However, Tillich's *dialectical conception of spiritual being* included movement in God, not immutability, finding in the Trinitarian tradition of divine imaging a sense of "Spiritual Presence" as a drive for self-transcendence that privileges dynamics over form.[34]

As in Schelling, Tillich deemed the divine-demonic dialectic to be intrinsic to divine being, not just creaturely being. The difference between divine and human substance is not between simple and composite being, but between Spirit with a capital S—which always turns demonic destructiveness to creative ends, making room for novelty in history—and spirit with a small s, which as "finite freedom" can contradict its essential selfhood, notably when human beings live a lie by patterning their self-image on thinghood. As in Augustine, the problem is not things as such but alienating use of them (*ST* III, 74). The classical divide in kind between creator and creation in a Schellingian ontotheology is upheld as that between unconditioned and conditioned being–becoming.

Because Christian National Socialists in Germany invoked the doctrine of creation to affirm Aryan superiority, their theological opponents—notably Barth—relegated that doctrine to auxiliary status. Primary for Barth were doctrines of revelation and reconciliation. Only with the ecological movement did the doctrine of creation again come to the fore. Christian apologists still sought reasons for our faith and found in Jesus the God-man a definitive indication of the Spirit directing salvation history. Tillich deals with the Genesis story by stressing its symbolic meaning. He said no to reading Genesis literally as a protoscientific text and yes to the theological conclusion that, in essence, what we are is good as created. The "split between essence and existence," which is how he describes the Fall, coincides well-nigh inevitably but accidentally, as it were, with the moment of creation. We are not *necessarily* sinful (*ST* II, 29–44). The "Fall" leaves our powers of formal reasoning intact, but in history logical interchanges are existential-dialectical, not formal-essential.

Where Augustine stressed sin as pride and the Son as archetypal incarnation of humble servanthood, Tillich emphasized the Hegelian theme of estrangement and reconciliation in "the depth dimension" of incarnate spiritual being. The Christ, not Christianity, is unique in that *Jesus as the Christ*, one with the Holy Spirit, "sacrifices" his finite selfhood to the eruption in time of the divinely instituted promise of cosmic reconciliation (*ST* I, 136).[35] Tillich reconstrues the Lutheran doctrine of justification by grace through faith as affirmation of "the courage to be" in spite of anxiety over possibly not being.[36] Our "finite freedom" can only overcome the temptation of fixating on our finitude if we acknowledge our participation in God, "the Ground of Being," which turns temptations into occasions for deeper faith in the dialectic of faith and doubt.

The dynamic of the possibility of negation, not just privation, is key to understanding sin and grace, when we accept our unacceptability. The original confession that Jesus is the Christ inaugurates God's Kingdom when we participate in his "New Being." The Christ Event reunites essence with existence in a process of "essentialization" (*CB*, 163–67; *ST* II, 118–36; III, 406–22). Participation through faith and love is key to any theology of predestination. Tillich roundly declares any doctrine of double predestination a mistake. It cannot symbolize any genuinely divine decree, since the very idea of such "violates both the divine love and the divine power ... Eternal condemnation is a contradiction in terms. It establishes an eternal split within being-itself," giving the demonic an undialectically everlasting final word. It draws false conclusions from abstract ideas, missing the symbolic nature of religious discourse, as do "all logical theological consequences which are not rooted in existential participation" (*ST* I, 285–86).

Like many before Wittgenstein, Tillich had a classically *essentialist theory of meaning*, setting much store by formal definitions and taking a primary use of words to denote objects. Starting with an Augustinian notion of the barely expressible mystery of being, he assumed that words are articulations of deeper unverbalized thoughts. Words "point" to depths of meaning, and when it comes to testing existential truth, there is no substitute for being within the circle of faith—that is, a community responsive to revelatory moments that participates in meaning-giving Spiritual Presence. Cognitive theological confusion is often due to missing the necessarily *symbolic nature of genuinely religious language.* Secular atheism stems from a misconstrual of the correct referent of "God" as "Being-itself" or "the Ground of being" (*ST* I, 235–38). Such misconstrual is practically inevitable because thought entails abstraction from the objects of thought.

Augustinian insistence on the mystery of divine being rejects all attempts to make human logic the yardstick of what God wills and does. Among contemporary linguistic analytic philosophers, ontology is generally considered an epiphenomenal part of culture. Tillich resisted that conclusion as an aberration owing to the triumph of "technical reason" in a society unaware of its roots (*ST* I, 72–75). He insisted that every use of language presupposes some ontology and that through ontology a unified theology of *religion and culture* is, in principle, always achievable. Language is the primary exemplification of culture. In his view, a "baptized" Hellenistic ontology rightly informs our theological vocabulary. Fluidity in meaning comes with the symbolic use of language when matters of ultimate concern are being articulated. Such usage rules out biblical literalism.

As an expression of the spiritual dimension of human being, according to Tillich, religion is the meaning-giving "substance" of culture, and culture is the totality of expressive forms, including instituional religious forms, embodied in successive times and places. The substance, religion in essence, is dynamic, not static. The eternal dialectic of the divine power of being works creatively beneath and behind the scenes, not tied forever to any one temporal order or dogmatic formulation. In Tillich, *the Protestant Principle* is a reminder, against the hubris of medieval Christendom and modern religious culture, that traditional Christian forms are as much part of our cultural history, in need of transformation, as non-Christian ones. To him the medieval high point of the Christ of culture was in art and architecture, not ecclesiology.

In religion, "the latent effect of the Spiritual Presence comes from and drives toward a manifestation of it in a historical community, a church" (*ST* III, 247). True religion disrupts the destructive fixities of formal culture and institutional hegemonies, as Gospel does of Law, recalling us to participate in the life of the latent Church (*ST* III, 152–55). Evident in religion and culture is a principle of "convergence of the holy and the secular." The self-transcending spiritual move is temporal, toward the future, not a timelessly eternal present. In the historical dialectic between separation and reunion, both transformation and deformation occur. Cognitively, this allows for new truth; practically, it allows social injustices that occasion prophetic protests (*ST* III, 78–84).

As often as not, protest comes from the religious or "depth dimension" of a culture, not religious institutions. With reference to slavery, for instance, the call for relative justice, according to Tillich, was prompted more by Stoic philosophy than by early Church practice.[37] Especially in modern culture, the transforming Logos is sometimes hidden in secular challenges to contemporary atrocities.[38] To him Picasso's *Guernica* was "one of the most truly Protestant paintings of the twentieth century,"[39] owing its inspiration to the "God above 'God'" (*CB*, 182), In "post-Christian" times, we inherit from the Reformation the task of addressing the fallibly human side of all religious cultures. What is new compared to Augustine's time is not that we inherit a religious culture in need of transformation, but that that culture in Euro-America was ostensibly Christian.

Tillich adamantly opposed any hint of triumphalism. But he found in the biblical notion of *kairos* or historically fulfilled time grounds for social reformation, including the emancipation of slaves. He was disappointed that the post–First World War era failed to realize a "kairotic" moment, when Christian socialism would prevail in Germany over Marxism and Nazism. He became convinced that any coming of the Kingdom in time is always only fragmentary. In the main, his eschatology ran along Johannine lines, with notions of individual participation in eternal life drawn from the cultural mythology assumed by all biblical authors. Of the two kingdoms, on his reading, while the heavenly always outlasts any earthly one, it is always more latent than manifest.[40]

Tillich's rejection of nineteenth-century evolutionary optimism and belief in historical progress meant that, for him, the Book of History became again, as in Augustine, primarily a book of personal history framed by the global biblical narrative. His sense of *kairos* did not condone utopianism. The social aspect of human being is implicit in his dialectical conception of being a self and being a part. But like Augustine, Tillich regarded any community as a group of individuals, sharing social structures but lacking a corporately centred self with a will of its own. The polar term to "self" is "world," not group (*ST* III, 312). Under conditions of existential estrangement, our no to God's will can seemingly conquer the yes of the Incarnate Word. But the Resurrection asserts God's power to absorb all demonic destructiveness and bring good out of evil. In a realized eschatology, we know even less than did Augustine how this may be so, but we can be sure that, in the end, God's yes absorbs and transforms every finite no.

While Tillich acknowledged that "Catholic substance" and the Protestant Principle are both universal (e.g., *ST* III, 122), his own predilections were Protestant Lutheran. Especially following the trauma of his experience as an army chaplain during the First World War, he denounced as idolatry quasi-religious nationalism and industrial capitalism. He admitted that his sacramental sense of Eucharistic presence was underdeveloped (*ST* III, 5). For him, "the symbol of symbols" is the Cross.[41] Time for change is signalled by changes in the material circumstances of life, as during the Industrial Revolution. That key cultural changes are due to divine creativity is evident from the fact that we cannot arbitrarily invent new symbols.[42] Meaningful symbols are given in response to revelation, not projected out of thin air.

The ontological priority of dynamics over form meant to most critical thinkers in Tillich's time that cultural institutions such as marriage are social constructs, not mandated by eternal laws of nature, contrary to what Augustine supposed.[43] Tillich's thinking was both essentialist and existentialist on such topics. Classical essentialists privilege what they consider the original meanings of terms such as marriage. Traditionalists invoke "natural law" to mean that God wills marriage to be the union of a man and a woman for procreation. However, conceptions of what counts as natural have changed.[44] In Tillichian thinking, marriage, as a viable biblical symbol of God's relation to Israel, though not a sacrament, is divinely rooted in creation. If modern geneticists could demonstrate that received differentiations between "male" and "female" are inadequate, then same-sex attractions might count as natural. But for Tillich, what is essentially natural, however construed, is existentially ambiguous (see, e.g., *ST* I, 186; *ST* III, 47, 123). Love and justice are principles not reducible to formulae eternally governing intercourse and sacramental blessings. The Protestant Principle goes against conservative legalism on such issues.

A more thoroughly constructivist approach, such as that adopted by feminist critics of Tillich, classifies marriage as no more than a social convention protecting property rights. Tillich might add that, when rhetoric escalates, fanatics project onto others, whom they wish to purge, what they repress in themselves (*CB*, 50). In this instance, repressed on one side might be fear of licentiousness, and, on the other, fear that to prescribe disembodied love is to prescribe frustration.[45]

By Niebuhr's criteria, Tillich belongs with Augustine among those who, for the most part, reckon the Christ to be the transformer of culture. He affirms the essential goodness of creation, "the split between essence and existence" in fallen history, and ultimate reconciliation with the Ground of Being through participation in *the New Being* of Jesus the Christ. As in Augustine, Jesus' mediating role turns on his identification as "the Word made flesh." Tillich's generation wrestled with the contrast between "the Jesus of history" and "the Christ of faith" but did not fully absorb the impact of literary-critical analyses that give as much attention to the Gospel message as to the messenger.

As a preacher, Tillich affirmed the sacrament of the Word; so, as in Augustinian research, his sermons are an important resource among his collected works. He always preached from biblical texts. If *the* vehicle of culture is language, then the way to start transforming a culture is to "baptize" its language. For Tillich this entails driving home the "real" meaning of God-talk in relation to everyday, existential concerns. His sermon "The Eternal Now" addresses individual expectations for the future, framed by memory of the past, to find healing in God's eternal "presence." The eternal is not endless time or timelessness, but "a dimension of time which cuts into time and gives us our time" in ways that bring us healing and hope in spite of despair.[46]

Transforming or Baptizing Culture

Both Augustine's and Tillich's apologetic concern was more with transforming culture than with sectarian purity of faith. In the Augustinian tradition, "Christ and culture" is part of the wider topic of God and the world. The core conviction is that the Trinity is always present in every historical moment as Creator, Judge, Inspirer, Redeemer, Community Builder, and Grace-Giver, in such a way that, in this life, good may come out of evil and, in the end, good will prevail. The Christ is *the* historical agent of and way to this. He is the Prince of Peace mediating the divine-human ordering of wills (however construed) toward the *summum bonum*. Life in this world is a pilgrimage of prodigals. Perfect bliss is realized, if at all, in moments that leave behind the primarily penal reality of historical existence since the Fall. As Tillich described "theonomy," truly grounded love can use compulsion against the obdurate but cannot coerce loving responses (*LPJ,* 114). Means must be congruent with ends. Divine power is not one more in a series of finite causes. It is what warrants just judgments and gives reality to all powers, as grace superimposed on or undergirding nature and culture. In contrast to developmentally minded liberation theologians, Augustine and Tillich were primarily oriented toward individual transcendence of our sinful situation.

In recent years, proponents of narrative theology and others have questioned whether Christian doctrine requires "ontotheological" underpinning. Questions raised relate to theology and the sciences, theories of meaning, missiological insights into inculturation, narrative structure, and lessons for dogmatics drawn from modern biblical criticism, all of which have some bearing on doctrines of creation, corruption, and redemption, which Niebuhr flagged as critical to any theology of transformation. The metaphysical question of evil, so critical for Augustine and Tillich, receives less attention.

Concerning creation, the question is how to relate *theological and scientific* insights. Tillich and Barth held that theology is independent of the sciences. Properly understood, there can be no competition between scientific and theological ideas, whether about genesis and geology or ethics and genetics. The disciplines deal with essentially different dimensions of being. Contemporary philosophers of religion, such as Nancey Murphy, criticize this assertion. She follows Ian Barbour in rejecting both scientistic cultural imperialism and the cosmological schizophrenia of existentialistic theologies.[47] The mistake on both sides, in her view, has been to presuppose a metaphor of building knowledge on foundations of assured axioms, be they derived from revelation or direct experience. The shared epistemological model was of hierarchies of knowledge, disagreements being over what belongs at the "top" or "bottom," whether or how theology should be included, and what to make of "religious" experience.[48]

In actual practice, Murphy points out, we operate in what is better described as a web of more or less overlapping disciplinary discourses, tied to experience mostly at the margins. We relinquish our "controlling beliefs," which are usually several removes from "direct" experience, only reluctantly. We tolerate dissonant positions longer than theoretical purists would allow. Academic disciplines are partially independent, partially interdependent, and sometimes complementary. In modern times, the challenge to Christian apologetics has been from skepticism. To postmoderns or "postliberals," the perceived threat is from relativism (which is often linked to pluralism, historicism, and constructivism).

In addition to foundationalism,[49] traditional responses to such challenges relied on questionable *theories of meaning and linguistic usage*. In particular, the essentialist theory of meaning presupposed in Tillich's answers to existential questions has been queried by George Lindbeck. He argues that Tillich's "experiential-expressivist" account of linguistic usage misses the point of Wittgenstein's strictures against picture theories of meaning.[50] This is a significant failing because, as noted above, language, with art, was Tillich's entrée to meaning in culture. Historically, in his view, terms lose their pristine meanings owing to existential alienation. The revelation of New Being only fragmentarily restores our sense of essential "God-manhood." It relativizes but does not dispel the ambiguities that bedevil debates about religion and culture.

An alternative conception of how experience and expression connect, consistent with Murphy's web metaphor, draws on Wittgenstein's conception of language-games and Mikhail Bakhtin's "dialogism." The latter's studies of folklore and modern novels are important for postmodern critiques of literature, including biblical literature.[51] Both point to pneumatological corollaries to traditional two-natures christologies and theologies of the Word.[52] Less known to systematic theologians, Bakhtin's metalinguistic observations independently support Wittgenstein, without restricting us to his model of grammatical rules as key to the nature of doctrine.[53]

Bakhtin highlights the *narrative structure* of concrete existence as the most revealing point of contact with God's will in creation and redemption. His *dialogical* account of linguistic usage affirms orientational pluralism. Unlike dialectics, it does not limit reactions to yes or no, but allows for the whole range of human responses registered in everyday discourse. In his locution, the technical languages of academic disciplines, including the sciences and dogmatic theology, are "monological," abstracting from the complexity of real life. In earlier times, folklore offered carnivalesque critiques of the official positions of church and state. Since the Renaissance, major critiques have been mounted in the distinctive genre of modern novels by such authors as Dickens and Dostoevsky.[54]

As Bakhtin pointed out, experience is not epistemologically prior to expression. We do not make inferences about a formally fixed "nature," to which we refer in languages only approximating "the truth." The truth is that we are already in the world, not projecting private thoughts onto some world "outside." That we have experiences is due to the common, multivoiced languages that we imbibe with our mother's milk. Everyday exchanges are "polyphonic." Ordinary discourse, as in Gospel sayings attributed to Jesus, has connotations that are never completely the same for all involved. Tone, manner, and silences are as real parts of actual conversations as what we jointly affirm. Differences matter. Axiomatic is the otherness of others. We cannot see ourselves from behind, as others do. We owe our full sense of self to how we interact with them. What is real are all the possibilities and actualities of life for all of us – possibilities that are eventuated in living language, which is "unfinalizable." As long as we keep talking, there is no closure on possible connotations and connections. Fighting for one definition of marriage for all in same-sex debates, for instance, or for the hegemony of one academic discipline for all accounts of self and world, is futile.

No single discipline covers all our experience in and of the world. Overlapping academic disciplines contribute to our webs of meaning. To paraphrase Whitehead, the philosophical theology learned in seminaries today becomes common parlance in the pews tomorrow.[55] The same is true of science: gravitation and genome theory filter into ordinary discourse to suggest currently more plausible construals of God's rule in nature than Platonic ideas.[56] Because we are not monads but members of communities, we share spatio-temporal ("chronotopical") configurations, which account for different genres of inquiry. Our philosophies of life are in the everyday languages we speak, not in any metadiscourse. These points are important for any adequate account of doctrine and for any conception of the meaning- and truth-giving power of the Spirit.

When discourse is of historical existence, human beings are imaginative responders to networks of meaning, rather than projectors of ideas out of nothing but individual psyches. In rare moments, some hear "God's voice," addressing us through others in *confessional contexts*. (An example from literature is Alyosha Karamazov telling his brother Ivan in God's name that he is not a murderer.)[57] According to Bakhtin, we all have an ideal of being perfectly understood, against which we measure relationships and expectations. Some identify this measure with God or "the Absolute," others with "the future" as determined by our peers, and still others with the fruits of future scientific research. However understood, in every dialogical event there is always this "third" voice carried by inherited communications and reworked for present purposes. As in Jesus' parable of the Pharisee and the Publican, cited by Bakhtin, the one who goes away justified does not fail—as the unjustified does—to hear any voice but his own. His sense of setting and tone reorient him at that moment to a "higher," reconciling perspective, unlike that of the one who, ostensibly in the same position, heeds only himself (Luke 18:9–14). The divinely justifying moment is dialogical. The self-justifying stance is monological.[58]

Dialogue is an overused term. Bakhtin's challenge is to understand what it means to *be* dialogical. It means attending to more than one source of tradition and culture, allowing for overlapping times—God's time, biblical time, ancient and modern times—that impinge on us in ways that require moments of mutual confession and commitment, when we respond creatively to affirm our identities in the everyday world. Feuerbach missed the asymmetry of divine–human interaction in dialogical encounters. The Christian proposal is of the cross for myself, but of beatitude or loving mercy for others. "What I must be for the other, God is for me."[59] That is the basis for our answerability to others, to our world, and to ourselves. When traditional religious language loses communicative power, a dialogical gesture may be the only authentic response, as in Dostoevsky's icon of the Christ kissing the Grand Inquisitor.

We have to engage in dialogue in order to become critically aware of our particular situation and to work through which versions of what doctrines and scientific theories should inform our judgments at any given time. Since the Bakhtin circle was barred from publicly discussing religious ideas, we get little direct guidance from him on how to recognize genuinely dialogical encounters with others and the Wholly Other. His politically approved work on Dostoevsky highlights paradigmatic *heroes* who *embody* theistic and atheistic *ideologies*. Chalcedonian christological terminology is latent but increasingly less part of the everyday exchanges recorded in modern literature. What Bakhtin offers is not another system, but pointers to where in his day great authors had "novel" insights—that is, God's good news for ordinary people.

With Wittgenstein, Bakhtin upholds the sense of meaning in life affirmed in *narrative theologies* that take their cues from Karl Barth and Hans Frei.[60] Frei argues that what renders the Christ salvifically present are "history-like" biblical narratives, not "onto-theologies."[61] However, as Tillich asserted and David Kelsey demonstrated,[62] no theologian avoids philosophical presuppositions entirely. With regard to philosophies of language, Bakhtin directs us to hear the extraordinary in the ordinary. That doesn't mean that poets never grope for the right words to adumbrate the mystery of divine presence. But we cannot use the symbolic meaning of some religious terms as a blanket excuse for discounting others' queries about meaning. Concerning sin and salvation, Tillich insists on a biblical understanding of ourselves as people, not things. Kierkegaard adds that we do not have a God's-eye view of personal truth. Bakhtin adds that God's truth cherishes our differences as we appropriate good news.

An ontological presupposition of any narrative account of salvific experience is that temporality is intrinsic to being. An important difference between Barth and Tillich is that Barth follows Kierkegaard in making "the Christ Event" *prototypical,* not *archetypal,* and thereby avoids lingering essentialism. With regard to Aristotelian categories of plot, setting, mood/tone, and character, arguably traditional salvation narratives have emphasized plot.[63] If the setting is the sinful world and the mood despair, hope depends on God coming to our aid. The New Testament plot is of Incarnation, conflict, death, and Resurrection. However, the redemptive impact of the narrative is due as much to character as to plot or tone—that is, to the presence of the Spirit in the agency of Jesus. In this connection, Tillich's focus on Jesus sacrificing his humanity undervalues the role of other relationships in the coming of God's rule. In the sequel to Peter's confession of the Christ, Tillich makes too little of graced human agency in sacramental "life according to the Spirit."

The eschatological thrust of the Christ prototype in Christian preaching sets our priorities when issues such as slavery or same-sex relationships are discussed. If religion is what concerns us unconditionedly, according to Tillich's definition, then part of the analytic job is to allow other disciplines to inform discussions of penultimate concerns. If we follow Bakhtin, the touchstone for wisdom is still a theory of meaning rooted in our languages. But in place of the visual metaphor of dimly seeing shadows cast by sunlight on the walls of our cave, he posits an audial metaphor of doubling voices juxtaposed to communicate a sense of salvific presence and absence in time. What abides is not the sun but grace and the call to answerability in harmony with others.[64]

Concerning soteriology, modern missiology reminds us that missionaries never "take" Jesus overseas. The Risen Lord is always already there. We can translate the Bible into local dialects because every language has the potential to participate in the *inculturation of God's Word*.[65] A biblical example of inculturation is the Fourth Gospel.[66] The Bible is the record of God's revelation in terms that others understand and pass on.[67] Saying "Amen" to passages from Paul's letters does not deny that the words are Paul's, nor does it make him infallible. God speaks through him in an ongoing community of discourse. Being true to revelation for Christians should mean being true to the Spirit in a way that does not monologically assume that, in God's world, "one cultural size fits all."

If we adopt the metaphor of *baptizing a culture* to describe the process of redemptive transformation in time, we must ask what in any given culture will die, what should be resurrected, and what is forever worth celebrating. If "the" Church is the Body of Christ in history, then it too, on its temporal side, must experience an ongoing process of dying and being raised to new life, as long as we are in this world. What "dies" is not just physical but finite spiritual conformations, such as philosophies giving priority to eternal forms and codes based on tribal or class mores. Some traditions are more lasting than others and can, for that reason, be thought eternal. But, Tillich insisted, making either religious or secular ideologies absolute is a sign of false consciousness (*PE,* 169).

Such considerations remind us that there is more to Christ the transformer of culture than the conversion of individual sinners. More than one facet of the Christ figure—humility or self-sacrifice—comes into play. Augustine reminds us that the work of the whole Trinity is involved. Tillich reminds us that God gives and engenders both love and justice, including restorative or creative justice, whenever we overcome estrangement from God's way for us (*LPJ,* 66). In this connection, Buddhists might complement our biblical picture with a sense of utter selflessness in the realization of infinite compassion, when communicating good news.[68]

Concerning the biblical portrait of the Christ who transforms culture, modern and postmodern theologians are still assimilating the scholarly judgment that Pauline *Messianic Spirit theology* predates—perhaps by a whole generation—Johaninne Logos theology. What is striking is how little attention Paul gave to the kinds of details about Jesus' person that fascinate historians. Perhaps we have in I Corinthians 13 a character portrait.[69] But Paul's focus is on pneumatology as key to life in messianic times. Our choice is between "life according to the flesh" and "life according to the Spirit."[70] Both Augustine and Tillich emphasized this choice in terms that appealed to the prevailing cultures of their times. Their model is of grounding theology in confessional Christian living in community, not limiting God's voice to what traditionalists say about the way.

A contemporary Trinitarian theology building on Pauline testimony might be less preoccupied with ontological implications than were Augustine and Tillich and more concerned with what it means to be called to be "the people of God." As the ecological movement insists, the baptismal metaphor of dying and rising with Christ applies to "the whole creation groaning in travail," not just to individuals being saved. The accent is on becoming imbued with the Christ-like Spirit as members of networks of churches aiming to be in the vanguard of universal renewal, living in anticipation of final judgment. The final test of truth is whether the churches are part of the Good News for others. In short, the challenging topic for a contemporary theology of culture is how we respond to the Trinity in a pluralistic world, where no single story commands universal assent, but the yearning is still for the peace which passes all understanding.

Notes

1 In Dorothy F. Donnelly, ed., *The City of God: A Collection of Critical Essays* (New York: Peter Lang, 1995), 135–49 at 144, re *City* XIX, 14–16.

2 On shifting connotations of these and related notions in Niebuhr's time, see Kathryn Tanner, *Theories of Culture: A New Agenda for Theology* (Minneapolis: Fortress, 1997), 3–24. On 61–62 she notes that for Niebuhr, "culture" is code for "the world" and situates Niebuhr as more "against culture" than, for example, Troeltsch.

3 H. Richard Niebuhr, *Christ and Culture* (New York: Harper Torchbooks, 1956), 207 (hereafter *C&C*).

4 C.N. Cochrane, *Christianity and Classical Culture: A Study of Thought and Action from Augustus to Augustine* (New York: Oxford University Press, Galaxy, 1957), 401.

5 In Augustine's Latin, *facere* is typically followed by *de*, not *ex*.

6 See A.D. Nock, *Conversion: The Old and the New in Religion from Alexander the Great to Augustine of Hippo* (Oxford: Clarendon, 1933), 7–14, on differences between primitive and prophetic religion.

7 This observation is based on years of introducing undergraduates to "Hinduism" and study tours of shrines and research centres in India. For a somewhat sweeping rumination on "Indo-European" culture and Augustine, according to Georges Dumèzil, see John Milbank, "Sacred Triads: Augustine and the Indo European Soul," in *Augustine and His Critics*, ed. Robert Dodaro and George Lawless (London: Routledge, 2000), 77–102.

8 See Cochrane, *Christianity and Classical Culture*, 407–9, on the Creator and "the creative principle."

9 See, e.g., Henry Chadwick, trans., *Saint Augustine: Confessions* (Oxford: Oxford University Press, 1991), VII, xii (18) 124–25; VIII, viii (20) 147; and note "amissio" in Marcus Dods, trans., *The City of God* (New York: Random House, 1950), XI, 10, 354 (hereafter *City*). Note 23, *Mali enim nulla natura est: sed amissio boni, mali nomen accepit.*

10 See Robert Crouse, *"Paucis Mutatis Verbis*: St. Augustine's Platonism," in Dodaro and Lawless, *Augustine and His Critics*, 37–50. On 42–43, he notes that Rist's attractive baptism metaphor needs considerable unpacking. John Rist, *Ancient Thought Baptized* (Cambridge: Cambridge University Press, 1994).

11 See James J. O'Donnell, "Augustine: His Time and Lives," in *The Cambridge Companion to Augustine*, ed. Eleonore Stump and Norman Kretzmann (Cambridge: Cambridge University Press, 2001), 8–25.

12 The Manichaeans acknowledged edited Pauline texts, not the canonical Gospels. See John J. O'Meara, *The Young Augustine* (London: Longman, 1954), 63; and J. Kevin Coyle, "Mani, Manichaeism," in *Augustine Through the Ages: An Encyclopedia*, ed. Allan D. Fitzgerald (Grand Rapids: Eerdmans, 1999), 520–25 at 524.

13 In Pamela Bright, ed. and trans., *Augustine and the Bible* (Notre Dame: University of Notre Dame Press, 1999), 74–103 at 75.

14 Footnote 5 on 99, citing her essay on "The Study of Augustine's Christology in the Twentieth Century," in *Augustine: From Rhetor to Theologian*, ed. Joanne McWilliam (Waterloo: Wilfrid Laurier University Press, 1992), 197.

15 See "Augustine at Ephesus?" in *One Lord, One Faith, One Baptism: Studies in Christian Ecclesiality and Ecumenism in Honor of J. Robert Wright*, ed. Marsha L. Dutton and Patrick Terrell Gray (Grand Rapids: Eerdmans, 2006), 56–67. She concludes that Augustine was well out of Ephesus.

16 See, e.g., the use of Letters 11 and 129 and Sermon 52 in Lewis Ayres, "The Fundamental Grammar of Augustine's Trinitarian Theology," in Dodaro and Lawless, *Augustine and His Critics*, 51–76.

17 See Edward R. Hardy, Jr., "The City of God," in *A Companion to the Study of St. Augustine*, ed. Roy Battenhouse (New York: Oxford University Press, 1955), 257–83.

18 E.g., *City*, I, xv, 21: "a community is nothing less than a harmonious collection of individuals."

19 Drive/urge: Ὁρμή or *nisus*. See R.H. Barrow, *Introduction to the City of God* (London: Faber & Faber, 1950), XIX: 11, 84, 224–25.

20 See Henry Chadwick's translator's note, *Confessions,* VII, ix, 15, 123, note 16.

21 See Giorgio Agamben, *The Time That Remains: A Commentary on the Letter to the Romans*, trans. Patricia Dailey (Stanford: Stanford University Press, 2005), 2–12.

22 See Alasdair MacIntyre, *Whose Justice? Which Rationality?* (Notre Dame: University of Notre Dame Press, 1988), 9; "the concept of timelessness is itself a concept with a history" and 398 re testing theses dialectically.

23 See C.K. Barrett, *The New Testament Background: Selected Documents* (London: SPCK, 1956), 209–16, excerpts from Philo and the *Epistle of Aristeas*.

24 Paul Tillich, *Biblical Religion and the Search for Ultimate Reality* (Chicago: University of Chicago Press, 1956), 2–5, on the dialectic between revelation and religion.

25 Note James Wetzel, "Free Will and Predestination," in Dodaro and Lawless, *Augustine and His Critics*, 124–41 at 134.

26 *City* V, VIII, 15, 261–62. On Manicheans and astrology, see O'Meara, *The Young Augustine*, 56, 64, 95.

27 So Karl Barth, *Church Dogmatics: The Doctrine of God*, II, 2, ed. G.W. Bromiley and T.F. Torrance (Edinburgh: T. & T. Clark, 1957), e.g., 122–23, 662–63.

28 See H. Wheeler Robinson, *Inspiration and Revelation in the Old Testament* (Oxford: Clarendon, 1962), 70–71, on sin and corporate personality.

29 See R.A. Markus, *Saeculum: History and Society in the Theology of St. Augustine* (Cambridge: Cambridge University Press, 1970), 5–13, 20–21, 27–53, 158–62.

30 See Paul Tillich, "The Two Types of Philosophy of Religion," reprinted in *Theology of Culture*, ed. Robert C. Kimball (New York: Oxford, 1959), 10–29.

31 For bibliographical data and exposition, see Peter Slater, "Religious and Theological Dialectics: Kierkegaard and Tillich," *Toronto Journal of Theology* 24, no. 1 (2008): 21–42.

32 See, e.g., *Kairos: Three Prophetic Challenges to the Church*, ed. Robert McAfee Brown (Grand Rapids: Eerdmans, 1990), for the Barmen Declaration and more recent texts from South Africa, Latin America, and elsewhere.

33 See Gandhi's reply to Tagore in *Young India*, excerpted in *Sources of Indian Tradition*, ed. William Theodore deBary (New York: Columbia University Press, 1958), 820–23.

34 Paul Tillich, *Systematic Theology*, 3 vols. (Chicago: University of Chicago Press, 1951, 1957, 1963), e.g., III:250 (hereafter *ST* I/II/III).

35 Note Paul Tillich, *Love, Power, and Justice* (New York: Oxford, 1954), hereafter *LPJ*. "In the loving person-to-person relationship Christianity manifests its superiority to any religious tradition" (27).

36 See Paul Tillich, *The Courage to Be* (New Haven: Yale University Press, 1952), 32–36 (hereafter CB).

37 *ST* III:263. Note also *LPJ*, 61. To liberals, Tillich noted, "Slavery in all forms contradicts justice."

38 So John B. Cobb, Jr., *Christ in a Pluralistic Age* (Philadelphia: Westminster, 1975), on Malraux and Christ as a "force field" for creative transformation in art, 31–65. Cobb's appeal, 140, to Jesus' self-consciousness would be disallowed by many historians.

39 Paul Tillich, *On Art and Architecture*, ed. John and Jane Dillenberger (New York: Crossroad, 1987), 95–96.

40 On "kairos" and "kairoi," see *ST* III:369–72, and Paul Tillich, *The Protestant Era*, trans. James Luther Adams (Chicago: University of Chicago Press), 148, 32–51. Note also his sermons, "We Live in Two Orders," and "You Are Accepted," in *The Shaking of the Foundations* (New York: Scribners, 1948), 12–23, 153–63.

41 Without naming him, Tillich acknowledged a debt to Eugene Fairweather, then his doctoral student, regarding "Catholic substance" in Protestantism, *Theology of Culture*, 169. Note *ST* II:153; "in the minds of the disciples and of the writers of the New Testament the Cross is both an event and a symbol and the Resurrection is both a symbol and an event."

42 See Robert Neville, *The Truth of Broken Symbols* (Albany: SUNY Press, 1996), x–xi, 1–75, 151–99.

43 See Richard A. Norris, Jr., "Some Notes on the Current Debate Regarding Homosexuality and the Place of Homosexuals in the Church," *Anglican Theological Review* 90, no. 3 (2008): 437–511.

44 Note in this connection Charles Taylor's conception of embedding and disembedding in *A Secular Age* (Cambridge, MA: Belknap, 2007), 146–53.

45 See, e.g., Alexander C. Irwin, *Eros Toward the World: Paul Tillich and the Theology of the Erotic* (Minneapolis: Augsburg Fortress, 1991), 121–52, on Judith Plaskow and others; Rosemary Radford Ruether, *Religion and Sexism: Images of Women in the Jewish and Christian Tradition* (New York: Simon and Schuster, 1974), 252–53, on projection; Beverly Wildung Harrison, *Making the Connections: Essays in Feminist Social Ethics*, ed. Carol S. Robb (Boston: Beacon, 1985), 106–7, on "tepid" public church support for gay rights.

46 Paul Tillich, *The Eternal Now* (London: SCM, 1963), 111.

47 Nancey Murphy, "Postmodern Apologetics, or Why Theologians *Must* Pay Attention to Science," and James E. Loder and W. Jim Neidhart, "Barth, Bohr, and Dialectic," in W. Mark Richardson and Wesley Wildman, eds., *Religion and Science: History, Method, Dialogue* (New York: Routledge, 1996), 105–20 and 271–89. Ian G. Barbour, *Religion in an Age of Science* (New York: Harper and Row, 1990), 4–30, 206, on Tillich and the Fall. Note also J. Wentzel van Huyssteen, *The Shaping of Rationality: Toward Interdisciplinarity in Theology and Science* (Grand Rapids: Eerdmans, 1999), e.g., 4, 17–63, 102.

48 See Tillich on Schleiermacher and Otto, *ST* I:40–43, 108–15. On nuances usually ignored, see George P. Schner, SJ, "The Appeal to Experience," *Theological Studies* 53 (1992): 40–59.

49 See, e.g., John E. Thiel, *Nonfoundationalism* (Minneapolis: Augsburg Fortress, 1994).

50 Note George A. Lindbeck, *The Nature of Doctrine: Religion and Theology in a Post-Liberal Age* (Philadelphia: Westminster, 1984), 24, 30–32, on Tillich. Regarding Wittgenstein on Augustine, see Fergus Kerr, *Theology After Wittgenstein* (Oxford: Blackwell, 1986), 42–43; also 145–47 on mental pictures and grammar.

51 For expositions of Bakhtin's leading ideas in relation to biblical criticism, see Barbara Green, *How Are the Mighty Fallen? A Dialogical Study of King Saul in I Samuel* (London: Sheffield, 2003).

52 On the Chalcedonian presupposition of Bakhtinian thought, see Alexandar Mihailovic, *Corporeal Words: Mikhail Bakhtin's Theology of Discourse* (Evanston: Northwestern University Press, 1996), 1–16. Note Jane Barter Moulaison, *Lord, Giver of Life: Toward a Pneumatological Complement to George Lindbeck's Theory of Doctrine* (Waterloo: Wilfrid Laurier University Press, 2007), 4–8, 44–47.

53 For exposition and extensive references, see Peter Slater, "Bakhtin on Hearing God's Voice," *Modern Theology* 23, no. 1: 1–25.

54 He also revered Shakespeare, Cervantes, and Goethe and wrote a dissertation on Rabelais.

55 Whitehead's observation was that the philosophy of today is the common sense of tomorrow. See, e.g., *Process and Reality*, ed. David Ray Griffin and Donald W. Sherburne (New York: Macmillan Free Press, 1979), 13.

56 On the subject of controlling beliefs and plausibility, see Nicholas Wolterstorrf in Richardson and Wildman, *Religion and Science*, 145. He talks of entitled belief rather than "rationality."

57 Fyodor Dostoevsky, *The Brothers Karamazov*, ed. Manuel Komroff (New York: Signet, 1958), XL8, 565.

58 See Lecture Notes, Appendix A, in *Bakhtin and Religion: A Feeling for Faith*, ed. Susan M. Felch and Paul J. Contino (Evanston: Northwestern University Press, 2001), 208.

59 Besides Felch and Contino, see Mikhail Bakhtin, *Art and Answerablity*, trans. Vadim Lupinov (Austin: University of Texas Press, 1990), 56.

60 See David E. Demson, *Hans Frei and Karl Barth: Different Ways of Reading Scripture* (Grand Rapids: Eerdmans, 1997), including bibliography.

61 See also Ronald F. Thiemann, *Revelation and Theology: The Gospel as Narrated Promise* (Notre Dame: University of Notre Dame Press, 1985), 78–91, 150–56. Note van Huyssteen, *The Shaping of Rationality*, 48, citing Joseph Rouse: "we must understand narrative here not as a literary form into which knowledge is written, but as ... a way of comprehending the temporality and locatedness of one's actions in their very enactment."

62 See David H. Kelsey's analysis in *Proving Doctrine: The Uses of Scripture in Recent Theology* (Harrisburg: Trinity Press International, 1999).

63 On ways and story elements, see Peter Slater, *The Dynamics of Religion* (San Francisco: Harper and Row, 1978), 47–63.

64 John Milbank, "'Postmodern Critical Augustinianism': A Short *Summa* in Forty-Two Responses to Unasked Questions," *Modern Theology* 7, no. 3 (1991): 225–37 at 228. Millbank appeals to Augustine's *De Musica* re harmony.

65 See Lamin Sanneh, *Translating the Message: The Missionary Impact of Culture* (Maryknoll: Orbis, 1989), 1–6.

66 On inculturation, see David J. Bosch, *Transforming Mission: Paradigm Shifts in Theology of Mission* (Maryknoll: Orbis, 1992), 447–57, and Stephen B. Bevans and Roger P. Schroeder, *Constants in Context: A Theology of Mission for Today* (Maryknoll: Orbis, 2004), 385–89.

67 See, e.g., Jacques Dupuis, SJ, *Toward a Christian Theology of Religious Pluralism* (Maryknoll: Orbis, 1997), on shifting paradigms, 185–200.

68 See, e.g., Aloysius Pieris, SJ, *Love Meets Wisdom: A Christian Experience of Buddhism* (Maryknoll: Orbis, 1990), 110–35, on "Gnostic Agape."

69 See, in this connection, a forthcoming work on Pauline ethics by Ann Jervis.

70 The definitive study of Pauline terminology is Rudolf Bultmann's *Theology of the New Testament* 2, trans. Kendrick Grobel (London: SCM, 1955).

8

Hooker on Divinization
Our Participation of Christ[1]

✠ ✠ ✠

DAVID NEELANDS

RICHARD HOOKER in his account of justification and sanctification took very seriously the significance of glorification. In this he was, like some other Reformation figures, informed by the Patristic notion of *theosis* or divinization. *Theosis* also links Hooker's account of God's grace with his Christology. To ignore this aspect of his account of engraced human existence is to miss his use of the logic of *theosis* to confirm the anti-Pelagianism of the Reformation.

Glorification

For Richard Hooker, glorification is intimately tied to his account of justification and to the sanctification that inevitably accompanies it. The connection, through the faith that is required as much for glorification as for justification, is described in one of the earliest of Hooker's compositions:

> because the last of the graces of God doth so follow the first, that he glorifieth none, but whom he hath justified, nor justifieth any, but whom he hath called to a true, effectual, and lively faith in Christ Jesus, therefore S. *Jude* exhorting us to *build our selves,* mentioneth here expresly only faith, as the thing wherein we must be edified, for that faith is the ground and the glorie of all the welfare of this building.[2]

When Hooker came to write on justification, the surprising Reformation *topos* for his defence for the controversial view that many of our ancestors

137

who lived and died in papist errors were nevertheless participants in God's salvation, he offered a scholastic overview of God's work of grace in the redeemed—work that includes both sanctification and glorification as well as justification:

> There is a glorifyinge righteousnes of men in the Worlde to comme, and there is a justefying and a sanctefyinge righteousnes here. *The righteousnes wherewith we shalbe clothed* in the world to comme, is both perfecte and inherente: that whereby here we are justefied is perfecte but not inherente, that whereby we are sanctified, inherent but not perfecte.[3]

As has been pointed out,[4] in this passage Richard Hooker once again grafted a Reformation confessional branch onto a scholastic tree: in one paragraph, he summarized the Lutheran revolution on the meaning of "justification," he acknowledged the Calvinist refinement on the sanctification that always accompanies justification, and he framed both with the Augustinian account of the continuity between the beginning and continuation of this process and its consummation in blessedness in the world to come.

For Hooker, the sanctification known in this life by the justified is connected in a continuum with the glory to be known in the world to come, and anticipates it. According to the medieval maxim, *grace is the beginning of glory in us*:

> by steppes and degrees they receave the complete measure of all such divine grace, as doth sanctifie and save throughout, till the daie of theire finall exaltation to a state of fellowship in glorie, with him whose pertakers they are now in those thinges that tende to glorie.[5]

In this continuum, the sanctified person will come to the perfection of the angels, who can no longer decline from loving God, but "being rapt with the love of his beauty, they cleave inseparably for ever unto him." This glory by anticipation is the meaning of Jesus' prayer that God's will be done on earth as in heaven:

> our Saviour himselfe being to set downe the perfect *idea* of that which wee are to pray and wish for on earth, [Matthew 6:10] did not teach to pray or wish for more then onely that here it might be with us, as with them it is in heaven.[6]

Theosis *or Divinization*

This bold affirmation accompanied a revival in Hooker of the spirituality of deification or divinization—a pattern well established in the Patristic period both among the Greek authors and in Augustine.[7] Though this idea has occasionally been considered as showing the inherent Pelagianism of Greek Christian spirituality, it actually shows the very opposite: the emphasis in the Greek authors on divinization filled a role very much like that of Augustine's insistence on the need for grace preventing, following, and perfecting human agency. For Gregory of Nyssa, for example, divinization was a doctrine that showed precisely his anti-Pelagian bent: salvation in divinization is so far beyond the power of the human creature that *only* God's aid could make it conceivable, let alone possible.[8]

At first glance, this pattern of deification or *theosis* seems remote from most of the spirituality of the Reformation, which emphasized human solidarity with Adam in sin and the need for *healing* grace. Deification had, in fact, been suggested in certain passages of Calvin,[9] and there has been a recent scholarly debate about the bearing of deification on Calvin's thought.[10]

For his part, Hooker is never in doubt about the grievous consequences of our solidarity with Adam: we "participate Adam" in that we are causally connected with him in a sinful human nature: "Adam is in us as an originall cause of our nature and of that corruption of nature which causeth death."[11]

Hooker could have spoken of a sort of "divinization through creation" since he affirms that all creatures participate in the Trinity as creatures,[12] echoing a pattern of thought from Thomas and Augustine.[13] He usually refrains, however, from using these terms, since our actual condition is one of corruption in our solidarity with Adam. The rational creature indeed desires naturally the bliss of glory, which can be expressed in terms of union with God and sharing the divine life: it cannot achieve it without further aid from God.[14] And Hooker indeed speaks of a *divinization of desire*:

> Moreover, desire tendeth unto union with that it desireth. If then in him we be blessed, it is by force of participation and conjunction with him. Againe, it is not the possession of any good thing can make them happie which have it, unlesse they injoye the thing wherewith they are possessed. Then are we happie therfore when fully we injoy God, as an object wherein the power of our soules are satisfied even with everlasting delight: so that although we be men, yet by being unto God united we live as it were the life of God.[15]

But the creature cannot achieve such union without further aid from God. Such a *natural divinization* would be by desire only, not by effect. Divinization must be a *divinization through grace*.

Habitus *and Created/Uncreated Grace*

A scholastic development that haunted the sixteenth century was summed up in the vocabulary of *habitus* and the related distinction *created/uncreated grace*.[16] The notion of grace in the human being as *habitus* was developed to provide an adequate theology of infant baptism, to describe the grace that is given to an infant who is incapable of deliberately performing the act.[17] Though the idea seems to occur in the latter half of the twelfth century, the term "created grace" and the complementary term "uncreated grace" appeared in the *Summa* of Alexander of Hales, in about 1245. These terms were unknown in Peter Lombard and are not found in Augustine, Peter's major source.

In the thirteenth century, however, both Bonaventure and Thomas made use of the concept of created grace. When the Spirit dwells in the human being, the human being is changed, and the *habitus* results from this indwelling. God is the cause of the *habitus*, which arrives at the very moment God gives himself. The *habitus* is "nothing less than the will of God expressing itself unceasingly within the complex reality of the being of man."[18]

Luther accepted only uncreated grace, rejecting "created grace" as implying a Pelagianism—a capacity in the creature to do good works without the aid of God's grace.[19] Calvin, who revived some aspects of the medieval scholastic account of grace in sanctification, was careful to avoid any suggestion that such grace was a "thing" possessed by the human being, and therefore meritorious. In this, he criticized both Augustine and Thomas.[20] Neither the term "created grace" nor the term "*habitus*" was used by the Council of Trent, though Trent confirmed, with Augustine, that when God crowns our merits, he crowns his own gifts.[21]

Thus Luther had returned to the position of Peter Lombard, and was condemned for doing so. Richard Hooker, in effect, agreed with Luther but found the correct view in Thomas Aquinas, who had been improperly identified as the source of the view now treated as Pelagian. Thomas had used the term *habitus* and had distinguished three senses of grace, a distinction Hooker twice borrowed: grace is first the undeserved love and favour of God Himself toward us; second, it is God's offered means of *outward* instruction; and third, it is the created grace that works *inwardly*.[22]

Hooker rejects a fourth sense of "grace," which he attributes not to Thomas but to "the schoolmen which follow Thomas"—that is, the view that God's grace involves a "formall habite, or inherent qualitie which maketh the person of man acceptable, perfecteth the substance of his minde, and causeth the vertuous actions thereof to be meritorious."[23] Hooker correctly saw that for Thomas, grace is a reality but is not an object.[24]

His point is clearly to agree that faith *as a habitual grace* is given by God simultaneously with the gift of His favour,[25] and this is imparted by degrees, but to reject any merit in the works of the person so justified in that gift of faith itself. This was also Calvin's point.

It is clear that human participation through election to life in Christ— both through Christ's elevating Incarnation and through his saving death— offers to human creatures participation in the whole Christ, including his divinized humanity, and a growth in that participation to the point of divinization or glory of the redeemed human being.

We also, nevertheless, especially through the sacraments, "participate Christ's humanity"; and the creaturely nature, without losing its creature- liness or changing its nature, has been divinized in the Incarnation: "by vertue of this grace man is reallie made God, a creature is exalted above the dignitie of all creatures and hath all creatures els under it."[26]

In fact, it might be said without exaggeration that the whole account that Hooker gives of the gracious work of God in human salvation through human participation in Christ is a gloss on II Peter 1:4, and may even be articulated in Trinitarian form using the language of II Corinthians 13:13:

> Life as all other guiftes and benefites groweth originalie from the father and commeth not to us but by the Sonne, nor by the Sonne to anie of us in particular but through the Spirit. For this cause the Apostle wisheth to the Church of Corinth the grace of our Lord Jesus Christ, and the love of God, and the fellowship of the holie Ghost. Which three St Peter compre- hendeth in one, the *participation of the divine* nature. Wee are therefore in God through Christ eternallie accordinge to that intent and purpose whereby wee were chosen to be made his in this present world before the world it selfe was made, wee are in God through the knowledge which is had of us and the love which is borne towardes us from everlastinge.[27]

Also related to the account of glorification is a relationship between justification and "reward" that distances Hooker further from the sensitiv- ities of the earlier Reformation. It is clear that Hooker remains, to the very end of his life, on the Protestant side because of his insistence on "impu- tation" and because of his acute sensitivities about any *merit* in human action. This, for all that justification and the beginning of sanctification are without regard to anything in the human being other than the gift of faith, does not lead him to deny that glorification is in the form of a reward:

Hee bestoweth now [after sin] eternall life as his owne free and undeserved gifte, together alsoe with that generall inheritance and lott of eternall life, great varieties of rewards proportioned to the verie degrees of those labours, which to performe, he himselfe by his grace inableth.[28]

To Angells and men there was allotted a three fold perfection, a perfection of the end whereunto they might come, eternall life, a perfection of dutie whereby they should come, which dutie was obedience and a perfection of State or qualitie for performance of that dutie. The first was ordained, the second required, and the third given. For presupposing that the will of God did determine to bestowe eternall life in the nature of a reward, and that rewards grow from voluntarie duties, and voluntarie duties from free agents: it followeth, that whose end was æternall life, their state must needes implie freedome and libertie of will.[29]

Both Thomas Rogers and Henry Bullinger had noted scriptural warrant for the view that God *rewards* human beings for good works done after justification with both temporal and eternal rewards.[30] And the homily on fasting, possibly by Archbishop Parker, both denied merit in human works and spoke of rewards greater than these works.[31] But these isolated observations were not incorporated into any larger picture of sanctification and glorification; they seem to have been attempts to come to some terms with the clear references in Scripture to reward. The Council of Trent was, however, far bolder in asserting the Augustinian maxim,[32] and this Tridentine precedent may have had a chilling effect on Hooker. John Donne, in the next century, would fearlessly exploit the language of crowning and works:

The ends crown our works, but thou crown'st our ends,
For at our end begins our endlesse rest.[33]

If so, it did not lead Hooker to silence: in this special sense of "reward," Hooker on at least one occasion was prepared to speak of human "merit." In discussing regular set Christian fasts, Hooker censures those, like Ambrose and Augustine, who have spoken of the *merits* of fasting, but strongly supports the virtues of organized fasts and declines to disagree with the ancient use of the vocabulary of "merit"—provided it is used carefully, and not literally—for such works of satisfaction:

I will not in this place dispute …whether trulie it may not be said that pœnitent both weeping and fasting are meanes to blot out sinne, meanes whereby through Gods unspeakeable and undeserved mercie wee obteine or procure to our selves pardon, which attainment unto anie gracious benefit by him bestowed the phrase of antiquitie useth to expresse by the name of merit.[34]

Hooker was apparently prepared to accept *merit* only in a metaphorical sense, and then only because of its use among early Christian writers. The "rewards" obtained for the quality of earthly life are in no literal sense "merited." The punishments may be. Hooker is prepared to use the word "reward" readily, the word "merit" only reluctantly.

Furthermore, the original plan of God to "determine and bestow eternal life in the nature of a reward" was not abrogated by human disobedience, but the actual sinful state of the human race in history made any simple and literal notion of meriting salvation impossible:

> The beste thinges we do have some what in them to be pardoned, howe then can we do any thinge meritorious and worthy to be rewarded? ... we acknowledg a dutyfull necessitye of doinge well but the meritorious dignitye of well doinge we utterly renounce.[35]

> ... cursed I say, be that man which beleeveth not as the *Church of England,* that without Gods preventing and helping grace, wee are nothing att all able to doe the workes of pietie which are acceptable in his sight.[36]

> The naturall powers and faculties therefore of mans minde are through our native corruption soe weakened and of themselves soe averse from God, that without the influence of his speciall grace, they bring forth nothing in his sight acceptable, noe nott the blossoms or least buds *that tende to the fruit of eternall life.*[37]

> Wee deserve Gods grace noe more then the vessell doeth deserve the water which is putt into it.[38]

As noted elsewhere,[39] for Hooker it remains of the utmost importance that human beings know that salvation for them remains a matter of punishment and reward, as Augustine had insisted. Preaching, for example, is important in giving a knowledge of God, not because right belief is the condition of justification, but because ignorance leads to *iniquity* and knowledge to *virtue:*

> because therefore want of the knowledg of God is the cause of all iniquitie amongst men, as contrariwise the verie ground of all our happines and the seed of whatsoever perfect vertue groweth from us is a right opinion touchinge thinges divine.[40]

In line with this view, Hooker held that the moral duty taught by divine law is necessary to the life to come.[41] This view was objected to in the *Christian Letter*, as compromising the Protestant view of salvation through faith in Christ alone and as obscuring the real motive to morality, "*the glorie of God our Father: his great mercies in Christ: his love to us: example to others,* [and not] that we must do it to merit or to make perfitt that which Christ hath done for us."[42] Hooker's marginal notes reveal by how much he accepted the account of his Protestant predecessors but continued to assert the consistency between this view and the complementary view that final salvation was in the nature of a reward:

> A thing necessarie as you graunt that by good workes we shold seeke gods glory, shew our selves thankfull for his mercyes in Christ, answere his loving kindnes towardes us and give other men good example. If then these things be necessarie unto eternall life and workes necessarily to be done for these ends, how should workes bee but necessary unto the last end seing the next and nerest cannot be attained without them. And is there neither heaven nor hell neither reward nor punishment hereafter to be respected here in the leading of our lives?[43]

Again, in defending the prayer of the *Book of Common Prayer* that prayed for deliverance "from sudden death," Hooker alludes to the relationship between the actions of our life before death and the reward and punishments of everlasting life: "Our good or evell estate after death dependeth most upon the qualitie of our lives."[44]

Similarly, in defending the prayer that we may be delivered "from all adversity," Hooker argues that, in the sense of sin as *crime*, we may be preserved from all sin.[45] Precisely such crimes, which are acknowledged by all men, both Christians and pagans, interrupt the process of justification and sanctification in us, and exclude us not only from the visible church but also from salvation.[46] A *Christian Letter* objected again to this view and wondered if Hooker could possibly mean that Scripture approved the view that such virtues, though taught by the light of reason, were of such necessity "that the wante of them exclude from salvation."[47] Hooker's manuscript note, otherwise a little obscure, refers to his insistence that eternal reward and punishment depend upon the quality of life. To deny this principle would be a great boon to the cruel and the wicked:

> A doctrine which would well have pleased Caligula Nero and such other monsters to heare. Had thapostles taught this it might have advanced them happily to honor. The contrary doctrine [that is, that the quality of a person's life has a bearing on eternal life] hath cost many saincts and martyrs their lives.[48]

Hooker goes on to explain that the works of the heathens are not acceptable, since they are not justified, but that "morall workes done in faith hope and charitie are accepted and rewarded with God," the want of such virtues and the presence of such crimes bringing punishment, both for heathen and for the justified.[49] To deny these rewards and punishments puts the Reformed Christian in the position of the Atheist, whose error is precisely to deny "the joyes of the kingdome of heaven and the endlesse paines of the wicked."[50]

The Value of Theosis

Reference has been made, in passing, to two texts in Hooker that refer directly to divinization or *theosis*, and to others that suggest it. A third will come.[51] The texts come, respectively, from Hooker's treatise in Book I on Reason and Human Law, his treatment of the unity of Christ with the Church and the individual "in this present world," and his treatment of the hypostatic union. All three occurrences are found at important junctures, and all three reinforce important links between the grace of God and Christ in the redeemed, but they do not suggest that the defence of *theosis* itself was an important controversial topic for Hooker. Rather, the assumption is part of his apparatus to deal with grace and Christology.

Hooker's extended christological treatise in Book V ends with a treatment, highly dependent on Thomas Aquinas,[52] of the three "gifts" Christ has received: the gift of eternal generation, the gift of union, and the gift of unction. The second, the "gift of union," which has bestowed supernatural gifts on human nature, is the one most closely linked to the theme of *theosis*, since in participating in Christ's humanity through Christ's church and Christ's sacraments, the creature participates in Christ's divinity, and hence the Trinity itself.[53]

We have suggested that the pursuit of the scholastic account of the relation of sanctification to glorification leads Hooker to speak in similar terms; but the real heart of his account of *theosis* is his treatment of our union with Christ; in salvation, we participate Christ and in so doing are, as it were, assimilated to the triune mystery that comes to dwell in the Church and its members. The human creature never loses its creatureliness; we are never absorbed into God, but through the Incarnation of the Christ of grace, the grace of God transforms the creature and leads the creature to a glory that the creature has not earned, but that brings eternal life, as if a reward. Yet this deification is not a turning of the creature into God, but a taking on of the creature in Christ. The creature remains a creature, dependent on God in all ways; but through the deification of our nature by the indwelling of the divine Word in it, the creature shares God's glory as an associate:

Finalie sith God hath deified our nature, though not by turninge it into him selfe, yeat by makinge it his owne inseparable habitation, wee cannot now conceive how God should without man either exercise divine power or receive the glorie of divine praise. For man is in both an associate of Deitie.[54]

Notes

1   I was Joanne McWilliam's student as a basic degree student, and she helped open my eyes to the meaning of early Christian writers, such as Cyprian and Augustine, who have become the base of my studies. Later I was her colleague as a teacher in the Faculty of Divinity at Trinity and a guest in her reading group.

2   *The Second Sermon Upon Part of S. Jude 14* (Folger Library Edition 5:44.15–21, hereafter FLE). Compare Romans 8:30; in the *ordo salutis,* faith is not mentioned, but justification, which implies faith, is.

3   *A Learned Discourse of Justification, Workes, and How the Foundation of Faith Is Overthrowne ("Justification")* 3 (FLE 5:109.6–11).

4   See David Neelands, "Justification and Richard Hooker the Pastor," in *Lutheran and Anglican: Essays in Honour of Egil Grislis* (Winnipeg: St. John's College, 2009), where this point is made, and where Hooker's general accounts of both justification and sanctification are given, with references to Calvin and Luther. To the end of his life, Hooker continued to treat justification in a way that honoured both the revolution of Martin Luther and the heritage of scholastic theology (Dublin Fragments 16, FLE 4:117–19).

5   *Of the Lawes of Ecclesiasticall Politie* V.56.13 (FLE 2:244.19–23).

6   I.4.1 (FLE 1:70.1–4).

7   G.W.H. Lampe refers to sources in the philosophy of Plato and Plotinos, and examples of the use of the idea in Irenaeus, Origen, Cyril of Alexandria, Gregory of Nyssa, Dionysios, and Maximus among the Greek authors, and in Tertullian, Ambrose, and Augustine among the Latins. Hubert Cunliffe-Jones, ed., *History of Christian Doctrine* (London: Continuum, 2006), 149ff.

8   For Augustine, see Henri Rondet, *The Grace of Christ: A Brief History of the Theology of Grace,* ed. and trans. Tad W. Guzie (Westminster: Newman, 1967), 91–95.

9   "Christ is not outside us but dwells within us. Not only does he cleave to us by an indivisible bond of fellowship, but with wonderful communion, day by day, he grows more and more into one body with us, until he becomes completely one with us." [1545 French version: "in one same substance"] *Institutes* 3.2.24 (I: 569–71). François Wendel, *Calvin: The Origin and Development of His Religious Thought* (London: Collins, 1963), 236f. Calvin addresses 2 Peter 1:4 at least twice in the *Institutes.* "Indeed, Peter declares that believers are called in this to become partakers of the divine nature. How is this? ... If the Lord will share his glory, power and righteousness with the elect—nay, will give himself to be enjoyed by them and, what is more excellent will somehow make them to become one with himself"; *Institutes* 3.25.10 (II:1005). Calvin criticizes Osiander for twisting this text "from the heavenly life to the present state"; the heavenly state is interpreted as becoming "like" God; 3.11.11 (I:737–38).

10 Carl Mosser, "The Greatest Possible Blessing: Calvin and Deification," *Scottish Journal of Theology* 55, no. 1 (2002): 36–57 at 39–40. Jonathan Slater, "Salvation as Participation in the Humanity of the Mediator in Calvin's *Institutes of the Christian Religion:* a Reply to Carl Mosser," *Scottish Journal of Theology* 58, no. 1 (2005): 39–58. Marcus Johnson has offered a mediating view, noting that Calvin can speak of *coniunctionem* in a far more intimate sense than Slater allows, as in *Inst.* 3.11.10; Johnson, "Eating by Believing: Union with Christ in the Soteriology of John Calvin," Ph.D. diss., St. Michael's College, 2007, 111–17, esp. n280.

11 V.56.7 (FLE 2:240.3–4).

12 V.56.55 (FLE 2:236.25–237.25).

13 G.W. Morrel treats *deification* in Anglicanism as *simply* the "Greek patristic influence in so much Anglican thinking," not recognizing it in Augustine and Thomas as well as in the eastern writers. Morrel, "The Systematic Theology of Richard Hooker," Ph.D. diss., Pacific School of Theology, 1967, 60. Others have identified *deification* as implied in John Wesley's re-creation of Anglicanism: "The doctrine of *theosis* is at the foundation of Wesley's Protestantism." Mark Mealey, "Taste and See That the Lord Is Good: John Wesley in the Christian Tradition of Spiritual Sensation," Th.D. diss., Wycliffe College and University of Toronto, 2006, 195.

14 See David Neelands, "Hooker of Scripture, Reason, and 'Tradition,'" in *Richard Hooker and the Construction of Christian Community,* ed. A.S. McGrade (Tempe: Medieval and Renaissance Texts and Studies, 1997), 83–85.

15 I.11.2 (FLE 1:112.13–20).

16 A remarkably lucid treatment of this distinction and the problems it caused is included in the summary of a mid-twentieth-century ecumenical gathering at Chevetogne, translated into English in C. Moeller and G. Phillips, *The Theology of Grace in the Oecumenical Movement,* trans. R.A. Wilson (London: Mowbray, 1961), which has informed this paper and provided most of the citations from medieval and ancient sources.

17 The term *habitus* first appears in Alan of Lille (PL 210.666), rejecting the position of Anselm (*De Conc. Virg.* 29) that baptized infants do not have grace. The germs of the idea, however, were already present in Augustine, who acknowledged that the Holy Spirit indwells baptized infants but denied that this indwelling was yet in actuality. Augustine, *Epistle* 187.6, 21, 26, in *Saint Augustine's Letters,* Vol. 4, trans. Sr. Wilfrid Parsons (Washington: Catholic University of America, 1955), 232–33, 237–38, 241.

18 Moeller and Phillips, *Theology of Grace,* 20.

19 Martin Luther, *Randbemarkung* on SSPL I, dist. 17, *Werke* (Weimar, 1893), 9, 41–42; Moeller and Phillips, *Theology of Grace,* 21; E.L Mascall, *The Openness of Being: Natural Theology Today* (London: Darton, Longman Todd, 1971) [Gifford Lectures 1970–71], 226–67.

20 *Institutes* 3.14.11 (I:778); 3.15.7 (I:794).

21 Moeller and Phillips, *Theology of Grace,* 22; Mascall, *Openness of Being,* 227.

22 *Dublin* 10 (FLE 4:109.7–10 & *g*); *Dublin* 17 (FLE 4:118.22–29). In *Dublin* 2 (FLE 4:103.31–104.3), Hooker uses the distinction inward/outward with respect to grace.

23 *Dublin,* 17 (FLE 4:118.22–29); cf. 10 (FLE 4:109.7–10 & *g*) and 16 (FLE 4:117.4–9). *Summa Theologiae* I–II. q 109, a. 2. Note Hooker's use of the distinction inward/outward at *Dublin* 2 (FLE 4:103.31–104.3).

24 *Summa Theologiae* I–II.110.1; II–II.23.2; Moeller and Phillips, *Theology of Grace,* 19.

25 That sanctification involves an internal *habitual quality* of the soul Hooker had made clear in such passages as "wee participate Christ partelie by imputation, as when those thinges which he did and suffered for us are imputed to us for right-eousnes; partlie by habitual and reall infusion, as when grace is inwardlie bestowed while wee are on earth and afterwardes more fully both our soules and bodies made like unto his in glorie." V.56.11 (FLE 2:243.4–9).

26 V.54.3 (FLE 2:222.21–23).

27 V.56.7 (FLE 2.238.12–23).

28 *Dublin* 31 (FLE 4:141.3–7).

29 *Dublin* 28 (FLE 4:135.30–136.8).

30 Thomas Rogers, *The Catholic Doctrine of the Church of England* (Cambridge, 1854), 117; Henry Bullinger, *Decades* (Cambridge, 1849–52) III, 9 (ii, 320ff), IV, 5 (iii, 204).

31 Homilies, second Book, no. 4: "An Homily of Good Works: And First of Fasting," *The Two Books of Homilies* [ed. John Griffiths, anonymous in original publication] (Oxford, 1859), 279–80.

32 "yet no Christian should ever either rely on or glory in himself, and not in the Lord, whose goodness is all so great that he desires his own gifts to be their mer-its." Council of Trent, session 6, Decree of Justification, 16. See Augustine, *On Grace and Free Will,* 15 (Nicene and Post-Nicene Fathers 1 5.450).

33 Deign at my hands this crown of prayer and praise,
    Weav'd in my low devout melancholy,
    Thou which of good, hast, yea art treasury,
    All changing unchanged Ancient of days,
    But do not, with a vile crown of frail bays,
    Reward my muse's white sincerity,
    But what thy thorny crown gained, that give me,
    A crown of Glory, which doth flower always;
    The ends crown our works, but thou crown'st our ends,
    For at our end begins our endlesse rest,
    The first last end, now zealously possest,
    With a strong sober thirst, my soul attends.
    'Tis time that heart and voice be lifted high,
    Salvation to all that will is nigh.   John Donne, *La Corona*

34 V.72.9 (FLE 2:391.24–392.2). See also *Justification* 21: "the aunciente fathers use merytting for obteyninge and in that sence they of Wittenberge [i.e., Wurtem-berg] have in their confession *we teach that good workes commaunded of god are nec-essarily to be don and that by the free kindnes of god they meytt their certen rewardes*" (FLE 5:130.13–17). Keble goes too far in claiming that Hooker accepts "merit" as a qualification for a supernatural blessing but denies merit as the ground of depend-ence. Keble edition (1888), Editor's Preface, 54 (i, cviii and n2).

35 *Justification* 7 (FLE 5:116.5–11). This text was quoted by the Georges to show Hooker's anti-Pelagianism. This it certainly does. But the Georges fail to take notice of the other part of Hooker's account: Augustine's view that we receive sal-vation finally as a reward. Charles H. and Katherine George, *The Protestant Mind of the English Reformation 1570–1640* (Princeton: Princeton University Press, 1961), 45. Hooker argues that Adam would have received it "as a reward," even though he

would have required grace and could not have achieved it naturally; this character of salvation is not eroded by the actual sinful state of the human race; in some sense salvation remains a reward, and the loss of salvation a punishment.

36 *Dublin* 1 (FLE 4:101.2–6).

37 *Dublin* 2 (FLE 4:103.12–17).

38 *Dublin* 46 (FLE 4:165.18–20). This text was quoted by Malone to contrast the rejection of merit in Hooker and in William Perkins. Malone rightly points out that Hooker emphasizes faith in his rejection of merit, whereas Perkins emphasized the sovereignty of God and predestination. Michael T. Malone, "The Doctrine of Predestination in the Thought of William Perkins and Richard Hooker," *Anglican Theological Review* 52 (1970): 108, 112. As Malone notes, Perkins and Hooker have many points of agreement on the precise doctrines of predestination, as well as differences. But for Hooker, as for Augustine, it is the life of the human being in grace that is emphasized more than the eternal foreknowledge and election of God.

39 Neelands, "Justification."

40 V.18.1 (FLE 2:65.8–12).

41 I.16.7 (FLE 1:141.5–8).

42 *A Christian Letter* 6 (FLE 4:22.8–11).

43 Autograph Notes on *A Christian Letter* 6 (FLE 4: 22.18–23.3). Hooker refers to Augustine's *On Faith and Works* (FLE 4:19.21). The editors suggest Chapters 1 to 14, but especially Chapter 9.

44 V.46.1 (FLE 2:184.5–6).

45 V.48.12 (FLE 2:200.6–11). This distinction between crimes and other sins, and their effect, is an important one, possibly borrowed from Thomas Aquinas, who held that sin was "compatible with virtue," in the sense that mortal sin could coexist with the *habit* of acquired virtue, and venial sin with the *habit* of infused virtue as well. This means that a sinful human being might nonetheless be free from vicious acts, especially serious crimes. *Summa Theologiae* I–II, q. 71, a. 4 (i, 899). See also Hooker's view that heresies and crimes exclude from salvation yet errors and faults do not. III.1.13 (FLE 1:204.30–205.4).

46 III.1.7 (FLE 1:198.4–5).

47 *Christian Letter* 3 (FLE 4:13.24).

48 Autograph Notes to *A Christian Letter* 3 (FLE 4:13.27–14.2).

49 Autograph Notes (FLE 4:14.21–23).

50 V.2.1 (FLE 2:23.15–16).

51 I.11.2 (FLE 1:112.13–20) V.56.7 (FLE 2:238.12–23); V.54.5 (FLE 2:224.14–18).

52 *Summa Theologiae* III.7–8.

53 David Neelands, "Christology and the Sacraments," in *A Companion to Richard Hooker*, ed. Torrance Kirby (Leiden: Brill, 2008), 373.

54 V.54.5 (FLE 2.224:14–18).

9

Logos Ecclesiology Revisited
The Church of the Triune God

✠ ✠ ✠

MICHAEL A. FAHEY, SJ

The Church's "One" Foundation

A popular Latin manual of theology widely used internationally in Catholic seminaries in the mid-twentieth century right up to Vatican II described the founding or institution of the Church—as did many other treatises on the Church—as the achievement of Jesus during his public life culminating at his Crucifixion. The thesis's formulation read: "Christus tradidit Apostolis regendi, docendi et sanctificandi potestatem, cui sese submitterent homines obligavit: unde auctor est societatis hierarchicae quam Ecclesiam appelavit."[1] This articulation of the role of Jesus Christ in the foundational act of the Church was heavily influenced by the Counter-Reformation theologian Robert Bellarmine, who described the Church as a visible, "perfect" society. One of the consequences of this way of describing the founding of the Church as the work of the Incarnate Logos (sometimes referred to as an "incarnationist" description of the Church's origin) is the failure to incorporate the Trinitarian roles that contributed to the new People of God, the community of the faithful. Those influenced by the Christ-centred way of seeing the emergence of the Church often even envisaged Jesus as providing, as it were, a kind of "blueprint ecclesiology." Jesus was seen as having established the structural characteristics of what in fact emerged historically more slowly under the inspiration of the Holy Spirit, such as the ongoing Petrine ministry, the episcopal office, ordination of priests, and so on.[2] Others, in part influenced by the concept of doctrinal "trajectories," considered that some of what was present in the mind of Jesus potentially came to be only gradually, under the inspiration of the Holy Spirit during the gestation period of the Early Church, as the Church grew in wisdom and grace.[3] For some, the intentions of Jesus and the goals of his preaching and miracle working focused on activities in Galilee and Judea. For them, the Church was born at the Crucifixion when blood and water poured forth from the heart of Christ (*nativitas Ecclesiae ex corde Iesu in cruce*).[4] The outpouring of the Holy Spirit at the first Pentecost was seen as more of a subsequent strengthening for an already existent nascent Church but not its moment of foundation. Gradually, however, both because of the writings of ecclesiologists and a closer reading of biblical descriptions about the emergence of the Church, the role of the believer's anointing by the Holy Spirit and the conferral of charisms were stressed. But even then, except in rare instances, the fully Trinitarian nature of the Church's inception (including in particular the role of God the Father) was not explicitly articulated.

The Trinity and the Church

The Trinitarian nature of the Church's origin was never completely obscured even in the late medieval period. As an illustration of this, one can appeal to the passage in the First Meditation of the Second Week in St Ignatius of Loyola's *Spiritual Exercises* (1522–24), where he invites the retreatant to imagine the Blessed Trinity in a kind of joint consultation planning the first stage of the establishment of the Church. "The three Divine Persons, observing the whole surface of the earth covered with men who are all on the road to hell together, decreed from all eternity that the Second Person would assume the nature of man for the salvation of the human race."[5]

When the opening chapter of Vatican II's *Lumen gentium* (LG), the Dogmatic Constitution on the Church (not, however, the rejected draft first offered by the Theological Preparatory Committee), richly highlights the Trinitarian origin of the Church through a plethora of New Testament citations, one detects a dramatic reappropriation of neglected material. The Church is a product of the Trinity, not only the result of the Incarnate Logos (see, *Lumen gentium* nos. 2, 3, and 4). Typical formulations of this new emphasis read as follows: "The eternal Father, in accordance with the utterly free and mysterious design of his wisdom and goodness ... determined to call together in the holy Church those who believe in Christ." "All the just from the time of Adam, 'from Abel, the just one, to the last of the elect,' will be gathered together with the Father in the universal church" (LG no. 2). Moving on from the role of God the Father, the conciliar text continues: "The Son, accordingly, came, sent by the Father, who before the foundation of the world chose us and predestined us in him to be his adopted sons and daughters ... To carry out the will of the Father, Christ inaugurated the kingdom of heaven on earth and revealed his mystery to us ... The Church—that is, the kingdom of Christ already present in mystery—grows visibly in the world through the power of God" (LG no. 3). And finally, rounding off the Trinitarian character of the Church's call to being, the council states: "When the work which the Father gave the Son to do on earth (see Jn 17:4) was completed, the Holy Spirit was sent on the day of Pentecost to sanctify the Church continually, and so that believers might have access to the Father through Christ in the one Spirit (see Eph 2:18)" (LG no. 4). The introduction to the Constitution on the Church concludes with a citation from St Cyprian of Carthage: "Hence the universal Church is seen to be 'a people made one by the unity of the Father, the Son and the Holy Spirit'" (LG no. 4). In short, the Church proceeds from the Trinity: the Father's universal saving plan, the Son's mission, and the Holy Spirit's ongoing sanctifying work.

How is one to explain this distinctive assignment of the Church's emergence to all the Persons of the Triune God? In part it may be due to a closer study of the biblical revelation about the Church's origin, especially the stress on the charismatic gifts of the Holy Spirit to the Church, or it may be due to reaction to the critiques of the Eastern Orthodox Church regarding Western Christianity's "Christomonism" that ultimately results in an inadequate Pneumatology. Catholic ecclesiologist Yves Congar responded to Orthodox objections and in so doing helped eliminate what seemed to be pure Christomonism.[6]

Ecumenical Consensus Statements

In the years following Vatican II, the Trinitarian focus of *Lumen gentium* was taken up and expanded in a variety of bilateral and multilateral ecumenical consensus statements. One recent example is the 2006 Anglican/ Orthodox Cyprus Statement (CS) titled "The Church of the Triune God," which extends to some 100 pages and 281 numbers.[7] The first section is a nuanced articulation of what Christianity confesses regarding the Triune God. The exposition then points to how each Person of the Trinity is involved in the creation of the Church. "It was in response to the revelatory and saving economy of the Blessed Trinity, celebrated and experienced by the Church in the sacraments of baptism and Eucharist, that the Church was led to formulate the doctrine of the Holy Trinity" (CS I, 11). In other words, paradoxically, the articulation about the Trinity emerges from the worship and life of the Church. Some might wonder why, in a document devoted to the Church, the ecumenical participants present a lengthy and heady description of the Triune God. The answer is provided in an early paragraph: "All our theology of the Church presupposes the eternal priority of this mystery of communion in the life of God. If God were not eternally a communion of love, the *koinonia* of believers would not be what it is, a real participation in the divine life, a *theosis*" (CS I, 4). Section II goes on to situate the Logos within the Triune God and then discusses the relationship between Christ and the Holy Spirit. It stresses the need to relate more closely the connection between Christology and Pneumatology. This is not surprising given the fact, as we have noted, that the Christian East claims that the Christian West has marginalized the mission of the Holy Spirit not only in its Eucharistic liturgies but also in theological reflection. At this point the text focuses on humanity and the Church. The Cyprus Statement notes: "Trinitarian theology has as much to say about humanity as about God ... This is why the theology of the Trinity is not a matter of detached speculation" (CS II, 23). It is clear how today serious explanation of the Church's origin surely contains a Trinitarian perspective.

This same kind of Trinitarian emphasis is notable, though more succinctly expressed, in the text of the Faith and Order Commission titled *The Nature and Mission of the Church* (NMC), published at the ninth General Assembly of the World Council of Churches held in Porto Alegre, Brazil, in February 2006.[8] This document is divided into six parts, the first section of which is titled "The Church of the Triune God," comprising twenty-six numbers. Some of the document's segments are especially noteworthy, as when it states: "The Almighty God, who calls the Church into being and unites it to himself through his Word and the Holy Spirit, is the Triune God, Father, Son and Holy Spirit. In its relationship to God the Church is related to each of these divine 'Persons' in a particular way. These particular relations signify different dimensions of the Church's life" (NMC no. 14). "Among scriptural images of the Church, some become particularly prominent, referring to the Trinitarian dimensions of the Church. Among these, the images of the 'people of God' and the 'body of Christ' are particularly important, accompanied by the imagery of 'temple' or 'house' of the Spirit. It must be noted, however, that none of these images is exclusive but all of them implicitly or explicitly include the other Trinitarian dimensions as well" (NMC no. 16).

Further examples of this Trinitarian perspective can be noted in a wide variety of ecumenical consensus statements, as for instance the Reformed/Roman Catholic Consultation's document assessing its discussions from

1984 to 1990, which culminated in a text titled "Toward a Common Understanding of the Church" (TCU).[9] The work of Christ is said to reveal that he is the Son within the Trinity. The consensus statement concludes: "Finally, the work of Jesus, the Son, reveals to us the role of the Spirit of God who is common to him and to the Father: it reveals to us that God is triune" (TCU no. 74).

Similarly, the text of the Methodist/Roman Catholic Consultation "Towards a Statement on the Church" (TSC) that summarized its discussions spanning the years 1982 to 1986: "As the assembly of God's people gathered in Christ by the Holy Spirit, the Church is not a self-appointed, self-initiated community. It originated in the redemptive act of God in Christ, and it lives in union with Christ's death and resurrection, comforted, guided, and empowered by the Holy Spirit" (TSC no. 3).[10]

The Contribution of Theologians

My task in these reflections is to indicate how this emphasis on Trinitarian ecclesiology developed gradually even before Vatican II and how this focus has been further developed by individual theologians.

One of the earliest modern studies stressing the Trinitarian aspect of the Church's foundation was published by Roland de Pury shortly after the Second World War at the Protestant Theological Faculty at Neuchâtel, Switzerland.[11] He brought together the three roles of the Trinity by describing Christ as the foundation of the Church as house of God, the Holy Spirit as its founder, and God the Father as the owner. Pury drew heavily on a variety of New Testament epistles: "Christ was faithful over God's house as a son. And we are [God's] house, if we hold fast our confidence and pride in our hope" (Hebrews 3:6). He also cited Paul's statement: "Do you not know that you are God's temple?" (I Corinthians 3:16). Again: "You are God's field, God's building" (I Corinthians 3:9). And finally, "In [Christ Jesus] you also are built into it for a dwelling place in the Spirit" (Ephesians 2:22). Christ may indeed be the cornerstone of the Church, but it requires a designer and an overseer.[12]

Some forty years later in an adjacent setting along Lake Geneva at the World Council of Churches' Ecumenical Institute at Bossey, Switzerland, an Italian Catholic theologian by the name of Bruno Forte summarized in a lecture—later published in Italian in 1983 and eventually in 1991 in English—ecclesiological developments achieved ecumenically by exegetes and theologians.[13] Drawing upon formulations of Vatican II and later theological contributions, Forte stressed that the Church receives the Holy Spirit through Christ from the Father. He argued that it would be better to refer to the faithful not as "the people of God" but rather, more specifically, as "the people of the Triune God." Forte stressed the disadvantages of a "visibilist" conception of the Church in the pre-Vatican II period, a conception that tended to obscure the mystical, hidden mystery aspect of the origin and nature of the Church. Thus he applauded "the rediscovery of the Trinitarian foundation of the Church, by virtue of which the Trinity is the origin, form and goal of the reality of the Church" (*Church*, 62).

One of the Catholic theologians whom Forte may well have had in mind was Romano Guardini (1885–1968) whose emphasis through his liturgical and doctrinal investigations led him to articulate an ecclesiology strongly Trinitarian in character.[14]

Another contribution to the explicit Trinitarian articulation of the Church's origin was the impact of Orthodox theology, especially the Russian Orthodox theology mediated in Paris through various Russian émigré theologians who settled at the Institute of St. Sergius.[15] Through their dialogue with Catholic theologians (in a common language) the Orthodox promoted a vigorous Pneumatology that awakened Latin Catholics to several neglected aspects of the mission of the Holy Spirit, and ultimately to new perspectives on the Church of the Trinity. In particular, two Orthodox theologians who influenced this development were A.S. Khomiakov (1804–60)[16] and Nicholas Afanasiev (1893–1966).[17] In more recent times, Orthodox ecclesiological perspectives with a Trinitarian emphasis have been mediated through the Romanian Orthodox theologian Dumitru Staniloae.[18]

An unusual phenomenon in recent theological reflections on the Trinity is the connection with non-Catholic sources. Whereas Catholic contributions to this theme have been modest, one of the leading authors on Trinity and its relationship to the Church is the Bosnian-born Evangelical theologian Miroslav Volf, a former student of Joseph Ratzinger (now Pope Benedict XVI), who now teaches as the Henry B. Wright Professor of Theology at Yale University. In his *After Our Likeness: The Church as the Image of the Trinity*, he articulated at considerable length the themes touched upon by Forte regarding the Trinitarian role in the creation of the Church.[19]

Another major contributor to this doctrine is the Finnish Pentecostal ecumenist Veli-Matti Kärkkäinen, Professor of Systematic Theology at Fuller Theological Seminary in Pasadena, California, and Privatdozent of Ecumenics at the University of Helsinki. After a year's sabbatical at the Institute of Cultural and Ecumenical Research, Collegeville, Minnesota, he published a valuable series of books that have pertinence to both Catholics and Pentecostals.[20]

Catholic publications on the Church and Trinity, as has been noted, have been far fewer. Notable exceptions are publications by two women theologians, one Australian (Anne Hunt) and one American (Carmina Magnusen [Chapp]), who have explored these themes.[21]

Conclusion

The benefits of stressing the involvement of the Trinity in the formation of the Church are numerous. Such an emphasis provides a much needed antidote to widespread discouragement and even disillusionment in the face of the Church's sinful and tepid members at a time of growing transparency. If the Church is seen as originating in the hidden and timeless reaches of the Triune God's plan for humanity, then it will surely perdure despite the intransigencies of human beings. This provides a hopeful and reassuring consolation even in a time of unfaithfulness. Linking the two mysteries of Trinity and Church also makes accessible a more profound understanding of the dynamics of the eucharistic liturgy, which consistently, if sometimes obliquely, addresses all three Persons. Ecumenically, this emphasis has unveiled a rich consensus in the understanding of the profound nature of the Church. It also illustrates to those who insist that Vatican II "made no changes" that, on the contrary, the pursuit of *aggiornamento* does eventuate in significant memory recall even at the core of Christian faith.

These reflections regarding a reappropriation of the Trinity's role in the establishment of the Church are dedicated to my late esteemed colleague Professor Joanne McWilliam, whose persistent research favoured the promotion of forgotten teachings. Her special interest was the theology of Augustine of Hippo, and her symposium on that bishop's theology produced a valuable volume titled *Augustine: From Rhetor to Theologian* (1992).[22] Both Joanne and her husband, Peter Slater, were active members of the Princeton-based American Theological Society, for which she served a term as its president. Her theological insights will be sadly missed both there and in the wider academic community.

Notes

1 *Sacrae Theologiae Summa, I: Theologia fundamentalis,* ed. Michaele Nicolau, sj, and Ioachim Salaverri, sj (Madrid: Biblioteca de Autores Christianos, 1958), thesis 3, 542.

2 See Aelred Cody, "The Foundation of the Church: Biblical Criticism for Ecumenical Discussion," *Theological Studies* 34 (1973): 3–18.

3 James M. Robinson and Helmut Koester, eds., *Trajectories Through Early Christianity* (Philadelphia: Fortress, 1971).

4 See the study of the Dutch theologian Sebastian Tromp, sj, *De nativitate Ecclesiae ex Corde Iesu in Cruce* (Rome: Gregorian University, 1932). Karl Rahner's 1936 doctoral dissertation at the University of Innsbruck addressed a similar theme: "E latere Christi: Der Ursprung der Kirche als zweiter Eva aus der Seite Christi des zweiten Adam," newly published in his *Sämtliche Werke*, Vol. 3 (Zurich: Benziger, 1996), 3–84.

5 *Spiritual Exercises*, no. 102. See also Jean Daniélou, "La spiritualité trinitaire de saint Ignace," *Christus* 11 (1956): 354–72.

6 See Yves Congar, "Pneumatologie ou 'Christomonisme' dans la tradition latine," *Ephemerides Theologicae Lovanienses* 45 (1969): 394–416.

7 Anglican-Orthodox Dialogue, *The Church of the Triune God: The Cyprus Statement Agreed by the International Commission for Anglican-Orthodox Theological Dialogue 2006* (London: Anglican Communion Office, 2006). On this text, see my commentary "*The Church of the Triune God*: The Anglican-Orthodox Cyprus Agreed Statement of 2006," in *We Are All Brothers, 3: A Collection of Essays in Honor of Archbishop Vsevelos of Scopelos*, ed. Jack Figel (Fairfax: Eastern Christian Publications, 2008), 209–22.

8 The first draft of the text was *The Nature and Purpose of the Church*. Faith and Order Paper 181 (Geneva: WCC, 1998), which was referred to member churches and others by the 1998 WCC General Assembly at Harare. In the light of responses it received, the Faith and Order Commission published a revised text in 2005, with a new title, *The Nature and Mission of the Church*. Faith and Order Paper 198 (Geneva: WCC, 2005). On this second, revised text, see *Receiving "The Nature and Mission of the Church": Ecclesial Reality and Ecumenical Horizons for the Twenty-First Century*, Ecclesiological Investigations, Vol. 1, eds. Paul M. Collins and Michael A. Fahey (London: T. & T. Clark, 2008).

9 See the text "Toward a Common Understanding of the Church," in *Deepening Communion: International Ecumenical Documents with Roman Catholic Participation*, ed. William Rusch and Jeffrey Gros (Washington: United States Catholic Conference, 1998), 179–229.

10 "Towards a Statement on the Church," in Rusch and Gros, *Deepening Communion*, 235–54.

11 Roland de Pury, *La maison de Dieu: Éléments d'une ecclésiologie trinitaire*, Cahiers théologiques de l'actualité protestante 14 (Neuchâtel: Delachaux et Niestlé, 1946).

12 See Michael A. Fahey, "Christ the Living Stone," *Toronto Journal of Theology* 16 (2000): 63–68.

13 Bruno Forte, *The Church: Icon of the Trinity: A Brief Study*, trans. Robert Paolucci (Boston: St. Paul Books and Media, 1991; Italian original 1983). Hereafter *Church*.

14 See Josef Kreiml, *Die Selbstoffenbarung Gottes in Jesus Christus: Zur Christologie und Ekklesiologie Romano Guardini* (Regensburg: Roderer, 2001). Also, Robert Krieg, *Romano Guardini: A Precursor of Vatican II* (Notre Dame: University of Notre Dame Press, 1997).

15 Alexis Kniazef, *L'Institut Saint-Serge: De l'académie autrefois au rayonnement d'aujourd'hui* (Paris: Beauchesne, 1974).

16 Paul Patrick O'Leary, *The Triune Church: A Study in the Ecclesiology of A.S. Xomjakov* (Fribourg: Editions universitaires, 1982). This theologian's name is usually transcribed as A.S. Khomiakov.

17 Nicholas Afanasiev, *The Church of the Holy Spirit,* trans. Vitaly Permiakov (Notre Dame: University of Notre Dame Press, 2007; posthumous Russian original 1971; French version 1975).

18 See the dissertation on Dumitru Staniloae by Radu Bordeianu, "The Trinitarian Ecclesiology of Dumitru Staniloae and Its Significance for Contemporary Orthodox/Catholic Dialogue," Ph.D. diss., Marquette University, 2006.

19 Miroslav Volf, *After Our Likeness: The Church as the Image of the Trinity* (Grand Rapids: Eerdmans, 1998) esp. Chapter 5: "Trinity and Church," 191–220. See a subsequent volume edited by Miroslav Volf and Michael Welker, *God's Life in Trinity* (Minneapolis: Fortress, 2006).

20 See especially Veli-Matti Kärkkäinen, *The Trinity: Global Perspectives* (Louisville: Westminster John Knox, 2007).

21 Anne Hunt, *The Trinity and the Paschal Mystery: A Development in Recent Catholic Theology* (Collegeville: Liturgical, 1997); also the more specialized analysis based on the theological synthesis of Edward Kilmartin by Carmina Magnusen, *Encounters with the Triune God: An Introduction to the Theology of Edward J. Kilmartin, SJ* (Bethesda: International Scholars, 1998).

22 See my contribution to this publication, "Augustine's Ecclesiology Revisited," in *Augustine: From Rhetor to Theologian,* ed. Joanne McWilliam (Waterloo: Wilfrid Laurier University Press, 1992), 173–81.

PART TWO

Christology and Ethics

10

Deep Christology
Ecological Soundings

✠ ✠ ✠

ELIZABETH A. JOHNSON, CSJ

Then they told what had happened on the road, and how they had
recognized him in the breaking of the bread.   —Luke 24:35

STARTING IN the last quarter of the twentieth century, the rise
of attention to planet Earth, both in wonder at its intricate community of
life and in mounting concern about its devastation at human hands, has
opened a new frontier for theological reflection.[1] The narrow anthropocentric focus that has characterized Western theology since the Reformation
is beginning to broaden to include once again the natural world of which
human beings are the product, in which they are embedded, and for which
they are responsible. This wider scope puts theology back in tune with
major themes of biblical, Patristic, and medieval theology, allowing it to
play melodies about the cosmos that have not been heard for centuries.[2] The
impact of this turn to the heavens and the earth has so far been felt most
keenly in the area of ethics. Questions of economic and social justice as
they affect the environment; the need for sustainable development that
preserves resources to the seventh generation; naming the sins of biocide,
ecocide, and geocide; promoting biophilic virtue while restraining greed
and selfishness: these and similar issues of personal and systemic behaviour are gaining a secure seat at the table of ethical reflection.

Systematic theology, which reflects on the rational, affective, and
practical meanings of Christian symbols, has come more lately to the

conversation. Nevertheless, it has started to probe the elements of belief for their intrinsic impulses which can ground and motivate the moral imperative to care for the earth. To date the lion's share of attention has rightly been focused on the doctrine of creation. Since the whole natural world is created by God, who saw that it was "very good" (Genesis 1:31), nature is more than a mere backdrop for the human drama of sin and redemption, more than simply an instrument for supplying human needs. It is God's beloved evolutionary handiwork, indwelt by the Spirit of life, with an intrinsic value all its own. This faith perspective flows into the mandate that human actions must honour the integrity of creation at every scale. When Pope John Paul II writes that "respect for life and for the dignity of the human person extends to the rest of creation,"[3] it signals a new chapter in the dialogue between creation faith and ethics.

Christianity, of course, encompasses more than belief in the one God who creates the world. It pivots around the life, death, and Resurrection of Jesus of Nazareth, cherished as Emmanuel, God with us. Thus Christology, too, must contribute its own colourful square to the great planetary quilt that we humans need produce to cover the earth with a blanket of care.[4] In this essay I propose to take soundings in this regard, exploring key lines of thinking that connect Christology with ecological ethics in a potentially fruitful way.

A Methodological Question

At the outset I am puzzled by the question of how to proceed. Since the birth of modern biblical scholarship some two centuries ago, scholars have been using the best empirical methods they can hone to explore concrete details of the life of Jesus of Nazareth along with the ways that memories of him were shaped and passed on by the early communities of disciples. By employing classical tools of historical and literary research to place Gospel texts in their contexts, this work has yielded a wealth of insight into the story of Jesus and the origins of Christianity in the specific circumstances of first-century Palestine. One of the powerful results has been the rediscovery of the Jesus of the Synoptic Gospels, read now not primarily in the light of later doctrinal development but in their own historical circumstances. The result is a portrait of Jesus as an eschatological Jewish prophet, sage, and healer in his own time and place, crucified for historically political reasons, and proclaimed to be risen in categories indigenous to Jewish expectations of the end-time.

The results of this Christology "from below," received and interpreted in the Church, have been inestimable. Pastorally, this method has allowed the Gospel to be preached in a way that respects the importance of critical thinking in the lives of contemporary Christian people. Correlating history with faith, Christology "from below" allows a kind of mutual light to be shed back and forth between historical reasoning and the dynamism of faith in people's lives. Here it is not thought in some simplistic way that history "grounds" faith or gives rise to faith, which is always a gracious gift from God. But when received in a faith context, historical Jesus research can indeed strengthen as well as challenge faith, by intelligibly narrating, interpreting, and drawing out the significance of points of belief. Divine presence and action in the world are not so intangible as to leave no discernible historical traces for the mind to follow in the spirit of our age.

But the results are even more wide-ranging than this. By giving us clues that Jesus of Nazareth was one kind of person and not another, that he taught specific things about the compassion of God and not something else, that he engaged in a prophetic ministry and not another, that he called people to one kind of response and not another, Jesus research is providing new imaginative fodder for Christian life and practice in every dimension. What is the mission of the Church, that community of disciples which "is the only real reliquary of Jesus,"[5] called in the Spirit to carry Christ's words and deeds forward in time? What virtues, what patterns of spirituality and ethics, mark a good Christian life? If Jesus belongs to the definition of God, what does his concrete human history reveal about the ineffable shape of divine love? Future historians will note how the renaissance in Jesus studies effected nothing short of a "revolution" in major areas of theology.[6]

One of the most significant breakthroughs has emerged where the Gospel portraits of Jesus are read in situations of gross poverty and violent oppression. There it becomes clear in a whole new way that Jesus' ministry, centred on the coming Kingdom of God, announced in word and deed the divine will for salvation to people whom society had cast out and marginalized as of no account. In parable and beatitude his words announced a reversal of who is first and who is last in the Kingdom of Heaven. In healings, exorcisms, and table companionship so inclusive that it gave scandal, his deeds enacted this love, providing a joyous foretaste of what salvation would entail. In the end, his death by state execution was the price he paid for fidelity to this ministry. The women and men who had accompanied him around Galilee and up to Jerusalem became surprised witnesses of his new presence by the resurrecting power of the God of life. Filled with the Spirit, they and all disciples since then have been called to follow the Way, working for life where it is throttled and gagged amid the changing circumstances of history. For those oppressed, this is nothing short of good news. For the Church, it makes social justice an essential element of its mission.

Here is where I grapple with the question of method, because these gains cannot be allowed to slip from view when the conversation turns to the broader natural world. Yet that danger exists. On the one hand, until recently liberation theologians concerned with the well-being of the poor dealt little if at all with ecological problems. On the other hand, most theologians who dialogue with science and many who address ecological issues focus on the natural world without much attention to the plight of the poor. When the latter deal with Christology, the Incarnation of the Word into earthly flesh takes centre stage. To pursue this, however, one needs to start in heaven and come to earth, which shifts attention away from the concrete challenge of the ministry of Jesus. Is this just a case of Christology "from below" in tension with a Christology "from above"? Or is there a way to keep the Synoptics and John comfortably knitted together in view of the earth and the needs of its many creatures? In writing this essay I attempt to move toward that goal. After discussing the profound ecological implications of the doctrines of Incarnation and Resurrection, I return to the ministerial Jesus seeking the compassionate christic paradigm that would afford a unified vision.

Deep Incarnation

"The Word became flesh and dwelt among us, full of grace and truth" (John 1:14). Making use of an already existing Logos hymn that itself was shaped by the late Jewish Wisdom tradition, the Prologue of John's Gospel proclaims a defining belief of Christian faith. Note that this text speaks not of the Word who existed before creation becoming human, *anthropos*, but rather of the Word becoming flesh, *sarx*, a broader reality. Note, too, that here the flesh is not identified with sinfulness and contrasted with a spiritual mode of being, as in the older *sarx-pneuma* Christology of Paul. Rather, *sarx* in John signifies what is material, perishable, transient—in a word, finite, the opposite of divinity clothed in majesty. All emphasis here is on the entry of the Word into the realm of earthy existence. Put into historical context, the anti-Gnostic tone of this hymn is unmistakable.[7] It protests against the idea that in Christ the Wisdom of God simply made an appearance while remaining untouched by the contamination of matter. Taking the ancient theme of God's dwelling among the people of Israel a step further, it affirms that in a new and saving event the Word *became* flesh, entered into the sphere of the material and mortal to shed light on all from within.

In truth, the configuration of *sarx* that the Word became was precisely human, which explains the strong emphasis on salvation for human beings in most christological reflection. In our day, however, the human race itself is being repositioned as an intrinsic part of the evolutionary network of life on our planet, which in turn is a part of the solar system, which came into being as a later chapter of cosmic history. Tracing how this natural history is shifting the location of anthropology opens a way to broader insight.

The prevailing theory in science today is that everything we know exists comes from a single indecipherable instant. The universe began 13.7 billion years ago when a single numinous speck exploded in what is rather inelegantly called the Big Bang, an outpouring of matter and energy that is still going on. This material expanded according to a precisely calibrated rate, unfurling neither too fast nor too slow. Its lumpy unevenness allowed swirling galaxies to form as gravity pulled particles together and their dense friction ignited the stars. Roughly 5 billion years ago, some of those giant, aging stars died in great supernova explosions that cooked simpler atoms into heavier metals such as carbon, spewing this debris into the cosmos. Following the original pattern of explosion and attraction, some of this cloud of dust and gas reformed and reignited to become our sun, a second-generation star. Some of it coalesced into chunks too small to catch fire, forming the planets of our solar system, including Earth. Then 3 billion years ago, another momentous change took place when the material of this planet so arranged itself that it burst into self-replicating creatures: the advent of life.

Out of the Big Bang the stars; out of the stardust the earth; out of the molecules of the earth, life. They were single-celled creatures at first, for millions of years. Then out of their life and death an advancing tide, fragile but unstoppable: creatures that live in shells, fish, amphibians, insects, flowers, birds, reptiles, and mammals, among whom have recently emerged human beings, we primates whose brains are so richly textured that we experience self-reflective consciousness and freedom—in classical terms, mind and will. As this story of the universe makes clear, everything is connected with everything else; nothing conceivable is isolated. What makes our blood red? Scientist and theologian Arthur Peacocke explains: "Every atom of iron in our blood would not be there had it not been produced in some galactic explosion billions of years ago and eventually condensed to form the iron in the crust of the earth from which we have emerged."[8] Quite literally, human beings are made of stardust. Furthermore, the story of life's evolution makes evident that we share with all other living creatures on our planet a common genetic ancestry. Bacteria, pine trees, blueberries, horses, the great grey whales—we are all genetic kin in the great community of life.

Repositioning the human phenomenon with regard to its historical, ongoing relationship to planetary and cosmic matter has far-reaching implications. It rearranges the landscape of our imagination to know that human connection to nature is so deep that we cannot properly define our identity without including the whole great sweep of cosmic evolution. Biologically, too, the common ancestry of humans and the rest of life in the original cells and our subsequent adaptive interactions make clear that humans do not stand alone. We evolved relationally; we exist symbiotically; our existence depends on interaction with the rest of the natural world.

This contemporary scientific perspective that so carefully repositions the human race has been further undergirded by philosophy. A dualistic philosophy that assesses spirit and matter as separate and opposed elements; a spiritual Platonism that looks upon matter as dark, chaotic, and anti-divine; or a materialism that reduces all consciousness to its physical substratum: none of these will do. But a philosophy that envisions spirit and matter as one in origin, history, and goal makes room for the scientific story as part of its own self-understanding. As detailed by Karl Rahner, the origin and the goal are the creative and recreative acts of the God of life at the beginning and end of time. The history comes about because the Creator imbues matter with the capacity for essential self-transcendence, which allows it to emerge again and again into radically new forms. Matter, zesty with self-transcendence, evolves to life, then to consciousness (animals), then to spirit (self-reflective consciousness in humans). Empowered by the uncategorizable dynamism of divine being, nature has in recent times emerged into a species that is self-aware and deliberately purposive. Human thought and love, we learn, are not something injected into the universe from without, but are the flowering in us of deeply cosmic energies. In the human species nature itself becomes not only conscious but open to fulfillment in grace and glory. In their inspirited corporeality, in turn, human beings are an element of the cosmos, taken from the ground (Genesis 2:7), never to be isolated from it.[9]

Repositioning anthropology along these lines provides the condition to rethink the scope and significance of the Incarnation in an ecological direction.

"The statement of God's *Incarnation*—of his becoming *material*—is the most basic statement of Christology,"[10] asserts Rahner bluntly. If so, the flesh that the Wisdom of God became as a human being is part of the vast body of the cosmos. The phrase "deep incarnation," coined by Niels Gregersen, is starting to be used in Christology to signify this radical divine reach into the very tissue of biological existence and the wider system of nature.[11] In becoming flesh the Wisdom of God lays hold of matter in the form of a human being, a species in which matter has become conscious of itself. This matter is part of the history of the cosmos, not detachable from the unity of the world. "Born of a woman and the Hebrew gene pool,"[12] the Word's embodied self became a creature of the earth, a complex unit of minerals and fluids, an item in the carbon, oxygen, and nitrogen cycles, a moment in the biological evolution of this planet. The atoms comprising Jesus' body were once part of other creatures. The genetic structure of the cells in his body was kin to the grasses, the fish, the whole community of life that descended from common ancestors in the ancient seas. Like all human beings, Jesus carried within himself "the signature of the supernovas and the geology and life history of the Earth."[13] The *sarx* of John 1:14 thus reaches beyond Jesus and beyond all other human beings to encompass the whole biological world of living creatures and the cosmic dust of which they are composed.

This framework has theologically staggering implications. For theology of God, the incarnation entails something not at all self-evident for monotheistic belief. Here the transcendent God who creates the world *ex nihilo* chooses to join that world in the flesh so that it becomes a part of God's own divine history. It is instructive to watch Rahner wax eloquent against the cryptic, erroneous idea that Jesus' human nature was no more than a disguise, a suit of clothes that could be shrugged off, a puppet pulled by divine strings, livery donned while a certain job is being done, a masquerade in borrowed plumes, an exterior material wrapped around his core.[14] To the contrary, by becoming incarnate, Holy Mystery acquires a genuine time, a life story, a death, and does so as a participant in the history of the cosmos. Hence, "the climax of salvation history is not the detachment from earth of the human being as spirit in order to come to God, but the descending and irreversible entrance of God into the world, the coming of the divine Logos in the flesh, the taking on of matter so that it itself becomes a permanent reality of God."[15] Becoming part of the material world allows the living God to be graciously present in a profound way not otherwise possible.

Conversely, the matter that the Word became, in all its finitude and perishing, is fundamentally blessed. Praising Christ for "the simple concrete act of your redemptive immersion in matter," Teilhard de Chardin expresses this insight in his famous lyrical *Hymn to Matter*, harsh, perilous, mighty, universal, impenetrable, and mortal though this material stuff be: "I acclaim you as the divine *milieu*, charged with creative power, as the ocean stirred by the Spirit, as the clay moulded and infused with life by the incarnate Word."[16] Rather than being a barrier that distances the divine, the matter of this world can function as a mediation to the immediacy of God. Hence it is by carrying out their creative responsibilities in and through the world, not by fleeing it, that human beings set out on the road to redemption.

These reflections flow clearly toward significant ecological implications. "Deep" interpretation understands John 1:14 to be saying that the Word of God entered into solidarity not only with all humanity but also with the whole biophysical world of which human beings are a part and on which their existence depends. Hence the Incarnation, a densely specific expression of the love of God already poured out in creation, confers dignity on the whole of earthly reality in its corporal and material dimensions, and on the cosmos in which the earth dynamically exists. The logic of this dignity leads in a clear direction. In place of spiritual contempt for matter, we ally ourselves with the living God in loving matter. In place of exclusively anthropological concern, we see that non-human creatures are also worthy of moral consideration. In place of granting nature secondary value because God became "human," we embrace the whole of nature, which evolves and sustains all creatures, humankind and the incarnate Word included. In the face of ecological wastefulness, we name wanton pollution, profligate consumption, and human-induced extinctions nothing less than grievous sins. The great universe is embodied in us, and we are its interiority, "stardust, earth stuff, beings literally conceived in far-off parts of the universe and seeded here on this planet to make a difference to the cosmos, to strike a chord, play a variation on the great themes of its music that has never been heard before."[17] How tragic when that music shatters and destroys the flesh that the Word became.

Deep Resurrection

When the noted American naturalist John Muir came across a dead bear in Yosemite, he bitterly complained about those whose belief had no room in heaven for such a noble creature: "Not content with taking all of earth, they also claim the celestial country as the only ones who possess the kinds of souls for which that imponderable empire was planned." But, he figured, God's "charity is broad enough for bears."[18] What is the status of the natural world in view of hope for redemption, and how does this affect ecological ethics? A narrowly anthropocentric theology answers this question in a way that would earn Muir's scorn. Only those with rational, immortal souls are eligible to go to heaven. Consequently, while human beings are called to be good stewards of creation, their neglect or abuse of the natural world does not raise too many eyebrows. Since nature is not redeemable, it does not have lasting worth. To the contrary, a "deep" reading of the Resurrection of Jesus Christ sees that the whole cosmos is destined for redemption, which adds another pull for care of the earth to the christological narrative.

Thanks to its original context in Jewish eschatological expectation, the proclamation that Jesus is risen from the dead has always connoted corporeality as an essential element. Far from the Greek dualism that envisioned the human being as composed of separable body and soul, Hebrew anthropology knew only of the body-person, dust of the earth and breath of God in unbreakable unity. The full-bodied reality of the Resurrection of Jesus Christ is the necessary correlate. It is not his soul alone that is saved from death, but his whole body-person-self. As Rahner observes, in the Incarnation the divine Logos became material, and in the consummation of his finite reality he does not strip off this materiality but retains it eternally.[19] The resurrection of the *body*, therefore, is indigenous to this central christological belief.

What this means in the concrete is not seriously imaginable to we who still live within the time-space grid of our known universe. It certainly does not mean that Jesus' corpse was resuscitated to resume life in our present state of biological existence, along the lines of the Lazarus story. Such naive physicality, presented in stained glass windows and Easter sermons, pervades popular thinking, but it does not bear up to critical scrutiny. Yet the Resurrection does have much to do with physicality. The empty tomb stands as a historical marker for the love of God, which is stronger than death and which acts with a power that reaches into biological existence itself. Theology tends to use the language of transformation for this event, but as Anthony Kelly observes, "the problem with transformation is that we cannot imagine what it means before it happens."[20] As a seed is unrecognizable in the mature plant into which it sprouts; as solar and astral bodies differ significantly from terrestrial bodies; as that which is perishable becomes inconceivably imperishable; as a creature of dust comes to bear the image of heaven; as those who are asleep in the grave suddenly become startlingly awake,[21] so too life in the eternal embrace of God is unimaginable. The angel, a streak of lightning in the tomb, says simply, "he has been raised" (Matthew 28:6).

For Jesus, this means the abiding, redeemed validity of his human historical existence in God's presence forever.[22] The joy that breaks out at Easter is also based on the realization that his destiny is not meant for him alone but for the whole human race. The risen Christ, "firstborn of the dead" (Colossians 1:18), signals the blessed future awaiting all who go down into the grave. As when at harvest time the first grapes to be gathered point to the abundance to follow, Christ, "the first fruits of those who have fallen asleep" (I Corinthians 15:20) gives assurance to those of us still hanging on the vine. In view of the solidarity of the human race, his destiny means that our hope does not merely clutch at a possibility but stands on an irrevocable ground of what has already transpired in him. Anthropologically, this means that for human beings salvation is not escape of the human spirit from an existence embedded in matter, but resurrection of the body, the whole body-person, dust and breath together.

"Deep" resurrection pushes interpretation beyond its human scope to include a future for the whole natural world. "In Christ's resurrection the earth itself arose,"[23] declared Ambrose of Milan, and this insight provides a crucial linchpin for ecological care. The reasoning runs like this. If this person, Jesus of Nazareth, composed of star stuff and earth stuff, whose life was a genuine part of the historical and biological community of Earth, whose body existed in a network of relationships extending to the whole physical universe, if such "a piece of this world, real to the core"[24] at death surrendered his life in love to the living God and is now forever with God in glory, this signals embryonically the redemption not just of other human beings but of the whole creation. The whole natural world, all of matter in its endless permutations, will not be left behind or rejected but will likewise be transfigured by the resurrecting action of the Creator Spirit.

Theologians point out that were this not the case, if God simply created the world, valued it for a time, and then let it be annihilated, we would face a moral crisis: God as Creator would fail the test of love, which desires life abundant for the beloved. So one might conclude from creation alone that there is more ahead. But the Resurrection narrative bruits this beyond mere implication. Starting with a humiliated body laid in a tomb, it tells of the creative power of divine love "triumphing over the crucifying power of evil and the burying power of death."[25] The tomb's emptiness signals the cosmic realism of God's transforming action: Christ is not only firstborn of the dead but also "firstborn of all creation" (Colossians 1:15). In a beautiful synergy of visual and verbal poetry, the Roman Catholic liturgy of the Easter Vigil symbolizes this with cosmic and earthy symbols of light and dark, new fire, flowers and greens, water and oil, bread and wine. The

Exsultet, sung once a year on this night, shouts: "Exult, all creation, around God's throne," for Jesus Christ is risen! The proclamation continues:

> Rejoice, O earth, in shining splendor,
> radiant in the brightness of your King!
> Christ has conquered! Glory fills you!
> Darkness vanishes forever!

The risen Christ embodies the ultimate hope of the earth and all creation. The final transformation of history is the salvation of everything, even of matter, even of bodily life, even of the whole cosmos, into the mystery of God.

As with the Resurrection of Jesus and all the human dead, cosmic redemption is neither imaginable nor empirically verifiable. But it stems from the logic of faith in God who creates and indwells the world, embraces it in Incarnation, and loves and values the whole evolving shebang. The Resurrection unveils yet another dimension of divine relationship to the world, making clear that ultimately divine purpose is cosmocentric and biocentric, not merely anthropocentric. In its light, hope of salvation for sinful, mortal human beings expands to becomes a cosmic hope, a shared hope.

Broadening the circle of redemption to include the natural world sets ethics strongly on the road to moral concern for "otherkind" (all the living creatures with whom humans share this planet) and for the life-sustaining systems of water, land, and air that sustain us all. We need to work, personally and as a matter of public policy, for the well-being and fulfillment of all our neighbours in creation, all of whom are destined for salvation into the mystery of God.

One way to forge an intelligible connection between this hope and ecological ethics has been pioneered by John Haught, whose argument incorporates the scientific story of the universe itself. The long sweep of cosmic history and the evolution of life on our planet reveal, when you think about it, that from its explosive beginning the universe has been filled with promise. As its own natural processes have worked out, more has continuously come from less: more organized forms, with more beauty and capacity for action. In a very real way the cosmos has been seeded with expectation, pregnant with surprise. Its story has been one of restless adventure, ever on the go, experimenting with this and that as it keeps giving birth to the new, bringing forth things never seen before. Undergirding this wild, ambiguous, transient, and exciting undertaking is the Spirit of God, the power of the future, who continually creates the world by empowering the world to make itself. And the process is not finished yet. Since nature carries the future within itself, positively glows with it, human action that aborts nature's possibilities by wreaking harm on ecosystems is nothing less than a profound violation. It shortchanges nature's promise, killing off what might yet be. In so doing, "such negligence amounts to a frustration of God's own creative envisagement of the future of this vast universe."[26] In view of the divine will to create and save an entire complex *universe*, our ethics must be shaped by a growing sense of being forever a part of it and its still developing promise. In accord with the promise that embraces all reality and that is glimpsed most explicitly in Christ's resurrection, we find an ever deepening solidarity with the entire universe and its future in God.

The Christic Paradigm Writ Large

As the above reflections show, theology that explores the deep significance of Incarnation and Resurrection beyond their anthropological meaning can add specific Christian insight to the value of the natural world and motivation for its care. This in itself would be a good contribution. But it would be a shame if this line of reflection went forward without reference to the Jesus of the Gospels and the oceans of scholarship that have flowed around his ministry and death in the last half-century. The narrative of the historical Jesus is suited to the spiritual temper of this age and has the capacity to capture the imagination of contemporary people. In addition, it has energized liberating practices for justice and peace that ecological concerns can ill afford to do without. How to forge a strong link between Christology focused on the earthly Jesus of Nazareth and Christology focused on the cosmic Christ?

One tool that serves to forge this link is the concept of the "christic paradigm" developed by Sallie McFague. Drawn from the Gospel story of Jesus, this paradigm is shaped by his ministry, with its preaching of the reign of God and the embodiment of the Kingdom's approach in his compassionate love, all the way to the cross. Faithful to its roots, the paradigm keeps firmly in view that as far as the living God is concerned, "liberating, healing, and inclusive love is the meaning of it all."[27] Consequently, concern for all those who suffer, and in particular for the millions of the earth's poor people deprived of life's necessities, must characterize Church teaching, theology, and spirituality. Since social systems are a form of embodiment, being structural extensions of the decisions of human persons and thus sharing in human sin and grace, the divine intention expressed through Jesus achieves a certain fullness only to the degree that social systems themselves (political, economic, cultural) embody inclusive love for the most disregarded.[28]

Upon reflection it becomes apparent that the importance of bodily physicality is intrinsic to this paradigm. Jesus' healing practices placed people's physical suffering at the centre of importance; he engaged his own spittle and warm touch to convey health. And how he fed people! Large numbers on hillsides and smaller groups in homes where he was generous host and table companion knew and appreciated his concern for their bodily needs. His orientation to earthiness did not stop there but pervaded his preaching as well. Set within an agrarian culture, his parables are salted with reference to seeds and vineyards, plowing and harvesting, lost sheep, rain, and sunsets, even to the point where he did not hesitate to speak movingly of God's care for the wildflowers and sparrows. Citing Isaiah, he proclaimed, along with good news for the poor and freedom for the oppressed, a year of favour from the Lord, this last evoking the covenant tradition of sabbath year and Jubilee when the land was allowed to rest and recharge (Luke 4:18–19). The reign of God about which his ministry pivots is all-inclusive and, in the prophetic spirit of the lion lying down with the lamb, promotes reverence for all creatures. With ecological awareness, we observe the christic paradigm take on physical, ecological dimensions.

The scientific story of cosmic expansion and the evolution of life on earth already underscores the radical interrelatedness of all things. Interpreting this natural world through the lens of the christic paradigm allows for the claim that the direction of creation itself is toward inclusive, healing love for all. *Write the signature of this christic paradigm, drawn from Gospel mercy, across the cosmos.* Then Incarnation underscores the dignity of what is physical, for bodies matter to God: all bodies, not only those beautiful and full of life but also those damaged, violated, starving, dying, bodies of humankind and otherkind alike. Then Resurrection grounds the promise of fulfillment of all the bodies in creation, not only those that succeed in their time but also those that are disparaged, judged unimportant or unacceptable, broken, pushed into extinction. Then the ethical implication of this dynamic inscription brings social justice and the integrity of creation into a tight embrace.

Since divine love embraces all, especially the needy and outcast, this includes the planet itself, its many different ecosystems and the creatures that inhabit them. If nature be the new poor, then solidarity with the poor and the option for their flourishing extend to encompass the earth itself and its distressed myriads of creatures. In the ecological ethic that results, Jesus' great command to love your neighbour as yourself extends to include all members of the earth community. "Who is my neighbor?" asks Brian Patrick. He answers: "The Samaritan? The outcast? The enemy? Yes, yes, of course. But it is also the whale, the dolphin, and the rain forest. Our neighbor is the entire community of life, the entire universe. We must love it all as our very self."[29] If liberating, healing, and inclusive love is the meaning of it all, Jesus' inclusive compassion for the unincluded embraces all of nature, all that share the evolutionary web of life on this planet.

As theology takes steps to expand its vision of justice and mercy in this ecological direction, the well-being of the outcast human poor must also be reframed as more than simply a social good to be struggled for. In an original argument, liberation theologian Juan Luis Segundo shows how this is thinkable by connecting social justice with the divine goal for the evolution of the earth itself. Central to Jesus' mission, he writes, was preaching the good news of the reign of God with its central reality of divine love. Integral to this message is the surprisingly inclusive character of this love, bent especially over poor and marginalized people. This message and the struggle to embody it historically receive an absolute value through the Resurrection of Jesus, which validates his person and mission. It becomes clear that plenitude of life for all, including the poor, is God's original and ultimate intent in creating the world. The particular material content of Jesus' ministry—in other words, his proclaiming the kingdom of God in word and deed—manifests the ultimate divine purpose that gives order and direction to the world, not just to a slice of the world but to the whole world in its evolutionary history. Those who believe in Christ make a wager that love as Jesus enfleshed it is ultimately worthwhile; it is the meaning encoded at the heart of the universe itself. In the light of this conviction, disciples can risk the struggle for life in a world where death due to entrenched poverty and violent injustice are a daily possibility for millions. In doing so they, the community of the Church, are working in history to enflesh the Kingdom of God, thereby moving evolution in the direction passionately desired by divine intent. Thus, "the integration of the poor into a humanizing web of social and global interconnectedness is crucial to the progress of planetary evolution."[30] It tips the balance to grace, spirit, life. Such concern is inherent in the evolutionary intent of God as revealed in the life and preaching of Jesus Christ.

Inscribing the christic paradigm across the natural world gives nature religious importance while giving social justice global scope and urgent evolutionary significance. Action for justice for the earth and all its poor is faith's appropriate response. The benefit for ecological theology is that insights about the sacredness of matter drawn from Incarnation and Resurrection, which tend to be rightly mystical and beautiful, remain tethered to a historical point in time and space, to the life and death of Jesus of Nazareth, to suffering and desperate need, to practical and critical effect.

Conclusion

In a well-known parable told by Teilhard de Chardin, the human race is on a ship moving through an uncharted sea. For millennia, human beings lived in the hold of the ship, unaware of the larger evolutionary processes moving the boat. Now the passengers have come on deck, where they see a tiller, navigational instruments, charts. They have crossed a threshold. To an important degree, human beings are now able to speculate on the direction of the evolutionary process and even to drive the ship toward a conscious goal. Will they act responsibly and steer in a goodly direction? Or will they crash the ship onto the rocks?[31]

Christology has a great deal to contribute to a flourishing outcome, if it too comes up onto the deck. There is much more richness to be explored than this essay has covered. The ecological significance of the cross is one such area. No exception to perhaps the only ironclad rule in all of nature, Jesus died, his life ending in a spasm of state violence. Contemporary theology is rich in reflections on the power of this death to disclose the self-emptying, compassionate nature of divine love that suffers with the agony of the human race. Ecological theology goes deeper in connecting divine suffering with the natural world, making the case that the living God bears the cost of new life through endless millennia of evolution, from the extinction of species to every sparrow that falls to the ground.[32] To be in solidarity with divine care amid creation's groaning (Romans 8:22), believers must enter the list of those who act compassionately for ecological well-being, enduring the suffering this entails. Another avenue that joins the highest of orthodox doctrine with care for the whole creation is Wisdom Christology, found very early in the New Testament. Its connection between the crucified, earthly Jesus and the divine figure of Sophia through whom all things are created moved early Christian reflection in an irreversibly cosmic direction. The redemption themes in the Hebrew Bible that shaped the christological titles of Messiah, Son of David, and Son of God are yet a third source. The long-desired king was expected to bring peace and prosperity to the people, which good could not be separated from the flourishing of their land and animals and trees. There are no doubt more christological tropes awaiting exploration. The soundings in this essay make clear that the traditional anthropological focus of Christology does not exhaust its potential. Interpreted with an eye toward the wonder and distress of the natural world as we know it today, the meaning of Jesus Christ provides rich resources for an ecological ethic. Theologians owe this buzzing, blooming, bleeding world no less.

Notes

1   This essay is dedicated to the memory of Joanne McWilliam, first woman president of the American Theological Society, for whom I have the greatest respect and admiration. *Vivit!*

2   Details in Dieter Hessel and Rosemary Radford Ruether, eds., *Christianity and Ecology* (Cambridge: Harvard University Press, 2000), 3–21. Harvard University ran a series of ten international conferences on world religions and ecology, each of which issued a volume such as the above: *Islam and Ecology, Hinduism and Ecology,* and so on—excellent resources.

3   John Paul II, "The Ecological Crisis: A Common Responsibility," in Drew Christiansen and Walter Grazer, eds., *And God Saw That It Was Good: Catholic Theology and the Environment* (Washington: United States Catholic Conference, 1996), 215–22 at 222. For key statements by Christian and Jewish leaders, consult the National Religious Partnership for the Environment at http://www.nrpe.org.

4   The metaphor is from Sallie McFague, "An Earthly Theological Agenda," in *Ecofeminism and the Sacred,* ed. Carol Adams (New York: Continuum, 1993), 84–98 at 89.

5   Edward Schillebeeckx, *Christ: The Experience of Jesus as Lord* (New York: Seabury, 1980), 641.

6   The claim to revolution is made by Walter Kasper, Jürgen Moltmann, Hans Küng, Jon Sobrino, and Leander Keck, among others; see Elizabeth Johnson, "The Word Was Made Flesh and Dwelt Among Us: The Impact of Jesus Research on Christian Faith," in *Jesus: A Colloquium in the Holy Land,* ed. Doris Donnelly (New York: Continuum, 2001), 146–66.

7   Commentary on the prologue by Rudolf Schnackenberg, *The Gospel According to John* (New York: Herder and Herder, 1968), 225–65.

8   Arthur Peacocke, "Theology and Science Today," in *Cosmos as Creation,* ed. Ted Peters (Nashville: Abingdon, 1989), 28–43 at 32.

9   Karl Rahner, "The Unity of Spirit and Matter in the Christian Understanding of Faith," *Theological Investigations* VI (New York: Crossroad, 1982), 153–77 at 172. See in that volume his "The Secret of Life," 141–52.

10   Karl Rahner, "Christology Within an Evolutionary View of the World," *Theological Investigations* V (New York: Seabury, 1975), 157–92 at 176–77.

11   Niels Gregersen, "The Cross of Christ in an Evolutionary World," *Dialog: A Journal of Theology* 40 (2001): 192–207 at 205; see also Denis Edwards, *Ecology at the Heart of Faith* (Maryknoll: Orbis, 2006), 58–60.

12   David Toolan, *At Home in the Cosmos* (Maryknoll: Orbis, 2003), 206.

13   Sean McDonagh, *To Care for the Earth* (Santa Fe: Bear, 1986), 118–19.

14   Karl Rahner, "On the Theology of the Incarnation," *Theological Investigations* IV (New York: Seabury, 1974), 105–120 at 116, 118, and passim.

15   Rahner, "The Unity of Spirit and Matter," 160; emended for inclusivity.

16   Teilhard de Chardin, *Hymn of the Universe* (New York: Harper and Row, 1961), 70.

17 Toolan, *At Home in the Cosmos,* 214.

18 Cited in James Nash, *Loving Nature: Ecological Integrity and Christian Responsibility* (Nashville: Abingdon, 1991), 124.

19 Rahner, "The Unity of Spirit and Matter," 170.

20 Anthony Kelly, *Eschatology and Hope* (Maryknoll: Orbis, 2006), 85.

21 Paul piles on these metaphors in 1 Corinthians 15, exasperated at questions about the resurrected body.

22 Karl Rahner, *Foundations of Christian Faith* (New York: Seabury, 1978), 266.

23 *De excessu fratris sui,* bk. 1, in *Patrologiae Latina* 16:1354; cited in Kelly, *Eschatology and Hope,* 177.

25 Rahner, "Dogmatic Questions on Easter," *Theological Investigations* IV: 121–33 at 128.

25 Kelly, *Eschatology and Hope,* 94.

26 John Haught, "Ecology and Eschatology," in Christiansen and Grazer, *And God Saw That It Was Good,* 47–64 at 60.

27 Sallie McFague, *The Body of God: An Ecological Theology* (Minneapolis: Fortress, 1993), 161.

28 Thomas Clarke, ed., *Above Every Name: The Lordship of Christ and Social Systems* (New York: Paulist, 1980), 5–6 and passim.

29 Brian Patrick, cited in Michael Dowd, *Earthspirit* (Mystic: Twenty-Third, 1991), 40; see also Anne Clifford, "Toward an Ecological Theology of God," in Christiansen and Grazer, *And God Saw That It Was Good,* 19–46 at 34–36.

30 Here I am indebted to my student Miguel Lambino, SJ, and the insights in his doctoral dissertation, "The Liberationist Influence in the Evolutionary Christology of Juan Luis Segundo," Fordham University, 2000. See Juan Luis Segundo, *An Evolutionary Approach to Jesus of Nazareth* (Maryknoll: Orbis, 1988).

31 Teilhard de Chardin, *Activation of Energy* (New York: Harcourt Brace Jovanovich, 1971), 73–74.

32 Arthur Peacocke, "The Cost of New Life," in *The Work of Love: Creation as Kenosis,* ed. John Polkinghorne (Grand Rapids: Eerdmans, 2001), 21–42.

11
Neither Male nor Female
Christology beyond Dimorphism

✝ ✝ ✝

PAMELA DICKEY YOUNG

I AM DELIGHTED to be asked to write about Christology in a volume for Joanne McWilliam. The fact that Joanne's theological views often differed from mine never meant that she was any less supportive of me as a person and as a scholar. I greatly appreciated her wisdom and her wry sense of humour in questioning ideas. I don't expect she would agree with the position developed in this chapter, but I do know we would have had a good discussion about it, and I regret that this discussion will never take place.

From the beginnings of second-wave feminist Christian theology, the maleness of Jesus was treated as an issue, and rightly so. The maleness of Jesus was used to justify and subordinate. That Jesus was male somehow meant singling out maleness as better than femaleness. Women could not be ordained because they did not model the body of Jesus down to its penis. Some churches claimed this not only as a man-made rule, but also as a divine sanction, for after all, God had chosen to become incarnate in a male, not in a female. Maleness was not only next to godliness but also itself the Incarnation of God. Therefore, maleness was the superior form of humanity and femaleness never quite attained normative status. Feminists saw the maleness of Jesus as a problem that had to be discussed.

Now of course, this is not the whole story, and feminists in the 1980s and into the 1990s who saw something in the Christian tradition beyond its apparent sexism sought in a variety of ways to answer Rosemary

Ruether's question: "Can a male savior save women?"[1] Feminists who stayed in the Christian tradition sought a Christology beyond patriarchy, a Christology in which the maleness of Jesus was incidental rather than essential to the whole project. While those who left the tradition, or who could not find anything useful within it, understood the maleness of Jesus as more than a stumbling block—indeed, as a massive roadblock—those who stayed downplayed Jesus' maleness. The maleness of Jesus was a stubborn fact, but it was not all there was to say about Jesus. And so we took refuge in finding the meaning of Jesus beyond or outside of his maleness.

In this chapter I will return once more to the maleness of Jesus. Through the use of a theoretical lens informed by feminist and queer theories, I will read the maleness of Jesus not just as a useful tool for patriarchy but as the creation of patriarchy precisely to enforce a social structure of superordination and subordination. Maleness and femaleness are not so much stubborn facts as they are a way of thinking about the world. As I will argue below, the moment one accepts this sexual bifurcation or dimorphism as a given, not as a construction, a whole system of superiors and subordinates falls into place, whether we find that desirable or problematic and whether we seek to argue against that system or not.[2]

Questioning Sexual Dimorphism

It has become an accepted part of the study of much Christian theology today to question the gender roles into which religious traditions often slot males and females and to criticize the ways in which those gender roles inscribe certain attitudes toward people on the basis of maleness and femaleness. We tend to see gender roles as social fabrications rather than as inherently given. We do not, for the most part, question our assumption that, however constructed our gender roles might be, they still depend on a notion of the bifurcation of humanity into male and female sexes and an ensuing view of sexual complementarity that relates men and women as opposite parts of one whole. When this notion of complementarity is invoked, it brings with it a system that devalues women in relation to men and that has no place for non-heterosexual relationships because they violate the notion of the complementary wholeness of male and female humanity.

What would happen to christological studies if sex were a socially constructed category, parallel to the construction of gender? When I first pose this question to my students, many do not even understand the notion.

They quickly retreat to biological arguments in the same way that the arguments against gay and lesbian marriage are constructed. Males and females are biologically different. Reproduction, among other things, depends on this difference. It seems obvious to them that though gender is socially constructed, sex is a biological category. As Christine Delphy says: "We now see gender as the *content* with sex as the *container*."[3] We take sex as the given on which gender differences are predicated and to which they are assigned. As Westerners, we assume maleness and femaleness from the very beginning as a decisive division of humanity and then we use them as a sorting mechanism to provide categories into which to put people. At a child's birth (or now, even sometimes before birth!), one of the first questions, if not *the* first question, we ask is "Is it a boy or a girl?" For all our thinking that we have overcome some of the worst of stereotyping by gender, we still look for a blue or pink blanket to give us what we take to be a piece of vital advice about the newborn. As a society, we depend heavily on sex differences so that we will know how to address people, how to treat them, where to slot them. We are uncomfortable when we do not know if the person with whom we are interacting is male or female.

Contrary to this notion of the naturalness of biological bifurcation into male and female (sexual dimorphism), an increasing number of theorists argue that it is the fact that we continue to see gender divisions as important that pushes us to place so much emphasis on the biological differences between male and female. For Christine Delphy, for instance, gender precedes sex.[4] She does not deny the biological characteristics necessary for reproduction. But she does question why these characteristics should have given rise to the bifurcated division on which so much social difference has been predicated. We emphasize sex, she argues, because so much has depended and still continues to depend on gendered views of the human world. But sex is not entirely self-evident. How does one decide for certain what counts as male or female? By penis or lack thereof? By (in)ability to bear children? By chromosomal exploration? Delphy makes the claim that sex, like gender, is socially, not biologically, constructed. For the purposes of reproduction we could emphasize sexual differences for a certain part of human life. But it remains that we emphasize these sex differences throughout life. Such an emphasis would not seem to be required for reproduction alone. This leads to a question about why we have been so fixated on this difference, which in turn leads to the suspicion that social ends beyond reproduction are being served.

Delphy asks why sex difference is emphasized as bifurcated and binary.[5] Her suspicion is that these binary differences are seen to be so important in order to keep certain social values in place—social values that still give males priority over females and that value heterosexuality above "same"-sex relationships. Why are we so insistent on male and female as the most basic categories into which to sort humans? Sorting people into these two categories as all-important and all-encompassing separates them from one another in a singular way that recognizes only one sort of difference. Such absolute differentiation would seem to be useful only if we are proposing to treat people differently based on these categories. Furthermore, to place people into two categories for the purposes of difference of treatment and expectations of conduct also means that, because the difference is seen as absolute and unbridgeable, certain interactions between those who fall into the same category (all men, all women) might also be seen as inappropriate or problematical.

Sex bifurcated as male and female may be an interpretation—that is, it may *not* be an unquestionable matter of natural importance. Writes Christine Gudorf: "Until the last few decades, human sexuality was usually understood as a fixed phenomenon. It was thought to endure over time in roughly the same form, with the same properties. But recently we have come to see in sexuality, as in other areas of human existence from forms of energy to the organization of space, that our categories for classification are not naturally occurring, but the result of human artifice."[6] As Georgia Warnke notes in response to the argument that procreation is what shows us how important and natural this bifurcation is: How often do we really *want* to reproduce?[7] There are certainly good arguments that might be made about treating pregnant persons and those who have recently given birth differently from other persons. But then the dichotomy would be pregnant and recently delivered persons in one category and the rest of humanity in another. Most of our lives, especially in the twenty-first century in the West, are non-reproductive. If reproduction is the key to a certain difference of treatment, then in relation to some specific difference of treatment concerning childbirth, we should concentrate on reproduction, not on sex, as a sorting tool. As to treating mothers differently from fathers in the matter of child rearing, we enter again into a realm that is now usually considered a social, not an inherent difference. We could then divide humans into primary caregivers and secondary caregivers, not males and females. The possibility of categorization is not simple and binary, but complex and endless.

In establishing maleness and femaleness as crucial and opposite categories, we also set up a category that has become central in both theological discussions of the relationships between men and women and theological interpretations of sexuality—the category of sexual comple-

mentarity. Many religious groups offer the "naturalness" of sexual complementarity as one of the chief reasons to oppose gay and lesbian marriage.[8]
In this argument, sexual complementarity is seen as biological and, therefore, as crucial for reproduction. But arguments about complementarity
extend beyond reproduction to such areas as child rearing and claiming
that normative families need both male and female influences for their
social well-being. In this way, assumed biological differences quickly take
on social purposes.

Like Delphy, Judith Butler thinks that sex is a social construction. Butler is one of the main influences in queer theory, a theory (or theories)
that, drawing from a variety of postmodern influences, sees all our categories (including sex and gender) as human constructions that are open
to deconstruction and critique. Especially in queer theory, the normative-
ness of sexuality as straight, heterosexual, and procreative, and the cultural assumptions made on that basis, are closely questioned. Butler is well
known for her discussion of sex and gender as performances rather than
as essential or inherent descriptors of who or what one "is." Socially constructed norms and conventions constrain our performances of our own sex
and gender (which may or may not conform to those norms). There are
many ways to perform sex and gender, not just two.

If sex and gender are both socially constructed, it follows that human
identities are destabilized. We are not male and female essences existing
through time, but temporal identities who are continuously being constituted and reconstituted according to the influences and norms around us.

Rereading the "Maleness" of Jesus in Christian Tradition

Many of our feminist Christologies have read sex as the container for gender. We accepted sex/gender dimorphism and sought to make the male
Jesus the container for a non-patriarchal Christology. If we critique the
whole notion that the maleness of Jesus is a divine given or a fact that
cannot be changed, do we learn anything new about Christology?

Jesus is not "male." Rather, the Christian tradition has read him as
"male" in order to create and reinforce a social order wherein males are
seen as more important than females. Such a social order also has the effect
of insisting on sexual complementarity, which disadvantages women, who
must be joined to men in order to gain the privileges of maleness, and
which disallows all sexual relationships that are not part of a patriarchal,
heterosexual, potentially procreative marriage. Jesus' "maleness" is an
instrument of control in the Christian tradition.

There is a sense in which Jesus is not always "male" in the Christian tradition, if maleness means a reading or interpretation of Jesus that stresses sexual bifurcation. There is little evidence, for example, that the Gospels read Jesus as "male" in certain normative ways. What I mean is that in the Gospels, Jesus is exempt from the category maleness in a variety of ways even while his maleness is still assumed and inscribed on the social order. Jesus was an unmarried man in a culture in which marriage was the norm. He associated with people who were not classified as "normative" and with whom dominant males did not associate—women, outcasts, sinners— thereby at least in some ways refusing the privileges and the constraints of "maleness." Maleness is arguably seen as much more important in Paul and in some of the later New Testament books—such as the pastoral epistles—than in the Gospels.

Even Paul occasionally presents a vision that the message of Jesus might be one that does not draw its meaning from the bifurcation of the sexes. If "there is no longer male and female" in Christ Jesus, we get a glimpse of the possibility that sex need not be a defining factor in understanding this new religious movement. It has always struck me as curious that the dominant reading of what it means to be human in Christianity is taken from Genesis rather than, say, from Galatians 3:26–28. So, the dominant trajectory about humanity has been the making of "male and female."[9] And then the notion that in Jesus Christ there is no longer "Jew or Greek ... slave or free ... male or female" has been interpreted in light of the assumed sexual bifurcation of Genesis and not the other way around. Thus the meaning given to the overcoming of divisions is traditionally seen as a problem to be solved because the most straightforward interpretation—that the divisions should not be seen as of any import in the new Christian order— is socially problematical. So instead of saying that maleness and femaleness are not important in light of the Gospel of Jesus, the Galatians text is often interpreted in ways that do not upset the social order.[10] A reading that does not emphasize sexual dimorphism would call into question interpretations of Galatians that present this text as an eschatological ideal, or read it in terms of the equality of potential salvation rather than as a teaching about the social order. The assumed sexual complementarity of Genesis infuses the reading of the New Testament, not vice versa.

In the Nicene Creed, despite all the English translations that have historically read in "maleness," the language actually offers an undifferentiated view of what Jesus became—"*homo factus est*" not "*vir factus est*." Jesus' "maleness," though it is undoubtedly assumed in cultures that by and large make and act on the assumption of bifurcation, is not always the main point about Jesus. Indeed, this is precisely what second-wave Christian feminists were building on in their attempts to create non-patriarchal Christologies, even though they too assumed the sexual bifurcation that underlay their thinking.

Peter Brown notes that up until the third century CE, male bodies and female bodies were generally considered equal if they were virginal.[11] Thomas Aquinas, following Aristotle, considered women to be misbegotten men.[12] Thus for Aquinas the distinction is not first between male and female, but between perfection and defect. The point I am making with these examples is that Christianity has not always universally bifurcated humans into males and females as the most crucial categories of difference. Other categories of difference might be virgin bodies/non-virgin bodies or men/misbegotten or deficient men. On close inspection, using the lens of suspicion about male–female bifurcation, we might also see humanity in more than two categories, not just sorted into superordinates and subordinates, but as more diverse and varied. Recognizing that there might be other ways to view humanity than simply in a sex-bifurcated fashion renders our readings of Christology, biblical texts, and Christian history more complex and problematic, but it may also give rise to new insights.

Over time, the dominant reading of Jesus' maleness comes more and more to be construed as crucial to understanding his significance. Earlier feminist Christologies assumed that they had to read over or through Jesus' maleness. What happens if we read Christology without having to think of sex as the "container" and instead think of sex as a construct?

We can't pretend that the category "sex" does not exist in our readings. To do so would only reinscribe normative maleness while pretending that the power dynamics, however socially constructed they are, have ceased to hold sway. Instead, we must take seriously the ways in which the categories male and female have been used to inscribe certain power relations; but at the same time, we must refuse to be limited by those categories.

The categories male and female are human constructions that are made for—or at least serve—a particular social order that advantages straight men over women and queer men. If we recognize sex, like gender, as a human construction, the question of the sex of Jesus cannot be made a question of some assumed "essential" maleness, nor can it be attributed to God's choice of maleness (and sexual complementarity) over femaleness.

Que(e)rying Christology[13]

Influenced by Butler and others, some Christologies have made use of queer theory in their constructions. These readings often involve the idea that Jesus is "queer," meaning that Jesus does not conform to the conventional or normative categories.

Lisa Isherwood reads Jesus as a model of transgression. His acts, because they are transgressive, can be labelled "queer." In using Jesus' acts as a model of transgression, queer people can come to love themselves and to act in similarly transgressive ways.[14] Similarly, in *Queering Christ,* Robert Goss wants to reclaim an embodied sexual Jesus in order to provide a Christology that is liberating for those who do not accede to heteronormativity. He claims that Jesus' solidarity with the oppressed extends also to solidarity with the sexually oppressed.[15] Following Marcella Althaus-Reid, Goss offers a variety of readings of Christ beyond heteronormativity. He combines this with Eleanor McLaughlin's notion of the transvestite Christ to paint a picture of "Christ's protean solidarity with all peoples, all economic and political locations, all genders, and all sexual orientations."[16] In this he comes to a "postmodern Queer Christ" who can challenge normative gender and sexual expressions.

Tricia Sheffield offers a transgendered reading of Jesus' body as queer through the Chalcedonian understanding of Jesus as both fully human and fully divine. Jesus' body is queer because "God is passing for human, and Jesus is passing for divine, and so they are both transgressively intertwined."[17] Jesus' queer body can disrupt traditional constructions of sex/gender and sexuality.[18] Karen Trimble Alliaume, drawing on Judith Butler, suggests that feminist Christology is a performance of Jesus "as citational practices rather than as attempts to replicate a standard."[19] For Alliaume, as for Butler, citation is not quite imitation, because the one cited, Jesus, is already a historical construction, thus destabilizing both Jesus and the one doing the citing.[20] Now, though it is helpful to see Jesus as already a historical construct and therefore not a single stable character, Alliaume's Christology, like many other Christologies dependent on queer theory, still takes Jesus (however destabilized) as the norm to be cited.

The Christologies briefly outlined above tend to concentrate on the person and example of Jesus. They tend to give the *person* of Jesus priority over the *work* of Jesus; and when they do talk about the work of Jesus they tend to see it in terms of an example to be repeated or cited. Thus the queering of Jesus that they accomplish is the queering of one individual in relation to many. Attempts to queer Jesus are important contributions to christological debate. In my view, however, they tend to begin in the wrong place. The question "Who is Jesus?" is an important but limited question. Beginning with this question runs the risk of neglecting to engage the full range of christological inquiry. The question "Who is Jesus?" only has meaning in relation to a matrix of meaning that also needs to ask and answer questions about God and humanity.[21] Otherwise, it is difficult to get from a queer Jesus (however interesting) to a position that has direct relevance or meaning for contemporary human beings. One is reminded of Daly's comment in response to the assertion that Jesus was a feminist: it does not matter if Jesus was a feminist, "I am."[22] The focus of Christology should not just be on Jesus, but on why Jesus should matter at all. There are plenty of transgressive actors out there to choose from. In my view, Christians are only interested in Jesus because of Jesus' effect on the earliest followers and, through the texts we have, on contemporary human beings. Unless we also explore Jesus' and our connections to God we cannot fully understand the salvific point of Christology. An excellent transgressive performance may be necessary, but it is not sufficient to account for why Christians would want to continue to focus on Jesus.

The specific point I want to make here is that the issue of sexual bifurcation in Christology will not be fully treated until we deal also with questions of God and humanity. Christian discourse about God, interestingly enough, provides one sort of model for talk of a personal being who cannot be slotted into the pattern of sexual bifurcation. Now, unquestionably this God is (generally) *gendered* male through the discourse about "him," so the model is incomplete. Nonetheless, in a search for discourse where sex is not front and centre, this is one place to look. If God can be seen as personal and yet not assigned a biological sex, perhaps we can talk about humans in that way, too. Indeed, in the parlance of queer theory, this makes God "queer"—that is, not easily assignable to a normative sex category. Our language about God is highly gendered because we draw it from our gendered language about people. Nonetheless, that this language has, for the most part, been able to avoid language about the sex of God leads me to see the possibilities of a language for human beings that does not rely on sexual differentiation.

If the categories male and female are social constructions, then seeing Jesus' sex as relevant to his salvific function is also a social construction that can, it follows, be reconstructed differently. Furthermore, all human beings, regardless of how they are classified according to sex or sexuality, should from a theological point of view have equal access to whatever is understood to be salvation.

Certainly feminist views have questioned whether Jesus' sex is of any importance in determining his salvific role in Christianity.[23] But this questioning could proceed still further and might well illuminate and reclaim such traditions as that of Gregory of Nyssa, who saw the sexual dimorphism of humanity as a result of the Fall.[24] Readings of the Christian tradition might be different if such readings assumed that bifurcation into sexes was a construction that needed (re)interpreting rather than an unquestionable given. If emphasizing or stressing or even noting Jesus' maleness is already a constructed assumption that needs questioning, then the starting place of Jesus' maleness itself becomes unstable. This means not that one cannot value embodiment, but rather that we need to recognize the multiple forms that bodies take instead of investing values in certain kinds of bodies by devaluing others. This in turn helps us avoid the idea that the straight male body is the norm to which all other bodies ought to aspire.

Constructing Christology

In my view, through the story of his life, death, and Resurrection as told in the Gospels, Jesus functions as one who re-presents God's grace. Using language that is familiar from Butler, one might say that Jesus performs God in the world. But here "performs" is not used to suggest imitation or citation, but a concrete embodiment of God in the world. If God is queer in the sense of not being easily categorized according to sex and sexuality, then the re-presentation of this God should be read in the same way. In this way one could, I think, talk about Jesus, too, as "queer," meaning that Jesus, too, should be left uncategorized with regard to sex and sexuality. If in the resurrection "they neither marry nor are given in marriage" (Mark 12:25), this also provides a clue to a reading that might suggest downplaying the importance of sexual dimorphism, not just in some eschatological future but also as a present desideratum.

In my view, though it is Jesus' role to perform or embody God, it is not a Christian's job to cite or perform Jesus, as some theologians, following Judith Butler's notions of citation and performance, would have us do (Alliaume). The problem with the notion of the imitation of Jesus, whether in its more historical forms or in forms influenced by postmodernism, is that this somehow suggests a replication of specific actions—you perform by repetition. But the danger of thinking of the task as repetition is that it leaves little room for the difference of action that any change in context demands. It risks understanding Jesus' specific acts as normative. The job of the

Christian, in my view, is not to perform Jesus in the sense of imitation or citation, but to perform what it means to be fully and authentically human in response to Jesus and the grace of God received through Jesus. I do not mean to suggest that the texts portraying Jesus' actions are useless or meaningless. Certainly readings of Jesus' acts as transgressive could well be one way to understand what it means to be fully human. But I give priority to the experience of God's grace, for it is that grace experienced in and through Jesus that gives one the possibility not just of replicating a past, but of genuine movement toward a new future. In that sense, I think, the actions of Jesus do not stand as examples to be cited but as challenges to be met by appropriate action in my own context.

Indeed, one of the problems I have with Butler is that it is not clear how or even whether I have much freedom or creativity.[25] I think that norms and conventions are influential, but that individuals also have freedom to enact those norms (Butler calls this "citation") or not. I do not have to accept and perform, even if in parody, the norms I am given. Here I take my cue from Alfred North Whitehead, whose theories allow both for social influence and for genuine newness or creativity.[26]

Unless I have sufficient human freedom both to make me accountable for my acts and to allow me to create as well as reinscribe, I do not see that I am any further ahead than if I were to agree with theologians such as Augustine or John Calvin about how limited my human freedoms are. If all I do is perform roles that are given to me, I am constantly mired in what the Christian tradition calls sin. I respond to the performance of God (i.e., respond to God's grace) not by citing someone else but by seeking full humanity for myself and others. I don't perform Jesus because of the inherent limitations in seeking to reproduce the actions of someone from a vastly different time and place. I encounter God as performed in/by Jesus and through this am drawn into relationship with God.

Seeing the categories "male" and "female" as social constructions does me little good unless this new way of seeing also allows me to remake my responses. As I see it, the promise of the Christian Gospel, the promise represented by Jesus, is the promise that things can be made anew, that new life is possible beyond the reinscription of older and less authentic ways of being.

If the categories of male and female are human constructions, then the way is opened to rethink Christian responses both to women and to sexuality. Feminist theology made much progress on the question of changing the status of women within Christianity, but it still (at least until recently) left intact the maintenance and justification of the difference between male and female, especially in relation to Christology. Leaving the male–female division unchallenged reinscribes normative heterosexuality. Even when some within the Christian tradition want to be open to those sexualities traditionally considered "non-normative," the main move has still been to read these sexualities in relation to the pattern of sexual dimorphism and sexual complementarity. Christians need to move beyond a response to queer sexualities that depends on talk about how God has created people as gay, lesbian, and so on, and into talk about the fluidity of sexual desire. The sexual ethics that would follow from such a change would concern recognizing the full humanity of all sexual actors rather than applying sexual rules according to how one is categorized.

Once we recognize both gender and sex as human constructs it is clearer that our talk about God—especially about God as gendered (if not sexed)—is also a human construction. This does not remove the problematic of using personal language for God, but it does mean that our language might come less and less to attribute sex differences to humans that then, along with hierarchicalized meanings, are also predicated of God. If we use human language to talk of God and if that language increasingly does not express a need to divide humans in terms of sex, then sex/gender talk will not automatically be used for God.

If we read the event of Jesus as about neither gender nor sex, this seems to me to open up definitions of the possibility of full humanity. I am not called to be fully female or fully male, fully straight or fully queer, but fully human. Indeed, the fact that "fully queer" might sound like an oxymoron to some readers signals the importance of changing our thinking about sex as well as about gender.

Conclusions

What, then, would be the central points of a Christology such as the one I wish to uphold here?

Christologies themselves are human constructs. They portray human understandings and constructions of God's relationship with the world. Christologies are interpretations. A Christology that is fully cognizant of the constructed nature of sexual difference is one that deconstructs the maleness of Jesus as a power play on behalf of maleness over femaleness and heteronormativity over "lesser" sexualities. To signify Jesus as "male" is already to place maleness as normative in relation to femaleness and to place heterosexuality as normative in relation to all other forms of sexuality. Even a Christology like the one I am espousing here that does not expect or require imitation of Jesus still needs to deconstruct the categories in which Jesus is understood in relation to God and in relation to human beings.

The main focus of Christology is not Jesus but the experience evoked by Jesus (and the God Jesus re-presents) and the effect of this experience on persons whose lives have been changed. In the New Testament texts about Jesus there are stories of people being called beyond themselves into a relationship with Jesus through whom they experience God in a new way. In my view I am not called to imitate Jesus or even to imitate the relationship with Jesus that another person has. I am called to enter into a relationship myself with the God Jesus re-presents.

Relationships can be used to reinscribe norms and rules, but they can also be places where one can work out oneself and one's own life in freedom and creativity. I do not perform Jesus; I perform myself. What frees me and allows me to be authentically human? I would say that the answer to this question is not imitation, but grace. The danger of thinking of Christology as performing Jesus is that it can lead to a relatively narrow view of what performance is required. It can lead to an idea that living the Christian life is like reading a book of rules from the life of Jesus (even if there is a wide variety of ways to construe those "rules"). For instance, it might be seen to be a glorification of the performance of suffering. Another danger of thinking of life as imitation of something that has gone before is that we might lose sight of the ways in which the world is different from earlier times; or we might assume that everyone is placed in the same way and has the same possibilities.

Social location is important, even crucial, to understanding what one is called to do by the God whom Jesus re-presents. As a well-educated and well-off woman in the developed world I have vastly more choices about enacting myself than someone bound by constraints of poverty or lack of education. And, of course, I am also bound by the constraints of my social location, as Butler and others make clear from the notions of citation and performance. But according to my view of Christology, constraints are not the only or the last word.

What do I learn from reading/encountering Jesus, then? I learn that grace or love surrounds me even when I've done nothing to earn it. I learn that I am valuable in and for myself and that everything else is valuable in and for itself. I learn that despite the constraints of time, place, socialization, and social expectations that surround me, I am not utterly bound by these. I learn that to respond to this love in gratitude makes the world a better place for all creatures.

Learning to be fully and authentically human, fully and authentically oneself, means developing and having an erotic connection to the world. I use *eros* here in the sense that it is used by Audre Lorde; it "provides the power that comes from sharing deeply any pursuit with another person. The sharing of joy, whether physical, emotional, psychic or intellectual, forms a bridge between the sharers that can be the basis for understanding much of what is not shared between them, and lessens the threat of their difference."[27] Despite Christian understandings of love as disinterested love, it has always seemed to me that the understanding of love to be gleaned from the Christian tradition is profoundly erotic.[28] If we reclaim the goodness of *eros*, the passionate connection of one to another, we might be able to reclaim the goodness of sex in the Christian tradition. And if sex is good for itself, for the connectedness it brings, then we do not have to reduce sex to procreation to make it licit. If we move beyond procreativity as the purpose of sex we can also move beyond one of the main purposes served in the Christian tradition by the bifurcation of humans into male and female. Of course *eros* can be misused, but the possibility of misuse is not a justification for rules that restrict the possibilities for its fulfillment.

As I learn to be fully and authentically human I have freedom to conform to the social categories I have been given or to manipulate those categories in creative ways. I can move beyond the categories male and female at the times when these categories are used to slot me into a specific place in the social order. If, in Christ Jesus, there is truly no male or female, then I do not have to use these humanly constructed categories to understand who I am as human and I do not have to use them to regulate my personal and sexual life.

If I subvert the category of maleness, then the maleness of Jesus can no longer hold meaning as a christological category. To talk about the maleness of Jesus says nothing of importance about Jesus but speaks volumes about the Church's investment in the category of maleness as a way to control "appropriate" gender roles and licit sexuality. Since quite early in its history, the more the Church became institutionalized, the more it sought to make itself acceptable, respectable, and powerful in the societies in which it found itself, and the more it sought to control sexuality and gender roles. To talk about the importance of Jesus' maleness is to talk about a politics that keeps women as secondary and that values heterosexual marriage for procreation.

This does not mean that I might not need to use these categories strategically. There are good feminist reasons to keep the categories "male" and "female" as useful categories of analysis that inform how we still continue to structure our religious traditions and society more broadly to the advantage of some and to the disadvantage of others. The point is not to cease using categories, but rather to see that they are interpretive categories rather than simple "givens." Recognizing the power of gender roles to control our interpretations has led to new ways of understanding Christology. Similarly, interrogating sex opens new possibilities for christological understanding.

Notes

1 Rosemary Radford Ruether, "Christology and Feminism: Can a Male Savior Save Women?" in *To Change the World: Christology and Cultural Criticism* (New York: Crossroad, 1981), 45–56.

2 Here I want to express my thanks to Stephanie Swift, who helped me with research into queer Christologies.

3 Christine Delphy, "Rethinking Sex and Gender," in *Feminism in the Study of Religion: A Reader*, ed. Darlene Juschka (New York: Continuum, 2001), 411–23 at 414.

4 Delphy, "Rethinking Sex and Gender," 411–23.

5 See also Judith Butler, *Undoing Gender* (New York: Routledge, 2004); Christine Gudorf, "The Erosion of Sexual Dimorphism: Challenges to Religion and Religious Ethics," *Journal of the American Academy of Religion* 69 (2001): 863–92.

6 Christine Gudorf, "The Social Construction of Sexuality: Implications for the Churches," in *God Forbid: Religion and Sex in American Public Life,* ed. Kathleen Sands (New York: Oxford University Press, 2000), 45.

7 Georgia Warnke, "Intersexuality and the Categories of Sex," *Hypatia* 16 (2001): 126–37.

8 See, for example, Canadian Conference of Catholic Bishops, "Brief by the Canadian Conference of Catholic Bishops to the Special Legislative Committee on Bill C–38, *The Civil Marriage Act*" (2005), http://www.cccb.ca/Files/CCCBBrief_BillC-38 .html, accessed 5 January 2009; and Evangelical Fellowship of Canada, "Submission to the Special Legislative Committee on Bill C-38 (CC38) *The Civil Marriage Act*" (2005), http://files.efc-canada.net/si/Marriage%20and%20Family/Brief%20%20C-38 %20Committee.pdf, accessed 5 January 2009.

9 For a critique of reading the Genesis texts as requiring complementarity, see Gwendolyn B. Sayler, "Adam and Eve / Adam and Steve? A Challenge to the Hermeneutical 'Complementarity' Argument," *Currents in Theology and Mission* 33 (2006): 406–14.

10 See, for example, J. Louis Martyn, *Galatians: A New Translation with Introduction and Commentary* (New York: Doubleday, 1997).

11 Peter Brown, "Bodies and Minds: Sexuality and Renunciation in Early Christianity," in *Sexualities in History: A Reader,* ed. Kim M. Phillips and Barry Reay (New York: Routledge, 2002), 129–40.

12 Thomas Aquinas, *Summa Theologiae*, I, q 92, 99.

13 The word, "que(e)rying" I take from Gary David Comstock and Susan E. Henking, eds., *Que(e)rying Religion: A Critical Anthology* (New York: Continuum, 1997).

14 Lisa Isherwood, "Queering Christ: Outrageous Acts and Theological Rebellions," *Literature and Theology* 15 (2001): 249–61.

15 Robert Goss, *Queering Christ: Beyond Jesus Acted Up* (Cleveland: Pilgrim, 2002), 140.

16 Ibid., 181.

17 Tricia Sheffield, "Performing Jesus: A Queer Counternarrative of Embodied Transgression," *Theology and Sexuality* 14 (2008): 233–58 at 243.

18 Sheffield, "Performing Jesus," 247.

19 Karen Trimble Alliaume, "Disturbingly Catholic: Thinking the Inordinate Body," in *Bodily Citations: Religion and Judith Butler*, ed. Ellen T. Armour and Susan M. St. Ville (New York: Columbia University Press, 2006), 93–119 at 102.

20 Alliaume, "Disturbingly Catholic," 114–15.

21 See Pamela Dickey Young, *Feminist Theology/Christian Theology: In Search of Method* (Minneapolis: Fortress, 1990), 42–54; idem, *Re-Creating the Church: Communities of Eros* (Philadelphia: Trinity Press International, 2000), 95–105.

22 Mary Daly, *Beyond God the Father*, with original reintroduction (1973; Boston: Beacon, 1985), 73.

23 See, for example, Rosemary Radford Ruether, *Sexism and Godtalk: Toward a Feminist Theology* (Boston: Beacon, 1993).

24 Rosemary Radford Ruether, *Women and Redemption: A Theological History* (Minneapolis: Fortress, 1998), 3.

25 See, for example, Judith Butler, "Undiagnosing Gender," in her *Undoing Gender* (New York: Routledge, 2004), 75–101 at 77 and 88.

26 Alfred North Whitehead, *Process and Reality: An Essay in Cosmology* (1929; New York: Free Press, 1978).

27 Audre Lorde, "Uses of the Erotic: The Erotic as Power," in *Weaving the Visions: New Patterns in Feminist Spirituality*, ed. Judith Plaskow and Carol P. Christ (San Francisco: Harper and Row, 208–13 at 210.

28 Dickey Young, *Re-Creating the Church*, 31–36.

12

Theological Implications of Mobile Hospitality

✛ ✛ ✛

DEIRDRE GOOD

JOANNE MCWILLIAM exemplified hospitality and charity wherever she was: in the welcome she and Peter Slater gave to others and in her openness to discussion and ideas at all times and places. This essay is a small way of honouring her memory.

Hospitality to strangers is a Christian virtue. By virtue, we mean something we esteem highly, a quality we try to practise. We did not, however, invent this particular virtue. In most countries of the world, strangers are shown hospitality.

Hospitality is a biblical mandate. Leviticus 19:33–34 instructs ancient Israelites, "When an alien resides with you in your land, you shall not oppress the alien. The alien who resides with you shall be to you as the citizen among you; you shall love the alien as yourself, for you were aliens in the land of Egypt: I am the LORD your God." And in the New Testament, the Epistle to the Hebrews 13:2 exhorts, "Do not neglect to show hospitality to strangers, for by doing that some have inadvertently entertained angels." Perhaps the author has the entertainment of angelic strangers by Abraham and Sarah (Genesis 18:1–3) or Lot (Genesis 19:1–14) or even Tobit (Tobit 12:1–20) in mind. The allusion in Hebrews is vague, but the practice of "love of strangers" is commended in a wider context of "letting brotherly love remain." The presumption is that those addressed should continue in a practice already evident among the letter's recipients. In a context of the itinerant ministry of disciples, hospitality is of course an important means of spreading the Gospel. But hospitality is not simply kindness to strangers. It has always been a virtue practised without regard to location. Indeed, Paul counsels "[p]ursuing hospitality to the stranger" in Romans 12:13 using an active verb. The odd NRSV translation, "extend hospitality to strangers," simply demonstrates how hard it is to dislocate hospitality. By this I mean not only that hospitality is not practised from a specific location, but also that this aspect of hospitality is not widely understood. Because this inconvenient feature of hospitality has been a neglected element of biblical texts, their interpretation and application, it is the focus of this essay.

Abraham in Biblical and Post-Biblical Tradition

If we suppose that Abraham is the paradigm of hospitality to strangers that the author of Hebrews has in mind, Genesis 18 might be a good place to begin. It preserves lengthy details of Abraham's encounter with three strangers.

> The LORD appeared to Abraham by the oaks of Mamre, as he sat at the entrance of his tent in the heat of the day. He looked up and saw three men standing near him. When he saw them, he ran from the tent entrance to meet them, and bowed down to the ground. He said, "My lord, if I find favor with you, do not pass by your servant. Let a little water be brought, and wash your feet, and rest yourselves under the tree. Let me bring a little bread, that you may refresh yourselves, and after that you may pass on—since you have come to your servant." So they said, "Do as you have said."
>
> And Abraham hastened into the tent to Sarah, and said, "Make ready quickly three measures of choice flour, knead it, and make cakes." Abraham ran to the herd, and took a calf, tender and good, and gave it to the servant, who hastened to prepare it. Then he took curds and milk and the calf that he had prepared, and set it before them; and he stood by them under the tree while they ate. They said to him, "Where is your wife Sarah?" And he said, "There, in the tent." Then one said, "I will surely return to you in due season, and your wife Sarah shall have a son." And Sarah was listening at the tent entrance behind him. (Genesis 18:1–10)

The practice and location of hospitality in this passage is clear: it is food offered to passing guests under the oaks of Mamre at some distance from Abraham's tent. Hence all the to-ing and fro-ing: a seated Abraham sees three travelling figures whom he runs to meet. Anxious to offer hospitality, he persuades them to rest under the tree and runs back to the tent to ask Sarah for cakes. Next he runs to the herd for a calf to be prepared by the servant for food. Then he takes cakes prepared by Sarah, and the calf, milk, and curds prepared by himself and the servant, and brings them to the visitors under the tree. They are all not so far from the tent that Sarah cannot hear the promise spoken by one of the three guests that she will have a son. This is the element of reciprocity shown by the guest or recipient of hospitality and a feature of the practice.

Christian icons of Abraham's hospitality often show the location of the table at which the three strangers ate as under a tree, with Abraham and Sarah looking on from either side. The tree as the location for hospitality is for the convenience of the strangers. Post-biblical tradition, however, alters Abraham's location. Instead of running to greet strangers and bringing hospitality to them, Abraham moves his dwelling.

According to the (first century BCE) Testament of Abraham, Abraham, the paradigm of hospitality, pitches a tent at the crossroads so as to welcome more strangers arriving from four different roads. Abraham thus welcomes rich and poor, kings and rulers, crippled and helpless, friends and strangers, neighbours and passers-by. "All on equal terms thus did the pious, holy, righteous and hospitable Abraham welcome them." The Testament of Abraham, like the *midrash* on Genesis, Genesis Rabbah 48,9, understands Abraham's behaviour to be typical, not exceptional, in that he wanted to serve travellers constantly. Similarly, the first-century writer Philo of Alexandria, describing Genesis 18, says Abraham ran out of his house and begged the strangers who were passing by his home to stay with him because he was so eager to extend hospitality to them. Aboth deR. Nathan 7 says that "Abraham … used to go out and look all around and when he found strangers he would invite them into his house." In fact, he built a mansion on the road where he would leave food and drink so that anyone who came by would eat and drink and bless God.

In all of these passages, hospitality is not primarily associated with the treatment of friends, neighbours, or members of one's own family. When Abraham catches sight of the messengers in the distance, he has no way of knowing who they are. The blessed have earned praise for welcoming the stranger. Indeed, in the Christian Bible, the word often used for hospitality is *philoxenia*, from the Greek for one who loves strangers. Part of the goodness in hospitality is in receiving a person outside the community from whom one has no immediate expectation of reciprocity. The person you help may never be in a position to help you—he or she may even bring you harm. Nevertheless, hosts are obliged to extend themselves.

Rahab and Women's Hospitality in Biblical and Post-Biblical Tradition

But Abraham is not the only example of hospitable behaviour in post-biblical tradition, though he may be the best known. In I Clement, an early writing of the Church Fathers, Abraham is a paradigm of faith and hospitality along with Lot and Rahab the harlot. According to I Clement, "the hospitable Rahab" hid the spies sent by Joshua to Jericho in order to spy out the country. For this action all under her roof were saved. The sign the spies gave her, namely, hanging out a scarlet thread from her house to identify and save "all that are yours under your roof," makes it clear that, for the writer of I Clement, "all who believe and hope on God shall have redemption through the blood of the Lord."

In this interpretive shift from biblical to post-biblical, from hospitality offered outside the house to hospitality offered in the home, we see a reflection of a movement from nomadic to urban. But within the biblical text itself, a shift has already taken place in regard to gender: the place from which a male head of household offers hospitality is different from that of women. While Abraham can be seen to run back and forth between strangers and flocks in public pursuit of provisions for hospitality, Sarah and servants are at home. Women extending hospitality in the Hebrew Bible exist in a somewhat protected physical space that we would identify as a household. For all intents and purposes they function as head of that (less public) household.

Elijah, for example, received hospitality from a foreign widow of Zarephath at her own expense in her house for considerable time according to I Kings 17–18, while the country was in the midst of a drought and while the prophet was battling foreign gods. Elijah assures her that her supplies will not run out until the end of the famine. When her son dies, he restores him to life through God's power. This is the element of reciprocity. Similarly, Elisha receives hospitality from a wealthy Shunammite widow according to II Kings 4:9–10. She sets aside a chamber for him with a desk, bed, lamp, and chair. She also and in turn receives the promise of a son and when he dies, Elisha, like his predecessor, restores him to life. In two cases, the more private sphere in which women are located becomes more public when a stranger is shown hospitality in it.

Rationale for Extending Hospitality

Throughout Leviticus and Deuteronomy, the Hebrew people are instructed again and again to take care of the less fortunate. Whether it is leaving a portion of one's crop unharvested so that the poor may come anonymously to partake, or one's attitude toward such charity, the Old Testament makes it clear that failure to take care of the poor and destitute is unacceptable. In Talmudic commentary on Numbers 28:2 we have a precursor to Matthew 25: God says to Israel, "'My children, whenever you give sustenance to the poor, I impute it to you as though you gave sustenance to Me.' Does God then eat and drink? No, but whenever you give food to the poor, G-d accounts it to you as if you gave food to G-d."

The reasons for this are fairly obvious; first, all of our blessings come from God and therefore we must share our good fortune with others; it is not our good fortune, after all, but luck and circumstance—blessings—that have afforded us enough food and clothing. To hoard it when other of God's children go hungry is unacceptable.

A second factor underlying the Talmudic injunctions is the fact that, since the fall of the First Temple in 587 BCE, the Jewish people have been largely diasporic. They have been wanderers and strangers in lands not their own. This becomes a complete diaspora only after the Roman conquest and destruction of the Second Temple, but it would be fair to say that for the bulk of their history as a collected people, the Israelites and Jews have been strangers themselves. As the chosen people, called to always be the one with the least, the one in need of charity, the Talmud nonetheless calls for these poor and destitute ones to give what they have.

Christian interpretation tends to locate hospitality in the home. Sr. Sarah Schwartzberg, in "Abraham's Hospitality to Strangers: A Model for Interreligious Dialogue," describes Abraham and Sarah as models of hospitality welcoming three strangers into their tent.[1] She has thus read Genesis 18 through a post-biblical lens. Her reading is actually a widespread misreading of the text. She continues: "They bring the strangers into their home, into a circle of compassion and concern, where they nourish them by both food and kindness. Hospitality is timely, gracious, and abundant. It is undiscriminating and welcomes all who come." Such interpretations rely exclusively on post-biblical traditions, neglecting the text's description of Abraham's hospitality offered under a tree. As we shall see, such a (Christian) reading neglects the mobile hospitality of Jesus. Before we explore other examples, we need to pause to consider ways in which our modern interpretive context has shaped interpretations like that of Schwartzberg.

Modern Assumptions about Hospitality to Strangers

We can all agree that hospitality is a Christian virtue. But why do we write books and articles about it? Hospitality is, after all, central to most religious traditions. Abraham's offering of food and protection to the three messengers in Genesis 18 became the paradigm for ancient Israelite, Jewish, and early Christian hospitality, as we have seen. We've noted that hospitality to strangers is a mandate in most non-Western societies. I have been welcomed into the houses of complete strangers in Matere Valley, Nairobi, and in the *favelas* of São Paulo, Brazil, in ways that I would never be welcomed into the apartments of strangers in Manhattan. We write articles and books about it because Western Christian communities struggle with welcoming the stranger, so we need to make the mandate for hospitality explicit. Think of discussions in parish communities about how to welcome visitors to Christmas. In preparing for Easter services in church I have heard the plaintive cry about strangers: "Who are these people and what are they doing in *our* church?"

We have to recognize that openness to strangers reflects a mindset that most of us who are Western don't intrinsically possess. This is probably why our discussions of hospitality can sometimes dwindle to stories of our hosting (non-Western) strangers in our homes. But if our discussions and practice of hospitality become questions of whom we welcome into our homes (and for how long and under what conditions), then we have lost the dynamic of exchange that hospitality presupposes. Hospitality has become a one-way street. We determine who is invited and who is excluded because it is our home, our castle. Such an interpretation is not about welcoming anyone—it is about control. Welcoming someone has become secondary to an assessment—a judgment by me as host about the kind of stranger that is welcome and the duration and type of welcome that is appropriate. If we reduce hospitality to an arbitration of who is and who is not welcomed by us as hosts into our homes, and under what conditions and for how long, is this not a diminution of the biblical mandate of hospitality to the point of distortion?

I believe this is also true of debates about conditions and circumstances under which people may approach the communion table. If we enter into such debates, we have already decided that there is such a debate about who is welcome and who is not. In my view, on this question, the evidence of the Gospels is unequivocal: Jesus practised open table fellowship with respect to God's hospitality. It wasn't his table. He was received as a stranger, welcomed as a guest, and gave hospitality at the tables of strangers or acquaintances. Sometimes he learned from others about brokering God's limitless inclusion.

Jesus and the Canaanite Woman

The Canaanite woman wrested from Jesus a concession that she could claim hospitality. When the story opens, Jesus has withdrawn outside the boundaries of Israel to the coastal regions of Tyre and Sidon. But he has not withdrawn beyond public notice. An anonymous woman cries out to Jesus in public and in a language he understands: "Have mercy on me, O Lord, Son of David; my daughter is severely possessed by a demon!" He makes no response. Then the disciples ask him to send her away and he tells her why: "I was sent only to the lost sheep of the house of Israel." Faced with her second plea for help, Jesus explains that his mission to Israel is not to be snatched away and thrown to the dogs. Only when the woman retorts that even the dogs eat crumbs that fall from their master's table does Jesus publicly acknowledge her faith. Her daughter is healed instantly. The organizational challenges faced by early Jewish Christian communities devolved upon setting and maintaining boundaries, and that is reflected in the New Testament documents. But the story of the Canaanite woman shows us something else. Matthew didn't go back through the manuscript and scrape out all the places where Jesus said he was sent only to the lost sheep of the house of Israel; instead he showed how Jesus, the ultimate paradigm for the believing community, was made to revisit and revise an assessment of who gets included in the Kingdom. Through her insistence, the Canaanite woman is finally shown hospitality by Jesus; by implication the Matthean community shows her hospitality, too.

The Parable of the Sheep and the Goats

By locating Jesus' encounter with the Canaanite woman before the judgment parable of Matthew 25:31–46, in which the Son of Man, seated on a throne, separates the nations into the sheep and the goats and identifies the sheep as heirs of the Kingdom of Jesus' father on the basis of their treatment of "the least of these my brethren," Matthew indicates implicitly that Jesus' notions of hospitality have changed. When Jesus identifies the care offered to the "least of these" with care given to himself, he challenges followers to put their focus on those who do not appear to have much to offer. He identifies responses to the most vulnerable ones (those who are hungry, thirsty, strangers, sick, or in prison) with responses to his own needs. In this extraordinary passage, Jesus does not identify a specific place for hospitality, but opens up the possibility that in every setting his followers might see an opportunity to offer hospitality to those ordinarily overlooked or undervalued.

Emmaus

In Luke's Gospel, journeys characterize and shape ministry; Jesus journeys to Jerusalem for most of the Gospel; while in Acts, disciples and apostles travel from Jerusalem to Samaria, to Europe, and eventually to Rome. Hospitality facilitates and defines Jesus' journey to Jerusalem; it identifies followers and disciples who listen and extend welcome (Mary and Martha, the mission of the Seventy, the Good Samaritan, Zacchaeus), and it solidifies opposition (some Pharisees and scribes).

Luke's Gospel shows a particular interest in and assumes the practice of hospitality without regard to location. The Gospel of Luke casts Jesus' birth, life, and ministry as a visit from God (1:68, 78–79). Yet Jesus was born in an animal trough, a place of dislocation. Luke is replete with stories of invitations and hospitality offered, withheld, expected, accepted, and rejected: Jesus' inaugural sermon (4:16–30); the call of Peter, James, and John (5:1–11); the stories of Zacchaeus (19:1–10), the woman who anoints Jesus' feet (7:36–50), the Prodigal Son (15:11–32), Lazarus and the rich man (16:19–31), the Good Samaritan (10:25–37), and Mary and Martha (10:38–42); the sending of the disciples with no provisions (9:1–6, 10:1–16); the series of banquet parables (14:1–24); and finally the disciples on the Emmaus Road, where an act of hospitality reveals that the risen Christ is with them (24:13–25).

A primary theme of the narrative is whether or not God's visit will be welcomed or rejected, and whether or not those who do welcome it will themselves commit to a practice of radical hospitality—not just for Jesus, but for all who have welcomed him. Will the poor and rich alike hear the invitation and join the new household they have been offered—the Kingdom of God? Will any of them, in turn, extend hospitality to others as a sign of their commitment to God's Kingdom? Luke frames Jesus' ministry as an invitation into that Kingdom and as an expectation of response, which includes extending hospitality.

The parables and stories that are recounted after Jesus "sets his face to go to Jerusalem" at 9:51 all take place on the journey to Jerusalem. Hence the welcome hospitality of Martha and Mary is not simply into their home but on the way to Jerusalem. So too is the hospitality offered to disciples as they are sent out and that offered by Zacchaeus to Jesus when he passes through Jericho. Injunctions to behaviour at meals are all within the context of the travel narrative and cannot be taken as examples of hospitality within the home.

In Luke 24:13–35, Luke describes two disciples walking from Jerusalem to the village of Emmaus after Jesus' Crucifixion. These two disciples have heard reports about Jesus' Resurrection, but they are slow to believe (24:18–25). A "stranger" joins them on their journey (24:18). Though they do not know it, the stranger is none other than the resurrected Jesus in an unrecognizable form (24:15–16). In this respect, Jesus' actions resemble the visit of strangers in Genesis 18. As the disciples arrive at their home in Emmaus, the stranger continues to travel onward. But the disciples insist that the stranger accept their hospitality, especially because the day is drawing to a close (24:28–29). Once inside, the hosts prepare a meal for the traveller. When the stranger breaks the bread, the disciples' "eyes [are] opened" and they recognize Jesus. At that point he vanishes from their sight (24:31). As a result, the two disciples believe fully in the resurrected Lord and return to Jerusalem to spread the good news to "the eleven and their companions" (24:33–35). Jesus forbids his disciples from evaluating hosts by their status. Christian guests must form deep and loyal bonds with people they encounter and not be looking constantly for better offers and more advantageous hosts. This story presents Luke's readers with implicit ethical directives for Christian hosts. The burning question in this passage is: Why does Jesus take on the form of a stranger? Surely Jesus' dramatic appearance and his interpretation of the Scriptures would have been just as effective and memorable had he appeared in a recognizable form from the beginning. (In several other post-Resurrection appearances recorded in the Gospels and Acts, the risen Jesus is recognizable from the outset.) Moreover, if Jesus is to take on an unrecognizable form, why does he not choose a more prestigious one—perhaps appearing as a priest or government official? Initially, Cleopas and the other disciple think the stranger is foolish, uninformed, and slow to understand. Yet to discover the truth about the resurrected Jesus, they are forced to listen to and learn from the unassuming stranger. It is only as these two disciples journey with the stranger, listen to him, extend hospitality to him, and break bread with him that they are able to experience the risen Lord and receive his message for them and for the other disciples. These two disciples in Emmaus become prime examples of Christian hosts. Rather than shunning strangers, Jesus' disciples would do well to journey alongside them. Rather than exclusively speaking to those they encounter along life's journeys, Jesus' disciples would do well to listen first. Rather than deeming others to be foolish, ignorant, and of no benefit, Jesus' disciples would do well to assume that God might have revealed himself to strangers. Rather than taking things at face value, Jesus' disciples should realize that the Spirit is at work in the world around them. Almost certainly Luke is inviting his readers to conclude that if they extend hospitality to strangers, as these two disciples did on the road to Emmaus, they too may be "entertain[ing] angels without knowing it" and thus experiencing the resurrected Jesus.

The practice of hospitality is not about being a good host: it is about participating in a continual exchange of the roles of stranger, guest, and host. It presupposes a network of relationships—an awareness of interdependence. We can see this best in the story of the two disciples encountering a stranger on the road to Emmaus. That stranger walks and talks along the road with them about recent events in Jerusalem. They offer him hospitality at the end of the day, whereupon, invited to stay as a guest, he assumes the position of host and is identified by them as he breaks bread. On the road to Emmaus and in a place that is not his, a homeless, resurrected Jesus moves fluidly between roles of stranger, host, and guest. Luke's Jesus offers Westerners the challenge of receiving and giving hospitality "to go."

Theological Implications of Mobile Hospitality

When we relocate the practice of Christian hospitality from who is and who is not welcome in our homes to the recognition that hospitality is offered and received in other places along the way, a different, more permeable dynamic opens up. But changing the location of the welcome is only half the solution. Offering someone food in a soup kitchen, while it is a good thing in itself, is not actually hospitality because it is not rooted in an exchange of roles. Abraham and Jesus confront our restrictive notions of hospitality, encouraging us to think about our human interdependence in giving and receiving hospitality on the way.

The Jewish theologian Martin Buber teaches us, in addition, something important about the practice of dislocated hospitality: in *I and Thou*, he advances the argument that all situations can be categorized under the two "essential" relationships: the I–It relation and the I–You or Thou relation.[2] All our dealings in the world are either relationships of objectification, exploitation, or relationships that call us out of our self-obsessed, self-controlled worlds into the "between." The I–Thou may exist not only between two human beings, but most famously, between the human being and, for example, a tree.

The I–Thou relationship for Buber is one of radical hospitality and receptivity. It is an openness to the other as Other, as some One whom I neither manipulate nor objectify. The I–Thou is a relation that takes me outside my enclosed inner world of experience and places me in the "between," where the other and I face each other in truth. There is no higher plane for this encounter; it does not "transport" you or take you away. It does change your orientation, however. It moves you. The religious for Buber is not an other-world or other-time carved out for religious matters; rather, it is having time, being in time, for the other. Everything is religious. To be in relation with God is not to go to church every Sunday; it is to face the other who faces you and calls to you. It is in the everyday that we find God, for God is All. Somehow, Buber manages to put forth a seemingly pantheistic philosophy that nevertheless remains truly Jewish and monotheistic. While suggesting that it is in our relations to created others that we find God, Buber does not simply reduce God to "others." In our createdness, we are created as able to respond to others in their being, rather than as objects to be used and manipulated. We fulfill our created purpose, we are most truly ourselves, when we face another in an I–Thou relationship, rather than an I–It one. Buber says, "Creation is not a hurdle on the road to God, it is the road itself. We are created along with one another and directed to a life with one another."[3]

Thus, the stranger appears to us, comes to us or we to them, and we can respond humanly, that is, in openness. "The ethical in its plain truth means to help God by loving his creation in his creatures, by loving it towards him." What is hospitality but welcoming? Recognizing that we are alone, all of us, and isolated in our own worlds, but nevertheless have this tremendous and mysterious capacity to respond to the other, we can acknowledge that our very createdness seems to exist for this purpose, and not for some sort of world-domination via I–It relations. Buber explains the confrontation between Jesus and the Pharisees with regard to the Greatest Commandment in this way:

> To the question which was the all-inclusive and fundamental commandment, the "great" commandment, Jesus replied by connecting the two Old Testament commandments between which above all the choice lay: "love God with all your might" and "love your neighbor as one like yourself." Both are to be "loved", God and the "neighbor" but in different ways. The neighbor is to be loved "as one like myself" (not "as I love myself"; in the last reality one does not love oneself) to whom, then, I should show love as I wish it may be shown to me. But God is to be loved with all my soul and all my might. By connecting the two Jesus brings to light the Old

Testament truth that God and man are not rivals. Exclusive love to God is, because he is God, inclusive love.[4]

It is in the encounter with the other in times and places not of our choosing that human priorities are displaced; in fact, human existence is grounded in contingency and powerlessness because of the claim of the Other. This chapter's focus is on the mobile aspects of the ancient practice of hospitality, the custom of welcoming travellers or strangers while committing to provide them with protection and provisions. Stressing mobile hospitality highlights that it is not a one-sided ministry: Jesus' disciples are called to be both exemplary hosts and exemplary guests as they carry out the ministry of Jesus in word and deed. Hospitality establishes a truly interdependent and reciprocal relationship that requires disciples, whether they are hosts or guests, to view the other, the stranger, as embodying a divine claim.

Notes

1 Sr. Sarah Schwartzberg, "Abraham's Hospitality to Strangers: A Model for Interreligious Dialogue," *Bulletin for Monastic Interreligious Dialogue* (July 2007). http://www.monasticdialog.com/a.php?id=817, accessed 31 December 2008.
2 Martin Buber, *I and Thou* (New York: T. & T. Clark, 1970), 62.
3 Martin Buber, *Between Man and Man* (London: Routledge and Kegan Paul, 1947), 60.
4 Ibid., 59–60.

13

Jesus Died for Our Sins
Redemption as an Ethic of Risk

✝ ✝ ✝

CYNTHIA CRYSDALE

Almighty God, Father of all mercies,
We your unworthy servants give you humble thanks
For all your goodness and loving-kindness
To us and to all whom you have made.
We bless you for our creation, preservation,
And all the blessings of this life;
But above all for your immeasurable love
In the redemption of the world by our Lord Jesus Christ ...[1]

 T HUS BEGINS the General Thanksgiving that is said in the
daily office of the Anglican Church. Above all we give thanks to God for the
love manifested in the redemption of the world through Jesus Christ. It is
a simple enough prayer, and the words roll easily off our tongues. But the
phrase "the redemption of the world by our Lord Jesus Christ" is anything
but simple. How to understand the work of Jesus, and the meaning of
"redemption," has been the subject of many theologies over the centuries.
And while much effort, and even blood, has been expended over the task
of debating and defining the *person* of Jesus as both divine and human,
yielding a number of creeds, the work of salvation has never been defined
in an official teaching of the Church. Instead, the work of Anselm of Can-
terbury, with his "satisfaction" theory of the atonement, has held sway for
over a thousand years, generating a number of hybrid offspring that reside
in the hearts and minds of many contemporary believers.[2]

In recent decades, new attention has been paid to theologies of redemption, known also as theories of atonement. A number of critiques have ensued, not only of Anselm's satisfaction theory but of its many derivatives as well. The key question seems to be whether the Christian *kerygma* can sustain an understanding of salvation that seems inherently to engage acts of violence. Christian feminists have unpacked the cult of suffering that ensues when the central narrative of the Gospel is about a father-figure God who wills the suffering and death of his Son.[3] As more and more "theologies from the underside" come to the fore, theologians who speak for the oppressed have revealed the triumphalistic cruelty of the cross as an instrument of imperialism.[4] The work of René Girard on scapegoating has provided a new angle from which both to understand and to criticize the violence of many atonement theories.[5] Most recently, theologians from the peace churches—Mennonites and Quakers—have raised the challenge again: How can a good God have instituted a transaction for the forgiveness of our sins that is primarily understood as a required act of violent sacrifice?[6]

It is beyond the scope of a single chapter to recount the history of the many images, metaphors, and theories that have explained the work of Christ on the cross over the years.[7] Even the current literature on the cross, atonement theory, and its revision presents a challenge for a single chapter.[8] The purpose of this chapter is to imagine new ways of envisioning how the work of Jesus—even and especially the fact of his execution on a Roman cross—might be the occasion for transformation in believers' lives today. After a short review of the "problems" with atonement theory, I will use the notions of an ethic of control and an ethic of risk to move beyond the idea of redemption as a transaction in which God solves the problem of human evil. Using the work of Sebastian Moore, I will then develop some ideas about how we can encounter the cross in ways that will reverse the cycle of decline and violence in our lives.[9]

Problems with Atonement

In a recent book of this title, Stephen Finlan alludes to contemporary literature that highlights the problems believers have with the traditional doctrines of atonement. He begins,

> The agenda is largely set by the widespread dismay regarding the received doctrines of atonement, for instance, such notions as these:
> • God's honor was damaged by human sin;
> • God demanded a bloody victim—innocent or guilty—to pay for human sin;

- God was persuaded to alter God's verdict against humanity when the Son of God offered to endure humanity's punishment;
- The death of the Son thus functioned as a payoff; salvation was purchased.[10]

Robert Daly, SJ, in reference to this quotation from Finlan, observes that "if this, or this kind of, atonement theory is central to our idea of God and of salvation, we are in deep trouble. In effect, this notion turns God into some combination of a great and fearsome judge, or offended lord, or temperamental spirit. It calls into question God's free will, or justice, or sanity."[11] Daly refers to the many metaphors that Paul used in an effort to explain the difference that Christ has made for the world. He indicates that Paul's switching among many images simply indicates Paul's apparent recognition that no one of them was sufficient. Daly goes on to highlight "the extent of the deformation that took place when theologians began to select just some of these metaphors and push them to their 'theological' conclusions."[12] This narrowing down became prevalent in the post-biblical world:

> Increasingly, an interpretation of Jesus' crucifixion, seen more and more as a transaction, indeed as a cultic, juridical, and even quasi-magical transaction, became the core message, while the actual teachings of Jesus, which had little, if anything, to do with such an interpretation, "became a secondary body of information" (Finlan, 57). It was a devolution, a reduction of atonement theory down to the idea that God deliberately intended Jesus' violent death (Finlan, 101, agreeing with Walter Wink).[13]

With Anselm's *Cur Deus Homo* (1098), this devolution progressed to the point where the devil is no longer the source of violence against humanity (as in earlier Patristic writers); God the Father himself is. "What is laid out, even taken for granted here and in so many of the traditional atonement theories of the Western church, is an inner-divine 'scenario of divine violence restrained by divine mercy, but a mercy that had to be mediated through violence.'"[14] In the end, what is so problematic about this development is the implication for our understanding of God: "What all this does, whether consciously or subconsciously, (and at odds with a mature Trinitarian theology ...) is to locate violence and the negotiation of violence within the divine."[15]

This outline of the problems with atonement is minimal. The purpose here is simply to highlight a number of points: (1) atonement theory has come under increasing scrutiny in recent theological work; (2) much of the scrutiny involves a deconstruction of the implicit violence that seems to have been incorporated long ago into our ways of understanding salvation; (3) an understanding of salvation involving a transaction in which God appeases God's self seems to be inextricably bound to this violence; and (4) this corrupts our understanding of the very nature of the divine, as if violence were somehow part of God's nature.

An Ethic of Control or an Ethic of Risk: Different Accounts of Moral Agency[16]

In *A Feminist Ethic of Risk* (1990), Sharon Welch delineated two different understandings of moral action.[17] Persons who function with an ethic of control assume that there are direct and immediate results from their moral choices. One does A and B is the clear result. Thus, moral agency is about controlling events and thereby producing predictable results. The image is of a "surgical strike" whereby the targeted menace is removed and dealt with once and for all. This view of moral action relies on "the equation of responsible action and control—the assumption that it is possible to guarantee the efficacy of one's actions."[18] Latent within this approach is the assumption of power, whereby one "defines action as the ability to attain, without substantial modification, desired results."[19] The objective and presumed result is the "eradication of evil."[20]

An ethic of control is tied not only to the politics of power and conquest but also to utopian aspirations. Ironically, such utopian hopes can actually subvert the cause of good:

> The aim of a final defeat of all evil forces, or the aim of finally meeting all human needs, does not appear as anything but praiseworthy on the surface. It is indeed surprising to find that such utopian goals as the defeat of evil and meeting of all needs can have, and often do have, highly dangerous consequences and that these constructions make peace less likely and justice seem less likely. This distortion of a seemingly positive goal operates in several ways. One is the inability to accept the prospect of long-term struggle. Seeking utopia, people turn to types of action that appear to offer immediacy and guarantees despite the dangers that may accompany these actions.[21]

Thus, it is not only power mongers and dictators who can succumb to assuming an ethic of control. Even those working for the oppressed, who are advocating for social justice, can think of themselves as eradicating evil in a decisive manner. The core of an ethic of control is not the cause being advocated but the expectation that clear and direct action will result.

In contrast, those who understand their moral agency within an ethic of risk accept that the consequences of their actions may be mixed. An ethic of risk is "responsible action within the limits of bounded power" and involves "persistent defiance and resistance in the face of repeated defeats."[22] This ethic acknowledges action that may yield only partial results. The goal of moral action is not complete success but the creation of new conditions of possibility for the future. An ethic of risk accepts the long-term struggle involved in oppressive situations. It is "an ethic that begins with the recognition that we cannot guarantee decisive changes in the near future or even in our lifetime."[23] Furthermore, "the ethic of risk is propelled by the equally vital recognition that to stop resisting, even when success is unimaginable, is to die," be it a physical death or the death of imagination and caring.[24]

Central to such moral action is engagement in a community of risk takers who are committed to the struggle over the long haul. An ethic of risk involves "strategic risk taking" in the face of overwhelming odds, and recognizes the irreparable damage of structural evil. "The ethic of risk is characterized by three elements, each of which is essential to maintain resistance in the face of overwhelming odds: a redefinition of responsible action, grounding in community, and strategic risk-taking. Responsible action does not mean the certain achievement of desired ends but the creation of a matrix in which further actions are possible, the creation of the conditions of possibility for desired changes."[25]

Welch's contrast between an ethic of control and an ethic of risk is a fertile starting point for understanding causal relations in an unfolding world, as a prolegomenon to grasping how evil *is* transformed *when* it is transformed. Before introducing the question of the resolution of evil, let us get a better grasp of two different notions of causation.[26]

While Welch is clearly critical of the hubris implicit in the ethic of control, in fact there are many events and relations in the world that occur with regularity, such that it is correct to assume that B will follow action A. Thus, to the degree that biological, ecological, and social routines operate regularly, there are cycles of cause and effect and patterns of co-operation in human community that make the predictability of "control" reasonable. The error comes in presuming that all of world process is determined by such singular direct causes. As a scientific, philosophical world view, this is the legacy of a mechanistic determinism left over from the era of Isaac Newton. The moral presumption of clear, decisive action is the stepchild of this one-sided view of how the world functions.

In fact, even the regularities on which we depend are conditioned. All things being equal, we can count on the climate to remain constant and the economy to hold steady. But, as we are all too aware in our current situation, both the climate and the economy can falter. If underlying conditions shift, then the schemes of recurrence that depend on these must shift as well. So when greenhouse gases accumulate, keeping warm air in the earth's atmosphere, the entire planet begins to compensate, such that oceans increase in temperature and age-old glaciers begin to melt. When the credit economy falters, the financing that made businesses and home ownership possible begins to crumble. The same occurs when disease undermines a person's metabolism such that cancer cells run rampant or immune systems fail in their defensive schemes.

The point is that everything that occurs in the world is subject to both regularity and probability. Much of what occurs, occurs according to predictable schemes of recurrence, whereby A causes B which causes C which in turns makes A happen again, creating a recurrent scheme of cause and effect. But the continuance of this regularity, or the possibility of something new emerging out of it, is subject to probability.

So when it comes to moral agency, there are situations where we can act with confidence that clear consequences will be the fruit of our actions. Assuming such "control" is not a matter of hubris. Assuming that *all* our actions will produce what we want them to produce does involve forgetting the fragility of our systems of regularity, a false assumption of control. Thus we need to balance this with the recognition of the "risk" inherent in all moral deliberation and action.

Let us explore this a bit further from the side of the agent who is acting. Questions for deliberation—What ought I to do in this situation?—do not come out of a vacuum but arise in conjunction with concrete discoveries of fact. My car won't start in the morning; what I ought to do depends on the reasons why it isn't working. A bit more seriously, I visit my mother and find her on the floor of her apartment, not breathing. My course of action must begin with at least a rudimentary determination of what has happened to her.

So "What am I to do?" (value judgments/decisions) and "What is the case?" (judgments of fact) are questions that often emerge simultaneously. And the validity of my actions relies on my accurate grasp of the facts of the situation. Still, judgments of value as well as decisions go beyond mere determinations of the current facts to determinations of the probable outcomes of various courses of action. Understanding my options involves grasping the regularities that can be counted on as well as grasping the unknown consequences of various courses of action. This latter determination involves calculating probabilities; and such probabilities, by their very nature, involve "risk."

Thus, for example, once I get my mother to a hospital I seek expert advice about her condition. There is a lot that I can count on to occur according to plan—the schemes of recurrence that make up her metabolism as well as the human patterns of co-operation that keep a hospital functioning. Other elements are less secure—a resuscitation process has got her breathing again, but it is unlikely that she will make it through the night without an artificial respirator. Intravenous medication may help her breathing but brings with it other side effects. No treatment at all, other than bed rest and vigilance from nursing staff, is also a possibility; repeated resuscitation, if necessary, would further damage her fragile heart.

Thus, the choices involved here all include considering both the schemes of recurrence on which we can count (an ethic of control) and the probabilities that affect the possible outcomes of various courses of action (an ethic of risk). The more accurate the predictions are, the more informed our choices will be. But no matter how accurate certain predictions are, moral agency has a peculiar uncertainty; we make judgments based on the likelihood of certain outcomes.

The point is to highlight an important feature of our world from two angles. First, events and the relationships among them involve regularities in which schemes of recurrence function predictably unless upset by newly emerging conditions. The stability of these predictable occurrences is never ultimately secure but depends on underlying conditions. Second, as subjects, we make decisions and seek to shift certain features of the realities in the world as it currently operates. Thus when we act as moral agents we consider both what can be counted on (the regularities that make an ethic of control viable, though not absolute) as well as the likelihood of shifting conditions so that something new will emerge.

On one hand, I am affirming Welch's distinction between an ethic of control and an ethic of risk. On the other, I am observing that the regularities that ground an ethic of control and the probabilities that ground the uncertainty of the consequences of our actions operate in a complementary interaction. The flaw that Welch has identified lies in the conception of moral action *as if* it were only a matter of direct causality: A always yields B in a linear and unchangeable sequence. Such an assumption is not only morally presumptuous but also factually incorrect. World process functions dialectically between the regularities that can be counted on, "all other things being equal," and the likelihood that all other things *are* equal. We effect change by choosing to shift probabilities so that new possibilities, even new regular schemes of co-operation, may emerge. Whatever change comes about, for good or for ill, occurs because new conditions of possibility are established, setting the stage for the emergence of new orders of regularity, not merely because a single action has a clear and unambiguous outcome.

Welch's critique of an ethic of control involves an analysis of the way hubris and power support this erroneous account of moral action. A one-sided presumption of an ethic of control can become a deceptive narrative that we tell ourselves, a rhetorical and psychic flourish that protects us from the true fragility of choice. Furthermore—and this is the heart of Welch's contribution—those who have more economic, political, and social power are more able to perpetuate this myth for themselves. Indeed, those with such power more often experience the efficacy of their choices and are more often protected from the vicissitudes and vulnerabilities of life, thereby masking the reality of risk/probability in the world.[27]

God and the Solution to the Problem of Evil: The Myth of Redemptive Violence[28]

The error of assuming that moral agency is only about decisive action that has clear and unambiguous consequences lends itself to what Walter Wink calls "the myth of redemptive violence."[29] Such myths go back to ancient Near Eastern traditions in which conflict between the gods sets the stage for a creation of the world, and they continue today.[30] Wink cites as the perfect example the cartoon depiction of Popeye and Olive Oyl. Olive Oyl is abducted by Pluto, and Popeye comes to her rescue but is beaten to a pulp by the villain until, at the last moment (when Pluto is, in effect, raping Olive Oyl), a can of spinach pops out of Popeye's pocket and into his mouth. Transformed by such a quick fix, he is able to rescue his beloved and trounce the villain.[31] Today such redemptive violence is perhaps more present in our culture in the form of video games. Nevertheless, the basic structure remains: clearly designated good guys combat and ultimately conquer the evil villain. The good guys inevitably win, the bad guys are irredeemably evil, and this justifies the violence against them. There is no ambiguity; there are no multiple outcomes of moral action. "Cartoon and comic heroes cast not shadows."[32]

> The myth of redemptive violence is the simplest, laziest, most exciting, uncomplicated, irrational, and primitive depiction of evil the world has ever known. Furthermore, its orientation to evil is one into which virtually all modern children (boys especially) are socialized in the process of maturation ... Once children have been indoctrinated into the expectations of a dominator society, they may never outgrow the need to locate all evil outside themselves.[33]

What Wink here calls "the Domination system" illustrates the erroneous aspects of the ethic of control. This system presumes that evil, when encountered, can be overcome through direct action. The most powerful of direct actions is violence, so that violence becomes the *modus operandi* of the domination system. The myth is that violence and control will be redemptive. The danger is that violence and control become ends in themselves to be preserved at all costs. The irony is that, instead of eradicating evil, the supposed solution simply perpetuates it.

Wink maintains that there is a tension in the biblical tradition between this domination system and what he calls a partnership community. Some parts of Hebrew Scripture reinforce a powerful Yahweh who orders his chosen people "to destroy, plunder, and kill all but the virgin daughters of their enemies, and to take these as sexual slaves, concubines, and involuntary wives."[34] In contrast to this tradition is the legacy of the Hebrew prophets, some of whom directly chastise Israel for its reliance on military power. Wink cites Abraham Heschel, who remarked that the prophets were the first people in history to regard a nation's reliance on force as evil.[35]

Wink further maintains that Jesus followed in this long line of prophetic voices, living counter to and speaking against the system of domination and the solution to evil that it promoted. This is the message of the Kingdom of God—that evil forces can be turned around not through force but by love. Jesus acted against the mores of his time. Through his preaching, his concern for the marginalized, his treatment of women, his breaking of ritual practices, and his insistence on love of enemies, culminating in his death on a Roman cross, Jesus embodied an alternative to domination.[36] Nevertheless, as contemporary scholars are pointing out, such an alternative quickly devolved, once again, into a narrative of domination, of a quick fix through decisive, even violent action.

Under such a lens, God becomes an agent of decisive action who rescued sinners by redemptive violence, in this case the sacrifice of his son on the cross. The Resurrection serves as evidence of the "success" of this plan. Jesus becomes the sacrificial scapegoat who takes on the violence of our sins and is rewarded for his willingness to do so. Theological efforts to the contrary, this transaction ultimately makes of God a bloodthirsty deity and perpetuates the myth of redemptive violence (on God's part) and redemptive suffering (on our part). Ironically, it doesn't resolve the problem of evil but only perpetuates it.

God and the Solution to the Problem of Evil: Jesus and an Ethic of Risk

It is possible to understand Jesus' life, death, and Resurrection in a way that illustrates resistance and surrender within an ethic of risk. In this light, there is no transaction whereby God "fixes" evil through decisive action. It is not that Jesus' death in itself constitutes the solution to the problem of evil. Rather, this interpretation retrieves the fullness of Jesus' work in his life, death, and Resurrection. Jesus' manner of living becomes central to the meaning of his death. He lived with a radical set of values on a daily basis, recognizing the dignity of all and using his persuasive powers in a transformative, healing way.[37] He surrendered to suffering, not as a transaction that would be rewarded with new life, but as the risk he had to take in choosing to live life in union with his Abba, father. He resisted the religious and political distortions of his day by living and declaring an alternative set of meanings.

Central to this new set of meanings is the intersection between who Jesus was and what he did. Jesus' actions and preaching arose out of his unclouded sense of identity as a son in relationship to his Abba-Father-God. Thus, Jesus did more than choose a radical way of life—he chose *himself* as a child of God. The most radical element of his resistance to the powers of his day was that he defined his life's meaning in light of his identity, as a beloved son empowered by divine relationship.

Jesus' death, then, is understood as the consequence of this radical choice of self and the way of life to which it led. It is also, therefore, the ultimate unveiling (apocalyptic) event. In one sense his mission failed; in another, there is a denouement here, an ironic reversal, in which the supposed victory of the destructive powers becomes the occasion for an alternative to the cycle of violence. By refusing to succumb, even in the face of death, to the definition others had of him, Jesus exposed the powers for what they were. Wink puts it as follows:

> Here was a person able to live out to the fullest what he felt was God's will. He chose to die rather than compromise with violence. The Powers threw at him every weapon in their arsenal. But they could not deflect him from the trail that he and God were blazing. Because he lived thus, we too can find our own path.
>
> Because they could not kill what was alive in him, the cross also revealed the impotence of death. Death is the Powers' final sanction. Jesus at his crucifixion neither fights the darkness nor flees under cover of it, but goes with it, goes into it. He enters the darkness, freely, voluntarily. The darkness is not dispelled or illuminated. It remains vast,

untamed, void. But he somehow encompasses it. It becomes the darkness of God. It is now possible to enter any darkness and trust God to wrest from it meaning, coherence, resurrection.[38]

In accepting death as the consequence of his (w)holy identity, Jesus reveals both the nature of God as well as the true ground of human identity. God is not like the powers that assume control through decisive, violent action. God is not a wrathful God who demands retributive justice at all costs. God refused to do battle with evil powers on their own terms. God would not use violence to achieve his own ends. Instead, by allowing Jesus' death, and in raising him from the dead, God revealed that there is a permanence and transcendence to human identity that evil cannot destroy. Authentic resistance involves claiming that identity, grounded in God, and refusing to capitulate to the denigrating definitions of others. Authentic resistance to evil thus becomes an embodied faith in eternal life, meaning confidence that one's self perdures in God's embrace in spite of oppressive treatment from others. "Jesus' death on the cross was like a black hole in space that sucked into its collapsing vortex the very meaning of the universe, until in the intensity of its compaction there was an explosive reversal, and the stuff of which galaxies are made was blown out into the universe. So Jesus as the cosmic Christ became universal, the truly Human One, and, as such, the bearer of our utmost possibilities for living."[39]

God's Solution to the Problem of Evil: Reversing the Cycle of Violence

In *The Crucified Is No Stranger,* Sebastian Moore develops a model of personal salvation as a drama that unfolds in believers' lives.[40] In this perspective, the problem of evil is the sin of self-destruction, whereby we all fail to embrace the deep hidden selves that we are, oriented to God. Instead we choose to deny our transcendent Eros, even killing the one-loved-by-another in order to avoid the challenges of self-transcendence. Jesus, as the only fully flourishing human, in union with God, represents this self that we crucify. "What if Jesus were the representative, the symbol, the embodiment, of this dreaded yet desired self of each of us, this destiny of being human…? The crucifixion of Jesus then becomes the central drama of man's refusal of his true self."[41]

This drama works itself out in two scenarios. The first is the actual historical drama in which Jesus, as embodiment of this (w)holy human flourishing, bears the brunt of human *ressentiment* against the good.[42] This is the drama we have reviewed through the lens of Wink's interpretation of the Domination system. There is also, then, the drama as it works itself out in the believer's life. This is the Christian who, "confronted with Jesus crucified, finds all the evil in his life becoming *explicit* as the willful destruction of this true self now for him in the man on the cross."[43]

Key to this drama is that it makes explicit what otherwise remains an obscure tendency to destroy what we could become. The death of Jesus is not just a coincident tragedy, it is his *murder*, the willful destruction that reveals the final outcome of the generic evil that otherwise remains diffuse. Because of Jesus' purity, all the evil is revealed on the side of those who will his death. "The evil thus restricted to the crucifiers becomes an *act*, arising in the human heart and proceeding to its destructive conclusion; an *act*, don't you see, and no longer an *atmosphere*."[44] Evil, thus taken to its extreme and made explicit in history, the murder of the sinless one, is revealed to be ultimately powerless, to exist *within* the purview of God's love.

In this approach, sin becomes not disobedience to a divine command but an innate conflict between who we are and who we can become. Operative in all our desires and aspirations is this "death wish." And its overcoming consists not in its demise but in its rise to power: evil taken to its full extent is shown to be ultimately powerless.

The full extent of evil, of this death wish, is manifested not only in the refusal of human self-transcendence but also in the destruction of any evidence that one might be called beyond the ordinary world of daily life:

> Evil is the inability of the death-wish to be simply a death-wish; its necessity to justify itself by removing the very *grounds* for requiring of us a more intensely personal life. This shows itself in the resentment that is sometimes felt in the presence of an exceptionally good and courageous man. The desire to remove him is the desire to remove an unusually eloquent piece of evidence for the fact that we are called to full personhood. The most passionately protected thing in us is our mediocrity, our fundamental indecision in respect of life. Its protection will require, and will not stop at, murder.[45]

Moore explains this process with the emphasis on evil and sin as an issue of *hubris*. Sin as pride leads to the ego needing to be in control, the ego refusing the call beyond itself to become a full creaturely yet transcendently oriented self. Jesus stands as the symbol of this self and, as crucified, makes explicit the results of the ego alienated from its source—pride taken to its full extreme.

But for some, the path to salvation may begin from the other side. There are some persons who, due to their social location, do not even have the ego to presume control. Many persons are socialized into believing that their identity lies solely in their usefulness to others. Economic, social, cultural, and political forces contribute to this message. For these persons, the self—the possibility of full human flourishing in communion with the Divine—has not been offered to them. This is not to say that such a self does not exist, only that the rejection of self comes in a different form, not as the ego taking charge but as the ego capitulating to others' definition of who is a full human person and who is not.[46]

For those who *begin* on the underside of social and psychological power, salvation has to do with discovering integral dignity and choosing this mystery of self by a *strengthened* ego. From this angle, one discovers in the drama of the cross a different story. One does indeed discover evil run to its full extreme. But in contemplating Jesus on the cross one discovers oneself, not as the crucifier who willed this death, but as the victim who has been slain. In this case, by identifying with Jesus as the crucified, one is able to name one's own victimization, to face the wounds that have hampered one's full human flourishing. Detrimental assumptions that one is constitutionally *unable* to be a creature in communion with God are unveiled as false presumptions. Resurrection is the revelation of God's loving embrace in spite of such oppressive powers. Eventually, one may come to see one's complicity in such victimization, but initially the crucified becomes one like me, a friend, not a stranger. Resurrection is God's embrace of one as loved in the face of powerful messages to the contrary.

Thus, some people discover themselves in the crucified Jesus as *crucifiers*, while others come to the challenge of new life through discovering themselves in Jesus as the *crucified*. Traditional interpretations have emphasized the former. Today, the rising voices of those from the underside of history highlight the latter route as important and viable. While salvation as forgiveness continues to be salient, the experience of resurrection life as empowerment is becoming a forceful transformative narrative for many today.

Sebastian Moore depicts the drama of salvation as one of discovering oneself in Jesus on the cross. To his explication of finding ourselves as crucifiers of perfect human flourishing, I have added the other side—the drama of finding ourselves as victims in Jesus crucified. Lest this sound like a purely intrapsychic exercise, let us note the perduring social cycle of violence in an ever widening circle of perpetrators and victims. Those who suffer oppression, be it social or economic or as the exercise of physical or sexual abuse, have a tendency to try to heal themselves in ways that simply perpetuate further violence. Thus, victims, in a distorted attempt to rectify unjust situations, end up becoming perpetrators of further violence, creating new victims, who in turn harm others in an effort to fix themselves. Thus we find a cycle of sin in which, often, our very attempts to promote justice or bring healing simply reinforce oppressive systems. So, perpetrators of self-destruction (leading to harm toward others) are often also victims of self-destruction (from harm done to them). Likewise, those socialized into serving the purposes of others can at times perpetuate their own self-destruction, sabotaging their own flourishing because such service is comfortable and familiar.

Stopping the cycle involves one person, at least, refusing to perpetuate it. The wounded person, rather than passing on pain, embraces the pain and finds healing. Such healing enables him to forgive, and such forgiveness frees his perpetrator from defensive living. Such a person, in turn, is freed to face her own pain and seek forgiveness for her harmful actions. So the cycle becomes not victim-perpetrator-victim but healed-forgiven-healed.

Redemption as an Ethic of Risk

Let me draw together the elements that have been emerging here. Redemption has been seen for some centuries as a transaction whereby Jesus' obedience and death on the cross are rewarded by winning for us freedom from the condemnation we deserve. While there are many versions of this theology of salvation, it remains one that lends itself to incorporating violence not only into our soteriology but also into the very nature of God. Sharon Welch's outline of an ethic of control along with Walter Wink's analysis of the myth of redemptive violence reveal the fault lines in some perduring theologies of redemption: Jesus' death seen as a final or decisive "fix" to the problem of evil can serve merely to perpetuate rather than to eradicate the cycles of violence and oppression that lie at the heart of the human dilemma. My own analysis of the dialectic between the regularities and the contingencies in the unfolding of world process reveals, on the side of the subject, that moral agency involves not just doing A so that B will follow, but making choices that seek to shift probabilities so that something new might emerge.

Central to this analysis is the term "conditions of possibility." When one operates without the hubris of assuming control, one intentionally seeks to set up new conditions of possibility for transformation. Rather than the eradication of evil, one takes as one's goal the long-term struggle to shift patterns of co-operation, to alter habitual attitudes and practices, to dismantle regularities that undergird systemic injustice. In doing this work for transformation one cannot know the outcomes of one's actions;

one simply chooses integrity, authenticity, and effective action in the hope that some faintly envisioned set of liberating values will emerge.

What does this have to do with our understanding of Jesus' work of salvation? Let us think of Jesus as the one who, in Sebastian Moore's terms, did not succumb to the fear that is at the heart of self-destruction. Instead he was the one person in history who lived out of communion with God to such a full extent that his ego ambitions did not destroy his deepest self-in-divine-relation. In fact, he was the one fully human being. As such he drew the anger and *ressentiment* of those living with an ethic of control, of those who assume that the power of domination is the road to fulfillment. The response of those enamoured of their mediocrity and cunning self-deceit (i.e., all of us) is to destroy this evidence of (w)holy human-in-divine relationship. The mystery of Jesus' work of salvation thus lies not only in his life but also in his response to this threat. He not only lived an integrated life in the embrace of God, but he did so *even in the face of evil*, manifest in the injustice of his trial and Crucifixion. The only one who justifiably *could* have retaliated did not. He chose to stop the cycle of revenge and violence by suffering evil rather than doing evil. Evil thus *fully manifested* as the intentional execution of the one and only pure victim in history exhausts its power. The ultimate failure of this kind of ethic of control, the hubris and power it falsely presumes, is revealed in the Resurrection and exaltation of the crucified one. Jesus is vindicated, and his followers are liberated, forgiven, and empowered in spite of their fear and failures.

Does any of this "fix" sin in a definitive way? Yes and no. It does not eradicate evil as would be presumed in an ethic of control. In fact it totally subverts the presumptions of such an ethic. Domination, power, quick fixes, decisive action; these are not the way of the God who raised Jesus from the dead. However, radically new conditions of possibility for transformation are definitively revealed. Within human history the work of domination, the full extent of evil, even of the human propensity to destroy the demand for self-transcendence at all costs, has been shown to be ultimately powerless. The love of the Creator God has been shown to *encompass* such evil, to be beyond it rather than its equal opposite. What occurs is not a grand *fix* but the establishment of the conditions of possibility for transformation.

The drama of Jesus' life, death, and Resurrection stands once and for all as the icon of both the failure of the power of evil and the extent of God's healing and forgiveness. By entering into this drama in facing our own self-destruction as well as our own victimization we can discover new possibilities of forgiveness and healing. Because Jesus opted to live with authenticity in his identity in God, the conditions of possibility are opened up for us to see our inauthenticity, self-destruction, and victimization and to dis-cover that none of these need have the final word. Indeed, there is noth-ing we might do that would be so cruel as to put us beyond the reach of God's love and forgiveness. Likewise, there is nothing we might suffer that would be so horrendous as to put us beyond the reach of God's love and healing.

This fact is now revealed once and for all. This is the *already* of our *already but not yet* eschatological hope. The conditions of possibility for transfor-mation have been established in history. The working out of the reversal of schemes of recurring violence and victimization has still to unfold. Hence we are called, not to quick fixes and assumptions of control, but to live in the sure confidence of the hope of transformation while making choices within an ethic of risk. Through offering healing and forgiveness we can turn the cycle of violence into a cycle of reconciliation and renewal. We thus, embraced by resurrection love, can shift the likelihood that others will in turn be transformed.

Conclusion

Eucharistic Prayer C, Rite II, in the *Book of Common Prayer* of the Episcopal Church begins as follows:

> God of all power, Ruler of the Universe, you are worthy of glory and praise.
> *Glory to you for ever and ever.*
> At your command all things came to be; the vast expanse of interstellar space, galaxies, suns, the planets in their courses, and this fragile earth, our island home.
> *By your will they were created and have their being.*
> From the primal elements you brought forth the human race, and blessed us with memory, reason, and skill. You made us the rulers of creation. But we turned against you, and betrayed your trust; and we turned against one another.
> *Have mercy, Lord, for we are sinners in your sight.*
> Again and again, you called us to return. Through the prophets and sages you revealed your righteous Law. And in the fullness of time you sent your only Son, born of a woman, to fulfill your Law, to open for us the way of freedom and peace.
> *By his blood, he reconciled us.*
> *By his wounds we are healed.*[47]

In this Eucharistic celebration we place ourselves in the drama of salvation history—from the creation of interstellar space to the mysteries of a final

Passover meal in Jerusalem. In the process we declare that Jesus' blood has reconciled us and his wounds have healed us. Exactly what it means to say that Jesus died for our sins remains implicit. Yet weekly, sometimes daily, we put ourselves into this drama in the hope of opening up possibilities for a new future. In this essay I have tried to indicate that what we are about in this process is not a matter of availing ourselves of some simple "fix" that protects us from the wrath of a violent God. Rather we enter into a process of healing and forgiveness that has already begun in the "risk" of the Incarnation, in the choice of the Incarnate One to claim his identity in the face of misunderstanding and jealousy, to suffer evil rather than to do evil, so that the perpetual cycle of violence might come to a full stop. We enter into this history of salvation in the same way, making choices in the face of the seemingly irreparable damage of systemic injustice, not presuming to eradicate evil, but confident that the hope of the Gospel will manifest itself in incremental changes, shifting the conditions of possibility so that transformation might occur.

Notes

1 *The Book of Common Prayer According to the Use of the Episcopal Church* (New York: Seabury Press, 1979), 101. Since this article is published in a book in memory of Joanne McWilliam, I thought it appropriate to begin with a prayer from the Anglican tradition, which she embraced in mid-life. I first knew Joanne in the 1970s at the University of St. Michael's College, where I completed both an M.A. and a Ph.D. in theology. Although I did not study with Joanne, in the gender consciousness-raising of the 1970s I came to know her at various "Women in Theology" meetings, where female students and professors encouraged one another in their endeavours. Joanne served as a mentor and guide for many. I regarded her as an "elder stateswoman" of the feminist movement. As such, she had little patience for those of us struggling to balance social expectations and professional aspirations. At one point, when I raised the issue of having children and pursuing an academic career, her response went something like this: "You just do what you have to do: get on their jackets, get them out the door and off to school, or whatever!" Years later, after Joanne had crossed Queen's Park to Trinity College and ordained priestly ministry, we met again through a job search at Trinity. Although I was not hired, Joanne stayed in touch and encouraged my scholarly work. We met regularly at scholarly meetings, and she sent me annual Christmas cards. Indeed, I believe that she wrote a letter of endorsement when I applied for my current job at an Episcopal seminary.

2 Elizabeth Johnson makes the following comment about Anselm's model of salvation: "I sometimes think that Anselm should be considered the most successful theologian of all time. Imagine having almost a one-thousand-year run for your theological construct! It was never declared a dogma but might just as well have been, so dominant has been its influence in theology, preaching, devotion, and the penitential system of the Church, up to our own day." "Jesus and Salvation," *Pro-*

ceedings, Forty-Ninth Annual Convention of the Catholic Theological Society of America 49 (1994): 1–18 at 5. See also Robert Daly, "Images of God and the Imitation of God: Problems with Atonement," *Theological Studies* 68 (2007): 36–51 at 45.

3 See Joann Carlson Brown and Carole R. Bohn, eds., *Christianity, Patriarchy, and Abuse: A Feminist Critique* (Cleveland: Pilgrim Press, 1989).

4 See Yacob Tesfai, ed., *The Scandal of a Crucified World: Perspectives on the Cross and Suffering* (Maryknoll: Orbis, 1994).

5 See René Girard, *Violence and the Sacred* (Baltimore: Johns Hopkins University Press, 1977); *Things Hidden Since the Foundation of the World,* with Jean-Michel Oghourlian and Guy Lefort (Stanford: Stanford University Press, 1987); *The Scapegoat* (Baltimore: Johns Hopkins University Press, 1986); and James G. Williams, ed., *The Girard Reader* (New York: Crossroad, 1996). See also Raymund Schwager, *Must There Be Scapegoats?* (San Francisco: Harper and Row, 1987); and *Jesus in the Drama of Salvation* (New York: Herder and Herder, 1999). See also the review articles by Leo Lefebure, "Victims, Violence, and the Sacred: The Thought of René Girard," *Christian Century* 113 (1996): 126–29; and "Beyond Scapegoating: A Conversation with René Girard and Ewart Cousins," *Christian Century* 115 (1998): 372–75. More recent works that deal with mimetic theory and the atonement include Anthony Bartlett, *Cross Purposes* (Harrisburg: Trinity, 2001); and S. Mark Heim, *Saved from Sacrifice* (Grand Rapids: Eerdmans, 2006).

6 See J. Denny Weaver, *The Nonviolent Atonement* (Grand Rapids: Eerdmans, 2001); and Brad Jersak and Michael Hardin, eds., *Stricken by God? Nonviolent Identification and the Victory of Christ* (Grand Rapids: Eerdmans, 2007).

7 See Peter Schmiechen, *Saving Power: Theories of Atonement and Forms of the Church* (Grand Rapids: Eerdmans, 2005); Elizabeth A. Dreyer, *The Cross in Christian Tradition: From Paul to Bonaventure* (New York: Paulist Press, 2000); Gerard S. Sloyan, *The Crucifixion of Jesus: History, Myth, Faith* (Minneapolis: Fortress, 1995); and Rosemary Radford Ruether, *Women and Redemption: A Theological History* (Minneapolis: Fortress, 1998).

8 For a recent review of the literature, see Michael Hardin, "Out of the Fog: New Horizons for Atonement Theory," in *Stricken by God?* 54–76.

9 I would like to thank Cynthia Stelle for her research assistance in preparing this article.

10 Stephen Finlan, *Problems with Atonement: The Origins of, and Controversy About, the Atonement Doctrine* (Collegeville: Liturgical Press, 2005), 1. Finlan goes on to say: "Most strategies for dealing with objections to these doctrines involve separating the objectionable from the biblical, either showing that the objectionable doctrines do not occur in the Bible, or that they do occur but are not objectionable when properly explained" (ibid.).

11 Daly, "Images of God," 41. He refers here to Finlan, 97–98.

12 Ibid., 42.

13 Ibid. See Walter Wink, *Naming the Powers: The Language of Power in the New Testament* (Philadelphia: Fortress, 1984); idem, *Unmasking the Powers: The Invisible Forces That Determine Human Existence* (Philadelphia: Fortress, 1986); idem, *Engaging the Powers: Discernment and Resistance in a World of Domination* (Minneapolis: Fortress, 1992); and idem, *The Powers That Be: Theology for a New Millenium* (New York: Doubleday, 1998).

14 Daly, "Images of God," 45. He is quoting Finlan, *Problems with Atonement,* 75.

15 Ibid., 45.

16 Portions of this section of the essay have appeared in some of my previous arti-cles, most notably "Risk Versus Control: Grounding a Feminist Ethic for the New Millennium," in *Themes in Feminist Theology for the New Millennium (III),* ed. Gaile M. Polhaus (Villanova: Villanova University Press, 2006): 1–22; and "Making a Way by Walking: Risk, Control, and Emergent Probability," *Théoforum* 38 (2007): in press.

17 Sharon D. Welch, *A Feminist Ethic of Risk* (Minneapolis: Fortress, 1990). A revised edition was published in 2000. The changes involve revisions to one particular chapter, "The Ethic of Control," where Welch had discussed the nuclear arms poli-cies of the 1980s. In the process, however, she has deleted much of her earlier description of an ethic of control. Thus, unless otherwise noted, my quotations are from the original version of 1990.

18 Ibid., 23.

19 Ibid.

20 Immediately after the 11 September 2001 events, both President Bush and Ben-jamin Netanyahu spoke of the "eradication" of evil in terms reflective of this ethic of control. See http://www.whitehouse.gov/news/releases/2001/09/20010915.html and http://www.americanrhetoric.com/speeches/netanyahu.htm. Accessed 13 Jan-uary 2009.

21 Welch, *A Feminist Ethic of Risk,* 33.

22 Ibid., 19 (2nd ed., 45).

23 Ibid., 20 (2nd ed., 46).

24 Ibid.

25 Ibid.

26 While Welch introduces her categories in a mainly prescriptive manner, indicat-ing that one *ought* to function with an ethic of risk rather than an ethic of con-trol, I have tried to ground these categories *descriptively.* In other words, the ethic of control is not always fraught with hubris—indeed, there are some choices we can make with confidence that there *will* be clear and predictable outcomes.

27 This is why the ethic of risk is a *feminist* ethic of risk. To the degree that feminism takes as its task the unmasking of dominance, particularly male dominance, it relies on the experiences of women from the underside of history. To the degree that women have found themselves, proportionately, in social, economic, and political roles that deny them moral agency, they are more aware of the fact that moral choice includes ambiguity, vulnerability, and risk. It is not that women have some essentially different way of making moral decisions (by risk rather than control) or that vulnerability in and of itself is a norm to be sought after. Rather, women and many others who suffer from the powerlessness of social class, race, or sexual orientation are able to be more honest about the risk inherent in all moral choice.

28 Portions of this section of the essay are a recasting of Chapter 3 of my book *Embrac-ing Travail: Retrieving the Cross Today* (New York: Continuum, 1999).

29 See Wink, *Engaging the Powers.*

30 One example from the ancient Near Eastern traditions would be the *Enuma Elish,* a story in which multiple gods compete for power. In the end, Marduk conquers

and kills Tiamat, and her carcass serves as the foundation of the world. See, for example, http://www.ancienttexts.org/library/mesopotamian/enuma.html. Full text available at http://www.sacred-texts.com/ane/enuma.htm. Accessed 13 January 2009.

31 To see examples of Popeye cartoons go to: http://www.youtube.com/watch?v=0av3 fmr0sDc. Accessed 13 January 2009.

32 Wink, *Engaging the Powers*, 19.

33 Ibid., 22. Cf. Karen Lebacqz, "Love Your Enemy: Sex, Power, and Christian Ethics," *Annual of the Society of Christian Ethics* (1990): 3–23.

34 Wink, *Engaging the Powers*, 44. He relies here on the work of Raine Eisler, *The Chalice and the Blade* (San Franscisco: Harper and Row, 1987).

35 See Wink, *Engaging the Powers*, 45. He here refers to Abraham Heschel, *The Prophets* (New York: Harper and Row, 1969), I:166. After citing Heschel he gives a long list of the many passages in which the prophets denounce the characteristics of domination. See Wink, *Engaging the Powers*, Chapter 2n59.

36 See ibid., Chapter 6.

37 See Carter Heyward's "re-imaging" of Jesus in *The Redemption of God: A Theology of Mutual Relation* (Lanham: University Press of America, 1982), Chapter 2. See especially her discussion of power, 41–44.

38 Wink, *Engaging the Powers*, 141.

39 Ibid., 143.

40 Sebastian Moore, *The Crucified Is No Stranger* (London: Darton, Longman, and Todd, 1977).

41 Ibid., x.

42 On *ressentiment*, see Max Scheler, *Ressentiment*, trans. W.H. Holdheim (New York: Schocken, 1972).

43 Moore, *The Crucified*, x.

44 Ibid., 2.

45 Ibid., 13.

46 Dolores Williams makes a similar point in her retrieval of a womanist notion of sin. "Feelings of personal 'unworthiness' expressed in the Black women's narratives used in this study indicate problems in women's self-esteem ... The womanist notion of sin in this essay takes seriously Black women's depleted self-esteem. Thus elevating and healing Black women's self-esteem figures into womanist notions of what constitutes salvation for the oppressed African-American community." See "A Womanist Perspective on Sin," in *A Troubling in My Soul: Womanist Perspectives on Evil and Suffering*, ed. Emilie Townes (Maryknoll: Orbis, 1993), 147.

47 *The Book of Common Prayer*, 370.

14

Lord of Two Cities
Christological or Political Realism
in Augustine's City of God?

✠ ✠ ✠

JANE BARTER MOULAISON

M Y ACQUAINTANCE with Joanne McWilliam was largely literary; we shared far more by way of letters and academic writings—and, perhaps most significantly, by reading the same authors—than we did in the few face-to-face conversations we had. The written word was, I believe, an appropriate medium of exchange for both of us, and indeed, in time it came to be the grammar of a friendship that I think we both cherished. Though I had studied Theology in Toronto, I did not have the occasion to study with her. It was not until I ventured to publish my dissertation in 2005 that Joanne befriended me. She befriended me in that classical sense that Augustine understood well—quite simply, she mentored me. She assisted me through the publication of my book with *Editions SR* of Wilfrid Laurier University Press, for which she served as series editor. She then supported me generously throughout my tenure review, and finally, and lastly, she contributed an article on theological education for a collection of essays I edited for the *Toronto Journal of Theology*. I like to think that we shared what Cicero and his reader/disciple Augustine agreed to be the "foundation for authentic friendship," which is an "agreement on divine things."[1]

Perhaps more than any other theologian, Augustine of Hippo has been marshalled to champion a broad range of causes, both theological and secular. One of the surprising areas in which Augustine has been appropriated is in political theory: his *City of God* is often read as a treatise on politics rather than as a work of theology.[2] What animates these conversations often has less to do with Augustine's own context than with our own. Such retrievals obviously seek just war principles; but more broadly, they reflect a desire to inquire after the nature of and limits to political action in a world that tends to be alternately self-assured and cynical about its efficacy and value. However, answers to such questions are not always easily found in Augustine, whose *City of God* is anything but a systematic political treatise. In her anthology, *Augustine: From Rhetor to Theologian*, Professor McWilliam critiques the old questions that dominated studies of Augustine's Christology as those stemming rather straightforwardly from Modernist debates within Catholic theology rather than from Augustine's Christology proper. Her survey of twentieth-century writings on Augustine's Christology sees in the loosening of his position as a direct authority for Western Christianity a greater measure of freedom in assessing his writings proper.[3] A similar phenomenon can be traced in Protestant appropriations of Augustine. Those liberal Protestants concerned with maintaining the Church's prominent position in the public square have found in Augustine's *City of God* not only a salutary description of the vexed nature of our political striving in a fallen world, but also a justification for the abiding status of the City of God's ministers within the earthly city. Yet a strong case for the relevance of an ecclesial voice in politics demands apologetic moves that either neglect or water down the particular status Augustine ascribes in the *City of God* to Christ as Lord of both cities. In this case, rather than conforming Christology to satisfy debates on the nature of Christ, we find among Augustine's modern Protestant readers a curious waning of Christology in the waxing of a full-fledged political theory.[4]

One of the most influential retrievals of Augustine for the purposes of Protestant political theory is that of Reinhold Niebuhr. Niebuhr considered Augustine the father of Christian realism—a chastened and unidealized account of the nature of the fallen political world and Christians' rueful yet necessary reconciliation with it. Niebuhr finds in Augustine an authority who grants Christian faith a rightful and even prominent moral place within the governance of the secular world because of its accurate account of the fallen nature of humans and because of the high ideals it upholds. In Niebuhr's hands, Augustine helps underwrite Christian participation within liberal democracy, viewed not merely as a necessary concession within the earthly city but as a positive Christian duty. However, the profound influence of Niebuhr's reading of Augustine has obscured several significant differences between his political theology and that of Augustine. Most significantly, in my view, a Niebuhrian reading of the *City of God* obscures the role that Christ as Lord of the two cities plays in these respective theologians' accounts of Christian responsibility and possibility.

Christian Realism

The definition of realism is a decidedly slippery one;[5] it can refer to moral, political, and epistemological arguments, each of which will claim a positive relation to the "Real" based upon different kinds of mediation. Niebuhr's appropriation of the term and his ascription of realism to Augustine in his famous essay "Augustine's Political Realism" claims to concern itself primarily with a moral and political definition that "denotes the disposition to take all factors in a social and a political situation, which offer resistance to established norms, into account, particularly the factors of self-interest and power."[6] Niebuhr wishes to eschew a naive idealism of the sort characterized by "loyalty to moral norms and ideals, rather than to self-interest, whether individual or collective."[7] Both here and throughout his writings, Niebuhr is unconcerned with what he terms the "rationalistic" account of realism, the underpinnings of which might be found in an epistemological (in modern philosophy) or metaphysical (in classical theology and philosophy) account of how the judgments we render in our moral, social, and linguistic representations conform to transcendent reality. Niebuhr's concern with the pragmatic and the political spurred him at least to defer such questions when appropriating the term. For him, Augustine's realism was rooted squarely in anthropology: we must have a realistic sense of the capacity of sinful humanity to transcend self-interest. Niebuhr thus finds within Augustine's anthropology a sensible account of the human condition, one that maintains that human sinfulness will inevitably impede any realization of the *Civitas Dei* on earth.

Niebuhr lauds Augustine's achievement as capable of establishing "the only real basis for a realistic estimate of the forces of recalcitrance which we must face on all levels of the human community, particularly for a realistic estimate of the spiritual dimension of these forces and of the comparative impotence of 'pure reason' against them."[8] Augustine's theology of original sin offers Niebuhr an account of the actual powers that limit political possibility—particularly peace, which Niebuhr, following Augustine, regards as ever precarious and even illusory within the earthly city: "The *civitas terrena* is described as constantly subject to an uneasy armistice between contending forces, with the danger that factional disputes may result in 'bloody insurrection' at any time."[9]

Pride

Both Niebuhr and Augustine see human pride as the form that original sin is most likely to take within the *civitas terrena* as humans seek to govern themselves and one another. Pride is the ultimate form of rebellion against God and fellow humans, for it consists of a perverse imitation of God that seeks to impose its own dominion on others. One of the consequences of pride, according to Augustine, is that persons arrogate to themselves the capacity to create a kind of political or social version of the good life that is divested of God's grace and that thus offers a truncated form of the good. For Augustine, it is a mark of human futility that humans seek "for themselves a happiness in this life, based upon a virtue which is as deceitful as it is proud."[10]

In *City of God*, pride names the character of the *libido dominandi*, the lust for rule, which is less an inherent weakness within the psyche than it is an improperly ordered desire, one that aims merely for personal glory rather than a higher good. Though Augustine does not altogether condemn the pursuit of glory, that vaunted classical ideal, recognizing that it produces certain ends that are necessary for the proper ordering of society, glory too can become turned in on itself, as the citizen seeks recognition and praise rather than the truth. Thus the quest for glory is too easily prone to becoming corrupted, and the virtues it seeks in the ordering of the self and society soon become vices in the seeking of praise rather than higher ends. Therefore, while glory can be useful in directing human will toward the recognition of others, such a quest soon becomes vain as it seeks ever its own ends. Humility is required in political life in order to direct glory away from the self and toward its true source, which is the God who has come by humbly taking on human form. As Augustine writes:

> [F]or, though that glory be not a luxurious woman, it is nevertheless puffed up, and has much vanity in it. Wherefore it is unworthy of the solidity and firmness of the virtues to represent them as serving this glory, so that Prudence shall provide nothing, Justice distribute nothing, Temperance moderate nothing, except to the end that men may be pleased and vain glory served. Nor will they be able to defend themselves from the charge of such baseness, whilst they, by way of being despisers of glory, disregard the judgment of other men, seem to themselves wise, and please themselves. For their virtue,—if, indeed, it is virtue at all,—is only in another way subjected to human praise; for he who seeks to please himself seeks still to please man. But he who, with true piety towards God, whom he loves, believes, and hopes in, fixes his attention more on those things in which he displeases himself, than on those things, if there are

any such, which please himself, or rather, not himself, but the truth, does not attribute that by which he can now please the truth to anything but to the mercy of Him whom he has feared to displease, giving thanks for what in him is healed, and pouring out prayers for the healing of that which is yet unhealed.[11]

Though the classical virtues might be put to use for the benefit of humankind in the keeping of order in the earthly city, they are so shaped by the prideful desire for human praise and reward that their potential use for proper governance is thoroughly limited. It is instead through the humbled authority of those who seek not glory that a rightly ordered city is approximated. Yet saintly virtue exceeds even this, for it displays a refusal to secure our hope in human striving, and instead finds hope solely in the grace and mercy of God.

Reinhold Niebuhr construes Pride very differently. For him, pride is no less dangerous a temptation within civil society, but he considers it so large a component of the human psyche as to be an inevitability. Niebuhr finds in "biblical religion" the only adequate description of humans' willful self-determination. Biblical faith does not try to sanitize the fact of human corruption, nor does it commend a program for reform. Instead, according to Niebuhr, the biblical faith, which looks unflinchingly at vice, judges pride as not merely a personal foible but a perennial political menace: "powerful self-love or, in modern terms, 'egocentricity,' this tendency of the self to make itself its own end or even to make itself the false center of whatever community it inhabits ... sows confusion into every human community."[12]

Niebuhr thus views pride as an elevation of the self, one's group, or one's class so as to claim a status of superiority by its very denial of the limitations of the self or community. Such pride arises from denial of and anxiety over one's creaturely and limited status. It is a theological malaise no less than a psychological one, for it attempts to usurp God's place and therefore is best understood as a form of idolatry. All groups and individuals are prone to the corrosive power of pride, and its effects can be seen in familial, collegial, national, and racial conflict. For two reasons, it is instructive to consider the latter briefly, as illustrative of Niebuhr's understanding of the ubiquity and dynamic of prideful self-assertion. First, Niebuhr was clearly viewed as *the* great American public theologian during the Civil Rights Movement,[13] even as he was skeptical that it would be able to attain its high aims of racial reconciliation. Second, racial conflict enables us to bring into relief some distinct differences in the respective anthropologies of Niebuhr and Augustine regarding the nature of both collective and individual sin.

Pride, according to Niebuhr, is a constant and a universal temptation. Each individual and each society is prone to excessive self-love. Though universal, pride for Niebuhr is also structural: "socio-economic conditions actually determine to a large degree that some men are tempted to pride and injustice, while others are encouraged to humility."[14] So, while a universal temptation, material conditions will afford certain groups the capacity to realize and execute their wills and dominate others. The prideful self-assertion of the powerful, in Niebuhr's estimate, has two consequences. One, it will incite a greater desire for mastery over one's fellow men and women. This he calls a "horizontal expansion." Two, it will also create a "vertical expansion" whereby the mastery of a particular group over others will soon be endowed with a sense of righteousness, a sense that divine favour attends worldly success. As Niebuhr writes: "Any one who stands is inclined to think that he stands by divine right. Every one who has achieved a high form of culture imagines that it is a necessary and final form of culture. It is the man who stands, who has achieved, who is honoured and approved of by his fellowmen, who mistakes the relative achievements and approvals of history for a final approval."[15]

Though Niebuhr attempts to account for the cumulative and corrosive nature of the sin of pride, as individuals and groups permit their own egotism to go unchecked, one gets the sense that he does not go far enough in naming the vicissitudes of particular historical conditions and agents that might in some cases allow sin to go unleashed, as in modern totalitarianism. Niebuhr's account also refuses the possibility of reconciliation, which some might argue characterized the recent Truth and Reconciliation processes in South Africa. In other words, Niebuhr's typology allows insufficient room for both forgiveness and atrocity, as well as for the myriad political possibilities in between. Thus Niebuhr could write rather formulaically that

> White men sin against Negroes in Africa and America more than Negroes sin against white men. Wherever the forces of nature, the accidents of history, or even the virtues of the possessors of power, endow an individual or a group with power, social prestige, intellectual eminence, or moral approval above their fellows, there is an ego that is allowed to expand … A too simple social radicalism does not recognize how quickly the poor, the weak, the despised of yesterday, may, on gaining a social victory over their detractors, exhibit the same arrogance and the same will-to-power which they abhorred in their opponents and which they were inclined to regard as a congenital sin of their enemies. Every victim of injustice makes the mistake of supposing that the sin from which he suffers is a particular vice of his oppressor.[16]

I would like, in response to this argument, and with Augustine, to defend a theology that postulates "the congenital sin of [our] enemies." That is to say, the sin of pride is not a fact of the human condition that is parcelled inevitably among persons or groups, and enacted each according to his/its ability. While Paul does certainly write that "all have sinned and have fallen short of the glory of God" (Romans 3:23), this is not an ontological description, but is instead a working out of the logic of salvation—which is singular—in the two very particular stories of human rebellion among those who have the Law, and those who are newly adopted by faith in Jesus Christ into God's covenant. In any case, Augustine's doctrine of original sin, whatever its flaws, is at least free of the abstraction that persists in Niebuhr's account of pride, which fails to distinguish adequately among historical injustices against neighbour, postulating instead a common flaw among oppressors and their victims who, though not equally culpable because of the disparity of their means for oppressing others, would likely be so had they the material resources and resourcefulness.

Augustine's doctrine of original sin has less the tenor of inevitability, as he explores the manner in which the historical inheritance of sin can indeed generate habits of malfeasance and arrogance toward others. It is in this sense that we inherit sin from our first ancestors—it precedes our willful participation in it. Yet our individual sin is always our own. There is no point at which the self is abstracted from culpability because this sin was perpetuated rather than created by the self. The self's sinning is somehow always something that is novel to the self and to its particular circumstances. This has to do with the complexity of desires, habits, and specific vices to which my inheritance and my will are likely to give rise. There is thus, in Augustine, a far more robust sense of the complex relationship between self and society and, therefore, also a more nuanced capacity to make distinctions about moral responsibility. As Hannah Arendt, herself an Augustinian, wrote: "Where all are guilty, no one is." For Augustine, though all have sinned, all are not juridically guilty.

Thus Augustine's writings distinguish between various kinds of corruption that the soul undergoes as it sins, as it turns away from God. In *City of God* Augustine writes:

> Thus there is a wickedness by which a man who is self-satisfied as if he were the light turns himself away from that true Light which, had man loved it, would have made him a sharer in the light; it was this wickedness which secretly preceded and was the cause of the bad act which was committed openly ... Therefore God forbade that which, when committed, could be defended by no pretence of sanctity. And I am willing to say that it is advantageous for the proud to fall into some open and manifest

sin, and so become displeasing to themselves, after they had already fallen by pleasing themselves. For when Peter wept and reproached himself, he was in a far healthier condition than when he boasted and was satisfied with himself. A verse of the psalm expressed this truth: fill their faces with shame, and they shall seek thy name, O Lord, meaning, "May those who pleased themselves in seeking their own glory find pleasure in Thee by seeking Thy name."[17]

There are a number of noteworthy things in this remarkable passage, especially when considered in relation to Niebuhr's account of the universal sin of pride. First is the very open and concrete nature of the acts that are named or alluded to here. The betrayal of Christ by Peter is a concrete sin for which the remedy is no less concrete—one might even say public. That is to say, there is less a sense of a hidden depravity in Augustine in the sense of a psychological disposition than there is a sense of a hidden entropy that draws men and women from the light on account of the Fall. Furthermore, there is also a rather straightforward remedy to the sin, once healthily revealed—that is, the refusal to allow sin to become hidden or private (*privatio*). The privation of the self from public confession and reconciliation is the cause of sin's festering and its proclivity for gaining strength. Peter's confession is part and parcel of his healing. Thus an awareness of sin is not an acknowledgment of inevitable and unwavering guilt; rather, it is—non-paradoxically for Augustine—a constitutive part of grace: "*Fill their faces with shame, and they shall seek thy name, O Lord.*" This distinctive understanding of the role of humility and even humiliation will bring into even sharper contrast the differences between Niebuhr's and Augustine's Christology and political theologies.

Humility

While Augustine's anthropology does indeed emphasize a proclivity toward sinfulness within political life that is consistent with the mature anthropology of Reinhold Niebuhr, one finds in Augustine less a sense of tragic necessity than a dynamic of degeneration predicated upon disordered desire that cultivates cumulatively degenerate moral habits. There is nothing inevitable about this decline; there is, instead, a gravitational pull that can exert itself when improper moral habits are unleashed. Thus the relationship of the individual to society is not part to whole or microcosm to macrocosm—a theme that is prominent within Niebuhr's typologies—but rather is better viewed more dynamically as the habits of the City shape (though without determining) its individuals, while the City comprises persons who are varied in their moral capacities. There is no easy dualism in the relationship between the righteous and the unrighteous, but neither is there a homogenization of the two cities. Augustine allows that both Babylon and Jerusalem are mixed entities, consisting of sinners but also those who are decidedly virtuous and for whom righteousness remains ever a possibility because Christ has reconciled us to God: "God being made a righteous man, has interceded with God for man who is a sinner; for though there is no harmony between the sinner and the righteous, there is a harmony between man and man. Therefore joining us to the likeness of his humanity, He took away the unlikeness of our iniquity, and having been made a partaker of our mortality, he made us partakers of his divinity."[18]

Humans require supernatural aid in order to be lifted toward ends that are godly, and those ends are never fully attained in the earthly city or within the Church—within Babylon or Jerusalem. Even so, such *potentia* is not a mere ideal toward which humans strive but a possibility that is given and capable of being grasped by virtue of God's own saving act in Christ. "And it is not in our power to live rightly unless we believe and pray we receive help from him who has given us the faith that we must be helped by him."[19]

The effective operating of Christ upon the Christian believer endows her with virtues quite unlike those considered effective or attractive within the earthly city. The civic virtues are not abandoned; but they are deemed lesser than the virtue of humility, arising from desire of God, that the saints attain. As Augustine lays out his task in the preface to *City of God:* "For I am aware what ability is requisite to persuade the proud how great is the virtue of humility, which raises us, not by a quite human arrogance, but by a divine grace, above all earthly dignities that totter on this shifting scene. For the King and Founder of this city of which we speak, has in Scripture uttered to His people a dictum of the divine law in these words: 'God resisteth the proud, but giveth grace unto the humble.'"[20]

It is within the Church that such unearthly virtue is formed, in which the ends of desire are not found in the work of securing the earthly city but rather in the rest of the eternal city. This pilgrim Church, the City of God, *in via*, is no mere haven from the heartless, rough-and-tumble world of politics; it is instead its own kind of political entity, one that confers upon its subjects glory of a different kind, a glory that is found in humility and a glory that is infused upon its subjects by God's gracious gift in Jesus Christ. In its witness, the City of God prays for the world, and such humble supplication is efficacious and transformative: "Witness the prayer of the whole city of God in its pilgrim state, for it cries to God by the mouth of all its members, 'Forgive us our debts as we forgive our debtors.' And this prayer is efficacious not for those whose faith is 'without works and dead,' but for those whose faith 'worketh by love.'"[21]

For Augustine, Christ exists not as an ideal whose principles point to a perfection that always exceeds our grasp; rather, Christ is the living God who points indeed to a future perfection but who truly conforms the will of humans in this pointing. Desire is not merely a longing for a distant and impossible perfection, but rather participation in the perfection, an attribute communicated to humans in joy: "The role of Christ is to be a perfecter of the will so that the will learns to desire not corruption but goodness. In this sense, he is the way because he is able to so direct desire that humans long for what is good and true. ('The consent of the will for what we want is called desire; joy is the name of the will's consent to the enjoyment of what we desire.')"[22]

The harmonious ordering of the will toward its rightful desire in God is made possible through Christ's own humble supplication. By taking on the human nature (Philemon 2:5–11), Christ offers a new kind of path for humans that is a desire for God and the well-being of others rather than of the self. More than a private virtue, such a life is thoroughly a public one in which the peace given in faith has objective effects in the political life of the body: "In its pilgrim state the heavenly city possesses this peace by faith; and by this faith it lives righteously when it refers to the attainment of that peace every good action towards God and man; for the life of the city is a social life."[23]

The ordering of one's desire toward higher ends is made possible, according to Augustine, through Christ's condescension, his humiliation in taking on human form. The effect of such humiliation is a reconciliation of persons to God and the concomitant capacity to abjure the prideful and arrogant *libido dominandi* and, through grace, to become themselves humble, living lives for others in renunciation and obedience.

> For we ourselves, who are His own city, are His most noble and worthy sacrifice, and it is this mystery we celebrate in our sacrifices, which are well known to the faithful, as we have explained in the preceding books. For through the prophets the oracles of God declared that the sacrifices which the Jews offered as a shadow of that which was to be would cease, and that the nations, from the rising to the setting of the sun, would offer one sacrifice. From these oracles, which we now see accomplished, we have made such selections as seemed suitable to our purpose in this work. And therefore, where there is not this righteousness whereby the one supreme God rules the obedient city according to His grace, so that it sacrifices to

none but Him, and whereby, in all the citizens of this obedient city, the soul consequently rules the body and reason the vices in the rightful order, so that, as the individual just man, so also the community and people of the just, live by faith, which works by love, that love whereby man loves God as He ought to be loved, and his neighbor as himself,—there, I say, there is not an assemblage associated by a common acknowledgment of right, and by a community of interests. But if there is not this, there is not a people, if our definition be true, and therefore there is no republic; for where there is no people there can be no republic.[24]

Peoplehood is thus defined by Augustine not as the sharing of a common mind or common interests; it is instead predicated by its calling, gathering, and ordering by Christ. Therefore, to become a people requires a renunciation of sacrifice within the city because of the one true and common sacrifice that is already given. In short, it is the becoming of a community, a people based upon forgiveness—a reconciliation imparted to them that they, the citizens, must now confer upon one another. Theologian John Milbank puts it very well when he writes: "[T]he only thing really like heavenly virtue is our constant attempt to compensate for, substitute for, even short-cut this total absence of virtue [i.e., in a human life dominated by conflict and violence], by not taking offense, assuming the guilt of others, doing what they should have done, beyond the bounds of any given 'responsibility.' Paradoxically, it is only in this exchange and sharing that any truly actual virtue exists."[25]

Humility and Christian Witness

Christian responsible leadership within the state (a responsibility that is clearly central to Christian witness according to Niebuhr), though at times necessary, is not mandated, or even preferable for Augustine. One ought not to seek out political or ecclesial office, but one ought also not flee it. Augustine is fully aware of the kinds of temptations that exist among those who seek the estate of political office, and thus he commends even here the "sweets of contemplation," not in the sense of a private retreat, but rather as a safeguarding of the soul and of the Church from improper and truncated desire:

So that he who loves to govern rather than to do good is no bishop. Accordingly no one is prohibited from the search after truth, for in this leisure may most laudably be spent; but it is unseemly to covet the high position requisite for governing the people, even though that position be held and that government be administered in a seemly manner. And therefore holy leisure is longed for by the love of truth; but it is the necessity of love to undertake requisite business. If no one imposes this burden upon us, we are free to sift and contemplate truth; but if it be laid upon us, we are necessitated for love's sake to undertake it. And yet not even in this case are we obliged wholly to relinquish the sweets of contemplation; for were these to be withdrawn, the burden might prove more than we could bear.[26]

Christian life, even a life in public office, lacks coherence without the "sweets of contemplation" not because it affords a mere respite from political struggles, but because prayer is efficacious in rightly ordering desire. Implicit in this claim is Augustine's Christology, which maintains that the ascent to higher ends is laid out for us by Christ, whose mediation ensures that our prayers are not in vain, but are effective in the elevation of the soul and in the sanctification of the City of God.

It is precisely for his "monasticism" that Niebuhr critiques Augustine. Niebuhr finds in Augustine an "excessive" sense of futility in worldly affairs, which limits the deployment of justice in human affairs. For example, Niebuhr sees Augustine's incapacity to make judgments against slavery as an instance of the general impotence of his political theory.[27] This inability to make distinctions between various types of goods, according to Niebuhr, rests in a problematic anthropology that is unable to recognize that the mixed nature of the two cities derives from a moral and spiritual struggle not between saints and sinners, but between the saint and the sinner *within each human being*. For Niebuhr, in other words, the spiritual struggle between the wheat and the tares is foremost an individual or psychological one and therefore requires an individual cure. The cure, according to Niebuhr, is the principle of *agape*. *Agape*, on Niebuhr's account, is a disposition toward the other that is a willing release of one's own self-gratifying egotism for the sake of the "higher good." This moral principle presented forcibly as an ideal within the Gospel is a standard that humans cannot attain but toward which they can certainly strive.

Humility and Realism

The case is often made that Niebuhr's realism is moral and political rather than epistemological. Niebuhr himself makes no efforts to provide a foundational underpinning to his theology or ethics. He is instead interested in the pragmatic and the relevant. Yet Niebuhr's lack of a self-consciously articulated ontology—one that is grounded within either a biblical or an apologetical account of the truth—has the effect of short-circuiting his moral and political claims. An abiding feature of Niebuhr's writings on pride is that it is spiritual and intellectual arrogance that gets in the way of a justly ordered city. Humility requires us to relinquish our claims to truth, which for Niebuhr can be attained only partially. Yet to frame humility as primarily an epistemological virtue is to unwittingly situate one's argument within a very specific account of the Real within theology and philosophy—and that is that it cannot be approached. Stanley Hauerwas remarks:

> From many Jewish and Catholic perspectives ... such an account of humility appears to be asking them to understand their convictions in terms laid down by Protestant liberal theology ... Humility ... becomes an extraordinary weapon to still debate by Niebuhrians. Anyone who challenges the fundamental structure of their assumptions automatically becomes "authoritarian." Niebuhr might "praise democracy's capacity to sustain conflict," but in effect the conflict democracy allows is well policed. Nowhere is that more evident than in the exclusion from the politics of democracy of any religious convictions that are not "humble."[28]

Humility is therefore an epistemological virtue for Niebuhr, one which denotes that Niebuhr's realism cannot claim to be grounded in any firm sense of what is true beyond the assurance of the self. As a result, realism also connotes a kind of immanentism in Niebuhr—it is a theology that is turned on the self.[29] For Augustine, both knowledge and will, though compromised by sin, still participate within an ontology of peace and abundance. Therefore, the category of realism, however popular a term when ascribed to Augustine, is seriously deficient because it fails to name that there exists, beyond the story of empires declining and falling, beyond the machinations of power and pride, a greater truth and a greater power—and this is a power arising from the peace and plenitude that is both the origin and destination of all cities. As Karl Hefty writes: "Yet [Augustine's] theology exceeds the category of realism, because, while he takes human sin and suffering as serious threats to happiness and to the beatific vision, they never obscure completely a still discernible peace of being. By plumbing to its depth this question of the condition of our being, he resists in a compelling way the shallow waters of the real."[30]

In this sense, humility has almost the opposite meaning for Augustine that it does for Niebuhr. Augustine views humility as that which is imparted by the humbled one. Humility is thus the capacity not to pass over the truth of Christ's revelation in silence but to be conformed to it. This is nothing less than an ontological conformation as sinner becomes endowed with heavenly gift, because the giver of that gift has poured out his love to humanity. Humility is not the chastening of confidence in the truth of one's own being and of the story of salvation that is imparted in the life, death, and Resurrection of Jesus Christ but is the actual conformity to that truth that we know even in our natures: "For he who laments the peace his nature has lost is stirred to do so by some relics of peace which make his nature friendly to itself."[31]

If there is a realism here, it is a realism grounded in the divine life itself. There are no appeals in Augustine for a theory that might correlate the two cities and their spheres, thus theorizing on the earthly city's relationship to a distant City of God; there is instead a relationship that is described only insofar as Christ is the Lord of both cities: all that falls outside of Christ's reign is nothingness. Or, as Gerald Bonner felicitously puts it: "[I]t is only by possessing, and being possessed by, God that the human soul can realize itself."[32] We might say, even as we hope, that such self-realization is also possible for cities. And that its form is the cross.

Notes

1   Augustine, "Letter 258: Augustine to Martianus," in *Augustine Letters 211–270*, translations and notes by Roland Teske, sj, ed. Boniface Ramsey (New York: New York City Press, 2005).

2   See, for example, secular political theorists Hans J. Morgenthau and Arthur Schlessinger Jr., the latter of whom famously quipped: "Whatever you say about Augustine, at least he would have not been much surprised by the outcome of the Russian Revolution." Arthur Schlessinger, "Niebuhr's Vision of our Time," in *New Republic* 162 (22 June 1946): 754. See also Hannah Arendt, whose appropriations of Augustine go far beyond the political program that is realism, but who nevertheless finds coherence in an Augustine stripped of his dogmatic, and particularly his christological, claims. See also Joanna Vecchiarelli Scott, "Hannah Arendt's Secular Augustinianism," in *History, Apocalypse, and the Secular Imagination*, ed. Mark Vesey, Karla Pollmann, and Allan Fitzgerald (Bowling Green: Philosophy Documentation Centre, 1999).

3   Joanne McWilliam, "The Study of Augustine's Christology in the Twentieth Century," in *Augustine: From Rhetor to Theologian*, ed. Joanne McWilliam (Waterloo: Wilfrid Laurier University Press, 1992), 197.

4   Such readings of Augustine that tend to pass over his Christology in favour of his political theory include several writers whose primary aim seemed to be to establish a theory of politics that seeks primarily to limit vice through the means of the state. As such, politics has less a creative power than a prohibitive one. Among the prominent Christian realists are John C. Bennet, John Foster Dulles, Kenneth Thompson, Martin Wight, and Herbert Butterfield. Eric Patterson characterizes Christian realism's aims and temper thus: "Christian realism was a practical, flexible, and ethical response to the liberal idealism of the day ... In a time of upheaval and uncertainty characterized by the rise of fascism and communism, the Second World War, atomic weapons, and the cold war, the prophetic voice of Christian

realism was heeded not only by those in positions of power, but also by many in the mass public." Eric Patterson, ed., *The Christian Realists, Reassessing the Contributions of Niebuhr and His Contemporaries* (Washington: University Press of America, 2003), 10. Though Augustinian realism was prominent in mid-twentieth-century readings, there have also been contemporary retrievals of Augustine as a remedy for the specific ills of North American politics. See, for example, Jean Bethke Elshtain, *Augustine and the Limits of Politics* (South Bend: Notre Dame University Press, 1995); and Eric Gregory, *Politics and the Order of Love* (Chicago: University of Chicago Press, 2008). Interestingly, one finds in Augustine studies another school that retrieves Augustine's *City of God* for far more theological ends. I am thinking here of the writings of such theologians as John Milbank, Graham Ward, and Catherine Pickstock, the so-called Radical Orthodox movement. Here we see a retrieval of Augustine by those who are more concerned with matters of doctrine than of apologetics.

5 See Stanley Hauerwas with Michael Broadway, "The Irony of Reinhold Niebuhr: The Ideological Character of 'Christian Realism,'" in Stanley Hauerwas, *Wilderness Wanderings: Probing Twentieth Century Philosophy and Theology* (Boulder: Westview, 1996), 48–61. See also Robin Lovin, *Reinhold Niebuhr and Christian Realism* (Cambridge: Cambridge University Press, 1995); and Kenneth Hamilton, "The Doctrine of Man in the Theology of Reinhold Niebuhr" (Ph.D. diss., Emmanuel College, Toronto, January 1965).

6 Reinhold Neibuhr, "Augustine's Political Realism," in *The City of God: A Collection of Critical Essays*, ed. Dorothy F. Donnelly (New York: Peter Lang, 1995), 119.

7 Ibid.

8 Ibid., 121.

9 Ibid., 122.

10 Augustine, *City of God*, trans. Marcus Dods, in *Nicene and Post-Nicene Fathers*, Vol. 2, ed. Philip Schaff (Peabody: Hendrickson, 2004), Book XIX, Chapter 4, 403.

11 Ibid., Book V, Chapter 20, 102.

12 Niebuhr, "Augustine's Political Realism," 121.

13 See Eyal J. Naveh, *Reinhold Niebuhr and Non-Utopian Liberalism: Beyond Illusion and Despair* (Sussex: Sussex University Press), 147 and 148.

14 Reinhold Niebuhr, *Theologian of Public Life*, ed. Larry Rasmussen (Minneapolis: Fortress, 1991), 154.

15 Ibid.

16 Ibid., 155.

17 Augustine of Hippo, *City of God*, trans. Gerald Walsh, Demetrious Zema, Grace Monahan, and Daniel Honan (New York: Doubleday, 1958), Book XIV, Chapter 13, 311.

18 Augustine of Hippo, *On the Holy Trinity*, trans. Marcus Dods, in *Nicene and Post-Nicene Fathers*, Vol. 3, ed. Philip Schaff (Peabody: Hendrickson, 2004), 4.2.4.

19 *City of God*, 403.

20 Ibid.,1.

21 Ibid., 419.

22 Ibid., 304.

23 Ibid., 412.

24 Ibid., 418.

25 John Milbank, *Theology and Social Theory* (Oxford: Blackwell, 1990), 411, cited in Michael J. Hollerich, "Milbank and Augustine," in Vesey et al., *History, Apocalypse, and the Secular Imagination*, 325.

26 *City of God*, 413.

27 Niebuhr, "Augustine's Political Realism," 123.

28 Stanley Hauerwas, "The Democratic Policing of Christianity," *Pro Ecclesia* 3 (1994): 227, 229.

29 Or, as Kenneth Hamilton writes, spelling out the incoherence of a realistic political theology that is not grounded in ontology: "By insisting upon the ideal of justice Niebuhr had drawn back from a consistently realistic interpretation of political action. On the other hand, by insisting realistically upon power being the chief concern of the political, he had made it impossible to disapprove of any political action on moral grounds. The sole criterion of the rightness of a political policy was whether it resulted finally in a better ordering of society." Hamilton, "The Doctrine of Man in the Theology of Reinhold Niebuhr," 283.

30 Karl Hefty, "Truth and Peace: Theology and the Body Politic in Augustine and Hobbes," in *Theology and the Political: The New Debate*, ed. Creston David, John Milbank, and Slavoj Žižek (Durham: Duke University Press, 2005), 438.

31 *City of God*, 410.

32 Gerald Bonner, *Freedom and Necessity: St. Augustine's Teaching on Divine Power and Human Freedom* (Washington: Catholic University Press, 2007), 57.

Curriculum Vitae
Joanne Elizabeth McWilliam

✠ ✠ ✠

Personal

Born Toronto, 10 December 1928
Married to C. Peter Slater, 6 June 1987
Four children:
 Leslie Mary Dewart/Giroday
 Elizabeth Jacqueline Dewart
 Sean McWilliam Dewart
 Gonzalo Duarte
 Twelve grandchildren

Ecclesiastical

Ordained priest in the Diocese of Toronto, 1988
Honorary Assistant, Christ Church, Deer Park, 1998–2008

Education

Oriole Park Public School, Toronto
Loretto Abbey
University of Toronto, B.A. 1951 (Honours Philosophy and History), M.A. 1953
 (Philosophy)
University of St Michael's College, M.A. 1966 (Theology), Ph.D. 1968 (Theology)

Appointments

1954–55 University of Detroit, lecturer in philosophy
1969–94 St. Michael's College and University of Toronto, successively lecturer,
     assistant professor, associate professor, professor of Religious Stud-
     ies, cross-appointed to Faculty of Theology

1990–94	Chair, Department of Religious Studies, University of Toronto
1969–94	Member of the Toronto School of Theology
1981–84	Director, Advanced Degree Studies, Toronto School of Theology
1987–94	Member of the Graduate Centre for the Study of Religion, University of Toronto
1987–90	Associate Director, Graduate Centre for the Study of Religion
1993–94	Director, Graduate Centre for the Study of Religion
1994–2008	Professor Emerita, University of Toronto
1994–99	Mary Crooke Hoffman Professor of Dogmatic Theology, General Seminary of the Episcopal Church, New York.

Honours

2003 Doctor of Divinity, *honoris causae*, Queen's University, Kingston, Ontario, Canada

Publications
Joanne Elizabeth McWilliam

✝ ✝ ✝

Books

The Theology of Grace of Theodore of Mopsuestia. Washington: Catholic University of
America Press, 1971.

Death and Resurrection in the Fathers. Wilmington: Michael Glazier; London: Geof-
frey Chapman, 1986.

Augustine: From Rhetor to Theologian. Editor. Waterloo: Wilfrid Laurier University
Press, 1992.

In progress: *Leah, Rachel and Bilhah: Studies of Augustine's Christology.*

Chapters in Books

"The Misuse of Tradition." In *Women and the Church: A Sourcebook,* edited by Michael
Higgins and D.R. Letson. Toronto: Griffin House, 1986.

"Augustine's Struggle with Time and History." In *Atti del congresso,* edited by George
Lawless. Rome: Augustinianum, 1987, 997–1012.

"Augustine and Christology." In *The Christological Foundation for Contemporary Theological Education,* edited by Joseph D. Ban. Macon: Mercer University Press,
1988, 83–99.

"The Context of the Eighth-Century Adoptionist Controversy." In *Conversion and
Continuity: Indigenous Christian Communities in Islamic Lands, Eighth to Eighteenth
Centuries,* edited by Michael Gervers and Ramzi Jibran Bakhazi. Toronto: Pon-
tifical Institute of Mediaeval Studies, 1990, 75–88.

"Weaving the Strands Together: A Decade in Augustine's Eucharistic Theology."
In *Collectanea Augustiniana: Mélanges Tarisius J. van Bavel,* edited by B. Bruning,
M. Lamberigts, and J. van Houtem. Leuven: Institut Historique Augustini-
enne, 1990, 497–506.

"The Study of Augustine's Christology in the Twentieth Century." In *Augustine: Rhetor to Theologian*, edited by Joanne McWilliam. Waterloo: Wilfrid Laurier University Press, 1992, 183–206.

"Augustine and Ambrose's 'sanam fidem.'" In *Festschrift José Oroz Reta*. Salamanca: Agustinos Recoletos, 1993, 385–397.

"A Response to Papers on *Apostolicae Curae*." In *Anglican Orders. Essays on the Centenary of Apostolicae Curae, 1896–1996*, edited by R. William Franklin. London: Mowbray, 1996, 114–117.

"Augustine's Early Trinitarian Thought." In *Essays in Medieval Philosophy and Theology in Memory of Walter H. Principe, CSB: Fortresses and Launching Pads*, edited by James Ginther and Carl N. Still. Aldershot: Ashgate, 2005, 9–18.

"Augustine at Ephesus?" In *One Lord, One Faith, One Baptism: Studies in Christian Ecclesiality and Ecumenism in Honor of J. Robert Wright*, edited by Marsha L. Dutton and Patrick Terrell Gray. Grand Rapids: Eerdmans, 2006, 56–67.

"The Nurturing Church." In *In God's Hands: Essays on the Church and Ecumenism in Honour of Michael A. Fahey, SJ*," edited by Jaroslav Z. Skira and Michael S. Attridge. Leuven: Leuven University Press/Peeters, 2006, 19–31.

"Augustine's Letters to Women." In *Feminist Interpretations of Augustine*, edited by Judith Chelius Stark. University Park: Pennsylvania State University Press, 2007, 189–202.

Encyclopedia Entries

"Pelagius, Pelagianism." In *Encyclopedia of Early Christianity*, edited by Michael McHugh et al. New York and London: Garland, 1990, 704–8.

"The Cassiciacum Dialogues" and individual entries on *Contra Academicos, De beata vita, De ordine*, and *Soliloquia*. In *Augustine through the Ages: An Encyclopedia*, edited by Allan Fitzgerald. San Francisco: Garland, 1999, 2–4, 94–95, 135–43, 602–3, and 806–7.

"Augustine of Hippo." In *The Dictionary of Historical Theology*, edited by Trevor A. Hart. Carlisle: Paternoster; and Grand Rapids: Eerdmans, 2000, 43–46.

"Anglican Modernism." In Hart, *The Dictionary of Historical Theology*, 368–70.

Articles

"Some Theological Implications of the Thought of R.D. Laing." *Studies in Religion/Sciences Religieuses* 3 (1973): 63–70.

"The Notion of 'Person' Underlying the Christology of Theodore of Mopsuestia." *Studia Patristica* 12 (= *Texte und untersuchungen zur Geschichte der altchristlichen Literatur*, Band 115), edited by E.A. Livingstone. Berlin: Akademie Verlag, 1975: 199–207.

"Moral Union in Christology before Nestorius." *Laval Théologique et Philosophique* 32 (1976): 283–99.

"The Influence of Theodore of Mopsuestia on Augustine's *Letter 187*." *Augustinian Studies* 10 (1979): 113–32.

"Christological Particularity: Need It Be a Scandal?" *Anglican Theological Review* 62 (1980): 64–74.

"The Christology of the Pelagian Controversy." *Studia Patristica* 18, edited by E.A. Livingstone. London: Pergamon, 1982: 1221–44.

"Augustine's Developing Understanding of the Cross." *Augustinian Studies* 15 (1984): 15–33.

"The Misuse of Tradition." *Grail* I (1985): 13–23.

"Patristic Scholarship in the Aftermath of the Modernist Crisis." *Anglican Theological Review* 68 (1986): 25–42.

"La Autobiografia de Casiciaco." *Augustinus* 31 = *San Agustín en Oxford* 2. Madrid, 1986: 41–78.

"The Cassiciacum Autobiography." *Studia Patristica* 19, edited by E.A. Livingstone. Kalamazoo: Cistercian, 1990: 14–43.

"Tradition before the Future." *Toronto Journal of Theology* 9, no. 2 (1993): 51–66.

"San Agustín y el *De fuga saeculi* de san Ambrosio." *Augustinus* 40 = *San Agustín en Oxford* 4. Madrid, 1995: 196–205.

"'Not painted only from another picture': Augustine, *De quantitate animae* 33.76." *Studia Patristica* 33, edited by E.A. Livingstone. Louvain: Peeters, 1996: 172–77.

"No pintado de otra pintura: analisis del *De quantite animae* 33.76 de Agustin." *Augustinus* 44 = *San Agustín en Oxford* 5. Madrid, 1999: 175–81.

"Letters to Demetrias: A Sidebar in the Pelagian Controversy." In Festschrift for Ellen Leonard, edited by Mary Rose D'Angelo and Anne Anderson. *Toronto Journal of Theology* 16, no. 1 (2000): 131–39.

"Augustín en Éfeso?" *Augustinus* 52 = San Augustín en Oxford 7. Madrid, 2007: 139–50.

"How Theological Is Theological Education?" *Toronto Journal of Theology*: *The Future of Theological Education in Canada,* Supplement 1 (2009): 131–40.

Index

✠ ✠ ✠

251